The Performativity of Value

The Performativity of Value

On the Citability of Cultural Commodities

Steve Sherlock

LEXINGTON BOOKS
Lanham • Boulder • New York • Toronto • Plymouth, UK

Published by Lexington Books
A wholly owned subsidiary of Rowman & Littlefield
4501 Forbes Boulevard, Suite 200, Lanham, Maryland 20706
www.rowman.com

10 Thornbury Road, Plymouth PL6 7PP, United Kingdom

British Library Cataloguing in Publication Information Available

Library of Congress Cataloging-in-Publication Data

Sherlock, Steve, 1958-
The performativity of value : on the citability of cultural commodities / Steve Sherlock.
p. cm.
Includes bibliographical references and index.
ISBN 978-0-7391-6861-5 (cloth) — ISBN 978-0-7391-6862-2 (electronic)
1. Value. 2. Group identity. 3. Commercial products. I. Title.
HB201.S563 2014
306.3'4—dc23
2013045646

™ The paper used in this publication meets the minimum requirements of American National Standard for Information Sciences Permanence of Paper for Printed Library Materials, ANSI/NISO Z39.48-1992.

Printed in the United States of America

Contents

Acknowledgments

I would like to thank Lexington Press for publishing this book. I would particularly like to thank Jana Hodges-Kluck, my editor at Lexington Press, for her expertise and time spent on this project, and her patience in bringing it to publication. I would like to thank my production editor, Catherine Mudge, as well as all the others associated with Lexington Press who worked on this project. I also thank the anonymous reviewers of this manuscript for contributing their time and helpful insights.

I would also like to acknowledge funding by the National Endowment of the Humanities for two summer seminars which contributed to my development as a scholar. The first was conducted in 1995 by Dr. Samuel Weber at UCLA, entitled "From the Work of Art to the Serializing of the Media: Communication and Signification in Walter Benjamin and Other Theorists." The second was conducted in 2001 by Dr. Alex Gelley at UC-Irvine, entitled "Walter Benjamin's Arcades Project: Commodity Fetishism and the Aesthetics of the City." I would like to thank both Dr. Weber and Dr. Gelley for these seminars, both of which contributed to my understanding of critical social theory and poststructuralism. I would also like to thank the graduate faculty at Notre Dame during my formative years of learning social theory—especially Dr. Fabio Dasilva and Dr. Fred Dallmayr.

I would like to thank the administration at Saginaw Valley State University for sabbatical support for this project. I also thank the administration, university faculty, my department colleagues, and the support staff at Saginaw Valley for their help and friendship over my career at the university.

Finally, I would like to thank all of my family members for their ongoing support and assistance, and I would especially like to thank my love, Michele, for her consideration and encouragement while I wrote this book.

I

Toward a Poststructuralist Theory of Value: Development of the Theoretical Approach

Chapter One

Introduction

Just as scholars might directly quote, or paraphrase, the words of Shakespeare into their own work—as Erving Goffman (1959) does in developing his theory of dramaturgy, or Jacques Derrida (1994) in his work on Marx—social actors routinely "cite" cultural commodities in everyday life. In fact, Shakespeare's words and works have themselves become cultural commodities circulating in the marketplace, purchased and cited by consumers seeking to valorize the situation into which they are recontextualized. The exchange value (Marx 1967) of such a cultural commodity derives not only from its function in delivering *another* value, such as "literary value," into the new situational context, but also from its use as a citational resource for the identity construction of the subjects involved.

As Mikhail Bakhtin and his associates argued, the words of others—as meaningful signs which pre-exist their users—are continually incorporated into the utterances of the self (Vološinov 1986). For the Bakhtin Circle, the subject necessarily takes an *evaluative* stance toward these "words of the other," as they are configured into particular syntactical formations within the utterances of self. Subjects can "report on" the words of co-present or distant others with approval or disdain, taking evaluative stances toward their implied cultural values. For V. N. Vološinov, "reported speech" is "*speech about speech*" (115; italics in the original), as in the case of a direct quote or a paraphrase of the words of others. However, in a more general sense, the very *selection* of particular words of others, in order to formulate one's own utterances, is already a kind of reported speech—in that subjects make evaluative choices regarding which words of others to "report upon." The words of others come to subjects with historically sedimented meanings and values, available as resources to incorporate into their own evaluative utterances.

This process can be seen as a kind of citational practice, where selected words of others are "cited," or "grafted" (Derrida 1988, 12), into the reporting utterances of the self. Bakhtin and his colleagues argued that every material, syntactically configured utterance issued by a subject not only enacts a relationship with others, but a relationship between the *values* of self and those of others (Vološinov 1976; Holquist 2004; MacCannell 1985). The citation of the words and images of the other thus involves a continual renegotiation of social values in everyday life. Given that language has itself increasingly become a "cultural" commodity within post-industrial economies—distributed in formats such as television shows, websites, films, or books—the *commodified* words of others can be reported upon, and evaluated, when re-cited by the subject.

In this book, the contributions of the Bakhtin Circle on reported speech are moved into a framework of "performative citationality," as developed through the work of Jacques Derrida and Judith Butler (see Derrida 1988; Butler 1993, 12; Nakassis 2012, 635). Using the work of the Bakhtin Circle, Butler's formulation regarding the performative citationality of gender is extended to the performative citationality of *value*—especially the re-citation of exchange value in everyday life. The first section of this book develops the theoretical frame which will be used. The second section applies the theoretical frame to the *description* of the contemporary U.S. cultural economy, while the third section applies the frame to its *critique*.

Jacques Derrida (1988) famously argued, in his discussion of John Austin's work on linguistic performatives, that any "mark" must be recognizable across social contexts in order to be meaningful—and thus is inherently separable from the intentionality of any particular subject. For Derrida, words or gestures, although uniquely singular *in* context, must also be repeatable and recognizable *across* contexts in order to have social meaning. He calls this unresolvable tension, between the singularity and repeatability of language, the "iterability" of language (7; 10).

Another way Derrida says this is that language must be "citable" across social contexts—spatially and temporally separable from the "presence" of the intentional subject who first utters or writes the words. Meaning must be abstractable from a situated use by an individual subject, and thus is beyond the intentional control of that subject. Words can be re-cited and re-interpreted by audiences in ways never intended by subjects. Thus, meaning can never be finally fixed, and is endlessly deferrable into unknown future contexts. In Derrida's terms, meaning is never quite "present," as assumed in the tradition of Western metaphysics (Derrida 1973; 1981). Derrida considers this insight to be applicable to any meaningful identity, including the social identity of subjects. Because any identity must be repeatable across contexts in order to be socially meaningful, it cannot be "identical" with itself across those differing spatial and temporal contexts.

Judith Butler extended this argument in her work on gendered identity. In *Gender Trouble* (1999), Butler argued that the social identity category of "gender" must be continually re-performed across situations in order to remain normative and socially meaningful. For Butler, this means that "gender" must be *re-cited* across situated contexts, as a kind of cultural script which must be continually recontextualized and re-performed in social interaction in order to remain normative. In her following works (1993; 1997), Butler increasingly incorporated Derrida's notions of iterability and citationality into her performativity theory (Kirby 2006, 87; Lloyd 2007, 115; Hollywood 2002; 95). This theoretical move brought an increased emphasis on Derrida's critique of the "presence" of meaning and identity. In addition, Butler reworked a term from Louis Althusser in arguing that gendered identity does not pre-exist language use, but rather is *interpellated from* situated re-citational practices (1997, 27). The "performative citationality" of gender means that the re-citation of this identity category in everyday life, to a greater or lesser extent, re-imposes its normative boundaries upon social action.

The thesis of this book is that just as in the case of gender, *any* "value" must be continually re-cited in order to remain meaningful and normative. Subcultural values are performative in that they are continually *re-enacted*—and thus re-emerge—through everyday citational practices. In this sense, it is less that pre-existing subcultural communities "hold" particular values, and more that patterns of social behavior lead to the re-interpellation of particular social identities, which are "grafted" with particular values. From this perspective, the values of subcultural communities do not reflect a pre-existing group consciousness, but rather are re-cited and re-emergent in situated linguistic practice.

A theory which emphasizes the performativity of value differs from a "representationalist" perspective, which assumes that language merely describes the pre-existing cultural values of individuals or groups, or that the exchange value of commodities pre-exists everyday economic transactions. In contrast to the representationalist perspective, the "performativity of value" suggests that subcultural values and exchange value only re-emerge *from* citational practices. It is also argued in the book that the performativity of value generally occurs in the manner described by the Bakhtin Circle—in material, syntactical configurations where subjects continually re-make their stances toward normative value domains. However, the work of the Bakhtin Circle, which greatly emphasized linguistic utterances, is extended to more generally include other types of social action involving material forms.

This book particularly explores the process of the re-citation of economic or exchange value by subjects. The "performativity" of exchange value refers to the idea that exchange value does not represent the pre-existing market value of meaningful material forms, but rather that—like any identity, value, or meaning—it is re-cited through situated practice in everyday life. In the sense that the "performative" brings into being that which it appears to merely represent, the re-citation of exchange value continually re-enacts the U.S. cultural economy.

In this cultural economy, where language itself has increasingly become a commodity in the syntactical forms of television shows, films, or Internet sites, exchange value is re-cited as subjects continually re-position themselves relative to those material forms. Exchange value is thus re-generated through re-citational practices, as cultural commodities are continually re-grafted into the utterances or behavioral practices of subjects. Corporations produce marketable material forms, or "institutional utterances," which are distributed to subjects for the construction of their individual identities. These citational resources allow consumers to align their individual identities with those of particular subcultural reference groups. Indeed, Miranda Joseph (2002) has argued that the very notion of "community" is complicit with capitalism's efforts to market different products to different identity groups, presumed to hold a variety of subcultural values.

Exchange value is thus performative in the sense that it is continually re-cited and re-produced in everyday life, as social actors use institutionally produced citational resources to construct social identities, and to negotiate social values with others. This book further asserts, agreeing with the argument of John Guillory (1993), that exchange value has become the *hegemonic* value in contemporary U.S. culture, relative to all other cultural values (323). In other words, exchange value has now grafted itself onto all other types of value in such a way that virtually no "value" can be signified today without a consideration of the worth of the material signifier in "representing" those values.

In addition, the theory of performative citationality as developed by Butler suggests a space for the *critique* of this consumer economy, dominated by the hegemony of exchange value. If, following Derrida, the identity of any individual or community is not entirely "present," then neither are the values which are normatively affiliated with that identity. Those political, moral, or ethnic values which are typically associated with particular social identities are also unstable. In this sense, the very necessity of the continual re-citation of exchange value suggests that there can never be—in the language of the Frankfurt School—a system of "total reification" (see Rose 1978; Buck-Morss 1979; Jay 1973).

As Butler shows in the case of gender, while the re-citation of social identity categories may reproduce existing social inequalities, it simultaneously opens the *possibility* for the resistance of normative identities and values in future recontextualizations. Butler thus argues that the "citationality" of gender means that while particular gendered performances are required by power, the very fact that they must be re-cited in order to remain normative opens a space for their alteration. In this Derridean sense, the meaning of gender categorizations are unstable, given that they are necessarily altered through their repetition in differing situational contexts.

This book suggests that this insight can be applied in a similar way to the re-citation of both subcultural values, and exchange value—and in this way develop a poststructuralist critique of the commodification of language in the United States. As meaningful social categories, all "values"—including exchange value—are necessarily altered through their performative re-citation. The utterances of subjects, in syntactical configurations with the commodified words of others, can thus either "re-site," or resist, normative values.

THE THEORETICAL POSITIONING OF THE BOOK

A constellation of theorists—Bakhtin, Derrida, Butler, Mead, Goffman, Adorno, Benjamin, and others—are used in developing the thesis of this book. The book attempts to bring together the contributions of each of these major theorists, along with some relevant secondary literatures, to show how contemporary social identity is constructed through the re-citation of cultural commodities, and how this process re-cites the system of exchange value in the contemporary U.S. cultural economy. It may be worthwhile then, for clarification, to quickly summarize how the thesis advanced in this book is positioned relative to the ideas of the major theorists used, and how their work is extended as the argument is developed.

Relative to the Work of the Bakhtin Circle

The book incorporates a number of key insights from the work of the Bakhtin Circle. In utterances, subjects wrap their words around the words of others in syntactical formations, thereby enacting a particular stance toward the values of others. For Bakhtin and his associates, the *materiality* of the utterance becomes the site of value negotiation between self and others. The book expands on this formulation in a number of ways.

First, subject not only respond to the words—and implied subcultural values—of others, but also respond to their *commodified* words. In their utterances, then, subjects also take a stand *toward the exchange value frame itself*. Subjects recite, or resist, the commodification of language—and the exchange value frame itself—to varying degrees, as enacted in their utterances. The material form of the cultural commodity—shaped by profit considerations—enters into the overall materiality of the subject's utterance in a particular, syntactical configuration. In this sense, subjects not only "report on" the implied subcultural values of the words and images of others, but also take a stand relative to their material, commodified form.

Second, this focus on *re-citation* brings the Bakhtinian work on reported speech into a more contemporary theoretical frame—that of performative citationality. Subjects not only report upon the pre-existing identities and values of others, but *continually* re-cite and re-enact them. Social identities and values must be re-cited in order to remain meaningful and normative. In addition, the work of the Bakhtin Circle on linguistics is extended to the citation of other meaningful material forms, such as images, events, or social objects.

The Bakhtin Circle also emphasized—influenced by Einstein's theory of relativity—that the referential contexts of both self and other were necessary to produce meaning (Holquist 2004, 20–21). The third way that the work of the Bakhtin Circle is extended in this book concerns how value is generated through the *grafting* of the referential contexts of self and other. In Derrida's sense, the exchange value of a meaningful material form is generated not through the intentionality of its producer, but as it crosses from the referential context of the other to that of the subject. The material configuration of the utterance grafts together, while re-differentiating, the subcultural perspectives of self and others. Like a quote, the cultural commodity brings together at least two referential contexts, while simultaneously re-enacting the differences between them. Indeed, the term "exchange value" already suggests travel across contexts.

Fourth, the work of the Bakhtin Circle is extended to include *institutional utterances*. Corporations "report" the images and words of others to the subject in the syntactical forms of television shows, films, websites, books, and other cultural commodities. The words and works of artists, writers, photographers, and others are appropriated by economic institutions, and marketed to consumers as citational resources for individual identity construction.

In chapters three, four, and five, these extensions of the Bakhtinian approach are used to *describe* the contemporary functioning of the U.S. cultural economy. In the sixth chapter, an additional theoretical move is made in order to *criticize* this version of the "performativity of exchange value." Specifically, the Derridean *critique of presence* is added to this formulation. As subjects cite the words of others in their own utterances, the normative assumption is that value becomes "present" as the subject experiences the words and images of others. However, as Butler's work on recontextualization suggests, such a re-citation of the words and images of others does not result in the stable presence of exchange value; rather, exchange value is never quite "present." In fact, this instability of exchange value is today revealed in the difficulties experienced by corporations in *measuring* the value of their brands (Muniesa 2011; Adkins and Lury 2011; Moor and Lury 2011).

Relative to the Work of Jacques Derrida

The book incorporates Derrida's critique of "presence," as well as his insights regarding the iterability of meaning. His work is extended in this book in a number of ways. First, Derrida's critique of the metaphysics of presence in Western philosophy and culture is extended to a critique of the temporality of *value* in the U.S. economy. For example, chapter three ends with a Derridean critique of the *presence of subcultural values*, and chapter six develops a critique of the *presence of exchange value* in the contemporary cultural economy. Although subcultural values, and exchange value, are considered to be "present" in cultural commodities—and in the experiences they deliver to the subject—the iterable nature of language means that value is never quite "present."

Second, Derrida's work on the iterability of meaning is extended to a thesis regarding the iterability of value. Like any meaning, the "meaning of value" is continually deferred. Just as Derrida reveals the necessary instability of any meaning as its material form crosses contexts, so the meanings of language-commodities cannot "represent" stable subcultural values, nor stable exchange values.

Third, these Derridean insights are used to *criticize the central ideology* of the contemporary cultural economy—that the commodification of language generates the presence of exchange value, which is "experienced" by consumers. Inasmuch as contemporary marketers and academic theorists speak of an increasing tendency toward the "co-creation" of value by consumers, their approach often re-cites the ideology fundamental to both Western metaphysics and contemporary capitalism—that value becomes "present" through product development and marketing.

Fourth, Derrida's work on the "aporia" of the promise—that what is promised can never actually be fulfilled (Caputo 1997)—is extended to the *promise of value*. In a performative sense, it is the claim or *promise* of the presence of value which is re-cited in consumer practices in everyday life—as opposed to its actual *presence*. Advertisements continually promise valorized experiences for Cartesian subjects, and consumers re-cite such promises in identity construction. As Haug (1986) has argued, the promises of advertising are betrayed when the commodity fails to fulfill these expectations, and their promised value never becomes present. Of course, whether ideological or not, in practice investors make real money on the temporary stabilization of the "value" of language—just as the temporary stabilization of meaning in everyday life enables communication. While Derrida's notion of citationality may allow for the *theoretical* critique of the presence of exchange value—and may even help explain the unpredictability of an economy based on the commodification of language—in everyday economic practice the cultural assumptions regarding presence largely go unquestioned.

Fifth, Derrida's *critique of the Cartesian subject* of Western metaphysics is extended to the "experiencing" subject who *consumes* the words and images of others. Both the Cartesian and the capitalist versions of subjectivity are together interpellated from today's commodified cultural forms. The ideology of presence governing Cartesian subjectivity thus comfortably coexists with the presence of exchange value in the cultural economy. The commodification of language extends the reach of *both* the Cartesian and exchange value frames, as it re-cites the temporality of presence. Alternately, the research of linguistic anthropologists in non-Western cultures shows that a different conception of subjectivity emerges from alternate linguistic forms (Strauss 1989).

To illustrate how capitalist and Cartesian subjectivities have developed together in Western culture, the example of tourism is used in the book. The commodification of visual experience has historically reinforced both of these types of subjectivity. In tourism, commodified objects and images of the other are subject to the "gaze" of experiencing, consuming subjects (see Foucault 1965; 1994; Mulvey 1989; Dworkin 1989), as they travel to exotic "sights/sites/cites." The tourism model is also extended to consider contemporary citational technologies which allow for mediated forms of "travel," such as television, film, and the Internet.

Finally, Derrida's notion regarding the *anticipation of an unknown future* is extended in the development of a critique of the *calculative* orientation toward the future as found in contemporary investment and marketing practices. As marketers and product designers attempt to co-create value, they anticipate and shape how language *will be* commodified—in order to distribute citational resources with market value in the future. As Callon (1998a) shows, a market-based economy requires a particular type of agency—that of calculative agents who are able to anticipate and predict the behavior of other actors relative to economic contracts. In contrast to this type of calculative "anticipation" of the future—that is, a continued unfolding of the ideology of presence—Derrida (2007) argues that a real "future" requires an anticipation of, and a kind of hesitant eagerness for, the unknown.

Relative to the Work of Judith Butler

This book adopts Butler's central insight that social identity categories, and relations between identities, must be re-cited in order to remain normative. This insight not only explains the persistence of normative identities and values, but also opens a space for their potential alteration. In addition, the book adopts Butler's reworking of the Althusserian notion of interpellation to show how identities do not pre-exist utterances, but are actually retroactively constructed from them.

Butler's work on the performative citationality of identity is extended in the book to the *performative citationality of value*—both of subcultural values, as well as exchange value. Bringing in the work of the Bakhtin Circle, we can see that subcultural values are re-cited as the material *utterances* of the subject re-align individual identity with that of larger valuing communities. The material utterances of subjects necessarily "take a stand" relative to the interpellated values of particular "imagined communities" (see Anderson 1991). Thus, the process of interpellation involves the ongoing re-construction of social identities, which normatively align with the *values* of particular groups. The re-citation of subcultural affiliation also re-cites the exchange value frame, as citational resources are assigned an exchange value in their functional effectiveness of representing these other "non-economic" cultural values.

Butler used the work of Michel Foucault and Jacques Lacan, as well as Derrida's work, in the development of her theory of performative citationality. A second way in which this book extends the ideas of Butler is through the incorporation of the work of the social psychology of the Bakhtin Circle and of George H. Mead, rather than the psychoanalytic framework of Lacan. The theoretical perspectives of Bakhtin and Mead allow for a more sociological development of a *theory of socialization* oriented toward childhood citational practices. Incorporating their theories of the self into a framework of citationality, the process of "learning to value" is explored. Along with some work in linguistic anthropology, Butler's notion of re-citation is used to consider how children learn to re-cite important subcultural values, as well as the exchange value frame. In doing so, the book re-envisions the field of social psychology within a theory of performative citationality, and emphasizes the emergent nature of values through situated behavioral practice. The use of Mead also underscores the point that citational practices can be anticipated and rehearsed, as part of the sedimented history of normative performances.

A third way that the work of Butler is extended regards the thesis that the (cultural) economy is itself re-performed through the re-citational process. Michel Callon (2007) has suggested that the formulas of economists, as used by investors, shape the nature of the economy itself. In other words, economic formulas which purport to merely describe economic conditions actually contribute to their emergence. In addition, the work of marketers becomes performative of the economy, as these agents of institutions appropriate subcultural values in the design and marketing of their brands (Lury 2004, 8). This book extends these arguments to suggest that the citational practices of *consumers* are also performative of value—particularly in those sectors of the U.S. economy involved in the commodification of culture (see Nakassis 2012). The re-citation of the commodified words and images of others, as individuals align their identities with those of subcultural groups, re-generates demand in the market and thus "re-performs" the cultural economy.

Fourth, while Butler's work is used in the second section of the book to *describe* the contemporary functioning of the U.S. cultural economy, in the third section it is used to develop a poststructural *critique* of the commodification of language—and thus explore the possibilities of resistance to the re-citation of the exchange value frame. As the Bakhtin Circle argues, every utterance—which reports on or re-cites the words of others—necessarily takes a stance toward their implied values. This position aligns with Butler's notion that *recontextualization* involves a space for the resistance of normative values, given that each utterance "re-takes" a stance toward normative identities and values.

Finally, Butler's work is extended to more strongly emphasize the *materiality of language*—consistent with the Bakhtin Circle's focus on the material, syntactical configurations of utterances. One important issue in the literature concerns whether Butler's formulation of performativity theory neglects issues of social class and political economy (Boucher 2008). This book argues for the continuing importance of class and material conditions to a theory of performativity, and attempts to show how a theory of the performativity of *value* might address some of the issues involved.

The thesis developed in this book argues that it is the *materiality* of language which both—using Butler's terms—"enables" and "constrains" everyday social interaction (1997, 16). The materiality of *institutional* utterances, driven by the marketability of language, particularly constrains social action and contributes to the reproduction of inequality. Material resources used in the process of everyday identity construction are unequally distributed, as are the differential rewards received in society for the use of various class-based citational "styles" (Bourdieu 1984). In this way, the *materiality* of language, as cultural commodity, constrains social opportunities—as mediated through normative citational practices and identity categories. On the other hand, the materiality of language also enables utterances to "play against" the constraints of normative material conditions.

Derrida's notion of iterability suggests that while a meaningful "mark" must be *recognizable* across situations, it is not *identical* with itself across those situations. While Derrida sees the repeatability of the mark as a structural and inherent feature of the mark, Butler wants to shift the focus to a *social* iterability—emphasizing the historical "sedimentation" of repetitions (1997, 145; 152). It is precisely an emphasis on the materiality of language which enables such a theoretical move. Normative re-citational practices enable the persistence of material, "institutionalized" social environments within which everyday citational practices occur. The citational practices of individuals both reproduce, as well as play against, these sedimented material environments. The meaningful materialities of social environments can be altered precisely because they cannot be identical across re-citational instances—even while materiality has to be recognizable across situations in order to remain meaningful.

The meaningful materiality of an utterance is always in tension with the interpretive context which emerges in part through *it* (see MacCannell 1985, 984–85; Hollywood 2002, 109; Kendon 1997)—as well as through the *other* meaningful materialities which typically accompany that utterance in a social situation. Because the mark differs from itself over repetitions, it also "differs" in its stance relative to the meaning of the situational context of which it is a part. In other words, when the materiality of the meaningful mark differs—to a greater or lesser extent—across situations, it carries the potential to disrupt the interpellated meaning of the *overall material constellation* into which it is grafted.

Thus, a repetition which signifies differently than expected can disrupt not only the meaning and value of that particular utterance, but also the normative interpretive *context* against which all of the materialities belonging to that situation are interpreted. In addition, the meaning and value of any or all of those *associated materialities*, in that social situation, are also potentially affected by the proximity of the "subversive" material form. Using Butler's famous example, a gender parody performed in a nightclub—as an utterance which repeats "with a difference"—might not only draw into question the meaning and value of the gendered performance itself, but also draw into question the normative identities and values of the audience, of the workers in the establishment, or of the nightclub itself as a certain "type of place."

For an utterance to have *normative* performative effect, the interpellated context which its materiality "calls forth" must align with that of the other meaningful materialities in the situation. However, as Butler has argued in a commentary on Bourdieu (2000), when a performance is misaligned with authorizing context, this does not mean that it fails to "work"; rather, it simply fails to "work" *as expected or authorized.* While a "deviant" performance may indeed be sanctioned by social authorities, or even appropriated within normative valuing frames, there is also the possibility—especially through repeated or widespread iterations of "frame-breaking" (see Goffman 1986, 493)—that the normative frame or valuing context is itself altered. Thus, an utterance whose materiality repeats "with a difference" may indeed "misfire," but it may also lead to a change in the interpretation of the material constellation into which it enters.

Relative to the Work of George Herbert Mead

Mead (1969) has shown the importance of language in the construction of the self, and revealed the ability of humans to anticipate the likely reactions of others to their considered actions. Mead's work also shows the importance of significant symbols in this regard, and how social actors can share definitions of situations, social objects, and concepts—thus enabling the coordination of social action. As a theory of contemporary social identity formation, this book seeks to update Mead's theory of self through the incorporation of contemporary work on the citational practices of social actors.

Research in linguistic anthropology has shown how "entextualized" strips of language—which have been materially prepared to "represent" particular cultural traditions (Bauman and Briggs 1990)—are ritually re-cited into new situational contexts. As children are socialized, they learn to recognize those entextualized forms which represent group values, as well as learn how to recontextualize those material forms in everyday social interactions. In Mead's (1969) sense, children learn to anticipate the normative responses of others to their citational practices, and thus align their utterances with group expectations. In the contemporary U.S. cultural economy, children *learn to value* as adults prioritize particular cultural commodities within the home. "Values," including exchange value, are reproduced over generations through normative re-citational practices. Mead's work on significant symbols and role-taking is thus brought into the framework of performative citationality.

What Mead's work restores to this framework is the notion that *re-citational performances can be anticipated.* While the poststructuralist tradition has been eager to move away from the notion of intentional subjectivity, it is clear that utterances can be rehearsed through internal conversations with self, and adjusted before actualized. Mead's notion of meaning—as an anticipation of the behavioral practices of others (Joas 1997, 105)—can help to restore the notion of "anticipation" to poststructuralist theory, without relocating "meaning" in a shared group consciousness which pre-exists behavioral practice. Rather, the moment of rehearsal or anticipation is itself *part* of the sedimentation of normative practices (see Schechner 1985). It is argued that while Mead's more pragmatic notion of meaning helps his theory largely escape the Derridean critique of presence, some of his work on significant symbols is in need of revision along contemporary poststructuralist lines.

Mead's notions of the "I" and the "me" phases of the self are retained within the theory of performative citationality developed in this book. The identity categories and subcultural affiliations interpellated from citational practices are the "me" of public social identity. While this identity is constraining, individuals always retain a freedom to actively respond, as "I," within and against those constraints. As Butler has shown, the active recitation of identity categories like gender necessarily dislocates the presence of social identity across spatial and temporal contexts—in Mead's language, the singularity of the "I" always disrupts the stable repeatability of the "me."

If, as Mead argued, we think of the "me" of the self in a language, then today we think of our identity through *commodified language*. In other words, the very language used to construct the self has increasingly become a commodity itself, with an exchange value. The "experiences" of self come to be ranked in an evaluative hierarchy as to their worth, and the "self" becomes an archive of purchased and valued experiences.

Relative to the Work of Erving Goffman

Goffman's (1961) notion of role distance is an important concept in this book. For Goffman, the social actor experiences, and often communicates, a sense of dislike for roles that they may be forced to play. Goffman sees the self as a stylized combination of role-embracing, and role-distancing, behaviors (Goffman, in Lemert, and Branaman 2003, 90). In a performance, material props may be used to communicate one's dissatisfaction with a role.

This concept is extended in the book to argue that citational resources are marketed precisely to enable consumers to play against, or distance one's self from, normative roles, identities, and subcultural values—as alternatives are simultaneously embraced. As interpellated from material forms, identities and values of individuals align to varying degree with dominant cultural valuing domains. Social identities thus become a site where normative values are re-cited or challenged. Cultural commodities have an exchange value not only as they function to *align* the self with particular subcultural groups, but also as they *distance* the self from others.

Extending the work of Goffman on role distance into a performativity frame, the book thus considers how particular linguistic forms can acquire an exchange value as oppositional citational resources, designed precisely to "play against" dominant cultural values. In other words, given that social roles are affiliated with particular social values, the phenomenon of "role distancing" can be extended to the notion of "value distancing." Resistance to normative roles occurs not only through *deviant* expressions of role distance—as in Goffman's classic example of the acting out of older boys on a merry-go-round (97–98)—but also through *consumption*, or the citation of commodified cultural resources.

As Ferrell (1999) has shown in his work on "cultural criminology," deviant behavior may also be considered as a stylized performance within a particular subculture, as a kind of deviant "aesthetics" (403–4; see also Ferrell and Sanders 1995; Hebdige 1996). In other words, there is an aesthetic to "delinquent" patterns of role-distancing (see Sherlock 2013), which builds a "linguistic market" (see Bourdieu 1991) for oppositional citational resources. Dissatisfaction with normative identities and values today occurs not only through law-breaking behaviors, but also through the citation of cultural commodities.

Even illicit drugs—as commodities designed to evoke alternative experiences and play against normative economic and political realities—acquire an exchange value in their function as oppositional citational resources. Like advertising generally, what is marketed as the drug experience is the *promise of a valorized experience* for a Cartesian subject. In other words, both normative *and* deviant citational resources can be assigned a market value, and re-cite the hegemonic "frame" of exchange value—even if they "play against" normative subcultural values. If, as Goffman (1986) suggests, "frames" organize social experience, then the exchange value "frame" organizes the commodification of both normative and deviant "experiences."

Relative to the Work of Theodor Adorno and Walter Benjamin

The Frankfurt School generally, and Adorno and Benjamin specifically, saw the culture of late capitalism as nearly completely commodified. Their work, influenced by Lukács (Jay 1973, 174–75), attempted to develop a critical theory by which the reification of consciousness could be resisted. They saw the culture industry as leading not to the liberation predicted by Marx, but rather as an increasingly entrenched system which led to the regression of the critical capacities of citizens.

This focus on the "reification of consciousness" is shifted in this book into a poststructuralist frame, emphasizing situated behavioral practice. As Butler argues, the political economy responsible for the commodification of culture is itself continually sustained through re-citational practices. This requirement for re-citation opens up the space for political resistance. In particular, it is argued that *aesthetic* constellations of materiality have a potential for the disruption of the normative materiality of cultural commodities—from which normative identities and values are interpellated.

Adorno's aesthetic theory, as interpreted by Christoph Menke (1998), becomes the basis for a critique of the commodification of language in the contemporary cultural economy, once moved into the frame of citationality. For Adorno, the materiality of art is seen as having the potential to generate an experience of "aesthetic negativity" (xi), and thus disrupt normative *meanings*. This book extends Adorno's aesthetic theory by arguing that the materiality of art has the potential to unsettle known *value* frames, including that of exchange value.

For example, the work of Henry Louis Gates (1988) on the historical use of "Signifyin(g)" (46) within the African-American community shows how literary syntactical forms can disrupt normative meanings; in a similar way, literary utterances—or any aesthetic constellation—can unsettle normative *values*. Artists, art critics, or even participants in everyday dialogue may issue strips of language which, when recontextualized in particular situations, have the aesthetic effect of disrupting dominant values—as well as disrupting the social identities normatively associated with those values. In this way, even today's "commodities" may have an aesthetic effect in unknown future material configurations.

Walter Benjamin's work was particularly focused on the potential of modern citational technologies, especially film, to disrupt the normative exchange value system (see Buck-Morss 1983; 1979; Caygill 1998; Cadava 1997; Jay 1973). Benjamin argued that while modern technologies may indeed re-cite dominant values, they also have the potential to initiate political change. Cultural commodities may be re-cited in future material configurations with the aesthetic effect of disrupting known values, including exchange value. The social identities of subjects are made ambiguous when interpellated from aesthetically configured forms of *unknown value*.

The materiality of aesthetic configurations introduces an element of chance into the future (see Derrida 2007, 360–61)—as opposed to those citational practices of calculative actors who seek to secure the future for investment purposes. Even as institutions attempt to commodify language into a "closed future" framed by economic contracts, the re-citation of language into aesthetic configurations potentially reopens the future. A different, Derridean sense of "anticipation" emerges with aesthetic configurations. This involves a kind of eagerness for an unknown—rather than a calculable—future (see Derrida 1994).

In this book, the work of Adorno and Benjamin on aesthetics is aligned with a Derridean critique of the presence of exchange value. This book also aligns the work of the Frankfurt School with Butler's notion of how *re-citational* practices can dislocate normative identities and values. In this constellation of theorists, art emerges as a kind of dissonant materiality—a repetition with a difference. By taking a resistant stance relative to the normative material configurations into which it enters, art disrupts the value contexts which normatively rule over those configurations. While the material form of the commodity tends toward the repetition of normative values, the exchange value of an aesthetically configured material form is less easily cited.

TERMS USED IN THE BOOK

U.S. Cultural Economy

While several of the theoretical ideas, and some of the empirical research, used in the book originated in other countries, they are selected here inasmuch as they seem to illustrate aspects of contemporary U.S. culture. The central thesis of this book is limited to an analysis of the United States. In other words, the claim of the book is that research on other (mainly Western) cultures is relevant to the analysis of the United States—rather than that the thesis developed in this book is necessarily generalizable to other countries. Having said this, it does seem that many of the features of the contemporary U.S. cultural economy also describe contemporary trends in the United Kingdom. As Lury (2004) puts it, citing Marilyn Strathern, "Describing the societies in which we live is a general Euro-American project" (163).

The term *cultural* economy is meant to direct attention toward the cultural or symbolic dimension of today's commodities, rather than their utilitarian functions—although it is true that the symbolic dimension of commodities cannot be strictly separated from their utility (Jhally 1987, 4–5). Haug (1986) has shown, in his work on commodity aesthetics, that manufactured goods like automobiles that are today marketed with symbolic language associating them with adventure or status. In fact, a celebrity's signature on a branded piece of clothing, or an athlete's endorsement of a pair of tennis shoes, usually multiplies the exchange value of that "object" many times over.

Clearly in these examples, the language or meaning associated with goods has currency in the cultural economy. For this reason, while this book focuses primarily on the marketing of words and images, social objects cannot be entirely excluded from the analysis; as Slater has noted, the strict dichotomy between the "materiality" of objects and the "immateriality" of signs has been a "dubious distinction that has plagued much social theory" (2003, 95). As mentioned, branded "objects" are certainly cited in the construction of contemporary social identity, and thus are included in the discussion of a "cultural" economy.

The term "cultural economy" is thus used as a kind of shorthand to refer to the marketing of images, events, status symbols, words, brands, and so forth—that is, the marketing of meaning in the contemporary U.S. economy. As Celia Lury has noted, the "symbolic or cultural aspects of material objects have come to take on a special importance and distinctive organization in contemporary Euro-American societies, so that consumer culture is said to be drenched in meaning" (1996, 226). While the phrase "commodification of language" is sometimes used instead of "cultural economy," the book argues for the inclusion of images, events, and other social objects beyond the more narrow sense of "language." Also, while it is true that cultural commodities serve other functions beyond that of identity construction, the thesis of the book focuses on how the commodification of language serves that function.

Syntactical/Constellation

The term "syntactical," as used in this book, refers to the material arrangement of the words of self and the words of others within an utterance. However, the term is not limited to the linguistic arrangement of words in a sentence, but more generally refers to how elements in *any* meaningful, material configuration are positioned relative to each other—as in how words in an advertisement are played off against its images. The more general term, "constellation," refers to the material configuration of multiple meaningful forms. The term "syntactical" is not used to exclude semantics, or to favor form over content, but rather to emphasize the Bakhtinian argument that evaluative intonation is imparted through the *way* in which the speech of others is reported.

Identity/Self

In this book, the term "identity" generally refers to what Mead (1969) called the "me" phase of the self. This social identity involves the categorization of an individual, by others, into culturally available identity categories. Subjects can internally anticipate such categorization by others through the role-taking process, and thus tentatively apply the category to themselves when considering various social actions. The broader term, "self," is also used in Mead's sense, as comprised of both the "I" and "me" phases. The "I" is the active response of the individual to the actual, or anticipated, imposition of social identity by others.

Exchange Value

In this book, the term "exchange value" is used interchangeably with the term "market value," or the worth of a meaningful material form in the U.S. cultural economy. It is retained from Marx in this book to particularly link with the work of the Frankfurt School, and their concern with the commodification of culture.

Bakhtin Circle

Given the contested nature of the authorship of some key works surrounding Mikhail Bakhtin and his colleagues, this general term is often used. The exception is when other researchers are cited who have chosen to grant authorship to Bakhtin himself. The term "Bakhtinian" is meant to describe the intellectual tradition of the entire group, regardless of the authorship of individual works.

Citation/Citational Resources/Citational Technologies

This term "citation" refers to the positioning of a subject relative to meaningful materiality. Subjects take a stand relative to the values of others through the strategic positioning of self—whether reporting on their words in an utterance, or through sitting in the front row and applauding during a cultural event. The values of others are cited, or reported, by subjects in particular ways, as individual identities are aligned with those of subcultural groups.

The term "citational utterances" refers to the syntactical, material formations which result as subjects report on the words and images of others in their own utterances. The term "citational resources" refers to the words and works of others which are culturally available for use in identity construction. As mentioned, this book is particularly concerned with the commodification of citational resources. The phrase "citational technologies" refers to the mechanisms by which citational resources are delivered to consumers. Today, language is moved across situational contexts via mobile phones, laptop computers, and other evolving technologies. These citational technologies, themselves part of the constellation of materiality in a social situation, deliver the materiality of language into particular situations with an "enabling constraint" (see Butler 1997, 16)—shaping and framing language as a commodity for use by the consuming individual.

Performativity/Performative Citationality

The term "performativity" is used as an alternative to "representationalism." In J.L. Austin's (1975) sense, a performative utterance is one which brings a social phenomenon into being through language use, as opposed to merely describing a pre-existing phenomenon. When the term "performativity" is used by itself, it includes the metaphysical presupposition that the meaning and value of that which is "performed" actually becomes "present." The term "performative citationality" is used to distinguish Butler's version of performativity theory, which draws upon Derrida's notions of iterability and citationality. The addition of the notion of "citationality" brings a critique of presence to performativity theory, and thus allows—within performativity theory—a space for a critique of the presence of value.

Constantine Nakassis (2012) uses the term "citational performativity" in an article showing how the "performativity" of brands depends on their citationality. That term is specifically used by Nakassis in a discussion of how for Celia Lury (2004), the "interface" of the brand allows for the formulation of a "feedback loop" between consumers and brand developers, which "links uniquely contextualized consumer enactments of brand identity to processes of brand design, manufacture, and marketing, and back again" (Nakassis 2012, 634). While the use of this related term, by Nakassis, refers specifically to Lury's point regarding the re-appropriation of consumer "post-purchase" practices back into brand development, the alternate term used in this book—"performative citationality"—will especially emphasize two related, though distinct, points. The first point is that the re-citation of cultural commodities by consumers normatively re-cites the hegemonic frame of the exchange value system itself, as well as the cultural ideology of the "presence" of exchange value. The second point concerns how the iterability involved in this practice potentially leads to the destabilization of that hegemonic frame, and creates a space for an intervention in the ongoing commodification of language in U.S. culture. In fact, Nakassis uses the term "performative citationality" later in his article, when characterizing the work of Derrida and Butler (635).

It is also important to clarify that two versions of "performativity theory" are now emerging across several academic disciplines. One of the versions, which we can increasingly find in marketing research and theory, will be employed in section II of this book in order to *describe* the functioning of the U.S. cultural economy. This "Austinian" version of performativity theory shares some assumptions with the ideology prevalent in today's marketplace, and with normative cultural practices—most notably, the metaphysical assumption that exchange value comes to be "present" when co-created by firms and consumers. The other version of performativity, as developed by Derrida and Butler, draws upon the notion of citationality in order to *criticize* this ideological assumption regarding identity and value; again, this version is distinguished by the use of the term "performative citationality." The critique of the performativity of exchange value appears in section III of this book, which also draws upon the work of the Frankfurt School on the commodification of culture.

The Commodification of Language

This book focuses on language as a commodity. This includes both the marketing of words, as well as the marketing of "language" in the broader sense—such as the distribution of images or branded objects. In Mead's sense, this process involves the marketing of "significant symbols," or shared meaning, inasmuch as this cultural dimension is perceived to "add value" to the merely utilitarian function of goods. It seems clear that as the U.S. economy has transitioned to a post-industrial economy, the "language-commodity" is traveling through its marketplace in an unprecedented way.

For example, we can see this trend when considering the increased number of websites, the rapid growth of the video game industry, or the development of new citational technologies to move words and images quickly across situational contexts. As Dean MacCannell (1976) has pointed out, increasingly in late capitalism it is meaningful "experiences" which are being marketed to consumers. In the U.S. cultural economy, the commodification of language generates exchange value through the delivery of such experiences. Finally, it should be noted that this book focuses specifically on how language-commodities are used in the *identity construction process*, rather than on other functions of language-commodities—such as how a purchased instruction manual is used to learn how to build or operate something.

The Materiality of Language

The argument of this book regarding the materiality of language follows the lead of Jacques Derrida—that "materiality" is that which enables the recognition of social forms across contexts, and thus enables them to be meaningful. Language is "material" in the sense that written words or spoken sounds are able to be recognized by all users in differing contexts. For example, a hand-drawn or photographed image of a house is recognizable because shapes and visual forms can be meaningfully repeated.

Of course, the "modality" of material forms differ; as Louis Althusser once put it, "the material existence of the ideology in an apparatus and its practices does not have the same modality as the material existence of a paving-stone or a rifle" (1971, 166). Clearly, some re-enactments of meaning stay "materialized" for longer durations than others. As used in this book, the list of "material," repeatable, and meaningful forms could thus include written marks, physical gestures, social objects, the sound of a voice, or digital images. Given the multiple modalities that material forms take, the term "meaningful materiality" will sometimes be used in this book to refer to not only spoken or written language, but also any materiality which bears a social or cultural meaning. In this sense, *cultural commodities* involve words or images in the form of websites, television shows, or other social forms which generally derive their economic value from the marketing of social meanings.

For Derrida, this suggests that the meaning-generating function of language is not tied to the subjective intentionality of users, or what subjects "intended to mean." Rather, meaning results from the ability of materiality to be recognized as "the same" across situational contexts—in the sense that a word or image can mean the same thing across iterations to different people. As Derrida argues, meaning is possible because of this "citational" aspect of language. The repeatable, material form can be quoted or cited into different contexts, and continue to repeat its meaning—even in the absence of any particular user. Cultural commodities, like books or websites, can acquire recognized economic value because shared meanings are possible across contexts. In this repeatable, stable form, economic "value" can be co-produced by consumers, and measured by economists.

The emphasis in this book on the materiality of language allows us to incorporate Bakhtin's view of language into a more poststructuralist frame, inasmuch as Bakhtin and his colleagues strongly emphasized the materiality of utterances. For the Bakhtin Circle, it was through the syntactical, material form of utterances where the values of subjects engaged with the values of others. Given that in the cultural economy subjects receive the words and images of others in an increasingly *commodified form*, the value negotiations between self and others increasingly occurs within—to use Butler's term—

the "enabling constraints" of the exchange value frame. Subjects are enabled to either reproduce, or resist, this constraining frame through utterances which continually take a stand relative to it.

CONTEMPORARY RELEVANCE OF THE BOOK

In the contemporary marketing literature, there is an increased recognition that consumers "co-create value" along with firms (Prahalad and Ramaswamy 2004). In the advanced capitalist economies of post-industrial nations—like those of the United States and the United Kingdom—corporations and market researchers have increasingly become attentive to the lifestyles and subcultural values of consumers. They now actively solicit customer input into production, product design, and marketing processes. As cultural commodities routinely take the social forms of websites, books, films, or television shows, the appropriation of words and images from everyday life have become essential to the (co)production of economic value.

Both marketers and marketing researchers have begun to adopt some of the terminology of performativity theory, as they describe the process of the co-creation of value. Increasingly, consumer subcultural values are incorporated into products and brands, which are then marketed back to consumers for use in the identity construction process. Inasmuch as it helps us to understand these processes, this literature contributes to an understanding of the performativity of exchange value in the contemporary cultural economy.

A number of theoretical contributions have recognized that the fields of both economics and marketing have become performative of the economy itself. Callon's (2007) work has shown that the formulas produced by economists themselves influence investment decisions, thus *bringing about* particular economic conditions. Others have argued that in today's marketing practices, the appropriation of consumer values into the development of brands has become performative of their market value (Lury 2004, Arvidsson 2006; Nakassis 2012). As mentioned above, Constantine Nakassis notes that for Celia Lury, the brand acts as an "interface" between consumer and marketers; as consumption patterns change, marketers are then able to adjust features of the brand to sustain their desirability (Nakassis 2012, 625). Nakassis recognizes that it is precisely the "citational" aspect of the brand—that consumers *re-cite* its continually co-constructed meaning in various situated contexts—which enables it to be performative of market value (625).

These arguments regarding the "performativity" of the contemporary economy align with the thesis of this book. This book explores how the practices of consumers re-perform, as well as potentially resist, the exchange value frame. In developing a *critique* of the increasing commodification of language and the "presence" of exchange value, this book extends the thesis of the "performativity of exchange value" in a specifically Derridean direction. The metaphysical assumption regarding the "presence of exchange value" persists as the central ideology of the contemporary cultural economy. As mentioned above, Adorno's work on aesthetics is also important in the development of a poststructuralist critique of the commodification of language, especially as his work is brought into a constellation with that of the Bakhtin Circle on the materiality of utterances.

Consumer demand for particular cultural commodities, normatively used as citational resources in the identity construction process, re-cites the cultural economy and the system of exchange value. The words and images of others, having been incorporated into the product development of cultural commodities, or integrated with branded goods, become citational resources for the utterances of subjects in everyday life. Subjects construct their individual identities as they both align themselves with, as well as distance themselves from, particular group identities and values. On the "consumption side," then, consumer practices are re-performative of exchange value—as subjects continually re-generate demand for the citational resources provided by economic institutions.

Just as alterity is controlled politically through a kind of "reporting on" the speech of the subordinated (see de Certeau 1988; Inoue 2006), it is also controlled *economically* as institutions shape the "words of others" into marketable utterances. The commodified words and images of others are reduced to syntactically arranged "consumption experiences" for subjects, and assigned an economic worth. Language is thereby reduced to the "enabling constraints" of commodity form, which limits its possibilities for future re-contextualizations. In other words, the citational resources used in self-construction today, and those citational resources left for future generations, are driven primarily by profit considerations based on the marketability of language.

In the United States, the process of commodification has been extended from the worth of manufactured goods in an industrial-based economy, to the marketing of meaning itself in the post-industrial economy. In such a cultural economy, every utterance potentially acquires an exchange value in the media market, as new technologies make language eminently "re-citable." Those types of language-based commodities which bring the most profit, as indicated by measured patterns of consumer behavior, are those most likely to be re-produced or "re-uttered" by corporations. The economic system which—as a measuring apparatus (see Barad 2007)—assigns a market worth to commodities simultaneously shapes the material forms which those cultural commodities take.

As the U.S. economy becomes increasingly "cultural," and meaning itself has become a commodity, the signification process has become central to capitalism—as well as to its critical analysis. Late capitalism involves the re-generation of exchange value through the continual re-commodification of language. While thinkers like Theodor Adorno saw how culture could itself become a commodity, this process has become even more accelerated and—with the increasing proliferation of the mass media—now includes the Internet as delivered on new citational technologies.

As social theory analyzes the production of economic and cultural value, then, it is necessary to move away from theories oriented toward the value of manufactured objects, toward a theory based in an analysis of the value of the meaningful "experiences" which commodified cultural forms now provide. Since commodities increasingly *are* language, the research and theories of semioticians, linguistic anthropologists, literary theorists, and others who work in areas dealing with the philosophy and rhetoric of language have become increasingly relevant to the *sociological* analysis of the U.S. cultural economy. This book attempts to contribute to the analysis of the nature of "value" in a cultural economy based on the copyrighting, marketing, and citation of commodified language—that is, the exchange value of words, images, events, and branded social objects. There is a gap in the field of sociology regarding a contemporary "theory of value" which seems to persist—despite the increased commodification of language in the U.S. economy, and despite the increased importance of cultural commodities for practices of identity construction today.

Chapter Two

Reported Speech and Citationality

In this chapter, the theoretical framework to be used in the book is developed. The work of the Bakhtin Circle, on both the "utterance" and "reported speech," is moved into the framework of performative citationality as developed by Judith Butler. Butler's version of performativity theory builds on Jacques Derrida's notion of iterability, and argues that identity categories must be re-cited in order to remain normative. While the Bakhtin Circle emphasized that values are negotiated in syntactical, material utterances, this insight is extended to argue that values must be *re-negotiated* and *re-cited* in order to remain normative. This formulation, developed in this chapter, will be used to explore the "performativity of subcultural values" in chapter three, and the "performativity of exchange value" in chapters four and five. In addition, Butler's formulation regarding the re-citation of identity categories opens a space regarding the potential alteration of normative identity categories through their recontextualization. This insight is extended in chapter six, as a critique of the commodification of language is developed.

THE NEGOTIATION OF VALUES IN UTTERANCES

For the Russian philosopher and literary theorist Mikhail Bakhtin, the concept of the "utterance" is central to the understanding of both self and social interaction (Holquist 2004, 59). Bakhtin argued that the "self" is constituted through the utterances of the subject, in interactive dialogues with others (see Gardiner 1992, 28). Through the choice of words to be included or excluded in the utterance, as well as through the manner of phrasing, particular relations with others are enacted and re-enacted in social interaction. For Bakhtin and his colleagues, relationships between self and others are thus continually re-negotiated through situated linguistic practices.

In their work, Bakhtin and his colleagues—the "Bakhtin Circle"—emphasized the *responsive* nature of the social utterances issued by self to an ongoing cultural dialogue (Holquist 2004, 60). Subjects respond to words received from others, which are part of the broader language system that precedes their birth. As Graham Allen (2000) points out, for Bakhtin, words are not only social in the sense that they establish relations with others when spoken, but also in the sense that they are signs drawn from a cultural linguistic system which pre-exists individual usage (21). Given that the values and attitudes of others differ from those of the self, the social utterances of subjects become a site of conflict or *value negotiation* between self and others (Holquist 2004, 37; 61; 65; Gardiner 1992, 28; Vološinov 1976, 103). For the Bakhtin Circle, the self is constructed as social actors enact an evaluative position or stance relative to the values of others, via utterances which both select, and respond to, particular "words of the other" in situated social encounters.

For the Bakhtin Circle, this process is clearly illustrated in the dialogical phenomenon of "reported speech." Reported speech concerns the way in which the words of others are characterized in the subject's own utterances, including the quotation and paraphrasing of their words (Vološinov 1986, 115). Generalizing beyond this concern with the direct or indirect reproduction of prior speech acts, it could be argued that the speech of subjects in everyday life always involves a kind of "reporting" on the words of others; indeed, the very selection of words into an utterance is already an evaluative choice. Words bearing historically negotiated meanings are thus, in everyday life, continually incorporated into the "authorial context" of the subject (Vološinov 1986, 116). To use a term from Jacques Derrida (see 1988, 12), the words of the other are "grafted" into the utterances of the self on an ongoing basis. Because of this, Vološinov suggests that the phenomenon of reported speech reveals a great deal about the variable *relationships* between self and others, such as their social statuses relative to each other.

The *way* in which the words of others are "reported" involves the representation and negotiation of values, and as such is a political matter. For example, the words of others might be distorted, reported upon in a mocking tone, or represented more neutrally; cultures and individuals vary in their use of particular syntactical forms to report, and "report on," the words of others (Vološinov 1986). Vološinov argues that standard syntactical practices emerge within different languages as to the normative ways in which the words of others are to be reported. Such practices reflect underlying cultural ideas about the relationship between self and other. For example, the extent to which a culture recognizes the self as uniquely individual, or as an undistinguished member of a larger social group, will be reflected in the particular linguistic, syntactical forms of reported speech (see Strauss 1989; Lee 1993).

For Vološinov, reported speech involves not only the "external" way that the speech of the other is reported in social situations, but also concerns the "inner" speech of the self (1986, 118). The internal dialogue of the self involves an ongoing engagement by self with these "words of the other"—as a kind of internal "reporting" on them. In this sense, cultural forms regulating reported speech, which themselves carry assumptions about the relationships between self and other, also affect the nature of the internal dialogue of the self.

For the Bakhtin Circle, reporting practices involving politicized words not only enact relationships between *specific* individuals, but also enact the relationship between the self and more *general* social norms and values. Reported speech given by subjects in various situations not only "takes a stand" relative to the values of co-present others, but also assumes a stance relative to the norms and values of the society at large—what the Bakhtin Circle alternately termed the "hero," the "superaddressee," or the "third" (see Vološinov 1976, 103; Clark and Holquist 1984, 205; MacCannell 1985, 980; Holquist 2004, 38). These terms generally refer to the normative discourse of the larger culture, which serves as the often unverbalized backdrop of assumptions relative to the interaction between self and co-present "addressee" (see Clark and Holquist 1984, 207). Any particular utterance therefore has to mediate between the values of the subject and the normative discourse of the culture, as well as take a position relative to the values of co-present others in a particular situation. In other words, the "superaddressee"—or the "generalized other" in Mead's (1969) sense—serves as the backdrop against which interactants politically negotiate social relationships.

After the self enacts a social position by reporting the words of others in various ways in "outer speech," the utterances of the subject will then be received by others. Of course, these others who receive and reply to the utterances of self are not only those who are physically co-present, but—especially in an age enabling the mass distribution of language—may be quite spatially and temporally distant from the situation in which they were uttered by self. The social "contexts" into which the (reporting) utterances of the self will later be grafted are often beyond the anticipation and the control of the subject making these utterances (Derrida 1988)—just as the words chosen and used by the self in constructing their own utterances had slipped well beyond the intentionality of prior users. Thus, the chain of "reported speech events" might best be thought of not in terms of the intentionality of individual subjects, but rather as a process involving a continuing re-citation, and recontextualization, of the words of others across situations.

This insight provides an important connection between the work of the Bakhtin Circle, Jacques Derrida, and Judith Butler. To "report on" the words of others involves a process of quoting, paraphrasing—or even just using—those words within the utterances of the self, while taking an evaluative stance toward their implied values. The words of others are thus "cited" in a favorable or unfavorable way in particular situations. Just as the "identity" of an academic work is constructed through a series of citational references with which the author agrees or disagrees, the social identity of the subject is constructed through the incorporation and evaluation of the words of others into one's own utterances—a process of citation. Butler's work is particularly concerned with how *gendered* identity categories are continually re-cited across situated contexts.

In a Derridean sense, it is because words can be re-cited *across* situations that social meanings, and thereby social values, are possible (see Derrida 1988). Before discussing more fully how the work of the members of the Bakhtin Circle on reported speech can be incorporated into a theory of performative citationality, however, it is first important to recognize the insistence of Bakhtin and his colleagues on the *materiality of the utterance*—and thus the materiality of re-citational practices.

THE MATERIALITY OF CITATIONAL PRACTICE

In *Marxism and the Philosophy of Language*, Vološinov (1986) emphasizes the importance of the materiality of the sign for human "experience." Experience, he argues, occurs through material signs, and consciousness itself is constituted "*only in the material embodiment of signs*" (Vološinov 1986, 11, italics in the original). Vološinov also emphasizes that meaning cannot be separated from its material embodiment. He suggests that the meaningful materiality of empirical reality is not only the basis of shared cultural meaning, but also is the basis of the self's "inner experience" (28). From this perspective, it is the meaningful *materiality* of the sign, as embodied in "objective" social forms, which is the basis for the formation of the self—as well as for the enactment of social relations between self and others. The values of self, relative to the values of others, are always constructed in an utterance in a syntactical form—that is, a particular material configuration of linguistic signs.

In this book, utterances will be considered as "material" in the sense expressed by Derrida in *Limited Inc* (1988), and in this way be linked to the position of the Bakhtin Circle. In that work, Derrida argues that every meaningful sign inherently must be able to function in the absence of any author or reader in order to be socially recognizable. Every sign, including those which represent social identities, carries the possibility of being removed from any particular context, and "grafted" or "cited" into a different context (1988, 7; 12)—a break from authorial context which is both spatial and temporal. For Derrida, the very nature of "understandability" already implies the temporal reproduction of linguistic forms from the past into the future, as well as across different spatial locations. This "iterability" means that every mark must be able to leave any context, and be insertable into any other context, if it is to be socially meaningful. Derrida thus describes "the possibility of disengagement and citational graft which belongs to the structure of every mark, spoken or written" (12).

In this sense, materiality is that which is recognized as "the same" across situational contexts, and given (shared) meaning. Of course, the "modality" (Althusser 1971)—or what Bruno Latour calls the "mutability" (in Bolt 2004, 24)—of material forms differ. The list of potentially meaningful material forms could thus include written marks, physical gestures, social objects, the sound of a voice, or digital images. It is in this sense that this book will speak of the "materiality of language"—as a *meaningful materiality* which is recognizable across situational contexts. "Language" will thus be considered in its broadest sense, including not only words, but also including any culturally meaningful "materiality"—such as images or social objects. It is also in this sense that we will consider language as a material *commodity*, which—in contemporary syntactical forms such as television shows, websites, or films—can come to have a (meaningful) exchange value across situated contexts.

We can thus see an affinity between the notion of reported speech in the Bakhtin Circle, and Derrida's notion of citational grafts. Both refer to the movement of meaningful materialities into another "context." For Vološinov, reported speech involves moving the words of others into the utterances of self; for Derrida, citational grafting involves the possibility of a meaningful mark carrying its meaning into a new context, when quoted or cited into that context. Given that these meaningful materialities can themselves acquire an exchange value, as well as "represent" other subcultural values, we can see that individual and institutional utterances are a site for the negotiation of values within a culture. Bringing Derrida's work on citationality and Bakhtin's work on the utterance together, we might thus consider how the images, objects and words of the other become "citational resources" for subjects, who establish their own social identities via material utterances which take an evaluative stance toward those resources.

When the words or images of others are "cited," the new syntactical arrangement socially positions the subject relative to cultural values, and—in Vološinov's sense of "inner speech"—becomes the basis for the subjective "experiences" of the subject. These syntactical configurations of meaningful materialities "play off" values against each other. Such configurations would include not only the sequencing of words in an utterance, but would also include the arrangement of words and images in a magazine advertisement, or the use of images and sounds together on a website. These material, syntactical arrangements not only provide citational resources for the construction of the self, but are themselves more or less marketable as the (material) basis of cultural experiences for others.

If, in a Derridean sense, the "identity" of meaningful marks can only occur through their repeatability *across* contexts, then the identity of such signs must be a function of the spatial and temporal *differentiation of* contexts. If identifiable meaning thus involves both the material grafting of marks into new contexts, as well as the differentiation of those contexts, an interesting question emerges as to whether it is more accurate to say—in Derrida's sense—that words have meaning "across contexts," or rather that *meaning emerges as contexts are both grafted together, and (re-)differentiated, in syntactically arranged material signs*. In addition, it might be worthwhile to remember here that for the Bakhtin Circle, the context against which an utterance makes sense is itself enacted *through* the utterance (MacCannell 1985, 984–85)—rather than pre-existing it. In this sense, the very presence of what appear to be autonomous and separable valuing contexts, which pre-exist their citation, is actually the *result* of particular syntactical arrangements of meaningful materialities (see Barad 2007).

This grafting of contexts occurs through socially meaningful material forms, which simultaneously *cite more than one (referential) context*—as in the case of reported speech, where the values of both self and other are grafted together. It is through the material form of utterances that subcultural values, such as religious or political values, are continually re-differentiated and re-negotiated. It is argued in this book that unequal social relations and hegemonic social values, including the system of exchange value, are re-cited or resisted through the *ongoing syntactical grafting of meaningful material forms*—in both institutional and individual utterances.

THE REPORTING OF SOCIAL IDENTITIES AND SOCIAL RELATIONSHIPS

Bakhtin, influenced by Albert Einstein's theory of relativity, argued that the meaning of social identity—like all meaning—requires two referential contexts (Holquist 2004, 20–21). The self, for the Bakhtin Circle, requires the other in order for this meaning to emerge. It is through the materiality of signs that the self cites the words of the other into its own unique utterance, thus bringing together—yet differentiating—these two referential contexts of self and other. The self encounters the "words of the other," in their materiality, and weaves them into its own responses. In this sense, the self emerges as "intertextual" (see Allen 2006), and constructed from an ongoing dialogue with others. The referential contexts of others are thus "grafted" with the referential context of self. As suggested above, the assertion that "meaning crosses contexts"—and as such is abstractable and repeatable—somewhat obscures the materiality of the grafting process, inasmuch as it is the *form* of the material sign which shapes *how* particular contexts are both united and differentiated. For Bakhtin, it is through the materiality of language—syntactical formations of linguistic signs—that the referential contexts of self and other(s) intersect.

To emphasize the "materiality of the graft" is to open the Derridean theory of citationality to the contribution of the Bakhtin Circle, which precisely emphasized how the syntactical arrangement of (material) words in utterances continually negotiates social relationships between self and others. Cultural values are grafted and situationally negotiated into particular hierarchies through utterances, as in reported speech. The subject grafts or cites the words of the other as they "report" on those words. When interactants in a social situation construct a dialogue using words from the larger culture, they actively craft relationships to each other against the backdrop of those larger cultural meanings and values. The self and co-present others select from the range of possible values from the larger culture to enact, and make relevant, to their situated interactions—necessarily taking an evaluative position toward those values.

The self thus encounters the words (and values) of others in their materiality. This not only includes those words of others addressed to them in everyday life, but also those words which are culturally available in the media—that is, "marks" of others not physically present. The responses of the subject may incorporate any of these "citational resources" into their own utterances, thus establishing and re-establishing relations with co-present others relative to larger cultural values. The "mark of the other" not only includes the ways the physical bodies of others meaningfully signify as they present themselves when co-present in a situation, but also—in the absence of the other—includes the books they've written, the music they've recorded, and other cultural commodities they may have produced. Utterances, as citational practices of the self which incorporate the signs of the other, thus (re-)enact particular social *relationships* with others.

The situational utterances issued by subjects continually re-incorporate the other in particular ways. The Bakhtin Circle argues that this incorporation of the perspective of the other, into the utterances of the self, is always a question of *proportion or ratio*—how much of the utterance of the self will remain "individual," and how much the utterance will "repeat" the referential perspective of another person (Holquist 2004, 29). The phenomenon of "reported speech," for example, directly speaks to the issue of *how* the values of the other are grafted with the values of the self in various proportions.

For example, the words of others can be reported verbatim with authorial neutrality on the part of self, or instead paraphrased with a great deal of added sarcasm. Syntactical forms of such citational reporting enact *political* relationships between self and other, and become mechanisms for value negotiation in everyday life. The material forms in which the words of others are reported, within the utterances of self (i.e., the citational grafts), enact the social *identities* of self and other in particular social relationships—such as the unequal relationship between gendered identities. The material form of any citational utterance both grafts together, and differentiates, the values of self and other—through the enactment of a hierarchy of values which are normatively taken to be associated with particular social identities.

It is important to note, however, that there is no necessary match between the *intended* meaning of one's utterances, and the *actual* responses of the other. While one's utterances may attempt to altercast the other in a particular way by re-citing a particular social relationship, as in the case of gender, there is no guarantee of its success. Subjects often anticipate one type of addressee, only to find another. In this sense, there can be no definitive addressee to an utterance, given that there can be no definitive correspondence between the anticipated response of another and their actual response. The social identity of the recipient cannot be secured in advance, but is only tentatively assumed. Thus, the "meaning" of the relationship implied by the utterance is only tentatively stated. Once an utterance is actually issued, the situation between self and other has necessarily changed from that anticipated by the subject.

When Derrida argues that a sign must be able to function in the *absence* of any addressee, his discussion speaks to the iterability of the mark; it is not to deny that subjects have ongoing relationships with *real* "addressees," who take up and respond to each other's utterances in everyday life. These are not incompatible positions: that an utterance expresses an ongoing situational relationship with an addressee (whose actions cannot be entirely predicted), and that the utterance must be made within repeatable, recognizable social forms which have the ability to function beyond any particular situational context.

What a Derridean reading adds to the framework of the Bakhtin Circle is to emphasize that the *meaning* of the relationship between self and other is not given once and for all in any particular utterance, but rather is continually deferred into the future. In Derridean terms, the meaning of a social relationship—like any meaning—is never quite "present" (see Derrida 1988; 1981). Utterances spoken or written in the past can, as material signs, always be reinterpreted. Future utterances can rewrite the meaning of past utterances. Thus, if an utterance may be said to posit or enact the "meaning of a relationship" between self and other (relative to normative cultural values), it is always a temporary, incomplete meaning. While, as the Bakhtin Circle argued, the (anticipated) "other" must be temporarily "closed" in order for identities to emerge at all (see Holquist 2004, 26–28; 84), it is also true that the meaning of those identities—as well as the meaning of the *relationship* between identities—is continually "torn apart" by the actual, situated responses of the other (see Vološinov 1986, 106).

REPORTED SPEECH AND CITATIONALITY

Derrida's work on citationality can be used to link the work of the Bakhtin Circle to the more contemporary theoretical work on performativity—especially the version of performativity theory developed by Judith Butler. In this section, Butler's insights regarding the "performativity of gender" will be extended into a more general theory regarding the performativity of all values, especially exchange value. Just as identity categories such as gender are re-cited in performative utterances across situational contexts, so are the values normatively associated with those identities. In "reporting on" the words and images of others in evaluative utterances, normative identity categories and cultural value discourses are recited or resisted.

As mentioned above, Derrida (1988) shows that for a speech act or any cultural form to be meaningful, and socially identifiable, it must be *citable*—that is, it must be repeatable across situational contexts. We find in Derrida's discussion of the citability of linguistic marks not only a dislocation of the autonomous, intentional subject normatively assumed in Western metaphysics, but also an alternative version of identity construction—which foregrounds a process by which the subject is constituted in a relationship with alterity. The construction of any meaningful social identity involves the repetition or re-citation of particular meaningful signs across situations, at the exclusion of other signs and meanings.

Butler, like Derrida, criticizes the notion of a sovereign, autonomous subject, arguing instead that the "subject" is an effect of citational practice (1997). For Butler, the citation of cultural scripts in everyday social performances constructs certain types of gendered subjects. Drawing upon the work of Michel Foucault, Butler argues that inasmuch as the subject is born into a system of normative citational practice which always already positions certain types of subjects, the subject is not entirely free to construct utterances according to a sovereign intentionality.

While gendered performances constitute and constrain the subject along gender lines, at the same time they make (gendered) *agency* possible—a kind of "enabling constraint" (1997, 16). This enabling constraint issues a social positionality—or, in Bakhtin's terms, a social "addressivity" (Holquist 2004, 48)—from which the subject responds. In a Derridean sense, even as re-citational practices attempt to re-establish stable social identities across contexts, regulated identities are necessarily disrupted because of the singularity of the situated re-citation; that is, repetition necessarily alters identity (Derrida 1988). Just as subjects cannot "fix" the intended meaning of their utterances, neither can a citational performance absolutely stabilize the social identity which is implied by the utterance. For Butler, then, while particular forms of speech acts re-enact particular kinds of subjects, they can never fully determine those subjects.

The kind of social agency which Butler (1999) envisions is situated between a determinism which involves the mere repetition of identity categories within a closed system, and that of a voluntaristic subject who is free to enact a social identity according to their own intentionality. The re-citationality of social performance *enables* the subject, but at the same time it *disrupts* the presence of that identity. We thus find Butler's position in line with Derrida's critique of the presence of the sovereign Cartesian subject.

Along with the notion of iterative citationality, Butler also agrees with Derrida's critique regarding J.L. Austin's notion of a performative speech act. In Austin's speech act theory, as Butler puts it, a "performative" is "that discursive practice that enacts or produces that which it names" (1993, 13)—such as in Austin's example of the pronouncement of a couple as "married." For Austin, the performative utterance does not merely describe a social situation, but rather brings one into being. As Butler notes, Derrida's (1988) critique of Austin moves the performative away from the (authoritative) control of the intentional subject, in the direction of the *citational* aspect of performatives—recognizing that performatives re-cite authoritative conventions. Butler states that, "If a performative provisionally succeeds . . . it is . . . only because that action echoes prior actions, *and accumulates the force of authority through the repetition or citation of a prior, authoritative set of practices*" (1993, 226–27; italics in the original).

For Butler, then, performances are not given by a sovereign subject; rather, they are re-enactments of prior performances which are socially recognizable and normatively re-enforced within a culture. It is Butler's thesis that gender is performative in this sense, given that the continual re-enactment of a gendered cultural script in turn continually re-constitutes the gendered subject. This behavioral re-enactment is not merely voluntary, however, but enforced by power within society—what Butler, influenced by Foucault, calls the "forced reiteration of norms" (1993, 94). The gendered subject is enabled as agent through this social ritual, yet is simultaneously constrained by—or "subject" to—the identity category.

This enabling constraint not only applies to the regulated form of one's own utterances, but also applies when others altercast them into particular social roles and social categories—as in Louis Althusser's well-known example of a citizen being "hailed" by a police officer on the street. For Althusser (1971), this process of "interpellation" occurs through the practice of re-citation—in Butler's words, "that continually repeated action of discourse by which subjects are formed in subjugation" (1997, 27). Hailing or interpellating a subject as a potential police suspect "works" as a performative because the action of the police officer cites prior instances of this practice—that is, it has become normative. In *Excitable Speech* (1997), Butler argues that hate speech precisely attempts to "interpellate" a subject into a subordinate position using such a practice—thus re-establishing a particular political relationship between subjects (2).

For Butler, the success of this attempt at altercasting the identity of others is not guaranteed in advance; she thereby criticizes the notion of a deterministic "discursive constitution" (19) of the other. Butler argues that one cannot totally guarantee an effective interpellation of the identity of the other, regardless of the level of social authority "behind" the citational practice. For Butler, attempts to altercast the other are not only acts of constraint, but simultaneously establish the social addressivity which enables the agency of subjects. She thus argues that while injurious speech attempts to position a subject within a stigmatized social category, there is no guarantee of its success. While constraining the other, it simultaneously constitutes, rather than removes, the social positionality of their agency.

Butler also argues that Althusser's notion of interpellation must be not be considered as originating from the "presence" of an authority figure, as in the case of the police. For Butler, Althusser retains such a metaphysical assumption regarding the "voice" of the authoritative, intentional subject (32–3). Instead, she argues that the effectiveness of the police officer's command is derived from the *re-citation* of a social convention, which re-establishes the authority (and identity) of the officer. In this book, the term "interpellation" will be used to refer to the way that particular re-citational practices position *both* social actor and addressee as certain types of individual subjects, as well as construct particular *collective* subjects who are assumed to share "subcultural values." In the Western ideology of "presence," these interpellated subjects are mistakenly taken to be the origin and motivator of the citational practices themselves—a move which disguises the process by which identity is itself enacted through citational practice (Butler 1997; Derrida 1988; Althusser 1971; Weber 1991).

Social conventions that interpellate racialized or gendered subject categories, for example, are repeated on an ongoing basis—a re-occurring social citationality which re-establishes these normative identity categories. As Butler notes, the category of gender, which both enables and limits the gendered subject, must be repeatedly *re-performed* in order to reconsolidate its effects. Citing Antonio Gramsci, Butler notes that "hegemonies" such as the discourse of gender operate only through "rearticulation" or repetition (1993, 132). Thus for Butler, a structure of inequality "only remains a structure through being reinstated as one" (1997, 139). We can see here the affinity of Butler's view of performativity with efforts in sociology to bridge the gap between agency and structure (see Giddens 1984).

Social relationships between self and other, then, are re-established through the repeated citation of those conventions which reinforce particular social identities of subjects and others. For Butler, however, agency includes not only the possibility of the repetition and reproduction of *normative* social identities and relationships, as in the case of re-establishing the gender hierarchy, but also the possibility of *dislocating* normative relationships through the same process. Butler argues that precisely because of the possibility of future repetitions in unknown situations, different social relationships are possible between self and others.

Just as one's utterances may attempt to interpellate an identity for others, these utterances simultaneously interpellate a social identity for self. Utterances issued from within situated and constraining identity categories—as in the case of gender—either "re-cite" and re-interpellate that normative category, or resist and interpellate an alternate identity which plays against the norm. If social identity is constituted through linguistic practices, and reproduced through a process of normative re-citationality, then alternative subjectivities become possible—through the dislocation of normative practices.

While the process of citationality necessarily restricts identity, for Butler it is only *through* the process of citationality that any possible "reconfiguration" can occur (1999, 185). In *Bodies That Matter*, Butler discusses what Gayatri Chakravorty Spivak has termed "an enabling violation" (Spivak, in Butler 1993, 122), noting that "The 'I' who would oppose its construction is always in some sense drawing from that construction to articulate its opposition; further, the 'I' draws what is called its 'agency' in part through being implicated in the very relations of power that it seeks to oppose" (Butler 1993, 122–23). The agency of subjects, while framed and limited by normative identity categories, can never be finally extinguished or determined through the process of interpellation.

For example, in her work on gendered performances, Butler shows how a performed parody may recontextualize "gender" and thus disrupt its normative meanings (1999, 186–89). For Butler, the spread of such practices of dislocation across a culture may force a "resignification" of the identity category itself, and open a possibility that future re-citations may signify differently. Butler thus argues that since structures of inequality—involving identity categories—are dependent upon re-citation for their continued functioning, it is precisely at the point of re-citation where their legitimacy might be most effectively challenged.

"Agency," for Butler, is thus linked to *possibility* (see 1999, 185; italics in the original); any situated repetition of identity categories reproduces or resists normative forms to varying degree. In their work, citing the contributions of Dwight Conquergood, Homi Bhabha, Jill Dolan, D. Soyini Madison, and others, Madison and Hamera also argue that performances carry the possibility of disrupting normative, sedimented citational practices (2006, xviii–xix). As Madison has noted, "Subversive performativity can disrupt the very citations that hegemonic performativity enacts" (Madison, quoted in Madison and Hamera 2006, xix). In fact, Butler has tied the question of moral responsibility to citational practices which either re-cite or resist normative constructions—as opposed to a morality situated within the autonomous consciousness and intended actions of a Cartesian subject (1997, 39).

While Butler thus follows Derrida's use of citationality as a way to criticize the sovereign subject of Western metaphysics, she also argues that Derrida loses the *social* dimension of citationality by locating it in the "*structure* of iterability"; that is, as an inherent feature of language. As noted above, Derrida (1988) shows in his critique of Austin that the meaning of a "performative" derives not from the intentionality of a subject, nor from the dictates of a particular context, but rather from its ability to move across contexts. For Derrida, this structural feature enables the repeatability and recognizability of the meaning of performances across contexts.

Butler, however, favors what she calls a "social" rather than a "structural" iterability (1997, 152). She argues that the force of the performative becomes "sedimented" (145) based on prior *social* repetitions. While it is true that social meaning depends upon repetition across contexts, Butler contends—though not without challenge (see Kirby 2006, 105)—that Derrida's "structural" formulation of iterability fails to give proper emphasis to the social character of these re-enactments, and thereby underestimates the potential for disruptive re-citational practices. For Butler, "structure" is just another name for the accumulated *social* force of normative citational practices, rather than an inherent (asocial) feature of the mark. Citational performance thus involves an ongoing "re-structuring" of meaning.

However, against Pierre Bourdieu, Butler (1997) simultaneously argues that this accumulated or sedimented social force cannot be guaranteed in advance through the intentionality of powerful social actors, or the "legitimate" authority of social institutions—inasmuch as re-citationality always carries the possibility of transformation. Butler thus attempts to retain a Derridean view of citationality, while at the same time recognizing that each instance of citational practice re-establishes a *social* relation between self and other—here coinciding with the position taken by the Bakhtin Circle in their discussion of reported speech.

An important aspect of Butler's argument is that, as we see in the case of gender, a social category pertaining to *group membership* enables and constrains the agency of individuals. When a social actor engages in citational practices—such as wearing particular types of clothing in accordance with normative gender roles—they are re-interpellated as a member of that particular community. In addition, particular social *values* are typically associated with interpellated group memberships and identity categories; for example, stereotypes about masculinity and femininity in the U.S. involve the attribution of particular social values to each gendered category. In this sense, citational practices which evoke identity categories such as gender *simultaneously interpellate particular social values*.

In this way, we might generalize beyond Butler's work on gender to suggest that *all social values are performative*. Citational practices in everyday life—whether words uttered, images displayed, or social objects positioned within the home—re-align the subject with particular valuing communities. For example, the placement of a religious object within the material environment of the home re-interpellates membership in that religious community, and re-aligns the identity of the subject with particular religious values. Given that words, objects, or images are normatively taken to "represent" particular subcultural values, their citation indicates membership in that valuing community. Engaging in re-citational practices, then, results in the re-interpellation of social identities, as well as the values normatively associated with those identities.

In this way, the work of the Bakhtin Circle on values can be linked to Butler's theory of performativity. Every utterance, which necessarily reports on and evaluates the speech of others, re-cites or resists normative value categories. The identity of the subject, as a "representative" member of a particular valuing community, is thus *re-interpellated through everyday utterances*. In a Derridean sense, the values of subjects—like any meanings—must be continually re-cited across situational contexts in order to remain meaningful. This re-citation of values is re-enacted through the material, syntactically-configured utterances of everyday life.

Judith Butler's approach allows us to move the work of the Bakhtin Circle, on how utterances negotiate the values of self and others, in a post-structuralist direction—that identity and value categories are interpellated from utterances, rather than pre-existing them. Normative identity and value categories re-emerge through a process of performative citationality. In turn, the work of the Bakhtin Circle allows us to extend Butler's work on the performativity of gender toward a more general thesis regarding the performativity of values. Social identity becomes an interpellated site where hierarchical arrangements of multiple social values are continually negotiated and displayed. To put it differently, social identities are interpellated from particular syntactical arrangements of material signs, as subjects respond from within, and to, the material environments constructed by the utterances of others.

AGENCY AND THE RE-CITATION OF VALUE

Agency and Enabling Constraints

The material form of meaningful signs always already depends on the interests of those who have prepared that materiality in such a way as to enter into particular contexts—as in the case of institutional utterances configured in marketable forms relative to the referential contexts of consumers. Bauman and Briggs (1990) have used the term "entextualization" to refer to the process of selecting a strip of language from the flow of everyday life, and readying it for insertion into another context (73). Particular material forms are entextualized in particular ways by institutions as citational resources, and marketed to subjects for use in identity construction. In this sense, economic forces shape normative material environments.

Incorporating Foucault's notion of "regulatory norms," Judith Butler similarly considers the materiality of the body to be an "effect of power" (1993, 2), where dominant economic and political forces shape *how* materiality communicates. As Foucault argues, power is invested in material forms (Butler 1993, 34–35; Foucault 1995). Adding the language of the Bakhtin Circle, we might say that cultural forms are shaped into particular material, syntactical constellations given the "regulatory norms" of a culture, and the workings of the political economy. These socially sedimented material forms, in turn, interpellate socially differentiated subjects.

The material, syntactical forms of language continually re-constitute, through normative citational practices, the political relationships between interpellated social identities. The prioritization of certain material forms in the culture thus relates to social hierarchies. Those material forms interpellating dominant cultural values are not only more often re-produced, but those economic networks which distribute or circulate these forms become "more institutionalized."

On the other hand, for Butler, the very citational practices which reproduce relations of power also enable the agency of subjects within these relations. Butler follows Derrida in arguing that the construction of any identity involves the "abjection" of excluded alterity (Butler 1993, 3). Given that any recognizable material sign always already holds its abjected "other" within, the social identity interpellated from such a sign is necessarily hybrid. This holds not only for the construction of social *identity*, but—in the Bakhtinian sense—simultaneously for the hybrid social *relationships* between self and others, as enacted through such identity categories. With their alterity within, such identities and relationships can never be finally secured in their "presence." Unequal social relationships between identities can be altered.

For Butler, the openness of the future to the continual recontextualization of identity categories means that there can be no final abjection or interpellation of the other into a subordinate social position. Butler thus argues that the "rematerialization" which occurs, as normative material signs are re-cited, offers the *possibility* of the dislocation of normative meanings and identities. For Butler, then, the identity that is enabled through the iterative re-citation of imposed categories can never be entirely stable or final.

Committed to the poststructuralist critique of the intentional, autonomous subject of the Cartesian metaphysical tradition, Butler states that "the question of agency is not to be answered through recourse to an 'I' that pre-exists signification. In other words, the enabling conditions for an assertion of 'I' are provided by the structure of signification" (1999, 183). As Butler puts it in a commentary on writing styles, citing the work of Monique Wittig, "gender itself is naturalized through grammatical norms" (1999, xix). With her notion of "enabling constraint," Butler attempts to steer a course through the difficult sociological opposition between agency and structure (see Lloyd 2007, 40). She supports neither the notion of a voluntaristic subject, nor a structurally determined one.

From Butler's perspective, "structure" is always re-cited and re-performed. In this way, Butler wants to oppose a "structural" determination of the subject as based on their positionality within a system—as in the case of Jean Baudrillard's determinant "code" (see Kellner 1991, 18–19; 28). On this point, she puts forth an argument similar to that of Anthony Giddens's (1984) work on structuration, or the work of Alexander, Giesen, and Mast (2006) on social performance. Those theorists insist that any "structure" must be continually re-performed in everyday life; as Giddens puts it, "structuration theory is based on the proposition that structure is always both enabling and constraining, in virtue of the inherent relation between structure and agency (and agency and power)" (1984, 169). Butler thus argues that agency is always a matter of re-enactment or re-citation, occurring within the material constraints that past citational practices have constructed—but which simultaneously enable new recontextualizations that have the potential to alter existing identities and values.

Citational Grafts and the Interpellation of Cultural Values

In a performative sense, "values" do not pre-exist their material enactment; rather, they emerge from particular material configurations—and are negotiated within those syntactical forms. From a performative perspective, neither the "values" of autonomous subjects, nor the "exchange value" of social objects, can be said to pre-exist their citational re-enactment. In addition, given the continual negotiation and contestation which occurs syntactically within material utterances, the values interpellated from those utterances are not "pure" value domains. Rather—in a Bakhtinian sense—a hybrid, or hierarchically arranged mix of values, are interpellated from any utterance (see Gardiner 28–29; 83–84; 107).

While a *representationalist* perspective assumes that value pre-exists its communicative expression, a *performative* perspective instead suggests that both subcultural values, and exchange value, are normatively re-enacted *through citational practices*. However, despite recent turns in contemporary marketing toward performativity theory—especially in the recognition of the co-creation of value by consumers (see Prahalad and Ramaswamy 2004)—the ideology of representationism persists in the U.S. cultural economy. In addition, while Derrida's version of citationality, resting on a notion of iterability, shows that value can never be fully "present," the metaphysical and ideological notion of the "presence of value" also persists in normative practice in the U.S. cultural economy. The theories of Bakhtin, Derrida, and Butler can be used both to *describe* the current workings of the U.S. cultural economy—in its ideological functioning—as well as contribute to its *critique and transformation*. In this section, it is shown how Bakhtin's work is compatible with the more critical version of performativity put forth by Judith Butler, as based on Derrida's notions of citationality and iterability.

In her essay, *The Temporality of Textuality: Bakhtin and Derrida*, Juliet Flower MacCannell (1985) argues that by revising Ferdinand de Saussure's notion of a "synchronic" system of language into a "scene or *synchronization*" (974, italics in the original), Bakhtin is able to show how utterances continually re-negotiate values in situated linguistic practice. Bakhtin demonstrates that "values" continually re-emerge *from* syntactical forms—as opposed to the notion that the material forms merely "represent" particular values as differentiated in a pre-existing linguistic system. In this sense, Bakhtin's work clearly does not re-enact the type of "presence" which is the target of Derrida's critique of Western metaphysics (970).

For Bakhtin, the differential meanings which make up the "synchronic" system of language always involve differing values (974). An utterance which re-cites a differential system of *meanings* thus also re-cites a differential system of social *values*. As MacCannell points out, for the Bakhtin Circle what is exchanged within the language system is not the pre-existing meanings expressing the thoughts of participants, but *words with values* (974). As Vološinov puts it, "In actuality we never say or hear *words*, we say and hear what is true or false, good or bad, important or unimportant, pleasant or unpleasant, and so on" (Vološinov 1986, 70, italics in the original).

In this view, material signs are always already "ideological" (10), or carry a particular "evaluative accent" or "intonation" (103). Thus, MacCannell argues that the evaluative utterance *enacts* the "synchronic" system. In other words, the self, by taking a "value stance" in an utterance, *puts into play* the system of differential values and meanings which Saussure calls the "synchronic." The "elements" in a linguistic system are not just differential to each other, but are hierarchically arranged or evaluated; that is, they are continually re-arranged through situated linguistic practice.

For Bakhtin, the relationship between the utterance and the valuing context against which it is interpreted is a reciprocal one—the interpretive context implied by the utterance does not pre-exist it, but rather re-emerges via the utterance (MacCannell 1985, 984-85). If "values," such as political values, economic value, or moral values, can be thought of as interpretive or valuing "contexts"—as the ground against which certain behaviors are evaluated—we can see that citational utterances continually re-evoke, or re-interpellate, such value contexts. In other words, the utterances of an individual subject continually conjure imagined collectivities, whose values and group identities the utterance is (ideologically) taken to "represent" (Butler 1997; Althusser 1971; MacCannell 1985, 984–85; see also Anderson 1991).

In the language of a theory of citationality, we can see that the syntactical forms of utterances, which graft the words of self with the words of others, necessarily interpellate differentiated, hierarchically arranged values and affiliated identities. In the utterance, the values of both self and other are negotiated in material form. In other words, it is not the case that an utterance interpellates a *single* valuing context against which it is interpreted; rather, any utterance necessarily initiates an interpellative re-grafting which involves differential values, arranged in a hierarchy. The syntactical, material form of reported speech necessarily *prioritizes* these differential valuing contexts, and thus simultaneously takes an evaluative stance relative to several cultural value discourses. The "synchronic," hierarchically–differentiated system of values interpellated from the utterance, to a greater or lesser degree, aligns with the normative value hierarchy within the culture—that is, the utterance "takes a stand" toward it.

At the same time, the social identities of individuals are also interpellated from such "hybrid" citational grafts; therefore, no individual social identity interpellated from an utterance can be a "pure" representative of a particular valuing community. In this sense, individual identity becomes a site of multiple, hierarchically–arranged values. The identity achieves some measure of stable social meaning through a consistent re-prioritization of multiple valuing contexts.

We can see here an affiliation with the line of thought developed in poststructuralism around Althusser's notion of "ideological interpellations" (Althusser 1971; Laclau 1977; Butler 1997). For example, Wolfreys (2004) has noted that for Slavoj Žižek and for Ernesto Laclau, the subject becomes the *site* where ideological discourse is consolidated. As Laclau puts it, "*what constitutes the unifying principle of an ideological discourse is the 'subject' interpellated and thus constituted through this discourse* . . . There are different types of interpellations (political, religious, familial, etc.) which coexist whilst being articulated within an ideological discourse in a relative unity" (Laclau, in Wolfreys 2004, 118; italics in Laclau).

In this regard, Bakhtin's work can be useful to emphasize the *materiality* of the process of "ideological interpellation." The syntactical forms of reported speech—in grafting the words of self with those of others—not only *unify*, but also *differentiate* interpellated "value contexts" in hierarchical fashion. Normative value and identity hierarchies not only are re-produced through the re-citation of normative material forms, but also can be challenged by the citation of materialities which are syntactically configured in alternative, non-normative forms.

As discussed above, Judith Butler endeavors to move Derrida's theory of "iterability" away from emphasizing the "structural" capability of an utterance to cross contexts, toward a more "social" iterability recognizing the sedimented, and politically motivated, meanings of utterances (see 1997, 148–52). We see here, as MacCannell reads Bakhtin, room for such a move. For Bakhtin, the differential contexts of identity and alterity—the two referential contexts "structurally necessary" for the production of meaning—are *put into play by the utterance itself.* These utterances, involving meaningful signs, contain socially sedimented meanings (and values). The relationships between these differentiated values are continually re-negotiated and restructured via the material form of the utterances themselves. Dominant social values and identity categories, such as gender, are continually re-cited and once again "put into play" in new utterances in new social situations—a *social* iterability. In this sense, to "materialize" utterances is to embrace or resist normative value hierarchies in a "scene of synchronization" (MacCannell 1985, 974)—or, echoing the language of performative citationality, a scene of "*re*-synchronization."

A system of differential values—those of self, other, and the normative culture—is thus continually "put into play" *materially* with every utterance. The stance taken by the subject relative to the values of co-participants in situated interaction, as well as toward those of the larger culture, shapes the syntactical form of utterances (see 980–82). In other words, after considering the implied values of words of co-present others received in dialogue—relative to the normative values of the culture—the subject replies with a citational utterance which simultaneously enacts a particular relationship to both.

Thus for Bakhtin, utterances do not express the thoughts of an autonomous subject, as much as establish and re-establish relationships between self and others—a position compatible with Derrida's critique of the "intentional" subject. Normative materialities have come to be differentiated as "representing" various cultural value domains, such as political, moral, ethnic, or religious values. Given that utterances always "report" on and use the words of others in their very formation, we can say that *citationality is the mechanism by which "values" are continually re-enacted and re-interpellated*—as the continuing "re-synchronization" of social relationships between self and others. The social identities of self and others become retroactive "representations" of larger valuing communities. The normative re-citation of material forms thus continually re-establishes normative social identities, as well as the normative relations between these "valuing" identities.

The words of the other thus come to the self not only with abstractable "dictionary meanings," but with meaningful *materialities* which always already imply particular social relationships involving particular social values—as when someone refers to normative gender categories. In the process of issuing one's own situated utterances—as responses to the words of the other—subjects are able to consider the general cultural implications of the words they select, as well as the situational implications relative to the values of fellow co-participants in everyday life. Co-participants in dialogue renegotiate their situated relationships using the normative citational resources of the larger culture, with their already-implied values.

There is an ongoing tension between *normatively* valued linguistic forms, and the *particular* intonation given to those forms in specific social situations by individuals—which may either reinforce, or undermine, those normative meanings. This formulation by the Bakhtin Circle is quite compatible with Derrida's notion of iterability, which precisely recognizes the tension between the contextual singularity, and the requisite repeatability, of any identifiable sign. Material forms can be taken as representations of stable and meaningful valuing contexts, yet also may dislocate those interpellated contexts when moved into new configurations with other material forms.

Identity and Value

Just as valuing contexts are interpellated from the entextualized utterances of the social actor, social identity is also interpellated from these utterances. The utterances of social actors simultaneously draw together two contexts—that of interpellated social *identity* categories and that of interpellated *value* domains. Reciprocally, the material sign is normatively taken as an entextualized *representative* of both contexts. Just as value genres, such as "political" or "religious" domains of value, become sedimented as repeatable and recognizable social categories across situations, so do social identity categories. Identity and value contexts are grafted together in entextualized material forms, and are thus interpellated together.

Through their utterances, embodied social actors thus become representatives of both social identity and value categories, earning (repeatable) reputations as "religious" or "family-oriented" types of people. The citation of a religious artifact in everyday life, for example, overlays the identity of the subject with religious values. Through such practices, the subject is taken as a representative of particular valuing communities, enacting a stance in relation to the values of others. This view regarding the interpellation of a group subject from citational practice inverts normative metaphysical assumptions regarding the relationship between the subcultural "consciousness" and social rituals.

Émile Durkheim's (1965) writings on the "elementary forms" of religion are interesting in this regard. Studying the beliefs of Australian clans, he notes that particular material "totems"—often animals or plants—are sacred to particular groups and provide the name (or identity) of the group (123). Drawings or paintings of the totem, which Durkheim refers to as "emblems," appear on everyday objects such as stones; these material objects become sacred inasmuch as they bear "*a design representing the totem*" of the group (140, italics in the original). While Durkheim's sociology in general emphasizes that "social facts"—like collectively held beliefs or values—exist as objective and autonomous social meanings which influence social action (1996), he also recognizes that "the emblem is not merely a convenient process for clarifying the sentiment society has of itself: it also serves to *create* this sentiment . . . It is by uttering the same cry, pronouncing the same word, or performing the same gesture in regard to the same object that they become and feel themselves to be in unison" (262, italics added).

In other words, while it is clear that for Durkheim a "collective consciousness" is what he calls a "social fact"—a sedimented cultural meaning and social force autonomous from individual consciousness—it is not altogether clear in Durkheim's study of religion whether the group consciousness actually motivates its material representation, or is interpellated *from* it. For Durkheim, the "material intermediaries," or emblems, "do not confine themselves to revealing the mental state with which they are associated; they aid in creating it" (263). Thus, the rituals relative to these materialities "gives the group consciousness of itself and consequently *makes it exist*" (263, italics added).

Durkheim argues that behavioral rituals in everyday life re-integrate members into the social group, and function to maintain its cohesion. This reading of Durkheim is quite compatible with a poststructuralist emphasis on citationality. The behavioral rituals relative to the meaningful materiality of sacred objects can be seen as *shared citational practices*, from which "collective values" are continually re-interpellated—making possible the normalization of citational references to an imagined collective community. Just as Butler argues that social identities such as gender must be continually re-cited in situated practices to remain normative, Durkheim notes that "these systems of emblems, which are necessary if society is to become conscious of itself, are no less indispensable for assuring the *continuation of this consciousness*" (263, italics added). For example, a Fourth-of-July parade in the United States, complete with quasi-sacred flags, is a normatively shared citational practice which re-interpellates an "imagined community" bound together by a sense of nationalism and patriotism (see Anderson 1991).

However, the detection of sociological patterns in citational practices—as in the case of youth citing differently than their elders (see Rochberg-Halton 1986)—should not lead to the assertion of "citational communities" which presumably share values *pre-existing* their shared citational practices. Rather, in a poststructuralist (and sometimes Durkheimian) sense, the emergence of shared citational practices help to "create" and sustain a sense of collective consciousness. Because of this, sociological research which studies the relationship between citational practices and variables such as age, gender, and so forth should consider the ways that differential citational practices are normatively grouped into "identities"—both by sociologists, as well as by social actors in everyday life. Put differently, contemporary sociology might focus less on the "influence" of pre-existing group values on their individual members, and focus more on the situated citational practices and interactional strategies by which social group memberships (and affiliated values) are re-cited—and through which ingroup/outgroup boundaries are continually redrawn.

In his study, Durkheim located the origin of religion in the experience of "crowd interaction"—that is, the "experience" of a social force larger than the individual (Turner, Beeghley, and Powers 2007, 304). This force, attributed in traditional cultures to the realm of the sacred—was then perceived as a "pre-existing" cause of events in everyday life—even though, according to Durkheim, the sense of the "larger force" was emergent *from* the interaction. Similarly, in the contemporary ideology of "presence," group identities and affiliated subcultural values—actually interpellated *from* citational practices—are instead perceived as the motivation of those very practices (Althusser 1971; Butler 1997; Weber 1991). From a poststructuralist point of view, as collectivities differ in what they cite as "sacred" or "profane," their differing group identities and values retroactively emerge.

Another contribution from Durkheim's model involves the persistence of the "quasi-sacred" nature of material representations into modern, secular cultures (Turner, Beeghley, and Powers 2007, 308). The modern discourses of value emerge with the prioritization of some "quasi-sacred" signs over other mundane signs, as re-enacted in citational rituals. Specific words, images, and objects of the other are re-cited as valuable through their social positioning and prioritization in time and space, as in the case of "quasi-sacred" objects prominently displayed in the home. Individual and group interpellations of identity occur through the hierarchical arrangement of valued or quasi-sacred signs; in other words, as displayed through citational rituals.

Through socialization processes, then, social actors are able to learn normative citational practices relative to valued material signs, as well as learn the identity attributions made to those who cite them—thus enabling subjects to take an active role in constructing their own social identities. Social actors envision themselves as members of valuing communities as they cite their way into them, grafting their social identity with the values of others engaged in similar citational practices—the citational practice itself taken as evidence of these shared values. As Vološinov has put it, "the whole formal structure of speech depends to a significant degree on what the relation of the utterance is to the assumed community of values belonging to the social milieu wherein the discourse figures" (1976, 103).

Of course, as the Bakhtin Circle has shown, the modern subject has *multiple*, competing reference group affiliations. In differing social situations, social actors "double-voice" (see Bakhtin 1984, 185) differing value domains through their citational practices. In other words, the voices of others are "heard" through the subject's voiced utterance—with varying levels of compatibility and value alignment. The unique value prioritization of any contemporary subject differs from that of others, as each individual's voicing of utterances simultaneously takes a unique stance relative to multiple cultural discourses. Thus, while each value genre itself—as socially meaningful—is repeatable and citable across situations by many different people, the "web of values" for any particular subject is a unique constellation (see Simmel, 1955). In this sense, social actors hold simultaneous "conversations" with many others, the consequence of which is that any interpellated identity simultaneously becomes positioned relative to multiple valuing contexts.

Thus, the utterances of self are not just double-voiced, but *multi-voiced*. If indeed the process of grafting multiple contexts via material signs produces "meaning," then we might say that the meaning of one's social identity refers to the hierarchical gathering of several valuing contexts together at the unique "site/cites" of the subject. A similar argument has been advanced in political theory regarding how a hegemonic ideology unifies multiple valuing discourses in the "identity" of the subject (Althusser 1971; Laclau 1977; Butler 1997; Wolfreys 2004). It is argued in this book that the exchange value discourse has emerged as such a unifying force in contemporary U.S. culture.

Social identity is interpellated from material utterances which are a unique combination of inclusions and exclusions—that is, some values are prioritized while others are abjected. As Butler shows, these inclusions and exclusions regarding the values of individual utterances are not entirely voluntary; they are both enabled by, and restricted by, normative identity categories such as race, class, and gender (see 1993). Normative identity categories thus arrive to subjects *already* grafted with particular value discourses. Subjects respond to, and from within, normative grafts of identity and value categories. Each of these normative contextual grafts enable certain behaviors, and restrict others. For example, Bourdieu (1984) shows how working-class identity is associated with "inferior values," resulting in the reproduction of social inequality in French schools and in the job market. The devaluation of the "cultural capital" of the poor in schools, in turn, restricts their later access to particular citational resources.

In Mead's (1969) sense, the "me," or "social identity," is not only interpellated by self and others from already *completed* utterances, but can also be interpellated by a social actor when *anticipating* future utterances. This moment of anticipation, however, should not be considered as belonging to a voluntaristic subject; rather, a subject's consideration of how others are likely to react toward an utterance is actually an "internal" repetition of past citational practices. The anticipatory rehearsal of a future citational practice thus belongs to a chain of re-enactments which give the social behavior meaning, falling in the gap between past and future actualizations of the considered behavior. In this sense, the moment of anticipation allows for a kind of "play" within the chain of re-enactments, where the *possibilities of recontextualization* can be considered—albeit within the constraints of existing material configurations, as well as the social constraints of the likely responses of others.

It is important here to distinguish between "social identity" and the "self." Using Mead's language (1969), the self is not limited to the social identity which is interpellated from a particular utterance (the "me"), but also includes an "I" phase. For Mead, this "I" phase—as in Bakhtin's formulation—keeps the self open to continual revision in new situations and therefore "unfinished." Reading Mead through poststructuralist theory, we can say that the self is thus comprised of both the "me"—the repeatable aspect of social identity as interpellated from particular entextualized forms—as well as the ongoing response (the "I") to such interpellated identity and value categorizations. The "self" continuously oscillates between the "I" and the "me" phases; but only the "me," or social identity, is interpellated from meaningful material forms. Because of the "I" phase, the self can never be identical with, or reduced to, a particular social identity; nor, in Derrida's sense, can the "me" remain identical with itself across contexts.

Mead's "anticipatory" phase of the act involves an awareness of how social identity will likely be interpellated from entextualized material forms, as well as how this entextualized identity is potentially repeatable in new situations. Thus, a person normatively refrains from a deviant act, knowing that their social identity will be entextualized by others in certain material forms (in words like "criminal," or in photographs in post offices, etc.). Subjects can anticipate how particular citational practices will likely interpellate a negative contextual framing—perhaps leading to the attribution of deviant values by others.

Identity must therefore be continually managed as an ongoing interplay between the anticipation of, and the retrospective interpretation of, that social identity. Responding to ongoing material constraints, a subject anticipates and actualizes syntactically arranged material utterances. These utterances by the subject incorporate, and play against, normative material configurations. It is from these constellations of meaningful materiality that social identity and affiliated values are continually re-interpellated.

The Anticipation of Citational Practice

The social psychology of George Herbert Mead emphasizes the human ability to anticipate the reactions of others to one's considered behavior, and make adjustments based on these anticipations (1969). Performativity theory and the critique of representationalism suggest that meaning, identity, and value do not pre-exist their behavioral enactment, but rather are interpellated from situated practice. The difficulty in incorporating Mead's work into a theory of performativity is to properly account for the fact that citational practices can be rehearsed and anticipated—without slipping back into the notion of the autonomous, intentional subject.

One of the goals of this book is to attempt such a task of incorporating Mead into a theory of performativity. It is argued that Mead's own view of "meaning" is helpful in this regard, in that for Mead "meaning" is located in a "social" awareness of the relationship between the actions of self and the likely social responses of others (Joas 1997, 105). In this formulation, meaning is not located in a self-reflective consciousness of an autonomous subject, but rather in shared, interactive "behavioural expectations" (116). If meaning, for Mead, involves the knowledge of normative patterns of behavior relative to shared material conditions—in other words, a knowledge of normative *citational practices*—then it seems a short step to move Mead's position into a poststructuralist framework, where the meanings of identity and value classifications are interpellated from such practices.

What Mead adds to the poststructuralist notions of "iterability" and "interpellation," then, is an appreciation that social behavior can be anticipated—because it is *normatively* patterned relative to meaningful material forms. The social *constraints* imposed by identity and value categorizations play out in intersubjective re-citational processes, where participants often have a shared awareness of the constraints "in play" in particular situations. To say that agency is *enabled*, through the imposition of an identity or value categorization, means that even given the social constraints of normative "re-citational expectations," a choice between behavioral alternatives always remains possible. As Anthony Giddens puts this point in his theory of structuration, "Each of the various forms of constraint are thus also, in varying ways, forms of enablement. They serve to open up certain possibilities of action at the same time as they restrict or deny others" (1984, 173–74). Mead's perspective thus helps shift the notion of "enabling constraint" away from individual consciousness, toward an *interactive* framework involving shared behavioral expectations.

Bakhtin's sociological version of how the self is constructed, in situations oriented toward others, is similar in many respects to that described by Mead. Indeed, Michael Holquist has commented that both Mead and Bakhtin try to develop a "language-based social psychology" (2004, 55). Both thinkers objected to theories of the self which abstracted from the situated corporality of lived existence (see Joas 1997; Holquist 2004). Like Bakhtin, Mead focused on how language allows for the coordination of human action—via "reciprocal expectations about behaviour" (Joas 1997, 114). This pragmatic concern with social action grounds Mead's theory of language—like Bakhtin's—in everyday, situated, social interaction. For Mead, these situated actions are the "precondition" of consciousness (Mead 1969, 18)—in contrast to the Western philosophical tradition which favors an autonomous consciousness preexisting behavioral practices. This approach aligns Mead with the more recent turn in poststructuralist theory toward situated linguistic practices—as in the case of Butler's work on performative citationality.

In *Mind, Self and Society* (1969), Mead asserts that social communication involves the interactive use of culturally shared "significant symbols" (46–47). It is through the use of significant symbols that humans can anticipate the reactions of others to their considered gestures. The responses of others which normatively take place in actual social situations, then, can be anticipated by social actors—allowing humans to envision and adjust their social actions before they occur.

For Mead, "meaning" concerns shared knowledge of the normative *responses* by both self and other to identifiable symbols. Significant symbols (or "significant gestures"), have an "identical" content (89), in that both self and other respond to them in the same way. For Mead, the social awareness of this shared, repeatable response to "significant" materiality—both anticipated and actualized—*is* meaning. Mead thus locates the possibility of "stable" meaning, across situational contexts, in the shared knowledge of social interactants relative to significant material forms. In this reading of Mead, meaning is not stable because of the inherently repeatable and "identity" of the sign. Rather, meaning becomes sedimented and stable through reoccurring social *responses* to material signs (i.e., normative citational practices), which can be anticipated.

Because of this situated, pragmatic focus, it could be argued that Mead's framework provides for the kind of *social* iterability sought by Butler (Butler 1997, 152), especially given Mead's focus on the interactive subject's "anticipation of," and "adjustment to," the potential citational practices of others. While the *anticipation* of the responses of others rehearses normative meanings (i.e., "identities" of signs), the *actualization* of this citational practice is always a situated event, which necessarily unsettles any assumed equivalence between the anticipated and actualized meanings.

For Mead, one's *social identity* is also a significant symbol—with a shared meaning to both self and others. He argues that the "meaning" of one's ongoing social identity (the "me") involves a continual anticipation of how others will react to self's utterances, and—in the language of citationality—how they will likely interpellate a particular social identity from those utterances. Mead, like Bakhtin, emphasized the importance of the *anticipated* response of the other in self-construction. From this perspective, human agency thus involves a consideration of the "attitude of the other" (Mead 1969, 162) toward citational practices *envisioned* as completed, as well as *actually* completed.

We can see here how Mead's framework can accommodate the theoretical shift away from "consciousness" toward "citationality." One's social identity, as a significant symbol with shared meaning, is interpellated *from* the citational practices of both self and others. Describing Mead's position in the essay "The Social Self," Joas notes that "our self-image results from the internal representation of others' responses to us" (Joas 1997, 110). Thus, to actively "construct" a particular social identity involves the attempt to anticipate, and influence, the social responses of others. The self's *own* citational practices involving particular material signs—using symbolic interactionist terms from Gregory Stone—"announce" particular social identities, as subjects attempt to influence the way that others will interpellate social identity from those signs. These others will then communicate (through *their* citational practices) whether or not they will indeed "place" the subject into the announced identity category (see Hewitt 2011, 77).

In Mead's perspective, the "me" is "linguistic" in the sense that we think about social identity in a language, using evaluative categories which have shared social meanings—such as a "patriotic" or "successful" person. Inasmuch as language itself—as a citational resource—has an exchange value in the contemporary cultural economy, this means that subjects think about the self in "commodified language." In the case of gender, for example, the images of women sold for profit in the media are the very same citational "resources" used in *gendered self-reflection*—such as the "experience" of masculinity through the objectification of women (see MacKinnon 1987; Mulvey 1989; Dworkin 1989).

Cultural commodities, such as television shows or Internet sites, have an exchange value which is considered to be the measure of their "worth"—both as an "experience" for the Cartesian subject, as well as in their function in "representing" a particular set of subcultural values. In a sense, one's social identity centers, or anchors, this hegemonic system of exchange value—as a kind of identity archive for the accumulation of valued experiences. The subject can experience the "worth" of citational experiences inasmuch as one is able to *anticipate the evaluative responses of others*—that is, social actors have a shared knowledge of the normative exchange value of the citational resource. Thus, the very language used to construct the "self" has an exchange value in the contemporary cultural economy. In this sense, the market worth of material signs, associated with the experience of certain subcultural values, presides over the construction of contemporary social identity.

CONCLUSION

In this chapter, the work of the Bakhtin Circle on reported speech was tied to that of Jacques Derrida and Judith Butler on citationality. Bakhtin and his colleagues showed how the values of self and others are negotiated through utterances. In reported speech, the words of others are quoted or paraphrased in particular syntactical forms, which reveal the subject's stance toward the cultural values implied by those words. It was argued that social identities and social values are negotiated materially, in syntactical formations involving the citation of, or reporting on, the words of others.

Derrida's work on the repeatability of meaning across situations was extended by Butler in her work on the performativity of gender. Gendered behavioral practices are continually re-cited by social actors across situated contexts, thus reproducing normative meanings and identities—as well as inequalities between identities. This chapter extended these insights to argue that values are performative in the same way, through re-citational practices from which identities and their affiliated subcultural values are continually re-interpellated. Bakhtin's work on the negotiation of values in utterances was incorporated into the poststructuralist framework of Butler and Derrida, to argue that the performative re-citation of values occurs in syntactical, material formations—utterances issued by subjects and social institutions.

The theoretical framework developed in chapter two was also enhanced by some insights from George Herbert Mead. Not only do values and identities emerge from actualized utterances, but these interpellations can be anticipated by subjects—and altered before their actualization. Because Mead's theory of meaning focuses on intersubjective behavioral practices, it is compatible with the poststructuralist frame advanced here—though not without some difficulty regarding the exact nature of agency within a theory of performative citationality.

The main goal of chapter two was to construct a theoretical frame showing that social identity is constructed through a process of citational performativity, through which the values affiliated with various social identities are negotiated. In this sense, social values are continually re-cited, or reproduced, through utterances—the "performativity of values." Rather than preexisting their behavioral re-enactment, as is assumed from a representationalist perspective, normative values and identities are continually re-performed and re-interpellated. Chapter three will focus on the performativity of *subcultural values*, such as religious, political, or ethnic group values, while chapters four and five will focus on the performativity of *exchange value*.

At this point it is important to distinguish between two differing "types" of performativity theories. The first, following the work of Austin (1975), argues that a performative utterance brings a phenomenon into being. Rather than simply describing a state of affairs, the performative utterance makes the state of affairs "present." From this point of view, subcultural values and exchange value are both manifest and measurable. While this theory has the advantage over representationalist theories in being able to better describe the current functioning of the U.S. cultural economy, it also reproduces the ideology of the "presence of value" which has become hegemonic to the culture.

The second version of performativity is that based on Derrida's notions of citationality and iterability, as developed by Judith Butler. This version emphasizes the ongoing *re-citation* of identities, norms, and values across contexts, showing that meanings and identities can never be fully "present" across situated contexts—precisely because of the temporal and spatial singularity of each iteration, and each context. This version of citational performativity, based on Derrida's notion of iterability, undermines the ideology that a state of affairs is fully "present" as a result of its performative enactment.

In this book, chapters three, four, and five—seeking to *describe* the contemporary U.S. cultural economy—argue that the first model of performativity theory not only is compatible with the contemporary functioning of the U.S. cultural economy, but has in some ways become integrated into it. For example, the marketing literature has increasingly referred to the "co-creation" of value by consumers—in a performative sense—where both companies and consumers together design products which make value present (see Prahalad and Ramaswamy 2004). This model—even while differing from a representationalist perspective—nonetheless re-assumes the "presence" of values, which are performatively enacted. The description of the contemporary economy in chapters three, four, and five attempts to show in what ways this "performativity of value" operates. In particular, it is argued that language itself has become an important commodity with its own exchange value, increasingly used as a citational resource in the construction of contemporary social identity.

Chapter six, however, attempts to develop a *critique* of the performatively enacted "presence of value" in the contemporary economy, and completes the turn toward the "citationality version" of performativity theory as developed by Derrida and Butler—what Butler has termed "performativity as citationality" (1993, 12; 21). Rather than simply describing how the contemporary economy is normatively re-performed, this chapter seeks to show how its future cannot be secured—in that the meaning of all values, including exchange value, is always deferred and never quite "present." This more critical version of performativity theory, in chapter six, is aligned with the critical theory of the Frankfurt School, particularly the writings of Walter Benjamin and Theodor Adorno. Thus while section II of the book, containing chapters three, four, and five, seeks to describe the "performativity" of value in the contemporary U.S. cultural economy, section III appeals to a model of performative citationality, based on Derrida's notion of iterability, in order to develop its critique.

II

The Performativity of Value: Description of the Contemporary U.S. Cultural Economy

Chapter Three

Citational Practices and the Performativity of Subcultural Values

In this chapter, it is argued that subcultural values are not located in a group consciousness, existing prior to their behavioral re-enactment. Rather, subcultural values are both reproduced, as well as resisted, through re-citational processes. Children "learn to value" as they are taught to cite those material forms prioritized by agents of socialization. It is through these citational practices that social identities and values are interpellated by self and others. Individual identities are aligned with group identities and values through citational utterances, which configure—or "report on"—the words, images, and social objects of others in particular ways.

In today's cultural economy, children are not only socialized into normative citational practices which reproduce particular subcultural values, but also into the metaphysical frame which assumes that value is "present" in cultural forms—a value which is to be "experienced" through an autonomous, Cartesian subjectivity. The material forms which children re-cite in contemporary U.S. culture are normatively configured to "represent" the presence of subcultural values and exchange value—as in the case of cultural commodities. This chapter *describes* how the "presence of subcultural values" is re-asserted through normative citational practices. The *critique* of this ideology regarding the presence of subcultural values is developed through Derrida and Butler's notion of performative citationality, and appears in chapter six.

IDEOLOGY AND NORMATIVE CITATIONAL PRACTICE

The Presence of Value

In his work, Jacques Derrida is critical of the type of subjectivity normatively constructed in the Western philosophical tradition. Western subjects are considered to be autonomous in their enlightened thoughts—thoughts considered logically prior to their representation in language. Derrida (1981; 1997) argued that this view of the subject rests on a philosophical model which favors speech over writing. Western philosophy has assumed an immediate connection between thought and spoken language—a "presence" of meaning (1997, 11–12). Derrida's critique of Western notions of subjectivity and self-identity exposes this assumption, as he alternately shows the importance of writing in the very constitution of meaning, and in the constitution of the identity of subjects themselves.

In semiotic terms, Western metaphysics has considered signs as necessary to employ when the referent is absent (Derrida 1988). For example, when an actual dog is absent, the material word "dog" is used as a signifier to refer to the absent dog—as "signified." The sign is thus normatively considered to be a "deferred presence" (1973, 138); in other words, used until the actual dog returns to our presence. As Derrida puts it, this metaphysical model "presupposes that the sign (which defers presence) is conceivable only *on the basis of* the presence that it defers and *in view of* the deferred presence one intends to reappropriate" (138; italics in the original). The sign—as mere representation of the actual thing—is considered to be "*secondary*" and "*provisional*" (138; italics in the original), as opposed to the primacy or presence of the thing itself. At the same time, however, these "provisional" signifiers, when *spoken*, were still considered to be "closer" to thought than written signifiers. Derrida quotes Aristotle, who argued that "spoken words . . . are the symbols of mental experience . . . and written words are the symbols of spoken words" (Aristotle, in Derrida 1997, 11). In his reading of Aristotle, Derrida thus concludes that within such a metaphysical model, "the voice, producer of *the first symbols*, has a relationship of essential and immediate proximity with the mind" (1997, 11; italics in the original), whereas writing is seen to be lacking this "presence" of meaning.

Derrida (1997) develops his critique of "presence" and "identity"—including the presence and identity of autonomous subjects—by building upon Ferdinand de Saussure's argument from his *Course in General Linguistics* (1974). In that work, Saussure showed that language and signification ultimately rest not on positive terms (i.e., the *identification* between signifier and signified), but on the *differential* relations between terms within a linguistic system. For Saussure, each signifier, and each signified, can derive its meaning only as it is set apart from, and differs from, all other signifiers and signifieds. In this view, the meaningful identity of a signifier comes not in its function of "representing" a particular signified, but rather emerges as it is distinguished from other signifiers within a linguistic system. The identity of meaningful elements is thus constituted only as a *function of these differences*.

Derrida argues that meaning—including the socially meaningful "identity" of things or people—can never be fully present either in the referent itself, in significations, or in the thoughts of subjects. Rather, meaning is always produced in a process of differentiation from what it is not; in other words, identity is socially constructed in a relationship with its "alterity." This alterity, as the difference necessary for identity to emerge, remains "within" any constructed identity—abjected or subordinated by that meaningful identity, yet always haunting it.

For Derrida, no signification—even that occurring in privileged speech—can construct a positive and identifiable meaning outside of this process of differentiation. Indeed, it is writing, for Derrida, which enables *repetition* to occur—a necessity for "identifiable" meaning to be established at all. Words must be repeatable across contexts in order to be socially recognizable, and thereby meaningful. For Derrida, it is this *possibility* of the repetition of any linguistic "mark" which allows for the mark to be recognizable as the "same" across contexts, and to signify the same thing in differing contexts (1988, 7). Derrida argues that meaning in language can never be firmly linked, in an immediate "present," to the intentionality or thoughts of the subject—inasmuch as words or other meaningful objects must be recognizable to other language users whether or not the subject is present. Rather, Derrida argues, language is fundamentally severed from its "original context," and thus from the control of any subjective intentionality, as it "disseminates" across contexts (Derrida 1981).

Instead of following the Western metaphysical tradition of linking language, in the form of speech, to intentional human consciousness, Derrida argues that *writing* is the model which illustrates the nature of all language—even speech. The very nature of writing is that it becomes radically free of its original context and of authorial intent, as it circulates across contexts. Writing precisely must be able to function in the *absence* of the author and the addressee (Derrida 1988). This capability of writing to travel across contexts makes shared meaning possible within a culture.

However, this also suggests that because the circulation of language into future contexts can neither be foreseen nor controlled ahead of time, meaning can never be absolutely guaranteed. Rather, meaning is continually "deferred" into yet-to-be-determined future contexts, and thus is never quite "present." This argument applies both to the "identity" or the meaning of particular words, as well as to the social identity of persons. In other words, social identity cannot be located in some kind of immediate present based on

Cartesian self-reflection or intentionality. Rather, like any identity, social identity must be recognizable across situational contexts in order to be sustained—and thus is necessarily subject to further recontextualizations in the future.

At the same time, however, Derrida argues—as Samuel Weber puts it—that this process of repetition "introduces an element of *heterogeneity*, or *otherness*, into the constitution of the same" (1996, 138; italics in the original). For Derrida, each repetition of meaningful materiality is not only recognizable as the "same," but simultaneously differs—temporally and spatially—from its last usage. What Derrida calls the "structure of iteration" (1988, 53) of the mark necessarily involves "*both* identity *and* difference" (53; italics in the original). While the meanings and identities of words, images, or gestures are sustained across contexts through repetition, they are never exactly the same, inasmuch as they occur in the singularity of situated contexts. Language thus involves the non-resolvable tension, or "aporia," between that repeatability across contexts which enables its identity, and its singularity in situated use (Derrida 1988; see also Norris 1984, 49).

It is important to note, however, that Derrida does not simply invert the speech/writing hierarchy in his approach, thereby privileging writing and relegating speech to the subordinate position—a mere reversal of the normative metaphysical positioning (Norris 1987, 56; Gasché 1986, 210). In other words, he does not privilege the moment of difference in iterability over the moment of identity. Rather, language includes both dimensions—situated use *and* repeatability. For Derrida, there is an ongoing tension between these dimensions of language.

Given that the construction of any social identity—whether that of a word, a text, or a person—necessarily involves a differentiation from other identifiable meanings, Derrida goes on to argue that the process of identity construction involves the exclusion or suppression of alternative meanings. These excluded meanings, as the alterity of the constructed identity, are "marked" by their absence—the "trace" of the other in identity construction. *Social* identities, such as gender or race, are thus constructed in a hierarchical fashion—privileging some favored significations and suppressing others. Derrida's critique of Western metaphysics thereby exposes the pretenses of any text—including essentialist discourses of race or gender—to the status of absolute truth or objective reality, given its own dependency on the very alterity it excludes. For Derrida, a "deconstructive" reading of any meaningful text involves revealing what is suppressed in the construction of that text's "identity" (Derrida 1989, 72; Derrida 1981; Culler 1982, 86).

Derrida's critique of Western metaphysics thus shows how the meaning of any materiality—including the materiality of language—is never quite "present." This argument can also be specifically extended to the meaning of "value." While it is normatively assumed that certain words or images reflect, or represent, the pre-existing values of a particular subculture—and are intentionally expressed by members of those groups—Derrida's notion of iterability challenges this assumption. For any meaningful material form to be recognizable as signifying a particular value—including exchange value—it must be repeatable and re-citable across contexts. On the other hand, the "valuable" is also singular in situated use precisely because of spatial and temporal differences between situated contexts. In this sense, there is no "presence" of value; rather, the "meaning of value"—like all meaning—is continually deferred. This argument applies both to subcultural values such as religious or political values, as well as to the exchange value of material forms. Although the metaphysics of capitalism suggests that cultural commodities deliver the "value" promised by their advertisements, this value always remains a *deferred promise*.

Despite the possibility of this Derridean-inspired critique, the normative belief in the U.S. is that cultural commodities deliver, or present, valued experiences to Cartesian subjects. This ideological belief, in the "presence of exchange value," has now become the basis of the contemporary cultural economy. Consumers assume that value is "present" in purchased commodities, as they position themselves relative to them. In other words, a process involving the citation of cultural commodities—taken to "represent" particular values and identities—has become an important dimension to the workings of today's cultural economy. While Derrida's work shows that the re-contextualization, or re-citation, of material forms has the *potential* to alter their meaning and value, in *normative practice* the ideology of the presence of value persists.

As social actors re-cite the material forms which they consider to represent subcultural values, they re-enact that "meaning of value," as well as interpellate a social identity from that material form. In this sense, we can speak of a "performativity of subcultural values," where to re-cite any subcultural value is to re-perform it in new situational contexts. Exchange value is re-performed as well, in that material forms considered of economic worth "cross contexts"—to be re-cited by consumers in the construction of their social identities. Even while Derrida's critique of presence shows that normative identities and values can be dislocated, normative citational practices typically re-cite the hegemonic frame of exchange value. While subcultural values or exchange value may not actually be "present" in cultural commodities, their normative material configurations encourage precisely this ideological interpellation, and rarely challenge its underlying metaphysical assumptions.

Cartesian Identity and the Experience of Value

An important reason why the "presence of value" remains a hegemonic assumption in the contemporary U.S. cultural economy—despite the possibility of a Derridean critique of this presence—has to do with the particular version of subjectivity "sedimented" in the materiality of the social environment, and continually re-cited in normative practice. Social identities interpellated from the utterances of others—which simultaneously "enable" and "constrain" the utterances of self (Butler 1997, 16)—not only involve identity categories like gender, but also involve the very notion of the individualistic subject as found in the Cartesian metaphysical tradition. In other words, the concept of an experiencing, individual subject is itself interpellated from particular grammatical or syntactical forms, normatively re-produced in citational practices. If Derrida is correct that Western philosophy and Western cultures have favored a metaphysics of presence, then we can find this privilege re-cited within those everyday citational forms which are "grammatically enforced."

Benjamin Lee and Greg Urban, in their introduction to *Semiotics, Self, and Society*, discuss some of the research regarding how "different cultures differentially encode understandings of what it means to be a self" (1989, 1). Cross-culturally, different linguistic forms are used to interpellate different kinds of "self," and differing relations between self and other (3). Lee and Urban also point out that the work of Benjamin Lee (1989) shows that "the Cartesian system is essentially a product of the language structures that the reflection process necessarily employs" (Lee and Urban 1989, 4). In other words, the metaphysical assumptions in the West regarding presence and subjectivity, as well as regarding particular relations between self and other, are *interpellated from particular syntactical forms*. The individualistic, Cartesian subject is re-cited as utterances re-employ these linguistic forms.

We can also see from the anthropological literature that alternative conceptions of the self are supported by alternative linguistic forms, which differ from those prevalent in contemporary U.S. interactions. In his work on Northern Cheyenne culture in southeastern Montana, Terry Strauss has shown that for Cheyenne speakers, "By dint of being addressed, even the inanimate object becomes a person, another self with which the speaker himself is dialogically engaged" (1989, 55). We see here an alternative to the strict Cartesian separation of subject and object found in the English language. To be socialized into a culture using these citational practices means learning to interpellate a self which differs from the individualistic, "ego-centered" self of Western cultures.

Strauss identifies several *linguistic features* found in the Northern Cheyenne language which interpellate different *cultural values* from those of the dominant Western culture. According to Strauss, pronouns used in the Northern Cheyenne language support what Milton Singer and Charles Peirce have called "tuism"—that is, "a philosophical understanding in which primary emphasis is placed on the second person, or 'tu,' rather than the first person, or ego" (53). As Strauss points out, in the Cheyenne language, one cannot refer to "a mother" as abstractable from context; rather, "She has to be a particular someone's mother" (65). However, the reference is less to an *ego's* mother, but in "tuistic" fashion the reference is to "the one who mothers me" (65). In other words, the linguistic form puts more of an emphasis on the other rather than the ego. Interestingly, Strauss notes an affinity here with the theory of the Bakhtin Circle, which also stressed the importance of the other in self-constitution (53). Strauss goes on to show how the usage of grammatical forms shift as members of the community begin to adopt more modern styles of communicating—with an accompanying loss of the "tuistical self" (67). The point here is that differing conceptions of "self" are intimately interwoven with particular linguistic forms. Citational practices evoking the words of others, as materialized into linguistic forms, not only interpellate a particular "kind of self," but a self which stands in particular *relationships* with others and their values (i.e., a self which accumulates "valuable individual experiences," or a self which values family and community).

Strauss's research also illustrates how the notion of "achievement" was traditionally interpreted within the Northern Cheyenne community, as a collective rather than an individual accomplishment—that is, within a web of supporting others (67). In contrast, Elinor Ochs (1997) has shown that "achievement" in the United States, as normatively constructed through language use, is a specifically *individual* accomplishment. She shows how linguistic forms, which differ cross-culturally, interpellate differing relationships between "self" and "mother"—with political implications regarding how "mothers" are valued or devalued in different cultures.

Ochs argues that language often does not index social identity directly, but rather as mediated through "certain pragmatic functions of language" (337). For example, Ochs notes that speaking in a soft tone or deferential way may index gender, but less directly than a pronoun such as "she" (340; 343). Similarly, Ochs shows how "baby talk" used by mothers in contemporary U.S. culture has implications for how the gendered category of "mother" is constructed and interpreted (351). As mothers use "baby talk" to report on what children mean, want, or have accomplished, the *individual* ego of the child emerges, and takes precedence over the mother's own voice. Ochs notes that particular ways of praising a child's accomplishments can "ignore or minimize the role of the mother in reaching a goal" (355). Such a deferential relationship of mother toward child, Ochs argues, leads to the devaluation of the contributions of mothers in the U.S. toward the achievements of their children, and to the cultural devaluation of "mothers" in general. In this study, we can see that as the material form of the mother's "reporting" utterance enacts a social identity for another, it simultaneously enacts a social identity for herself.

In this research, we find that a particular kind of *individual* ego of the child is "cited into existence" by the mother; as Ochs shows, it is an autonomous and "achieving" ego. The resultant identity of this "individual" ego obscures the role of the other's citational practices in its construction. In contrast, Ochs shows that in Samoan communities, praise is normatively responded to with an acknowledgment of the support and contributions of others (354). There, children are taught through language use to think of achievement as collaboratively, rather than individually, achieved.

This study by Ochs shows that a particular social identity is normatively interpellated from Western linguistic forms—that of an individualistic, accomplishing, and "experiencing" subject. This identity is interpellated from material utterances, which are then continually recontextualized into new situations. In the U.S., the normative framework for the interpretation of identity—continually re-interpellated from normative citational practices—is the metaphysical frame of Cartesian subjectivity and the "presence" of individual intentionality. The individual ego is thus *cited into existence,* and is continually re-cited through normative linguistic practices and particular syntactical configurations.

To be socialized into such an identity, through exposure to normative linguistic forms, is to learn that the individual self "accomplishes," or behaviorally acquires, a set of "valued" experiences. Individuals who are aligned with particular subcultural groups are said to have particular values and experiences. In other words, cultural *identity* categories are normatively grafted with particular *value* genres—both associated with the "experiences" of the individualized Cartesian subject. For example, a social identity as a "religious person" is interpellated when a subject cites a sacred text; this individual is said to have religious experiences, hold religious values, and serve as a representative of a religious community.

In this sense, to be socialized into normative linguistic practices is to learn to assert the "presence of values," as individually owned and experienced. Once "types of people" are categorized within particular social identities, aligning with normative value domains, their re-presentation in new situations is perceived as an incarnation of those values. In other words, a subject is recontextualized as a *representative* of a valuing community based on a previously earned reputation, and their "presence" is assumed to "re-site" the values of that subculture. In this ideological formulation, the assumption is that subjects, once acquiring a particular set of experiences and values, then transport those stable values into new situational contexts, and issue utterances which "reflect" those values. It is also assumed that the acquired experiences and values pre-exist any later situational expression of them.

Just as particular syntactical material forms can be used to interpellate a Cartesian identity which experiences "value" generally, so can *commodified* material forms interpellate a consuming or capitalist subject who is said to experience exchange value. The "capitalist subject," as interpellated from cultural commodities which have been configured into those material forms which generate profit, is an individual who experiences the worth of those forms in their function of delivering subcultural values.

As opposed to alternative material forms which may signify differently, the commodified material forms of Western cultures—from which a *Cartesian*, individualistic subject is interpellated—also support the interpellation of a consuming, *capitalist* subject who experiences "exchange value." Subjects in the contemporary cultural economy re-cite the discourse of exchange value whenever they position themselves relative to cultural commodities of economic worth, which are perceived as delivering valuable experiences. We thus find that in the contemporary cultural economy, the value of citational resources has come to be measured in terms of the "worth of the experience" they are said to provide to Cartesian subjects. In a discussion emphasizing the symbolic or cultural dimension of commodities in late capitalism, Dean MacCannell has noted that the "value" of today's cultural commodities "is not determined by the amount of labor required for their production. Their value is a function of the quality and quantity of *experience* they promise (1976, 23; italics in the original).

As the contemporary subject goes to a ticketed event to participate in a collective experience, or places a television set in a home in a particular neighborhood in order to watch a mediated event, "value" is created through particular configurations of meaningful materiality—as "experienced" by the subject. The "citation" of the event occurs from a situated subject position. As in the case of seats at a baseball game, such "experiencing positions" are differentially valued. An important component of the contemporary U.S. economy, then, concerns the strategic placement of cultural commodities in space and time relative to the Cartesian subject. It should also be noted, as Karen Barad's (2007) work suggests, that even the interpellation of particular spatial and temporal categories derives from material forms—here, as experiences closer or farther from the center of value as differentially positioned on a Cartesian grid.

As this temporal and spatial positioning is advertised, a valuable experience is promised. As we see clearly in the cases of the real estate market, or front row seating at an event, value has to do with the positioning of social "types" of subjects—as particular identity categories are interpellated from certain experiencing positions. Not only is the commodity assumed to be present in its value, but the viewer is "present" and socially positioned relative to differentially valued commodities.

In this sense, we might say that exchange value in the contemporary U.S. cultural economy involves the exchanging of "money for position," relative to commodified material signs. "Citational agency" thus has to do with *positioning* one's self, and one's utterances, within the material network of signs. Subjects continually negotiate, and are negotiated into, "enabling" and "constraining" *positions* within the culture from which to experience meaningful material forms. While at any *synchronic* moment we can speak of a system of "sign values," which locates subjects into a differential system of identity positions (see Baudrillard 1981; see also Kellner 1991, 21; 28), it is also true—in the language of citationality—that such a system must be continually *re-cited* and re-negotiated in everyday practice.

Traveling Subjects and Visual Experience

As Samuel Weber notes, Martin Heidegger (1977) argues that the modern, Cartesian subject views the world as a "picture," in an attempt to secure self-identity (1996, 81). In this process, the Cartesian perspective on self-reflection is extended *outward* onto the world. Thus we find, as described in John Berger's *Ways of Seeing* (1980), that European Renaissance paintings with "perspective" were valued as visual *experiences* for such an autonomous, individualistic subject. With the later emergence of capitalism, as John Guillory (1993) shows in his discussion of Howard Caygill's *Art of Judgement* (1989), such upper-class experiences of art came to acquire an "aesthetic value"—as "truth" was considered by the upper classes to be more fully "present" in the visual experience of art, as opposed to commodities (Guillory 1993, 316–17). This kind of "Cartesian subjectivity" not only favored a particular *spatial* arrangement centered by the subject, as in the use of perspective in art, but—as Derrida shows—also the *temporality* of "presence." Those objects which syntactically re-cited these spatial and temporal experiences of the Western subject came to be valued.

In a Bakhtinian sense, the dominant spatial and temporal orientations of a culture are often reproduced in evaluative utterances in the everyday interactions within that culture (Holquist 2004, 116). At times, Bakhtin extended his use of term "chronotope"—by which he meant the temporal and spatial assumptions within literary modes of narration—to "the relation *between* any text and its times" (113; italics in the original). The production and consumption of those meaningful material forms which reinforced the Cartesian "chronotope" became valued citational resources in the West. In other words, a particular *form* of visual experience comes to have a market value, as a citational resource for Cartesian subjects. Throughout Western history, we can find many cultural practices which reproduced the dominant chronotope of "presence," as anchored in a Cartesian-based subjectivity.

If citational practices involve rhetorically positioning one's responses relative to the words, images, and cultural artifacts of the other, then we can also consider how positioning one's gaze relative to the bodies of others—the *travel* experience—can be considered as a type of citational practice. In Western history, the Cartesian model of subjectivity has been reinforced by citational practices involving particular types of class-based visual experiences, as accumulated through physical and mediated travel. For example, Judith Adler has noted the historical connection between *travel* and *vision*, as it reinforces a subjectivity based on a "subjugation of a world of 'things'" (Adler, in Frow 1997, 91). As John Frow discusses, Adler's work shows that the practice of sightseeing in Western cultures, by the nineteenth century, was developing into a "general economy of looking" for the wealthier traveler, which would eventually form "the basis of modern tourism" (92). As Frow notes, John Urry has described these sightseeing practices as the "tourist gaze" (92). In the case of the 1900 Paris World Exposition, however, the reverse was true: "exotic" peoples from around the world traveled to Europe to participate in exhibits where they would be "gazed at" (Williams 1991; see also Urry 1990, 152).

Several theorists have contributed in establishing a connection between the modern Western subject and a particular way of viewing. John Urry, citing the work of Marshall Berman, discusses how Haussmann's construction of urban boulevards in late nineteenth century Paris permitted a particular type of gazing environment for subjects (1990, 136–37). As Mike Featherstone (1991) notes, Charles Baudelaire and Walter Benjamin linked the experience of modernity to the detached point of view of the "flaneur," who traveled through these emerging urban environments (72–73). As Urry puts it, "The strolling *flâneur* was a forerunner of the twentieth-century tourist" (138; italics in the original). Urry also credits Susan Sontag for linking the flâneur with modern photography (138).

In cities like Paris, the emerging retail stores at the turn of the twentieth century provided an exciting experience for gazing shoppers—where, as Rosalind Williams (1991) argues, the exoticism of the 1900 world exposition would continue in the "dream world" of modern consumerism. As Mike Featherstone (1991) has noted, for Walter Benjamin the Paris arcades were early iterations of modern department stores, or "temples in which goods were worshipped as fetishes" (73). In this sense, "commodity fetishism" might be understood as a certain *form of citationality*, where a gazing, modern consumer travels amidst "quasi-sacred" representations of alterity, experiencing their value. Featherstone cites the work of Susan Buck-Morss, who argues that for Benjamin and Baudelaire, this kind of gazing results in a perspective where "objects appear divorced from their context" (74).

In contemporary Western culture, time and place become abstractable and ahistorical, as experiences for the "present" subject. Thus a visit to a city like

Paris, or a film about it, become citational experiences merely to be consumed. Television and film today assemble a dizzying array of images from past, present, and future. As Norbert Bolz and Willem van Reijen put it, with such new technologies seeing has become "a montage of different times" (1996, 73). The hegemonic "temporality of presence" frames these images, often gathered from different historical periods, into the "present moment"—and positions them relative to the "present" subject. The proliferation of *images* thus becomes a central theme in the characterization of contemporary culture as postmodern—with video, as Frederic Jameson (2001) argues, being the hegemonic medium of postmodern culture (69). Siegfried Kracauer has also argued, according to Eduardo Cadava, that "the history of the world is in danger of becoming a rapidly expanding collection of images . . . readily available in the eternal present made possible by the technical media" (Cadava 1997, xxvii)—thus echoing Heidegger's notion of the "world as picture."

It is through the citational and syntactical form of the "gaze" that the other is objectified, which in turn interpellates a particular kind of viewing and experiencing subject. In such a political economy, the "other" is often not allowed to continue to speak for themselves; rather, their words and images become valued, consumable "experiences" for consuming subjects. For Plissart and Derrida (1989), to take a photograph is to reproduce the gaze of the photographer. They suggest that this citational practice assigns the subject a viewing position with the "right of inspection," holding the other as the object of the gaze. Today, we find this gaze re-enacted in the continued marketing of "primitive" or "exotic" artifacts (Torgovnick 1990), just as in previous world expositions.

The critique of the "male gaze," as developed within feminist theory (Mulvey 1989), now extends to the photographic objectification of women on the Internet. Dworkin (1989) and MacKinnon (1987) have argued that males use this kind of dominating, objectifying gaze in order to establish and experience their own gender identity; in other words, a particular citational practice involving images is used to construct identities and values. In the language of citationality, masculine identity, and the values of a masculine subculture, are re-interpellated together as the male subject positions himself relative to the syntactically arranged materiality of the image. The words of the woman are silenced; instead, her image is entextualized for marketability within the institutionalized, citational practices of the pornography industry.

Western citational practices thus normatively function within the already-framed assumptions of the dominant chronotope—which assume an autonomous, pre-existing, and experiencing subject. In other words, the type of Cartesian "perspectivism" described above has become sedimented in the *material forms* of normative social environments and normative citational resources. Indeed, such forms have come to be technologically extended in contemporary U.S. culture.

Souvenirs and Alterity

As discussed earlier, the incorporation of the words of the other into one's own utterances—as in the case of a direct quote—is a citational grafting of two contexts. The utterance of the subject grafts the two referential contexts of self and other; the quote marks indicating that the quoted text does not entirely belong to the referential context of the subject, but rather retains a continuing relationship to the referential context of the other. In the case of quotes, as well as for souvenirs taken during travel to the "sites of others," the words and objects of the other are grafted into the citational utterances of the subject—even as they continue to signify the values and identities of others. Souvenirs provide a good example of how alterity is commodified and "quoted" into the referential context of self (Sherlock 1998).

In his discussion of tourism, Jonathan Culler (1981) has noted that to a tourist, a souvenir taken from a visit to Paris is not just an object to be used, but also represents "France" (127). Thus, as Dean MacCannell and Culler both suggest, tourists become semioticians (Culler 1981, 128), looking for representations which signify the values of others. Given this, the tourism industry attempts to construct a certain set of semiotic associations for "quoting" or citing by the traveler. Souvenirs play an integral part in this endeavor.

Souvenirs are often shaped into those material forms which interpellate an interpretive context of leisure and exoticism. When the traveler, upon return, grafts the souvenir into the referential context of home or work, the artifact "plays against" the routinized context of everyday life. Travel thus provides citational resources for subjects who wish, upon their return, to "double-voice" (Bakhtin 1984, 185) their home context with the connotations of an exotic alterity. In the contemporary U.S. economy, such a citational grafting of the referential contexts of self and other simultaneously cites the discourse of exchange value; that is, the souvenir is normatively perceived as "valuable" or worthwhile in representing an experience for the subject. Using Culler's example, the souvenir not only grafts the referential context of the tourist to the Parisian context, but itself has an exchange value as a citational resource.

In a sense, souvenirs are taken by travelers as a means of documentation of their "liminal" travel experience—as the experience of that which is "out-of-the-ordinary" (see Urry 1990, 10). Journeying away from the referential context of self into that of the other, a souvenir may come to represent how far a traveler went into that "context of alterity" before returning to the safety and familiarity of the routine. This "exotic" citational practice, involving the "presence" of alterity, is taken to valorize the referential context of self. In a Derridean sense, the identity of the self is repeated "with a difference."

This tension between the repeatability of self-identity, and its dislocation through the citation of the words and objects of the other, has itself acquired a certain marketability in the contemporary cultural economy. Material forms "representing" the values of others acquire an exchange value as citational resources, or commodified "souvenirs" of the other. Their materiality plays against the material forms already found in one's home environment, which represent the "present" subcultural values of self. In other words, the presence of the values of alterity is played against the presence of the values of self, as interpellated from the syntactical arrangement of material forms.

Souvenirs acquired through travel enable a later re-citation of the context of alterity, as they become positioned in everyday home or work environments. Subjects not only change viewing positions through travel, but often return home with copies of this "sight" for later re-citation—in the form of photographs and other souvenirs. Just as music played in a car, or a celebrity poster placed in a teenager's bedroom, the exotic souvenir taken from travel generates experiential value for the subject—through the material grafting of the words and objects of others into the referential context of self.

Tourism thus allows subjects to venture onto the lands of the "other," yet in a controlled fashion. When the subject positions the exotic souvenir within the confines of the home context, the souvenir functions—to use Derrida's term—as a "supplement" relative to the normative context of the subject's everyday life. In other words, the souvenir is re-abjected as "exotic," relative to the normative. Thus souvenirs are not just "representative" of the leisure experience, but simultaneously *re-differentiate and re-constitute* the home discourse, as its alterity. In other words, the taking of a souvenir materially *re-enacts a prior differentiation*—that difference which abjected the "exotic" other in the first place, as the referential identity context of the subject was constructed. In this sense, souvenirs specifically, and travel experiences generally, re-perform the subcultural boundaries between valuing categories.

As with any citational resource which grafts the referential contexts of self and others, the souvenir occupies an ambiguous place "between" contexts. A souvenir, like a quote, seems to have experiential worth to the subject as a *material representation of the difference in valuing contexts*—the re-enacted differences in values between self and other. In placing the souvenir in the home or office, the subject re-cites what the other values, inasmuch as it differs from the normative valuations of the subject's everyday life. As discussed earlier, a material graft both *brings together* and *differentiates* contexts, as the utterances of the subject necessarily "take a stand" relative to the words and objects of others. This "journey into otherness" becomes a means of (re-)constituting one's own social identity, as the subject re-abjects the words and the objects of the other. In contemporary U.S. culture, these words and images of the other are marketed as commodified citational resources.

This kind of "citational exoticism" allows tourists to experience the other from a safe distance through commodification (see Frow 1997, 100). Like the vicarious experience of alterity as delivered through the mass media (hooks 1992b), commercial tourism allows the self to explore the words or objects of the other in a controlled manner. A tension between desire and security thus informs the travel excursion. Discussing the research on transgression during carnivals and fairs, Mike Featherstone (1991) has similarly noted that "the other which is excluded as part of the identity formation process becomes the object of desire" (79).

As in de Certeau's "scriptural economy" generally (1988), this kind of citational exoticism keeps the other in an abjected place for the Western viewer, thus reproducing the certainty and security of the Cartesian experience. As de Certeau has pointed out, the *form* by which the other is cited matters—utterances can be shaped in such a way so as to allow for the other to be cited, but simultaneously not be allowed to speak for themselves (155–56). For example, John Frow has commented on how exoticism perpetuates the unequal identities of the developed West, and its "underdeveloped" Other (101). It is at the material site/cite of the souvenir, or in the materiality of reported speech, where self and other "meet." As commodity, the subject can gaze upon the souvenir, valued for its representation of alterity, without actually encountering that alterity—thus continually re-citing a scene of abjection in the construction of Western identity. In the taking of a souvenir, the "danger" of alterity to the identity of the subject is syntactically and politically managed.

In this sense, the commodified words of the other, taken into the everyday utterances of subjects, can be seen as souvenirs of a certain "experience of the other." Lives of those from other subcultures, framed in commodity form precisely for the experience of consumers, provide a highly controlled encounter with alterity. Rather than a reciprocal dialogue, citational encounters with the commodified words of others become rankable consumptive "experiences" for subjects—as brief excursions from the normatively interpellated identities and the routinized citational practices of home subcultures. As Erving Goffman (1967) has shown in his work on "commercialized action" (262), contemporary movies or other mediated experiences offer a grafting of safety and danger, where a controlled (citational) "experience" retains a trace of vicarious adventure. In addition, today the travel experiences of others are increasingly being distributed back to subjects via emerging citational technologies, enabling a nearly continual vicarious experience of alterity. This process, involving the words and images of the other, also contributes to the re-production of the cultural economy, now heavily reliant upon such citational practices.

Mediated Travel and Citational Technologies

Tourism, heavily dependent upon the visual gaze, has thus become an important paradigm for understanding contemporary U.S. culture. According to Rojek and Urry (1997), it is ever more difficult to distinguish between the experience of tourism, and the experience of Western culture generally (3). Dean MacCannell (1976) also sees tourism as the best paradigm to understand the modern subject (1). An important reason for the relevance of the tourist paradigm for these theorists has to do with the increased commodification of visual experience in late capitalism—the modern subject "travels" across mediated, citable images as distributed through television, film, and now, the Internet (Sherlock 1999). The materiality of these commodities altercasts subjects into particular viewing or "gazing" positions (see Williamson 2005). Given that Internet use involves an encounter with the meaningful material forms produced by others, we can say that many online experiences have become a kind of mediated tourism designed for subjects to travel to—and consume the pleasures of—various *sites/sights of the other*.

In his work, John Thompson (1995) has argued that mediated experience is increasingly important in modernity for the construction of social identity (233). In his analysis of contemporary mediated experience, he notes that "Mediated experience is always *recontextualized experience* ;it is the experience of events which transpire in distant locales which are re-embedded, *via the reception and appropriation of media products*, in the practical contexts of daily life" (1995, 228; italics added). In a Derridean sense, the mediated experience allows the traveling subject to cross, or graft, contexts without the limits of spatial proximity. In this sense, advertising for a mediated "experience of the other" becomes the *advertisement of another (valuing) context*, which promises to valorize the referential context of self.

Images which come into the home from television, computers, mobile devices, and other emerging technologies increasingly provide the consumer with opportunities to graft contexts via mediated "travel." Non-local images today provide a vast array of resources which individuals can cite as they construct a social identity. This situated identity of the subject becomes the site at which local and mediated contexts are grafted together, and simultaneously differentiated. This type of mediated travel allows for seemingly unlimited possibilities of new experiences, no longer limited by regional resources (see Thompson 1995, 207). These mediated symbolic resources are not necessarily consistent with each other, leading to—in Thompson's words—"a discontinuous sequence of experiences which have varying degrees of relevance to the self" (230). Thus the "postmodern" self cites a montage of influences, and seeks an eclectic mix of new travel experiences. Many different aspects of identity are thus assembled from citational practices involving differing material signs—resulting in what Kenneth Gergen has termed the "saturated self" (1991).

These mediated experiences for the traveling subject are also often *vicarious* experiences—the second-hand "experience" of someone else's experience. In the contemporary television, film, and Internet industries, the subject can stay in the safe and secured citational location of the home even while vicariously consuming the "commercialized action" happening to others on the screen (Goffman 1967, 262). For Goffman, the business of contemporary mass media is to offer the promise of vicarious, fulfilling experiences to consumers. The social world for the economically fortunate thus becomes divided into the "safe" citational positions of home or business, and the more exciting world of vicariously consumed experiences, where *others* on the screen are shown in more dangerous citational positions (262).

Clearly, today the Internet is, to use Goffman's phrase, "where the action is" regarding the citational practices of self relative to cultural commodities. Not only do corporations position language-commodities and advertising on websites, but social networking and video-sharing sites have emerged where subjects can post their own content for the viewing pleasures of others. *Any* occurrence from everyday life can now be uploaded from self to others, making the "experiences" of any subject potentially marketable for the vicarious enjoyment of others—and vice versa. These sights/cites of the other are often *ranked* as experiences by viewers across the world, who express their approval or disapproval for that "sight." Such feedback on citational practices shapes a sense of normative value, as well as shapes the direction of future citational practices. While not every uploaded strip of language generates profit in actuality, they *potentially* do—thus the increased marketability and "citability" of language (see Weber 2008).

The extent to which the Internet becomes commercialized is a matter of ongoing economic and political negotiation, although it is already clear that its syntactical form, as a citational technology, is compatible with an advanced capitalist economy. As in the case of television, advertisers are drawn to those Internet sites where consumers are most often traveling, gazing, and finding citational resources to use in the construction of social identity. What makes many websites valuable is that they precisely become a site for the advertising of *other* commodities, as well as for other websites. A link to a different website becomes an advertisement for another value context. In this way, the "value" of the online experience is continually deferred, as *further* mediated travel is continually required. Sites become recognized places of commercial value, not only because of the citational resources they provide to Internet travelers, but also—like television (see Jhally 1987, 72)—because of the audiences delivered to advertisers who promise the "presence of value" elsewhere.

We thus find an increasing technological ability for today's subjects to look in on the "contexts of others," and to continually cite/sight each other's daily experiences. The travel experiences of others can now be posted to social media sites or texted to the subject, who can experience the words and images of others during their own daily travels. In contemporary U.S. culture, language—both as actual and potential commodity—is "traveling" to an unprecedented degree.

THE PERFORMATIVITY OF SUBCULTURAL VALUES

Learning to Value

As discussed earlier, every utterance can be seen as a variant of "reported speech," in that the utterances of self incorporate and recontextualize the "language of the other." For Bauman and Briggs (1990), the "strip" of language which has been selected for recontextualization into the utterances of self can be referred to as a "text," as distinguishable from the flow of everyday life—which they refer to as interactional "discourse." They define "entextualization" as "the process of rendering discourse extractable, of making a stretch of linguistic production into a unit—a *text*—that can be lifted out of its interactional setting" (Bauman & Briggs 1990, 73, italics in the original). In this sense, we might say that a selected strip of language is an entextualization (or text) which has been *readied for citation.*

As Michael Silverstein and Greg Urban (1996) note, these decontextualized strips are often thought to "represent" the culture of a social group (1-2)—whether in the writings of social scientists, or in the everyday communication practices within a community of users. This normative assumption coincides with Derrida's critique of the metaphysics of "presence," where the material sign is thought to carry the intentionality or consciousness of an absent subject—here, a collective subject—across contexts. In the case of the entextualized cultural artifact, the assumption is that the artifact becomes an authentic material representation of the collective values of the group. In this normative perspective, these artifacts can then be recontextualized into the utterances of subjects, as well as into institutional settings like museums—as signs taken to re-"present" particular subcultural values. We have seen that in the case of tourism, souvenirs are taken by travelers precisely to re-cite the subcultural values of others into the referential context of self.

To be socialized into a culture is to learn the "significant" entextualizations which are normatively taken to represent key values of one's own subcultural group, as well as learn which entextualizations assert alternative values—as associated with alterity. Social actors learn the meaning of material signifiers as they observe the normative reactions of others toward that material form—for George H. Mead (1969), a "role-taking" process. Culture thus becomes "reproducible" across contexts, and across generations, through learned citational practices relative to material forms. Children acquire social identities as they learn to prioritize, or cite, normatively valued social objects within a culture—including commodities (Sherlock 2004). Socialization involves both the learned recognition of normatively *decontextualized* meanings—repeatable and shareable across social contexts—as well as the learned ability to *recontextualize* these meanings in new and singular ways in evolving social situations. In recontextualization processes, subjects learn to strategically "cite" cultural texts in unique combinations in everyday life. Thus, we can *analytically* separate two aspects of socialization, although they are inseparable in practice. The first process involves learning the meanings of normative entextualizations, which are taken to represent community values. The second process involves the learning of *recontextualization strategies* which "bend" or shape these meanings in situated re-citational practices.

In addition, it must be kept in mind that, in a Bakhtinian sense, the (generic) context against which social utterances have meaning itself emerges through social interaction (MacCannell 1985, 984–85)—thus the recontextualization of utterances (texts) also involves the "recontextualization of contexts." In other words, interpretive (valuing) contexts, as valuing "genres" interpellated from recognizable material forms, are also subject to Derrida's rule of iterability. In their work, Bauman and Briggs argue that "context" is not to be understood as a exterior frame for discursive acts as pre-given by social norms or by social institutions, but rather is emergent from the situated negotiations of everyday life (1990, 68). Their point is not to deny the force or existence of social structural constraints on identity or action, but rather to recognize the *emergent* nature of context. In other words, while "valuing contexts" have normative meanings across situations, they emerge as hierarchically differentiated when negotiated through situated linguistic practice. In interaction strategy, participants in a situation cite others differently, shaping cultural meanings and values in politically strategic ways—thus evoking and grafting differing valuing contexts as they seek to influence others.

Briggs and Bauman, in their article "Genre, Intertextuality, and Social Power" (1992), elaborate on Bakhtin's notion of "genre" in a way useful to this discussion. Citing the work of William Hanks, they argue that while genres have traditionally been considered as literary categories—used to classify texts and their structural features—they might better be considered as "frames of reference" used in social interactions (141). In this sense, texts are both entextualized and recontextualized with reference to an interpellated valuing genre, as interpretive context. Employing this concept of genre, Briggs and Bauman show that entextualized forms can be used to evoke the authority of a cultural tradition (148). They show how the interpretation of an entextualized artifact is influenced by its association with a traditional valuing genre; thus, its recontextualization in interactional negotiations re-evokes that traditional valuing context. For Briggs and Bauman, genres "bear social, ideological, and political-economic connections" (147).

We can see that this argument applies to such valuing domains as ethnic, religious, or other subcultural values. As (re-cited) interpretive contexts, valuing genres are linked to particular collectivities (see 145). Various religious or other subcultural value genres are *interpellated from* the re-citation of texts and cultural artifacts—that is, from sedimented social practices. The re-citation of a cultural form interpellates the subject as a member in a "valuing community" (see 150)—which, in turn, serves as the interpretive frame for both the citational utterance, as well as for the social identity of the subject. In Althusser's terms, interpellation retroactively creates the imagined collective subject, as well as the affiliated generic values that the utterance is then taken to represent (see also Weber 1991). Valuing contexts or genres are reproduced or resisted in various ways, as the subcultural texts "representing" such genres are recontextualized into new situations.

Anthropological work on entextualization and recontextualization processes in cultures other than the United States may lend some insights into contemporary U.S. socialization processes—as an outline of the general way through which individual identity is aligned with community values. For example, in his work on the performance of traditional nativity plays in Mexico, Richard Bauman (1996) shows that the "text" of the play—first as script, then as cards used by actors, then as "rehearsals," and finally as "performance"—undergoes a series of recontextualizations. The script or text of the nativity play is continually *re-cited* along the way, continually re-evoking a religious context as the ground for its interpretation. Religious values and meanings are re-interpellated, as the script is re-cited in each of the sequential stages leading to the final performance—a re-citational ritual which continues a cultural "tradition." In other words, the script, as entextualized subcultural artifact, is continually recontextualized and re-cited, leading to a continued re-interpellation of shared subcultural values and collective identity.

Citing the work of William F. Hanks, Michael Silverstein and Greg Urban (1996) note that the generic "context"—evoked as ground to interpret a particular text—is also used *across* situations to interpret other artifacts (see 8). For example, the religious context which is interpellated from a nativity script can also be used as the interpretive backdrop for the interpretation of a statue or crucifix. In this way, the valuing genre is abstracted as a meaningful social category across its situated applications.

While it is true, as Bauman and Briggs point out, that generic contexts are situationally negotiated, it is also true that such re-citations are not entirely voluntary. In Butler's sense, citational practices "representing" cultural traditions are normatively enforced; in the example above, children may be required by parents to attend the nativity play. The process of socialization into a culture involves learning to entextualize and recontextualize words and texts under threat of social sanction.

To be socialized into a culture thus involves learning citational practices, relative to those material artifacts which evoke normative and hierarchically arranged value genres. In normative socialization, one learns to align one's individual identity with the identity and values of the larger community. In Bauman's example, growing up in a religious community means that a child is expected to re-cite the nativity play in their utterances, and one's social identity as "religious person" is interpellated from those citational practices. In this formulation, we have now come close to Durkheim's (1965) view of how religion "works": ritual behaviors are enacted relative to material "totems," which are taken to represent the collective sense of the "sacred" (Turner, Beegghley, and Powers 2007, 304–5). In this sense, re-citational practices which incorporate communally valued entextualizations can be viewed as ritual behaviors.

As Silverstein and Urban have pointed out, within a culture some texts are more important or authoritative than others (1996, 12). Cultural traditions are preserved through re-citational rituals involving valued texts. Social identity, as an affiliation with particular valuing communities, is constructed by citational reference to such authoritative texts. In fact, such authoritative texts *must* be re-cited in order to continually maintain their privileged status (12–13).

In everyday life, social actors construct social identities with varying degrees of commitment to the normative rituals involving valorized cultural texts. Using Goffman's (1961) terms, "role embracement" or "role distancing" may be interpellated given such varying levels of commitment to normative citational styles. As Igor Kopytoff (1986) has noted, in preindustrial communities there is a greater alignment of individual valuations with communal valuations than in modern cultures. In the language of citationality, there is less deviation of individual citational rituals from normative citational rituals—and less performative display of "role distance." For example, in the case of the nativity play, Bauman identified the "different orientations on the part of participants toward the authoritativeness of the script" (1996, 304). In that study, almost all members of the community were anxious to "show their embracement" of the religious authority of the script and re-cite it faithfully—the lone exception being the "Hermitaño" character in the nativity play who served as a "carnivalesque and subversive" figure (Briggs and Bauman 1992, 152).

In their work, Briggs and Bauman have drawn attention to the inevitable "intertextual distance" or "gap" (1992, 149) between any *situated* re-citation of an authoritative text and its *idealized* meaning. *How* a text is cited by subjects determines whether this gap is "minimized" or "maximized" (149–150). Those citational strategies which *minimize* the gap encourage the interpellation of a strong group identity, shared values, and cultural "tradition." The subject who aligns strongly with *collective* values thus uses those particular syntactical forms of "reporting speech," or citing texts, which are most loyal to tradition—as in the case of a direct quoting of an authoritative text.

In contrast, a citational practice which uses *individualizing* strategies, such as "avoiding direct discourse" (151), has a consequence of *maximizing* the distance or gap between citational instance and value genre, and supports "claims of individual creativity and innovation" (149). Briggs and Bauman thus show that *syntactical* features of utterances generate more or less "distance" from imagined communities, and their associated values. The uses of meaningful syntactical forms to either embrace community values, or to express an individual sense of "role distance," are learned through socialization.

In general, contemporary U.S. culture tolerates a great diversity of value genres—generally "maximizing the gap" between an individual's values, and any one homogenous set of traditional values. However, we still find that normative citational practices have emerged to reproduce a *dominant* value genre in the United States—that of exchange value. The discourse of exchange value has become hegemonic, even given the differentiation and diversity of other subcultural value genres, precisely because of the commodification of language. Those material forms which index membership in diverse subcultures are *themselves given a market value*, which can be abstracted across valuing genres and subcultures. Citational resources can be given an exchange value by which to rank subcultural artifacts against each other, as well as to hierarchically rank subcultural groups themselves. Citational resources taken to "represent" the values of various subcultural groups are unequally distributed by social class—as "cultural capital" in a market economy (see Bourdieu 1984).

For example, following Bourdieu and citing research by Shirley Brice Heath, Briggs and Bauman (1992) identify social class differences learned in modern schools regarding techniques of referencing particular imagined communities. They show that middle-class children, in their acquisition of cultural capital through education, build a repertoire of citational references to a historical "literary community"—thereby interpellating their social identity as a literate member of such a community in ways that working-class children do not (161). In other words, the generic identity category of "educated person" is achieved through the acquisition of the ability to cite literary texts—a citational skill which is unequally distributed.

While Pierre Bourdieu's (1984) work convincingly argues that social institutions like education regulate access to, and differentially reward, particular citational practices, Judith Butler has shown that the identities of such institutions are themselves the *result* of re-citational practices (1997, 147). As Crawford and Ostrom (1995) have suggested, social institutions themselves can be considered as recurring patterns of social behavior, and studied using terms drawn from linguistics to identify the "grammar of institutions." As discussed above, the syntactical practices of *economic* institutions materially shape the meanings and interpellated values of cultural commodities—and thus ultimately the identities of the consumers who cite them. In these utterances of economic institutions, commodities are entextualized into those material forms which maximize profit, and thereby re-evoke the hegemonic discourse of exchange value.

We thus find a link between the citational practices of *institutions* engaged in the production of cultural commodities, and the identity of *individuals* as consumers of citational resources. Just as upper-class students learn to cite their ways into *literary* communities and preferred educational statuses, other social actors learn to cite their way into other subcultural communities. Economic institutions are eager to provide citational resources to all. Both the hegemonic system of exchange value, as well as the unequal social positioning of actors within that system, are reproduced through the re-citation of cultural commodities.

In a diverse, modern culture like that of the United States, we find that individuals may engage in individualizing, role-distancing strategies relative to any one set of religious, ethnic, or political values. Conversely, modern individuals may "minimize the gap" between individual citational practices and those shared within a larger collectivity—whether a subculture or occupational bureaucracy. To be socialized into contemporary culture, then, is to learn citational practices which allow for individualized variations regarding the embracement of—as well as the distancing of self from—subcultural values and institutionally enforced regulations.

Learning to Re-Cite

If "meaning" involves an awareness of normative action relative to material forms, as suggested by the work of George H. Mead (see Joas 1997, 153; 105), then socialization into normative meanings involves learning to re-cite social forms in appropriate ways. As discussed above, in socialization processes subjects are taught, on the one hand, to decontextualize and abstract normative meanings. On the other hand, subjects are taught to recontextualize and alter meanings in new situational contexts, in such a way as to negotiate a desired outcome within that unique situation. In this section, these two aspects of socialization will be illustrated through the consideration of two relevant studies.

As discussed earlier, Derrida argued that Western philosophy and culture have favored a metaphysics of "presence," where meaning is assumed to be located in thought, and conveyed through language. In schools, students socialized into such a model would come to view texts as "containing" the meanings intended by authors. This meaning is assumed to be abstractable and stable across texts and contexts. In other words, students would learn to abstract dictionary-like definitions of words and generic features of texts, as well as to interpret such abstractions as "reflecting" or communicating the subjective intentionalities and values of authors. Techniques are thus predictably developed in Western schools in order to evaluate the ability of students to recognize "objective" meanings and values as "present" within texts (see Silverstein and Urban 1996, 9). In educational theory, the term "textualism" has been applied to such a model (Collins 1996, 204).

In a study of a Chicago grade school, James Collins (1996) notes that while readers with less-advanced skills focused on pronunciation exercises in the classroom, more "advanced" readers engaged in exercises designed to recognize literary themes. As Collins shows, both sets of exercises reinforced a textualist approach in differing ways. The "advanced" readers were taught to abstract "universal" literary themes from a particular text, while "less-advanced" readers were taught that their reading performances revealed a decontextualizable "ability to read"—an ability which could be "objectively" assessed independently of situational context (see also Mertz, 1996, 232).

Collins's study shows that the "presence" of these varying student abilities—whether the ability to read, or the ability to recognize literary themes—is related to the assumed presence and stability of meaning in the text itself. While, as Derrida and Butler argue, re-citational practices have the *potential* to disrupt normative meanings, in this particular study we find that the citation of literary texts in these classrooms instead *stabilized* the universal meanings and literary themes assumed by the textualist model. In turn, the text—as a citational resource assumed to "contain" meaning—was used to stabilize the *identities* of students, and rank them according to ability.

Considering the hypothetical futures of the "advanced readers" in the Collins study, we can imagine how their citational performances—which re-cited the literary themes "present" in various texts—could lead to an interpellation of the student as a good scholar. This meaningful social identity, of course, could itself be carried across situations, from classroom-to-classroom. In other words, the ability to abstract and cite normative meanings, or literary genres, during a classroom interpretation of a text enables a claimed membership in a "literary community." In the contrasting case of those students with lower-level reading skills, the lack of reading ability ultimately leads to a stigmatized social identity. This "abstractable" identity can also cross educational or employment contexts. In the case of either group of readers, we see that citational practices have implications for social identity.

As mentioned above, one aspect of socialization requires that youth engage in practices which display their ability to *decontextualize*, or abstract, meaning from particular cultural texts. Collins shows that this can involve either the abstraction of universal literary themes from texts, or the abstraction of a decontextualized ability to read. The other aspect of socialization involves the ability to recognize the political implications of the *recontextualization* of meaningful material forms, and to learn to differentially cite sources in unique situational negotiations.

Generally, social actors learn to cite socially relevant values in dialogue, linking their own utterances to prior speech acts. Citational practices contribute to an *emergent* interactive context, as actors recontextualize in what ways strips of prior discourse may be relevant to new situational negotiations. In other words, both material texts, as well as their implied (valuing) contexts, are strategically brought into new situated interactions.

As Elizabeth Mertz (1996) shows in a study of law school socialization in the United States, students learn to cite "precedent," or previous instances of discourse. Mertz notes that this skill does not involve a reading of the "universal" meaning of particular texts, but rather a learned style of reading where only *selected* aspects of prior texts are "made relevant" to the negotiation of current legal cases. To be socialized as a lawyer is to learn to *cite strategically*, or to "bend" meanings—extracted from previous cases—toward new politically oriented outcomes. As Mertz puts it, attorneys "struggle to succeed in imposing a particular *recontextualization* of precedent" (230, italics added). Generalizing beyond the Mertz study, we can see that such an ability is also used in everyday interactions, as social actors strategically "report on," or recontextualize, the words and images of others for particular purposes. This skill—recognizing how prior citational practices mean something new when recontextualized into a new situation—illustrates the Derridean point that meaning is not stable across contexts, but is necessarily altered in each situated use. Both students of law, and actors in everyday life, find that how and when a previously established meaning or value is cited is important to the outcome of the negotiation.

In the U.S. legal tradition, lower court decisions frame and limit the legal issues for the appellate courts—which is obviously not the case in everyday life. However, in a more general way we can say that the material forms of socially prior utterances necessarily shape the *possibilities* for their later recontextualizations in everyday life. In the syntactical arrangements of utterances and social objects, materiality is shaped into particular forms which influence—but do not determine—the ways in which these objects are likely to be recontextualized in later social interactions.

In both legal practice and in everyday life, the citation of "precedent," or of previous utterances, can reshape the meaning and value of those prior communicative acts. In other words, the value of a prior case changes as it becomes a precedent for the case at hand (see 234). In a Derridean sense, the meaning and value of the previously materialized utterances are continually *deferred*, and open to possible recontextualization and redefinition in unknown future situations. It is not so much that the meaning and value of cases is stable *across* contexts; rather, the meaning and value of any material sign is re-negotiated through a *grafting* of that "precedent" into subsequent interactions.

In socialization, then, subjects learn how to choose those particular "precedents," from the vast array of previously entextualized utterances of others, which are seen to be strategically relevant in everyday interactions within subcultural groups. For example, a particular team's baseball cap may be strategically recontextualized into street gang interactions—from which membership in that subculture is interpellated. Repeated citations of this "precedent" may become a normative gang ritual, which alters the meaning and value of the baseball cap (relative to the larger culture). Such a citational practice, as Mertz puts it in reference to the citation of legal texts in the law school classroom, "directs attention to *aspects of text that are ideologically significant*" (231, italics added).

Even young gang members become quickly aware that the normative meaning of a baseball cap has been "recontextualized" in this situation, with implications for the interpellation of social identity for its wearer. If a particular baseball cap were to become an important, quasi-sacred object within a street gang, we can see that its "authority" comes not from its *normative* referential content (i.e., the meaning of the hat in the larger culture), but from the way it comes to "index" membership in the subcultural group (see Silverstein 1976) as it "plays against" the normative meanings of the larger culture. Similarly, in law school, students learn that only certain legal aspects of previous cases are relevant to the present case (Mertz 1996, 240).

In this section, using the two school studies, we have analytically separated two aspects of socialization—first, learning to decontextualize social meanings so as to transport them across situations, and second, learning to recontextualize social meanings as relevant to new situations. In everyday practice, of course, these learned skills are in fact closely intertwined, and continually used in conjunction with each other. This holds not only for the re-citation of particular *texts*, but also for the re-citation of an interpretive *context* or valuing genre itself—inasmuch as the meaning of a contextual genre has to be linked to prior usages. Street gang members may recontextualize baseball caps or several other "texts" in the ongoing re-citation of the valuing "context" of gang affiliation.

Socialization thus involves learning how normative relationships between self and others are constructed through the *re-citation and recontextualization of meaningful materialities*. Robert Preucel, in his book *Archaeological Semiotics* (2006), has noted that the field of archaeology has begun to relocate its problematic by supplementing the study of "material culture" with the study of "materiality" (4–5). He defines "materiality" as "the social constitution of self and society by means of the object world" (5). In his book, he also notes a corresponding movement within the field of semiotics toward situated practice (8). In considering this convergence of interests in archeology and semiotics, Preucel stresses the importance of the "contextualization" of material entities for their meaning (8). He also notes the contributions of "pragmatic anthropology" as it builds upon Peircean semiotics, especially the concept of "indexicality" (68). In this tradition, Preucel points out, "It is widely accepted that linguistic forms often serve as indexes of social groups" (78).

We can clearly see here an affiliation of this anthropological problematic with Butler's notion that citational practices "interpellate" the social identities of self and other, as well as align individual identities with those of larger reference groups. This convergence can also be aided through a Bakhtinian emphasis on the materiality of citational resources, as the site for the re-negotiation of cultural values. In other words, there is an increasing recognition in scholarly literature as to the importance of socialization processes where subjects learn how to both decontextualize, and recontextualize, meaningful material forms. As Silverstein and Urban have put it, "textuality and entextualization practices turn out to be about 'identity'" (1996, 10).

Valuing contexts, as well as the social identities of actors, are *negotiated* in situational interactions. In other words, meaningful strips of language do not "index their contexts" once and for all, but rather context itself is continually renegotiated as social meanings are continually bent toward particular situational outcomes. Social actors, as John Gumperz (1997) has shown, learn to recognize "contextualization cues" used by others, in establishing and negotiating interactional context (231–32). Because social actors are simultaneously situated relative to multiple valuing contexts at the same time, participants in dialogue must continually re-prioritize or make relevant particular values—and communicate these strategic movements to each other (see also Duranti and Goodwin 1997, 5).

Thus subjects not only learn to re-cite or recontextualize *texts* within "pregiven" contexts (such as a classroom), but in turn re-establish the meaning and relevance of those *contexts* through the same citational practices. For example, to abstract a theme from a literary text in a classroom maneuver is to re-assert the *educational context*—as opposed to re-citing a prayer in a classroom which evokes an alternative religious context. Duranti and Goodwin have noted that "talk itself constitutes a main resource for the organization of context" (7–8). They cite the contributions of ethnomethodologists to this line of argument, given their recognition as to how social actors "negotiate or achieve a common context" (27). Duranti and Goodwin also cite the contribution of those conversation analysts who study how contexts shift in dialogue (30). In learning how to re-cite, then, subjects must learn to re-evoke normative contexts, in socially appropriate ways, when interacting with others. This not only includes the citation of situationally relevant words, but also the appropriate prioritization of those materialized props or social objects which evoke normative hierarchies of valuing contexts.

To be socialized into language use, then, involves learning how to use "contextualization cues" (Gumperz 1997, 231-32), and other normative conversational techniques (see Lucy 1993), which enable audiences to re-enact particular interpretive contexts through utterances. As the Bakhtin Circle has shown, the way in which the entextualized words of others are reported or cited involves the employment of particular syntactical forms. These forms interpellate the valuing contexts of self and others, which play against each other. As utterances incorporate the words of others in particular ways, normative valuing contexts are "re-cited." The ability to appropriately re-cite cultural values is learned through socialization.

Learning to Negotiate Identity and Values

In his work, George H. Mead (1969) locates the meaning of the material objects and signs that we encounter in everyday life in the normative responses of others toward them—in a social commonality of response which the social actor learns to anticipate (73–74; Joas 1997, 105). Social actors are thus socialized into a culture of common meanings, both regarding the physical uses of material objects, as well as regarding their more abstract significations—as when a child is advised to color in a coloring book rather than in a sacred text.

As discussed above, in citing material signs into new situations, the meaning of that sign crosses situational contexts. Similarly, the meaning of "value" is abstracted across contexts, as those material signs which are normatively taken as representative of particular value domains are cited into new situations. Subjects learn how others cite particular cultural forms, and thus learn to recognize their normative value. In re-citing this value in their own utterances, subjects adopt normative citational styles relative to cultural value discourses. The process of "learning to value," in accordance with community traditions, involves learning to recognize the value of normative forms, to produce such forms in normative citational styles, and to recontextualize valued forms into situated negotiations with others.

Subjects learn how to refer to meaningful materialities, and how to value them differentially. They learn to behave in culturally preferred ways relative to particular material forms; in David Graeber's words, one way to think about value is "as the importance of actions" (2001, 49). Citational practice thus becomes the social mechanism whereby the normative value domains, such as religious, ethnic, or political values, are reproduced—these practices become socially sedimented ways of ritually acting toward valued cultural forms. Value domains are thus re-produced as a *commonality of social response to material signs*—and in reference to which, in Mead's sense, social actors are able to anticipate the citational practices of others.

It is not only the materialized text which is taken to have value across situations, as a material representation of a collectively held cultural value, but the "valuing context" itself is re-assumed as the artifact is re-cited. These contexts are implied in the material *form* of the cultural artifact; indeed, meaningful materialities are usually produced precisely in order to evoke particular valuing contexts in future situations. For example, it is anticipated that the material form of a crucifix or a hymn will normatively signify a religious valuing domain. The value of the artifact, and the valuing (religious) context, reciprocally emerge in citational practices.

In this sense, within the representationalist framework still normative in U.S. culture, we can distinguish between two senses of "value"; first, the "functional value" of a text in more or less effectively representing the collectivity; and second, the collectively held "cultural value" which is said to pre-exist its material embodiment. Citational practices are normatively held to involve both the functional value of material citational resources, as well as the social values they signify.

As Mead argued, it is through "role taking" that we evaluate our impulses to act—themselves socially conditioned within the value order—in light of the anticipated value attributions of others. For Mead, like Bakhtin, this future-oriented nature of action always already involves values. The "social self" we present to others, in Mead's words, "must be recognized by others to have the very values which we want to have belong to it" (1969, 204). In other words, subjects align their situated citational practices with the normative value discourses in such as a way that a recognizable type of "valuing identity" can be interpellated—as supposedly motivating those citations. In Mead's (1969) terms, we anticipate the assessments which others will make of "me," and their attributions of values to "me." In Vološinov's words, "Intonation can be thoroughly understood only when one is in touch with the assumed value judgments of the given social group," as a "commonness of evaluations" (1976, 102).

Inasmuch as these social responses of others become organized or sedimented within a culture, we can speak of the *normative* valuations, or typifications, made by others regarding our utterances. Through the process of socialization, subjects become aware that in response to one's own citational practices, others will attribute to them a socially recognizable identity, and attribute subcultural values to that identity. The acting subject thus negotiates their citational moves relative to normative identity categories, as well as relative to the subcultural "values" normatively attributed to those social identities. Children learn the social typifications which accompany their citational practices. They learn that certain "types of people" engage in certain types of social behaviors, and learn to attribute particular values to those people. In this sense, to "entextualize," or syntactically incorporate, a value domain into an utterance already anticipates the "recontextualization" of the utterance by others.

As children learn language, they learn how to prioritize, or make relevant, certain behaviors or words in particular situations. Children learn what their parents think is important, as parents direct their attention toward particular material signs in situations. Children learn what words are to be re-cited in particular situations—thus learning to *anticipate the priorities of others relative to the meaningful materiality of language*. In family life, children learn to prioritize certain valued social objects in *spatial* arrangements in the home, as well as learn the *temporality* of priorities in everyday family interactions. Social actors learn to prioritize material signs in their own utterances by learning how significant others cite material signs, as well as how significant others interpellate value hierarchies and subcultural membership from those signs.

From a symbolic interactionist point of view, social actors are not simply socialized into the *structure* of a normative value system; rather values are *re-constructed* in everyday life through social interaction (see also Graeber 2001, xii). Vocabularies of normative values are strategically employed in specific social settings, as value is talked about, negotiated, and situationally re-enacted. As Herbert Blumer has noted, social interaction involves an interpretive process where meanings are emergent from *within* the situation, as opposed to "a mere automatic application of established meanings" (1969, 5). For example, family life can be considered as a "negotiated order"—a term associated with the work of Anselm Strauss (Hewitt and Shulman 2011, 164). Family members have to negotiate and prioritize citational practices—such as what television shows to watch, what type of electronic devices to purchase, or what events and "experiences" to enjoy. In this sense, family values are re-produced through citational practices.

In a diverse culture, value conflicts continually arise in everyday life, given the differing stances of individuals relative to the multiplicity of available value genres. An important aspect of interpersonal dialogue thus concerns the continual re-prioritization of values, and the negotiation of social relationships involving such values. For example, a parent may question a teen's citational selection of a rock poster, as opposed to a religious object, for a bedroom wall. We can see that politically negotiated outcomes regarding the prioritization of valuing contexts, as well as the implications of such outcomes for social relationships, occur through the meaningful material signs cited in social interaction.

Values are therefore not only negotiated within the syntactical form of particular utterances, as in the case of reported speech. Rather, the *entire material configuration* of an interactive situation is the site of value negotiation. The materiality of any particular utterance plays against the materialized utterances of others in the situation, as well as against the normative meanings of the other social objects in that material configuration. The citational practices or behavioral moves occur within the entire materiality of the "social situation."

The politics of value negotiation thus involves the strategic use of citational resources—such as the way that subjects report the words of others (see Vološinov 1986; Duranti and Goodwin 1997, 12). Bakhtin has used the term "double-voicing" to refer to the way that a speaker takes an evaluative stance relative to the words or voice of another *within* the speaker's own utterance (Bakhtin 1984, 185; Wortham and Locher 1999). This concept can also be extended to refer to the way that a citational utterance "reports on" the normative materiality of social environments—as comprised of the words, objects, and images "of the other." Value and identity negotiation between subcultures, with competing values, occurs through meaningful material forms themselves.

The Re-Citation of Reference Groups

The citation of a "reference group" involves the assertion of one's identity as a member of a collectivity. In such a citational practice, value differences within the referential subculture are glossed over in favor of a more unified typification of the supposedly shared values of that community. To borrow Benedict Anderson's term from his study of nationalism, the referential subculture is an "imagined community" (1991). However, given the diversity of contemporary U.S. culture, the subject simultaneously cites multiple, competing, subcultural reference groups—forming a "web" of citational affiliations (see Simmel 1955), or a hybrid mix of "value subjectivities" for each individual. The prioritization of such references occurs via material utterances which, as Bakhtin shows, enact the "synchronization" (MacCannell 1985) of a differentiated and hierarchical system of values.

When the subject experiences the "presence" of value in the contemporary cultural economy, it is not merely as an individual. Rather, subjects construct individual experience through the value genres and identity categories which align them with particular reference groups. For example, a subject may experience everyday life as the type of person who would put "family above business," or as someone who tries to keep "commercialism out of art." In the course of a day, social actors participate in several valuing spheres, re-constructing experiential identities relative to many differing, and even conflicting, imagined valuing communities.

Thus each social identity, interpellated through citational practice, necessarily involves different ratios of competing values. Because cultural commodities enter into differing material constellations, the same mass-produced form in different situations may interpellate differentially ranked values and identities. The ongoing citational practices of subjects are thus guided by, to use Derrida's term, a "logic of supplementarity" (1997, 215)—where some values are cited as dominant in identity construction, and other values are subordinated.

The very act of differentiating and prioritizing values divides the world of meaningful materiality into more or less "valuable" citational resources, which, in turn, interpellates a prioritizing subjectivity. This occurs on both individual and subcultural levels, as individuals *cite their way into* imagined communities with already-interpellated value hierarchies. Vikki Bell (1999), citing the work of Anne-Marie Fortier and of Jonathan and Daniel Boyarin, speaks of the "performativity of belonging," where the re-citation of the norms of the group "makes material the belongings they purport to simply describe" (3).

For example, membership in a family is re-cited as individuals daily position themselves relative to social objects taken to represent that membership, as well as issue material utterances which re-enact the alignment of individual identity with that of the family. Bringing Eugene Rochberg-Halton's (1986) study (discussed below) into the language of citationality, we can say that the home environment continually interpellates the family as a collective subject "possessing" a particular hierarchy of group values—given the way that material objects have been positioned and prioritized in the family's citational practices. Family values are thus continually re-constructed through the ongoing placement of material social objects within the spaces of the home.

One's individual experiences as a member of the family are constructed relative to this collective sense of family values. Thus, we may find that one family member becomes uncomfortable watching a particular television show in the living room with another family member, if the interpellated values of the show stand against those collective values. In other words, particular images or words from the television may, by entering into the normative material constellation from which the collective values are interpellated, create a kind of dissonance relative to normative group identity.

In this sense, politics involve the defense of the citational practices of one's self, or one's group, in order to maintain value distinctions. Just as, for Butler, gender is politically maintained through the enforced repetition of gendered citations, so are various value discourses and valuing communities *institutionally* maintained in the culture, through both the marketing of citational resources, as well as in the maintenance of the material environments in which citational practices occur. In the language of Pierre Bourdieu (1984), an institutionalized "linguistic market" emerges favoring particular kinds of cultural capital.

Using another example, we can see that the citation of particular values at a speaking engagement may index the speaker as a representative of the "kinds of values" supported by a sponsoring political community. Whether at a religious ceremony or political rally, a keynote speaker is taken to represent the pre-existing, collectively held values of the group. The positioning of the audience relative to the materiality of the speech—a citational practice—serves to ritually reinforce group solidarity. The alignment of the speaker's values with those of the group occurs *through* the meaningful materiality of the speech itself, as well as through the speaker's bodily "presence" at the event—another citational practice relative to that event.

In late capitalism, the citational resources used to interpellate group values are themselves commodifiable, in that they not only *represent* group values, but also are given an exchange value as to their ability to experientially *deliver* those values—that is, make the values "present." Thus each speech and each speaker, or each guest on a television talk show, is actually—or potentially—given an exchange value as to their functional worth in "delivering" various religious, political, or family values. For example, the worth of a citational resource for an audience might be measured by the functionality of the political speech in winning votes, the perceived intensity of the religious experience at a revival, or simply the entertainment value of an attraction for a family on a vacation. The point is that the *exchange value* of the citational resource is itself measured in terms of its capacity to deliver the experience of *other subcultural values*.

In *Against the Romance of Community*, Miranda Joseph (2002) has argued that capitalism itself is dependent upon the notion of "community" (xxxii), in that group identities are differentiated through their differing types of consumption (22; 30). In this sense, Joseph speaks of consumption as a "performative production" of both individual and community identity—rather than as a passive "consumerism" (34). While the dominant ideology is that community or subcultural values are unaffected by, or even resistant to, the exchange value system (9), in fact "capitalism is the very medium in which community is enacted" (xxxii).

As language itself becomes increasingly commodified, exchanged in the market, and assigned a worth in the U.S. cultural economy, the subjects who attempt to cite alternative values are thus faced with a dilemma. Those utterances which seek to signify, for example, a "religious" or "family" experience—outside of, or even opposed to, exchange value—must necessarily employ language which itself can become commodifiable and assigned a market value. Thus, it has become increasingly difficult for subjects to cite alternative valuing communities and discourses, inasmuch as their citation requires material forms which themselves have an economic worth.

As an indication of this difficulty, we today find people asserting that highly paid "televangelists"—once taken to "represent" a religious community—might instead represent the corruption of religious values, precisely because of their marketability. Others might assert that their favorite music artists and songs have been tainted through their association with advertised products. Even live events invoking values perceived to be oppositional toward commercialization, such as a religious revival or punk rock concert, are increasingly viewed with cynicism as they are heavily advertised, promoted, and thereby associated with exchange value.

In addition, the "measure" of the depth of religious or aesthetic experience itself is often given in the quantifying language of exchange value (see Guillory 1993, 323). For example, someone considering purchasing a painting for the wall of a home might not only consider the potential increase which the artwork brings to the marketability of the home, but may also attempt to quantify a measure of the "aesthetic value" of "experiencing" the work for a certain length of time. Works providing greater aesthetic experiences may well be "worth" the purchase price. In this sense, the exchange value discourse of the larger culture has become an pervasive reference, or frame, which is normatively grafted onto the everyday performativity of other values.

As Haug has shown (1986), the attribution of value to material goods is increased, along with the purchase price, precisely because of the aesthetic language which advertisers graft onto commodities. For Haug, sellers use aesthetic techniques, such as photography or music, to create a mythology or aura around the product. For example, in automobile advertising cars may be aligned with social status or adventure, beyond their mere use as transportation. For Haug, the exaggeration of what the consumer will "experience" following the purchase of the product has reached the point where the "aesthetic" experiences *promised* by material goods have become entirely separated from their "real" use-values. Haug argues that these promised experiences increasingly constitute a greater proportion of the exchange value of the product (16–17). Ironically, the *exchange value* of a citational resource increases as advertising successfully makes appeals to *other cultural values*—such as "individualism," "success," or "sexuality." The *promise* of the "presence" of other cultural values increases the exchange value of the cultural commodity.

In this way, a "valuing crisis" seems to have emerged for the contemporary subject, who experiences the difficulty of re-enacting subcultural values which somehow lie outside of the discourse of exchange value. Subjects find that the "presence" of *any* value is increasingly coterminous with the hegemonic "presence" of exchange value (see Guillory 1993, 323). The problem is that the signification of "non-economic" experiences and values cannot be separated from the commodifiable, material *form* of language in the cultural economy—from which exchange value is simultaneously interpellated. In this sense, any alternative values are always already "corrupted" because of the increased marketability of language itself.

In a Derridean sense, it is true that these alternative, "non-economic" value categories could never be, and have never been, pure types to begin with. However, in both popular perception and theoretical analysis, particular value categories have historically been regarded as separable domains. It is from *within* this traditional understanding that the contemporary subject now confronts a valuation crisis. While the market presents itself as simply a distributional mechanism—to deliver experiences aligning with the pre-existing values of subcultures and individuals—in so doing it necessarily disrupts the perceived "purity" of these alternative value categories.

Thus, to speak of the performativity of exchange value is to recognize that today, subjects cannot help but re-cite the exchange value frame—given the extent to which the culture has become commodified. In the contemporary cultural economy, virtually all utterances are potentially grafted with the hegemonic exchange value discourse. Not only do individuals re-cite the commodified words and images of others, but their own utterances may come to be marketable. The exchange value of language is thus potentially re-performed with every utterance—whether that utterance attempts to embrace, or attempts to resist, the enabling constraints of the cultural economy.

The Citation of Valued Social Objects

As mentioned, for Bakhtin the "synchronic" system of differentiated values between self and other is continually re-cited and re-negotiated through utterances. In the situated utterances of everyday life, individuals selectively cite material forms taken to represent various subcultural value discourses. Just as subcultural group identities are interpellated from citational practices which evoke competing value discourses or "genres" (Bakhtin 1984), so are individual identities "split" in various proportion between these culturally available value genres. One's social identity can never be a pure example of a particular genre—it can only be constructed in relation to alterity, and differentiated from social identities which are taken to represent other value discourses.

Bakhtin uses the concept of "ratio" to emphasize, as in the case of reported speech, that the values of self and the values of others always combine in some *proportion* in any utterance, as well as in the inner speech of the self (Holquist 2004, 29). Citational utterances, both anticipated as well as actualized, thus enact a "graft of values," or—to use Walter Benjamin's term—construct a unique "constellation" (Buck-Morss 1979) of values in varying proportion to each other. Extending this argument, the grafting of values applies not only within utterances, but also between utterances. In other words, individual identity is continually interpellated from a social environment comprised of multiple material forms—relative to the many group identities taken to be represented by those forms.

As discussed above, the material grafting of the values of self to the values of others in utterances involves the bringing together of at least two contexts in order to be meaningful. A subject grafts or cites the material signs produced by others into new utterances, taking an evaluative position relative toward normative identities and values by referencing those material signs in particular ways. In written or verbal *utterances*, this "referencing" or citational practice involves the syntactical construction of the utterance, as well as its positioning in sequences of interactional dialogue. In the case of meaningful *social objects*, this referencing involves the spatial and temporal positioning of these meaningful material objects relative to the subject.

For example, Rochberg-Halton (1986), relying heavily on the semiotic work of Charles Peirce, as well as the work of George Herbert Mead, has studied the construction of symbolically ordered environments in private homes. Rochberg-Halton argues that a material possession can serve as a "role model" or "reference" for a subject, inasmuch as the object can indicate or represent "certain values of the culture" (149). Rochberg-Halton here follows George H. Mead, arguing that "inanimate objects could serve as elements of the generalized other" (149), as subjects "take the attitude" of particular objects. These objects are associated with particular roles (150), which are patterns of social behavior taken to represent particular cultural values. In this sense, relationships to others can be enacted through the positioning of social objects, taken as material signs of particular social values. In his research, Rochberg-Halton specifically focuses on the arrangement of meaningful material objects in the home, given the differing values of their owners.

As Bakhtin would argue, every meaningful object has a social history involving others. Just as the "words of the other" become part of our own speech, the "objects of the other" are also incorporated into the citational practices of the subject. As in the case of reported speech, meaningful social objects signifying the values of others are grafted into the referential context of one's life, shaping one's own "inner values" in various proportion. Just as, for Vološinov, "inner speech" relies on the same objective signs found in external or outer speech with others, Rochberg-Halton points out—referring to Cooley and Mead—that internal conversations with self involve the social objects or "signs" distributed in home environments (155). In Bakhtinian terms, different individuals enact different "ratios" in regard to cultural value discourses through the placement of material objects in the home. For example, some people may place those social objects which predominantly reference "religious values" in prominent locations in the home, as opposed to status symbols referencing "exchange value."

While in the Rochberg-Halton study there were individual valuations which differed from the normative valuations of the larger culture, there were also *shared* behavioral practices patterned by sociological categories. For example, Rochberg-Halton points out that different family members valued items differently, especially across age categories (155–57). Specifically, Rochberg-Halton contrasts the "egocentric" placement practices of youth, who were very much concerned with their own emerging identities, with those of older adults (158). In Bakhtinian terms, these can be thought of as different hierarchical ratios involving differing value contexts—as indicated by the syntactical distribution of materialities within the home environment.

We can thus see how the spatial arrangements of social objects in a home might be seen as a *citational practice* of the subject, involving evaluative stances toward the "signs of the other"—as, for example, when a cherished photograph is placed in a prominent household location. After being stored for a time, such a photograph might be returned to the prominent location during a family gathering at a holiday—temporally situating the photograph to interpellate shared "family values." The citational practices of subjects thus involve the social positioning of material signs both spatially and temporally, interpellating a particular type of social identity which prioritizes—and also is taken to "represent"—the values normatively associated with these signs.

In this sense, we might reconsider "reference groups"—a term used in social psychology to refer to an intentional alignment of the values of self with the pre-existing values of particular social groups—along the lines of citational practice. Rather than seeing the spatial and temporal distribution of material signs as "representing" a prior group *consciousness*, we might speak of a more performative "citational referencing" of subcultural values, through the *material* positioning of signs relative to the subject. "Reference groups" thus become groups to be interpellated and *prioritized through citation*—a process which simultaneously interpellates the group identity, as well as those particular values which the groups are normatively taken to represent.

Thus, it is not only verbal or written *utterances* which enact what Bakhtin refers to as the ratio, or proportion, of the "values of self" relative to "values of others." Reading Rochberg-Halton's study through the language of citationality, we can see more generally that the materiality of social environments—which subjects (and social institutions) both construct and cite—also continually re-prioritizes cultural value discourses. As in the case of reported speech, the subject takes a stand relative to normative value discourses through the positioning and arrangement of meaningful material objects into particular configurations or constellations—relative to the social and physical positioning of the subject. The spatial and temporal positioning of material social objects, relative to the subject, thus grafts together the referential contexts of self and others in unique valuing ratios.

Just as situated material *utterances* necessarily signify in unique ways, so do the material configurations of *social objects*; in fact, both are meaningful materialities with differing "modalities" (see Althusser 1971). However, the *singularity* of such a particular citational grafting of objects is, in turn, subject to the "rules" of iterability—that is, in order to be recognizable and meaningful, the "value constellation" must be *repeatable* across situations. Thus, for example, norms regarding interior decorating emerge publicly, even as individual "value ratios" can be constructed through idiosyncratic citational practices in private homes.

The Normative Subject in Late Capitalism

As Berger and Luckmann argued in *The Social Construction of Reality* (1967), the dominant definition of reality is often "reified" (89), or taken for granted by members of a culture. Socialization into the reified worldview occurs through language, which continually reinforces a particular view of the world through the references made to social "realities" by actors. For Berger and Luckmann, the self internalizes normative social meanings, and thus a "subjective reality" (129) emerges. In the language of citationality, children are socialized into normative citational practices as they internalize the usual responses of others to their utterances. They learn the temporal and spatial prioritizations of material signs in their homes, neighborhood, and culture as they see what others pay attention to and value. From these normative citational practices, normative social identities are interpellated.

In contemporary U.S. culture, children learn to pay attention to and cite those material signs which are (ideologically) assumed to embody the "presence" of exchange value. Growing up in households where purchase decisions are made within the confines of particular family budgets, children learn to measure the worth of experiences against each other. Of course, in household decisions several cultural discourses come into play; for example, the perceived importance of entertainment experiences may be weighed against religious experiences as the family distributes its time. Yet even here the standardized measure of exchange value intrudes, in the consideration given by parents as to how the quality of various childhood experiences weigh against the labor experiences which ultimately finance them. It is not just that citational utterances "matter" to families, in that their meaningful materialities imply particular cultural values. It is also that citational utterances "count"—in that the exchange value of the citational experiences are weighed against the measurable constraints of family budgets. Parents thus attempt to guide youth through the maze of cultural commodities within social class restrictions, balancing the entertainment value of youth subcultural activities against other value discourses.

As Arlie Hochschild (2003) has shown, subjects also learn the emotions socially appropriate to various situations. Children learn to re-cite the appropriate emotion when engaging in particular citational practices; for example, that a day spent watching auto racing on a big-screen television should make them happy and excited, or that listening to the lyrics of particular songs should make them feel ashamed. These emotions are constructed in line with cultural and family value discourses regarding the supposed "presence" or "lack" of value in specific citational practices. The commodified words and images of others—like the televised race or popular song—are measured against the standard of exchange value, to the extent that they do or do not deliver worthwhile experiences to the normative subject.

The interpellated *worth* of subjective experiences, as measured within a hierarchy of exchange value, has become an important backdrop to the social typing of others and the construction of social identity—especially given the cultural belief that persons with higher incomes have better lifestyle experiences. Others attribute personality features to those who engage in particular citational practices, and assign them membership in particular valuing communities. The solicitation of desired value attributions thus becomes a taken-for-granted "motive" of social behavior (see Mills 2003). It is taken as natural that normative subjects organize their lives to maximize and collect these culturally valued experiences—a "reified" assumption into which succeeding generations are socialized (see Berger and Luckmann 1967). Contemporary socialization practices teach that the words of particular others—especially media figures—are rankable, marketable, and a source of valuable experience for subjects.

The words of the other—as representative of particular identities and cultural values—are *static*. In Derrida's sense, the normative meaning of a particular cultural form—such as a piece from a musician, or the words of a president—are abstractable from "original" context, and become citable in new contexts. Even while the living musician or president may be changing and evolving, their prior utterances become material forms with a sedimented historical meaning, and come to represent particular value domains. Thus, a subject can continually evoke famous media personalities as important influences in their own lives—even for decades—even though the cited other may have since become a very different person. As Thompson (1995) has noted, the relationship of "fans" with media celebrities is a one-sided, non-reciprocal relationship; in this sense, fans have their relationships with an entextualized form representing a valuing community, rather than with a person.

Following Goffman (1959), we can see that in the everyday presentation of self, citation practices are employed by the subject to prompt audiences to typify them within desirable identity categories. In addition, *self*-interpretation rests on the availability of desirable past experiences, or of past attributions by others, as evidence for particular self-categorizations. Thus subjects comb their own biographies and photo albums in order to construct their current identities, selectively citing valuable experiences of their past as evidence of their current status. Social actors also seek to anticipate and arrange valued experiences in the future, through the planned acquisition of fashionable citational resources. The normative contemporary subject thus attempts to build a "citational archive" of value, attempting to accumulate a lifetime of worthwhile, valued experiences to look back upon when assessing the "worth" of their life—as measured, again, in the language of exchange value. Each individualized subject thus emerges with a unique autobiography, or "constellation" of commodified citational experiences.

CONCLUSION:

CRITIQUE OF THE PRESENCE OF SUBCULTURAL VALUES

This chapter extended Butler's thesis regarding the performativity of gender into a more general thesis regarding the performativity of value. While chapters four and five will specifically address the performativity of exchange value, this chapter addressed the performativity of subcultural values. The main argument presented was that individuals align their social identities with subcultural groups through citational practices, which re-cite the values normatively associated with those subcultural groups. As opposed to a representational perspective which assumes that subcultural values pre-exist their expression, the chapter suggests that a performative perspective better describes how values and subcultural identities are constructed through situated, material utterances.

Just as Butler extended the work of Derrida in her work, this chapter began by extending Derrida's thesis regarding the metaphysics of "presence" in Western philosophy and culture into a thesis regarding the "presence" of subcultural values. Just as "presence" has been the dominant metaphysical assumption in the West, the assumed presence of subcultural values remains important for contemporary identity construction practices. The presence of subcultural values is today performatively re-enacted through the citation of cultural commodities, ideologically taken to "re-present" particular subcultural values.

The first section of the chapter concerned the socialization processes whereby this temporality of value (i.e., "presence") is reproduced, as children are taught normative citational practices. Subcultural values are performatively re-enacted by children as they learn to re-cite those meaningful material forms which represent important cultural values. Children are taught that value is "present" in particular material forms, and that the citation of these forms reveals that particular values are present within their own "selves." These practices can be seen as *performative* of subcultural values, in the sense that they actively reproduce these values—rather than simply representing them.

In addition to learning a particular temporality of value and how to re-cite it, children in Western cultures are also taught to use particular syntactical forms, which interpellate a particular type of subject. The notion of an individualistic, autonomous subject who "experiences" the value of social objects—a "Cartesian" subjectivity—is reinforced through utterances which materially re-enact these assumptions. Through citational practices, the individual Cartesian subject is aligned with the (Cartesian) subjectivity of a reference group, which is taken to collectively possess particular values.

The chapter next used the example of travel and tourism to show how the Cartesian version of subjectivity has been sustained throughout Western history, and continues into the present. Citational practices not only involve bringing the words of self and other together in syntactical formations, but also involve bringing the bodies of the subject into proximity with the bodies of the other—as in the case of travel. In Western history we find that a particular way of gazing at the other, in travel, has historically reinforced Cartesian subjectivity. The visual experience of a Cartesian subject involves the objectification of the other, as well as *reinforces the subcultural boundaries* between self and other. In "learning to travel," subjects learn to cite others in normative, syntactical formations which re-enact hegemonic identities and values.

The taking of souvenirs during travel also re-differentiates the referential contexts of self and other. Considered as "quotes" from another subculture, the souvenir valorizes the home context of the traveler by incorporating the exotic images or objects of the other (Sherlock 1998). As citational practice, the other is brought into the utterance of self in a controlled fashion. The incorporation of commodified words and images of others into the citational experiences of the Western subject continues today through mediated travel, involving citational technologies such as television, film, and the Internet.

The second section of the chapter directly addressed the processes involved in the interpellation of subcultural affiliation. An affinity was shown between the work of linguistic anthropologists on the entextualization of material artifacts, and the theoretical framework of this book on citational practice. Children are socialized so as to both recognize those meaningful material forms which represent key cultural values, as well as to recontextualize those forms in strategic ways in everyday interaction. Individual identity is aligned with subcultural identity and subcultural values through the citation of normative material forms.

Thus, the chapter focused on the performativity of subcultural values, emphasizing how these values and subcultural identities are interpellated from the material utterances of individuals and social institutions. As noted in the conclusion of chapter two, we must distinguish between the type of performativity operant in today's cultural economy—which rests on an ideology that subcultural values become actualized or "present" through citational utterances—and the version of performativity theory, supported by Derrida's notion of iterability, which is critical of this ideology. While this chapter described the former processes, we will now quickly consider their critique. In chapter six, we will return to a more comprehensive critique of the "presence of value," following our discussion of the performativity of exchange value in chapters four and five.

To return to the study of the nativity play discussed above, Bauman (1996) shows that despite the play being defined as an "authoritative" text—clearly representative of cultural tradition and religious values—each successive incarnation of the text was in fact *altered* as it was recontextualized. In a Derridean sense, while the repetition of any meaningful material form is necessary to maintain recognizability and meaning across iterations, each situated instantiation necessarily alters that meaning (and value). Thus, while the play was entextualized to "represent" religious values, each iteration necessarily altered both the repeated text, as well as the interpellated valuing context. The dislocation of the meaning of the entextualized artifact, as well as that of its interpellated contextual genre, also potentially unsettles the *identity of social actors* who cite the text in order to "experience its values." In other words, as the value of the text, as well as the valuing context of religion, are unsettled—to a greater or lesser extent—through particular recontextualization practices, so is the interpellated identity of both the individual and collective subjects who are socially positioned relative to that citational resource.

Derrida's version of citational performativity, based on the notion of iterability, argues that the meaning of any material sign can never be finally determined by intentionality (i.e., is never fully "present"). Rather, it is always deferrable and subject to later reinterpretations. From this perspective, social values—as meaningful—cannot be intentionally embodied into material signs, but rather are continually re-interpellated from them in situated negotiations. As such, they are always subject to reinterpretation in the future. The same argument also applies to the functional worth, or exchange value, of a material sign in representing a particular set of subcultural values. In this sense, the exchange value of meaningful material signs is never quite "present." However, while such iterability keeps open the *possibility* for alternative temporalities to materialize, in contemporary U.S. culture the hegemonic temporality of the "presence" of value persists—given the proliferation of commodified citational resources whose materiality re-enacts this temporality when re-cited.

Just as Derrida developed a critique of the assumptions regarding "presence" in Western metaphysics, a parallel critique of the presence of *value*—as experienced through the citation of cultural commodities—can also be developed. We might turn to Martin Jay's book *Songs of Experience* (2005) as a resource in the development of this critique of the Cartesian/capitalist experience of the presence of value. There, Jay criticizes the reduction of the category of "experience" to that of an individual, consuming (i.e., Cartesian) subject, pointing out that "phenomenologists, Critical Theorists, pragmatists, and poststructuralists alike" have all argued that experience—as a concept or category in philosophy—"cannot be reduced to what an isolated, contemplative, integrated subject has of an object that is entirely external to him or her" (403). John Guillory, citing the work of Joan Scott, as well that of Laclau and Mouffe, has also pointed out that a critique of the concept of "experience" in contemporary theory often accompanies a critique of "representation" (Guillory 1993, 10; 345–346n14).

Yet, while such a critique may have emerged in philosophy and social theory, it is precisely this reductive notion of "experience"—and its valorization—which prevails in cultural practices in late capitalism. Indeed, Jay points out that particular critical theorists—like Benjamin, Adorno, Heidegger, and some poststructuralists—have precisely seen "the commodification of experiences as one of the most prevalent tendencies of our age" (2005, 407). For Jay, and the philosophers he cites, this tendency toward commodification "is precisely the opposite of what many of the theorists in our survey have argued an experience should be, that is, something which can never be fully possessed by its owner" (407). Extending this critique of individual experience to that of "group experience," as in the case of a valuing community, Jay goes on to argue that the idea of a group "ownership of an experience"—which he sees as operating in contemporary identity politics—"forgets" that "experience involves an encounter with otherness" (408).

For Jay, such an "encounter with otherness" necessarily *dislocates* the identity of the experiencing subject. If, in a Derridean sense, "experience" is a meaningful category across contexts, it must itself necessarily be altered in the repetition of that meaning. Thus, the re-citation of the words of others by the subject—words perceived as representing particular subcultural values—does not simply reproduce those values. Rather, the "experience" of value(s) cannot be entirely stable or present across contexts. Instead, as the words of others are incorporated into the utterances of subjects, the subcultural values which they are taken to represent are necessarily altered. In this sense, the "experience" of group values cannot remain a stable reproduction of an identifiable, and present, meaning across contexts. Rather, the "experience" of any value, including the exchange value of commodities, necessarily involves the alteration of that value—as well as an alteration of the identities of self and other as interpellated from that meaningful material form.

Chapter Four

Citational Practices and the Performativity of Exchange Value

This chapter begins with a discussion of the *politics of reported speech*, and argues that an important dimension of power has to do with the ability to report on the words and images of others in particular ways. This insight is extended to describe how the *economics of reported speech* involves the marketing of the words and images of others in profitable ways. Language is commodified as economic institutions provide citational resources with which consumers construct their social identities. Inasmuch as the commodities which represent subcultural values also have an exchange value in the marketplace, the cultural economy is itself re-cited as consumers align their individual identities with subcultural identities and values. Citational resources are valued for both aligning, and distancing, one's identity with normative value discourses.

As the words and images of others are marketed, they travel across contexts into the referential contexts of consumers. These cultural commodities are normatively perceived as valorizing the referential context of self. The chapter considers how capitalist and Cartesian subjectivities are both re-cited in this process, as the subject experiences the "presence" of subcultural values as represented by the cultural commodity. The temporality of "presence" is re-cited as past events are cited, as live events are valorized, and as future value is promised.

THE CITATION OF CULTURAL COMMODITIES

The Politics of Reported Speech: Controlling Alterity

As the Bakhtin Circle argued, the utterances of the self necessarily mix one's own values with those of the other, enacting relationships between self and others (Vološinov 1986). The syntactical form in which the words of the other are cited amounts to a *political* re-framing of the "values of the other," with implications for these social relationships. The materiality of utterances is always already political, evoking and negotiating particular interpretive (valuing) contexts. In this sense, relationships of inequality between interactants can be materially re-enacted through citational practices, as the words, objects, and images of others are cited in particular ways. In this section, we consider the politics of how the words of the other are cited, or reported upon, within the utterance.

As subjects are socialized, they find a social hierarchy of approved and subordinated valuations already existing within the culture. The value claims of language become normalized into systems of cultural and subcultural discourse—genres which vary from informal subcultural vocabularies, to the more formal citational practices of law or science (Gardiner 1992, 81; Bakhtin 1986). As the Bakhtin Circle argues, culture is a site of these competing value systems or speech genres (Gardiner 1992, 73–74).

To say that these different, competing value genres are organized into a hierarchy suggests that, to use Derridean language, some discourses or meanings are dominant in any historical period, while others are devalued and considered as "supplemental" (Derrida 1981; 1997). Just as Bakhtin, Derrida, and Mead all argued that the self needs the other for its own constitution, it can similarly be argued that dominant speech genres need the subordinate speech genres for their very existence—what Derrida has called the "logic of the supplement" (1997, 215). However, dominant discourses tend to obscure their reliance on competing discourses; Bakhtin uses the term "monologism" to refer to a discourse which presents itself as the sole voice of "reality" or "truth" (Gardiner 1992, 26).

We can thus envision the relation between value discourses within a culture, as well as within a situated utterance, as a political question of "ratio" or "proportion" (Holquist 2004, 29). This ratio concerns the extent to which the syntactical configuration of an utterance or cultural text allows competing voices to be heard, and whether supplemental value discourses are acknowledged and respected as a legitimate part of the dominant discourse. The way that the citational practices of subjects in positions of power incorporate the "words of the other," then, becomes an important political question.

In *Marxism and the Philosophy of Language* (1986), Vološinov goes into great detail considering how different cultures employ different syntactical techniques regarding reported speech, which directly relates to the consideration which self gives to the autonomy of the language of the other. For example, some languages tend to require that direct quotations be used to keep the "integrity and authenticity" (119) of reported speech. This "direct discourse" creates clear boundaries between the speech of self and that of the other, minimizing the extent to which the speech of the other undergoes "penetration by the author's intentions" (119).

Direct discourse is subdivided by Vološinov into a "linear" or "pictorial style." In the first case of direct, linear quoting, the words of the other are given such deference that the self is allowed virtually no "individualization" in reporting. However, in the pictorial style, the authorial self adds "its own intonation—humor, irony, love or hate, enthusiasm or scorn" (121) to the speech of the other that it reports. "Indirect discourse," and the various mixes of direct and indirect discourse described by Vološinov, also involve both linear and pictorial styles when *paraphrasing* the words of another. Although the more linear styles of indirect discourse maintain a clear boundary between the words and perspective of self from those of others (130), the pictorial styles involve a greater dissolution of the "reporting" or "authorial" context—thus blurring the lines as to which are the words and values of the other in the subject's utterance, and which are the words and values of the reporting subject. Generally, Vološinov argues, modern cultures tend toward the pictorial discourse styles, supporting their "relativistic individualism" (123)—although he notes that different styles are required in differing institutional contexts. In short, the syntactical forms of citationality are important *political choices* in shaping the values of the self relative to the values of the other, as materialized in utterances.

Thus, a major variable distinguishing the many different styles of reported speech outlined by Vološinov concerns the extent to which the values of either the speaker, or of the other, are "allowed" to enter into the reporting process. Vološinov also points out that the use of quotation marks around a particular phrase used by the other may express a distancing of the author from the remark, or draw its truthfulness into question (131). In other words, speakers have techniques at their disposal, especially in modern syntax, by which to express the extent of their agreement, or disagreement, with the values of others which they are citing or reporting.

Because we are born into a language which already reflects the values of others, our linguistic utterances are already social. They can be considered as a kind of reported speech, in that the subject uses words received from others which are already sedimented with implied values. For the Bakhtin Circle, the political question of the utterance concerns what *stance* the author takes in relation to these words. This stance involves not only the semantic "content" of the utterance, but also the syntactical style or form by which the subject reports on the values and words of the other (i.e., showing ironic distancing, enthusiastic approval, etc.). In his analysis, Vološinov has revealed the political nature of the relationship between the referential (valuing) system of the self, and that of the other—as enacted within the utterance of the reporting subject. The utterance thus involves a tension between the values of the self and the values of others (both co-present and generalized).

The politics of syntactical form, when reporting upon the words of others, has also been demonstrated by the work of Michel de Certeau (1988) and Miyako Inoue (2006). These works illustrate how a subject can assert dominance over the other through the way in which the words of the other are reported. As they point out, the act of "not allowing others to speak for themselves" is an act of domination. De Certeau and Inoue both argue that forms of citationality can reproduce inequalities between individuals and groups. They show that various citational forms, such as historical accounts or newscasts, "report" the speech and values of alterity in ways favoring the powerful. Clearly, this discussion of the syntactical forms of *individual* utterances can be extended to the "utterances" and citational practices of larger social *institutions* (see Crawford and Ostrom 1995).

In his work, de Certeau (1988) identifies speech as the traditional "folk" voice—a voice which was increasingly excluded from being heard as printing technologies were developed in the West (132). As opposed to preindustrial cultures based in oral traditions, the very ideas of modernity and progress align with writing, in what he calls a "scriptural economy" (134). For de Certeau, in Western history writing was a practice linked to power (134).

In his analysis, de Certeau emphasizes that the historical implementation of this scriptural economy reproduces a Cartesian model regarding the "presence" of the autonomous Western subject. This Cartesian subject, as de Certeau puts it, confronts other entities as if a blank page on which to inscribe their thoughts and will—thus "producing a text and producing society as a text" (134). This Cartesian model, de Certeau argues, emerges with the secularization of modernity, in that a religious "presence" no longer functions in the subject position—speaking the divine word to passive believers (137). With this loss, the modern "subject" moves into the active role abandoned by the "First Speaker" (138). The power derived from this authorial positioning in modernity, de Certeau argues, is scriptural, and results in the subordination of those who lack the ability to establish their "presence" through writing (139).

The subordinated *voice* of preindustrial culture is simultaneously turned into the "other," or the alterity of modernity. Within the text of the modern scriptural economy, de Certeau points out, the "voice of the people" persists only as a voice from the past (132). However, the "return of the voice" of the excluded other takes a particular form—as *reported* speech. In other words, the excluded other is not allowed to speak for themselves; rather, the return of their voice is *managed and controlled* through the reporting techniques of the powerful. Like the scapegoated in the Greek polis (see Derrida 1981, 130), the "other" is strategically maintained within the community, but allowed only the *semblance* of participation. As Inoue (2006) puts it in her discussion of de Certeau, the "quotation" of the voice of the excluded other functions "as a textual strategy of containment and as the only means by which alterity—otherwise suppressed and excluded—can return to the text" (51).

The scriptural economy, which uses writing as a mechanism of extending its own domination, thus establishes the "voice of the people" as an exotic, outside force. It then attempts to reincorporate that excluded (and potentially dangerous element) in a controlled fashion. Yet from a Derridian perspective, instability exists within such a scriptural economy—even as it appears to expand its own powerful "presence." As Derrida has shown, the very citability on which the scriptural economy depends—writing which crosses contexts—inserts an element of unpredictability into the system. Thus, it is important to distinguish, as Derrida does, between "writing" as a mechanism of domination in a particular historical period, and "writing" (or the "mark") as a repeatable form which necessarily opens a possibility for the unsettling of stable identity (Derrida 1988). What Derrida means by "writing," then, in no way corresponds to what de Certeau refers to as the "scriptural economy"; rather, it is the basis of its critique. Indeed, de Certeau himself states that he is in agreement with Derrida's critique of presence (1988, 133).

In her work, Miyako Inoue (2006) extends this argument concerning the politics of citationality, as she discusses how the mass media in Japan have historically reported the speech of Japanese women. Drawing from the work of de Certeau, Vološinov, and Michel Foucault, Inoue shows that in the construction of modernity in Japan, many Japanese women were not allowed to speak for themselves; rather, mass media "reporting institutions" constructed a prototypical voice of the "modern" Japanese woman. Women were then pressured socially to incorporate the media's favored citational practices into their own utterances. Here we see that certain reporting practices of the media had implications for the citational practices of individual subjects.

Specifically, Inoue shows that the traditionally degraded "schoolgirl" speech, routinely cited by males as irrational and frivolous prior to industrialization, re-emerged in Japanese modernity as the gendered *voice of the consumer*, cited in popular magazines and on television (6–9). Women, especially in rural Japan, who had never even heard this type of speech were forced to confront it as the "voice" of the urban, sophisticated woman—a process Inoue refers to as the "*vicarious experience of women's language*" (21; italics in the original). The "modern" female in Japan, as consumer, was thus politically constructed using a particular *form* of reported speech. Thus, a syntactical, material form, and a "modern" type of citational agency, emerged together in Japan.

In Inoue's analysis, we can clearly see the politics of citationality and reported speech. The institutionalized utterances of the dominant group managed, and controlled, the excluded other with *metalanguage*—that is, speech about speech. As Inoue shows, reported speech is a "powerful linguistic apparatus to conquer alterity and thus to consolidate the modern self" (50). Her research gives an example of how producers of television shows, or editors of a newspaper, are able to speak as "voices of authority," re-incorporating—and thus re-framing—the speech of excluded others according to the dictates of the dominant group. Inoue argues that this maneuver disallows the excluded other from *contextualizing their own utterances*; as she puts it, "alterity, once cited, is deprived of its semiotic capacity to provide itself with *metalanguage* (an authoritative representation of what the cited voice means)" (53; italics in the original).

While no subject can control how their words will be recontextualized in the future, we can see that those excluded from access to media distributional networks will simultaneously be denied access to their own commodified words in future contexts—at least in terms of large-scale public discourse. If dominant others control their speech and meanings by "reporting it" in particular ways, then subjects whose words enter the media have no access to redirect its meaning in the public sphere. In other words, once language has been materially shaped into "institutional" forms, the ability to provide metalinguistic commentary on one's own utterances—to provide context for its future interpretation—is restricted.

Techniques of reporting the speech of others can also be used by institutional authorities to politically construct and manage stigmatized social identity. The entextualized utterances of a subject can be reported upon as "evidence" of their dysfunction or deviant character—thereby interpellating a deviant social identity from particular decontextualized utterances. For example, Hugh Mehan (1996) has shown that the social construction of a "learning disabled child"—an extextualization which interpellates a particular social identity—results from a process where the metalinguistic framings of a psychologist are given a higher legitimacy than those of the teacher, parent, or child themselves. Citing several studies, Mehan speaks of the "'politics of representation'" (253), which involves the political ability to frame the utterances of the child in reference to particular cultural discourses—in this case, the genre of "learning disability." In this way, any *ambiguous* utterances of a student, which might conceivably interpellate differing and competing interpretive contexts, are politically considered to "represent" only the context favored by the psychological authority. The identity of the child, once it is abstracted from the situated citational practices which construct it, is then normatively considered as a "context-free" identity which crosses situations (272). In this sense, power involves *normative control over citational practices*, through the use of dominant syntactical forms.

Of course, the social construction of the identity of a student as "learning disabled" is not normatively seen as a strategy or outcome of interactional politics, but rather as an objective assessment of the condition of the child. Importantly, the appearance of objectivity is itself constructed through citational practices, such as citing research, or citing particular social authorities. Along these lines, Wortham and Locher (1999) have shown that political reporters use particular syntactical forms, or "embedded metapragmatic constructions" (109), to maintain the appearance of objectivity while in fact disguising the political functioning of their utterances.

We can see in both the Inoue and Mehan studies that institutionalized practices of "reporting speech" have political implications for the social identities, and thus the social opportunities, of those subjects whose words are grafted into the utterances of the powerful. These processes involve taking the "words of the other," and framing them as representative of particular value or identity discourses. Applying the symbolic interactionist concept of "vocabularies of motive" (Mills 2003), Emerson and Messinger (1977) have shown that when everyday "troubles" are brought to "third-parties," like ministers or psychiatrists, the vocabulary of these authorities come to frame the trouble in alignment with normative religious or psychiatric discourses. Thus, we see again that in the metalinguistic or reporting practices of social authorities, the social actor becomes a "case" in the citational practices of those who are authorized to apply particular value discourses (see Foucault 1994).

An important part of the "politics of citationality" thus concerns who is allowed to cite whose words in particular social locations, and who has access to the institutionalized mechanisms of citation within a political economy. To be socialized into positions of authority is precisely to learn to engage in institutionalized citational practices, which configure words into those syntactical formulations which mobilize preferred institutional discourses. To be socialized into the culture, more generally, is to learn to anticipate the consequences of engaging in deviant citational practices, as well as the consequences of becoming "subject" to the reporting practices of powerful observers.

The Economics of Reported Speech: The Valorization of Context

In the last section we saw that an important dimension of power concerns the ability to cite or report upon the words of alterity in particular ways. We now turn our attention from the political to the economic institution. In this section, a parallel argument is made regarding the generation of exchange value.

Producers shape their cultural commodities—as institutional utterances—into material, marketable forms. This process detaches the words and images of others from one referential context, and markets them to consumers in order to valorize a different referential context. The words and images of the self and others become mere commodities in the marketplace.

Following Karen Barad's (2007) work, which elaborates on the quantum physics of Neils Bohr, we might say that within the cultural economy, the market becomes a kind of "measuring apparatus," which coordinates the exchange value of linguistic-based commodities. In quantum physics, as Barad discusses, the particular measuring apparatus used in a scientific experiment performs a particular "cut" in materiality during the measurement process—such that the material world obtains ontological determinacy as a *result* of this cut (127–28). This insight can be extended to describe the way that the measure of the exchange value of citational resources, within a market, generates the apparent "presence" of both subcultural values and exchange value.

Because the materiality of language will be assessed as to its market worth in the cultural economy, it is shaped by economic institutions into particular syntactical forms. Those material forms which are anticipated to sell will be those which ultimately are produced and distributed. In this sense, they are *readied for a favorable measurement* by the market research which guides the formulation of their syntactical, material forms. In other words, those particular syntactical forms are produced which will most readily mobilize favorable measurements (i.e., those which are likely to become popular commodities). While the exchange value of the cultural commodity is normatively seen, from a representationalist perspective, to "objectively" measure the pre-existing worth of the commodity, in fact—as quantum physics suggests—it is *emergent from the measuring process itself.*

One of the reasons that this "performativity" of exchange value is obscured is because of the nature of the "capitalist cut." This cut shapes material reality into those syntactical forms which simultaneously *reinforce Cartesian and representationalist notions* regarding subjects and objects (see 137–40). The performative nature of the economy is obscured when individual, Cartesian subjects are perceived to be "experiencing" the pre-existing value of autonomous objects—which in turn are taken to "represent" the values of various subcultures. Within the "phenomenon" created by the productive cut itself (140), exchange value is ideologically taken to be an "objective" measure of the extent to which other subcultural values—such as religiosity or ethnicity—are "present" in the measured material form. The exchange value apparatus is taken to measure the quality, or effectiveness, of cultural commodities in their function of representing these other, "non-economic" subcultural values—thus assigning one religious or political commodity a higher exchange value than another. The more expensive artifacts are often considered to be more "authentic" representations of particular subcultural values.

As capitalism emerged in the West, *separate* valuing domains, such as ethnic or religious values, proliferated in emerging urban areas as a result of the greater diversity of citational practices among urban residents. Joseph (2002) has argued that such differing valuing "communities" are in fact *complicit* with the development of capitalism, and necessary as identifiable consuming groups. These historical developments in the differentiation of valuing "markets" were a response to the emergence of industrial capitalism. In Barad's (2007) sense, the proliferation of "agentially separate" valuing contexts were historically enabled by the "agential cut" (see 174–75; 140) of the value measuring apparatus. Once multiple valuing contexts have been established between separate, identifiable subcultural groups and individuals, the differing values of others can "enter into negotiations" with the values of self—in the syntactical form of citational utterances. Within the Cartesian assumptions sustained by the material framing of the commodity system, the value preferences of others are materially played off against the values of self.

As the words, objects, and images of others are consumed, the "agential cut" (174–75) of the exchange value apparatus is itself re-cited, and thus is *materially extended.* Having historically evolved as hegemonic over other values, the exchange value measuring system now acts as an "enabling constraint" (Butler 1997, 16) relative to citational practices in everyday life. In this process, commodified "words of others" have been reduced to consumptive experiences for Cartesian subjects—as the most marketable cultural commodities are moved into the referential contexts of consumers.

The distribution of these types of linguistic-based commodities becomes increasingly institutionalized, responding to consumer demand for certain kinds of consumptive experiences—in order to sustain certain kinds of social identities. Consumer identity construction is affected by the ways in which cultural commodities are materially shaped by the "reporting practices" of larger economic institutions. Just as particular syntactical forms of reported speech are important *political* maneuvers in the maintenance of power—as we have seen in the work of de Certeau and Inoue—marketable forms of reported speech are increasingly the basis of the U.S. cultural *economy.* In a sense, the entire cultural economy is based on the re-citation of those material forms which signify the "presence of value"—a kind of "re-citational" economy.

The very concept of exchange value, or marketability, suggests travel between contexts—that is, to be "exchanged" *is* to change contexts. The "abstracting" language of commodity exchange becomes a discourse which *facilitates the travel* of commodities between individuals, or between communities—who are assumed to have different values. In a Saussurean sense, exchange value reigns over a system of differentiated subcultural values, as these subcultural differences are commodified, marketed, and moved with unprecedented technological capability. Thus, the marketing of cultural commodities today necessarily involves the transport of words, objects, and images into new situational contexts, as citational resources for valuing subjects. To anticipate value, or to recognize "market-ability," is to understand what a particular commodity would be worth in a different citational context, to a differently valuing subject.

As discussed earlier, Bauman and Briggs (1990) have used the term "entextualization" to refer to the ways in which language is selected and arranged in preparation for movement into another context; in today's cultural economy, the materiality of language is well-prepared for marketability. To "market" something is to entextualize it for travel in such a form which makes it valuable in a new context. While in this book we will mainly discuss the grafting of *commodities* into new contexts, other research has shown that the grafting of referential contexts also occurs in *advertising* (see Williamson 2005; Goldman 1992; Goldman and Papson 1996).

From a marketing perspective, the experiential "worth" of a commodity has to do with its *re-positioning* by a consumer, relative to the ongoing construction of their social identity. This re-positioning occurs either through the movement of commodities, as in bringing televised images into the consumer's home, or through the movement of the consumer relative to the commodity, as in attending events like music concerts. The value of the material commodity-sign is generated from its function in both *combining and re-differentiating contexts*—as the referential contexts of the Cartesian subject are played against the value contexts signified by the words and images of others. This graft of contexts simultaneously grafts with the hegemonic discourse of exchange value, as material forms are measured as to their functional worth in delivering the subcultural values of others to the subject.

Within the material conditions which frame the contemporary cultural economy, then, the exchange value of a commodity is perceived to be in its *movement* across situational contexts; that is, in the material re-grafting of contexts. Using a travel paradigm, objects gain or lose value as they circulate and are grafted into new social situations (see Appadurai 1986b). The perceived worth of a commodity has to do with the (re-)positioning of the material sign relative to the purchasing and experiencing subject. Such a Cartesian-based, experiencing subject is continually re-interpellated from the syntactical arrangement of the commodity form.

In the marketing of cultural meanings, popular brands or images generate profit through their movement into new situational contexts, where their alleged "presence" is said to add value. For example, much television programming in the United States has become a montage of celebrities "presenting themselves" on each other's shows. We also see product placement within shows, as well as one brand "sponsoring" the experience of another brand. All of these occurrences are examples of the commodified grafting of one context onto another.

A citational cross-referencing of the "value" of several commodities thus occurs, as when a soft drink company sponsors a movie, or vice versa. Television shows grafted into the home context, or music grafted into the car-driving context, are said to "add value" to the experiences of the subject. In this sense, drawing upon a term from Julia Kristeva, we can speak of the "intertextuality" (Allen 2006, 3) of the material forms generating exchange value. Cultural entrepreneurs are precisely in business to acquire an entextualized cultural form from one context, then transport it for grafting into another. Commodification is thus intimately involved with recontextualization, or the grafting of contexts in marketable material forms.

Like a quotation, the cultural commodity participates in at least two contexts simultaneously; while it moves into any new context, it continues to reference its "former" contexts. For example, a baseball program from a noteworthy game may become a showpiece for the home context, as it brings its ties to baseball history into the home. The contexts of home, baseball, and market worth are thus grafted into the one material sign, with interpellative implications for the social identity of the experiencing subject. In a sense, the object itself becomes a "marker" for another context (see Culler 1981, 132), "representing" the valuing context where it has been, and the travel experiences it has had. In her work, Annette Weiner argued that objects are valuable *because* of their histories (Graeber 2001, 34). Like a ticket stub or program from an event, the object testifies to the occasions at which it was "present."

Cultural commodities, just as in the case of quotations generally, exist simultaneously in at least two contexts, with their materiality functioning to graft them. This materiality which grafts contexts is continually assessed in terms of its exchange value in providing experiences for the subject, and also as a resource in identity construction. Its exchange value has to do with the way it "represents" one context while it valorizes another—in other words, in the unique way one valuing context is played off against another.

Of course, the production of the materiality of commodified language is largely based on considerations of exchange value in the first place. What gets produced in the cultural economy is what sells—re-enacting normative patterns of citational practice and identity construction. Thus, the array of citational resources normatively available within the culture is always already affected by exchange value. The construction of social identity, and the utterances of subjects, become limited by available citational resources. In other words, given that social situations and interactions are shaped by the materiality of the social world, the commodification of language limits the types of social identities which can be interpellated in those situations. In Mead's (1969) sense, the self is not only constructed through the exchange of language in social situations, but through *commodified* language with an exchange value.

As anthropologists like David Graeber (2001) have pointed out in regard to exchanges generally, and the Bakhtin Circle in regard to linguistic exchanges (see Vološinov 1986), exchange is not just about things, but about *relationships* between self and others. The normative grafting of exchange value with other valuing contexts affects social relationships. We find that the commodified words of particular others—such as those of a celebrity on a talk show, an actor in a movie, or a political commentator on a news show—are normatively considered by subjects to be "worth more" than the devalued, mundane conversations of everyday life. *All* language today—whether received face-to-face in everyday life, or as mediated through electronic technologies—becomes potentially measurable against a standard of exchange value. Other persons are interpellated as "exciting" or "interesting" inasmuch as their words are marketable. In short, the commodifiable words of others, in the material form of citational grafts, are reduced to experiences for modern and postmodern subjects.

For example, in Inoue's (2006) study, we have seen that the once-ridiculed schoolgirl voice later became a linguistic commodity. Consumers were positioned in order to cite these "words of the other" in the process of constructing their own identities. This citational practice was a mechanism which both interpellated the subject as "modern," and interpellated particular others—from magazines or television—as the celebrated providers of consumable and valuable experiences. In this process, these mediated "others" were reduced to the source of consumable material signs for the subject's experience.

When interpretive contexts are grafted together, as interpellated from citational practices, they enter into a relationship with each other—differentiated, yet combined. For example, listening to music while driving a car brings together the meaningful materiality of the driving situation with the meaningful materiality of the music. The "experience" of the positioned subject is said to be enhanced through the consumption of the music-commodity, as the "values" represented by the music enter into the referential context of the driving subject. If the drive to work is normatively perceived to be a mundane and routinized "context," the addition of the materialized music both valorizes it—and yet plays against it. The "work context" and the "leisure context" thus are simultaneously combined, and re-differentiated, as the materiality of the car, the music, and the subject are brought together in a situational configuration.

For Mead and Bakhtin, the human creation of meaning always involves bringing at least two referential contexts together (Joas 1997, 173; 182; Holquist 2004, 20–21). This implies that "value"—as meaningful—also requires at least two differentiated contexts, as interpellated from material forms. Thus, to cite the material "representative" of one context, in order to supplement another context, is an important basis for the construction of value. Of course, any two contexts could not exist separately in the first place unless *previously differentiated* through an initial process of exclusion. In a Derridean sense, the citational grafting of contexts involves a process whereby the alterity initially excluded from one of the referential contexts is re-presented into it.

One referential context is thus perceived to be enhanced or valorized by grafting "back in" that materiality which was left out of its initial construction—that is, its "alterity." In both a Derridean and a Freudian sense, this amounts to a kind of "return of the repressed," where the alterity which was abjected in the constructed identity of a particular valuing context "returns" to the subject. In the Derridean sense that the meaning of any identity is never quite "present," we might say that "value," as meaningful, is never quite present within any differentially constructed referential context. Indeed, it is precisely because value is never quite present in a particular context that the context can be valorized by the return of something which is lacking in it. This supposed "return" of alterity becomes a material, performative display of both the re-unification of, and the re-separation of, valuing contexts (i.e., a citational graft).

Valorization within the contemporary cultural economy thus has to do with the experience of a *different* valuing context, as it "adds value" to a supposedly initial or "original" context. The material form of the alterity, which is grafted into the existing material environment of the self, acquires an exchange value in its ability to deliver this "experience" of the other. In the example given above, it is precisely because the driving experience is not itself historically defined by music, that music is able to enhance the driving experience for subjects—thus developing a consumer demand for music in cars. In the formation of any referential identity, the alterity which is excluded from its construction simultaneously becomes a citational resource which has the potential to valorize it.

In this sense, it is the utterances of alterity, as citational resources for the subject, which enable the exchange value of cultural commodities. Differentiated valuing contexts come to be "represented" by differentiated social objects. Those objects excluded in the construction of any particular valuing context potentially return to valorize it when purchased as citational resources. It is the citational grafting behaviors of consumers in everyday life—both re-unifying, and re-differentiating, objects and contexts—which in fact re-enact or re-cite the cultural economy itself. In a Derridean sense, it is the process of "supplementarity"—where the "identity" of any value is achieved through the subordination of another (see Norris 1987, 34; Gasché

1986, 210)—which enables the valorization of the referential context of self by the words and images of the other. In short, the cultural economy is re-enacted as meaningful material commodities representing one valuing context are moved into another.

Fetishism and the Presence of Exchange Value

The citational practices used in contemporary U.S. culture interpellate a Cartesian subject, who prioritizes objects in the social environment to "experience." These objects are understood, within such a framework, to embody the "presence of value." In poststructuralist terms, the *Cartesian* subject (as an autonomous, experiencing individual), and the *capitalist* subject (as an individual with needs and desires satisfiable through commodities) converge—and are re-interpellated together via citational practices.

Cultural commodities, cited by consuming subjects, are taken as *representations of thepresence of subcultural values*—thus continuing the metaphysics and ideology of "presence." From a poststructuralist perspective, then, the critique of the "presence of value" in the commodity cannot be achieved through a Marxist labor theory of ("embodied") value. Rather, such a critique must show that the Cartesian type of "experiencing subject," who confronts the value of commodities, is *itself* continually re-interpellated from citational practices. The "materialistic" side of such a poststructuralist critique is to show how the syntactical forms of the material environment itself—from which interpellations of subcultural values, exchange value, and consumer identities are made—are shaped by institutional utterances driven by political economy and profit considerations.

It should be noted that Marx himself described such an "experiencing" subject when describing the phenomenon of "commodity fetishism"—in which a subject falsely perceives value in the object itself, rather than in terms of the labor time invested in its production (Marx 1967). Amariglio and Callari (1993) suggest that Marx came up with his theory of "commodity fetishism" to answer the question of unequal trade. If the value of goods rely upon the labor time which contributed to their production, then it must be explained why "rational" subjects would trade goods representing unequal amounts of labor time (204; 207). Amariglio and Callari argue that the phenomenon of "commodity fetishism" answered the question for Marx, in that the exchange partners "falsely" perceived value based on the properties of objects—rather than in terms of labor time (207).

Marx had derived the concept of "labor time" itself when considering how it was possible that things with "radical contextuality," (i.e., "use values"), could be exchanged between subjects (Keenan 1993, 162). For Marx (1967), the answer was that the system of exchange value "abstracted" from use value. This abstraction then becomes a "shared quality" by which unlike objects (e.g., coats and linens) could be exchanged (171)—inasmuch as the exchange value represents abstract human labor. But, as Keenan notes, given Marx's contention that abstract human labor "is *first possible only in a society where the commodity form is the general form* of the labor-product" (Marx, in Keenan 1993, 171, Keenan's emphasis), Marx's argument becomes teleological (171). The commodity form enables the notion of abstract human labor, which in turn is the mechanism which facilitates the exchange of the commodity form.

According to Amariglio and Callari (1993), Marx also appealed to the concept of commodity fetishism in a different way—not to explain unequal exchange as the misrecognition of labor time, but rather as the result of "valuing differences" between autonomous individuals. For trade to occur, in this version of commodity fetishism, two parties must *perceive* the exchange as fair—that is, "as an exchange of equivalents" (204). In actuality, however, there is no "guarantee that these acts of trade involve equal magnitudes of labor time" (204)—in fact, Amariglio and Callari state that for Engels, "the exchange of unequal quantities of actual labor time is *necessary*" in capitalism (206n31, italics in the original). Amariglio and Callari argue that this version of commodity fetishism "summarizes the qualities of *individuals* that transform the unequal exchange of actual labor time into an exchange of equivalents" (204, italics added). In other words, for exchange to work—in both Marx's theory, as well as in the larger commodity-based economy—what is needed is the *notion of subjects who value differently*.

Amariglio and Callari thus find within Marx's writings the argument that certain "types of subjects" are required for exchange in capitalism to occur. These subjects must "conceptualize use values as *objects*, separate and distinct from themselves, which potentially have the ability to satisfy perceived needs" (208, italics in the original). In other words, a "Cartesian" subject is required. As Heidegger has argued, the Cartesian subject of Western philosophy and culture precisely constitutes a type of subject who is separate from the objects they "experience" and objectify (Weber 1996; see also Amariglio and Callari 1993, 209).

Amariglio and Callari thus read in Marx the importance of this objectification process in establishing the type of subjectivity necessary for the exchange process to occur (202; 209). Agents in exchange see themselves as individuals who have unique needs; thus it becomes "natural" that they would *value objects differently*. All that is then required is the market system by which to "measure" these differential cultural values and enact the trade. For Amariglio and Callari, this type of (Cartesian) individualism is a *prerequisite* for the capitalist exchange of unequal labor times (208; 216).

To summarize, as an alternative to the illusions of commodity fetishism (i.e., that value is inherently "present" within objects themselves), Marx chose to appeal to "the concept of socially necessary labor time" (216) in explaining the possibility of exchange between "rational subjects." He also chose to appeal to the labor theory of value in explaining the "real source" of value and surplus value. Keenan, as discussed above, has shown some of the difficulties with this approach to explaining exchange (1993, 171). However, in their argument, Amariglio and Callari reveal that within the discourse of Marx another type of explanation emerges for the "perceived-as-equal" exchange of unequal labor times. This alternative explanation involves not the misrecognition of the real source of value, but rather the historical emergence in the West of the type of subject who constructs a particular self through objectification processes. We can recognize this move as a metaphysical positing of a "valuing consciousness" *as prior to valuing practices*. Whether Marx is "embracing" or "critically analyzing" this move might be disputed; the important point here concerns the *compatibility of capitalism with a particular version of subjectivity*—that of the individual, Cartesian subject who can experience the "value" of objects and the "values" which they are taken to represent.

Within such a discourse, it seems natural that objects are valued differently in different cultural or subcultural contexts (see Appadurai, 1986b). In other words, the worth of a social object may be interpreted differently given the differing subcultural values of various groups of collective subjects. Thus, from the perspective of one "valuing community," objects may appear to be over- or under-valued in another. As William Pietz (1993) has noted, the term "fetishism" was used by Protestant traders to refer to the trading practices of Africans. The Europeans believed that endowing material objects with supernatural qualities was an "irrational" trading practice (see also Foster 1993, 253). The exchange value of objects had to be negotiated between subjects with differing cultural values; the term "fetishism"—in its more anthropological sense—emerged to identify a "primitive" as opposed to an "enlightened" method of valuation.

Trade between so-called "primitive peoples" and Europeans illustrates the importance of the Enlightenment in the valuation process of capitalism. As Foster (1993) discusses, from the perspective of European traders, "primitive" peoples would not "assess value rationally" (255). Such a rejection of this "irrational" fusing of the sacred into material objects was an important component of the trading practices of Westerners, and of their "enlightened" self-identity. As the Europeans acquired the objects, they were taken out of their "religious context," and were re-evaluated as they crossed into an "enlightened" discourse—a process of recontextualization. The religious discourse of value came to occupy an abjected position within the enlightened discourse—as its alterity. The values of "primitive peoples" were interpreted as irrational, as were the social identities of the people themselves. As several commentators have pointed out, Western self-identity as "civilized" is constructed relative to its supposedly "primitive" or "savage" other (Taussig 1993; Horkheimer and Adorno 1972, 5; Pietz 1993, 139, 143).

For Pietz, then, the term "fetishism" refers to "a cross-culture situation formed by the ongoing encounter of the value codes of radically different social orders" (1985, 11). If it is necessary in capitalism that "unequal labor times" are to be perceived as "fairly" exchanged, it also seems "necessary" for the historical emergence of a term—like "fetishism"—to explain how and why objects are valued differently across individual and collective subjects. In the historical emergence of such "valuing identities," we find the hierarchical construction of different kinds of valuing subjects—those Europeans who use "rational" valuations, and those peoples who use "irrational" valuations based in religion. Such cross-cultural explanations of exchange assume the "presence" of differing communal values.

Along with the Western philosophical subject and the modern capitalist economy, then, emerges the idea that it is natural for autonomous individual and collective subjects to differ in their (pre-existing) values. It becomes necessary to assert the existence of multiple, separable, valuing domains. It can then be explained how over its "travel career," an object might gain or lose value depending upon which subjects are involved in the "valuing situation." As in the Pietz example, there come to be assumptions regarding the differing pre-existing values in the exchanges between differing "valuing communities." In this way, Georg Simmel's explanation of value makes sense; as Turner, Beeghley, and Powers describe it, "exchanges will occur only if both parties perceive that the object given is less valuable than the one received" (2007, 246). A particular trade which may not seem rational in a strictly economic sense is still explainable given the differing cultural values of the parties involved. In this sense, it is the differentiation of "pre-existing" values between individuals and groups which "explains" the basis of capitalist exchange. In other words, the functioning of the capitalist economy comfortably coincides with the Cartesian subject—as do metaphysical assumptions regarding the "presence" of exchange value in commodities.

Thus, Derrida's insight as to the privileging of "presence" in Cartesian self-identity and Western metaphysics can also be applied to economic valuation, and the assumed "presence of exchange value" in the capitalist marketplace. Today, the promotion of events such as fashion shows, film openings, and sporting events can be seen as claims of value—where the advertising marks the upcoming event with an anticipated *presence of value*. Commodities thus are present-ed as valuable relative to consumers from particular subcultural groups, who cite such material forms as they align their individual identities with those of the collectivity.

Following Derrida's critique, we could say that the assumption that value is "present" within cultural commodities is the *metaphysically based ideology of capitalism*. It appears that value is present, and available for subjects to purchase and "experience." In this sense, value can be seen as a *claim of presence*; in other words, the process of commodification involves the attributed "presence of exchange value." In Bakhtinian terms, the utterances of subjects, in citing cultural commodities, are "double-voiced" with an exchange value discourse (Bakhtin 1984, 185).

Consumers in the U.S. today make sense of the world through the exchange value schema, often interpreting their experiences based on their perceived exchange value—the "worth" of experiences relative to each other. Entextualized commodities—such as events, social objects, and language itself—are taken to "re-present" particular social values, and in turn are valued in the market for the experiences they provide when cited by the subject. Thus the "*ideology* of representation" (Norris 1987, 54, italics in the original)—which Derrida finds in the construction of "presence" in Western philosophy—continues in, and is compatible with, the contemporary U.S. cultural economy. This dominant, metaphysical, temporality of presence has become essential to the marketing of "valuable" experiences.

This same application of the "logic of presence," though simply inverted, can also be seen in those processes where value is said to be created through the "absence" of that which reduces it. In this case, the valued commodity is constructed through a process of exclusion; for example, the absence of something (i.e., crime) can make other things (i.e., real estate) more valuable. In the case of tourism, for example, sometimes value is generated by *including* particular visual cites/sites and experiences; sometimes, however, value is generated by *excluding* undesirable sights. In the latter case, the "touring" subject, seeking to incorporate only valued experiences in their excursion, participates in the re-citation of social boundaries, in order to exclude that which would compromise the security of their identity, and contaminate the quality of their experiences.

Continuing with the case of tourism, we can see that those luxury sites, where Western travelers vacation, are often physically secured against the "intrusion" of local peoples—who might disrupt the controlled experience and the supposed purity of the citational resource. Like security guards at a ticketed event, those who patrol the travel border sort out those who belong inside the valuable tourist site, and those to be left out. Often in exotic travel destinations outside of the U.S., the travelers are white, while the locals are not. Thus a racialized border is maintained—and "terror" is defined only from the perspective of white tourists, rather than from the perspective of the local population (see hooks 1992a). The citational resources provided to white tourists by the travel industry, perceived as generating "valuable experiences," thus re-interpellate racialized social identities, as well as the normative social relationships between them.

In the case of virtual travel on the Internet, we can find a similar situation regarding identity protection against the "presence" of threats. Hackers, viruses, and predators have come to terrorize online experiences, and economic value accrues to the more *secured* domains and experiences. Thus, computer security and privacy protection have become important components of the contemporary online economy. In addition, the dissemination of language over the Internet threatens proprietary rights regarding valued linguistic commodities—that "presence" of economic value which copyright laws seek to protect (see Poster 2001). Important questions have thus emerged in the U.S. cultural economy concerning the "travels" of language online, especially regarding threats to the presence of exchange value in the online environment.

The Hegemony of Exchange Value

John Guillory, reviewing the work of Howard Caygill, has argued that the separation of "exchange value" from "aesthetic value" is a historical development, corresponding to the emergence of the market economy. This process also involved the separation of the work of art from the commodity, and the academic discipline of aesthetics from that of political economy (Guillory 1993, 303; 308; Caygill 1989). For Guillory and Caygill, the positing of aesthetic value is a *result* of the historic emergence of an exchange value discourse (Guillory 1993, 303).

In his book *Cultural Capital*, Guillory (1993) summarizes Caygill's historical analysis of the modern correspondence of the "art of judgment" with exchange value discourse. Caygill argued that the emerging civil society in modern Europe—and its new moral philosophy—turned to the work of art as an attempt to regulate the also-emerging consumer society, and its potentially unrestrained desire for commodities (307). The new distinction between "art" and "commodity" suggested differences in moral values between the users of each, along class lines (308). In the language of citationality, we find here an interpellation of both class *identity* and moral *values*, from citational practices involving art or commodities. In other words, the materiality of art interpellated an upper-class identity grafted with the domain of moral values. In contrast, the materiality of the commodity was "consumed" by unrestrained, lower-class subjects.

Caygill shows that Adam Smith, in his earlier moral philosophy, had suggested that the market value of a commodity represented two things at once—the labor time necessary for the production of the commodity, as well as the amount of the "desire provoked in the consumer for the 'use' of that commodity" (Guillory 1993, 313). Here, money expressed both labor and desire, in "commensurate" amount or "proportion" (313). Caygill argues that because of the inadequacy of this formulation in explaining price (314), Adam Smith later moved toward dropping the consumption or "aesthetic" side altogether in his analysis of value, retaining only the "labor theory of value" famously taken up by Marx (315).

However, as Caygill points out, the consequence of such a separation of aesthetics from the analysis of exchange value is that it leaves a problem regarding the "aesthetic judgment" of the merits of a work of art, especially given that works of art continued—in Guillory's words—"to be exchanged in the marketplace as commodities which are commensurable with other commodities" (316). Caygill and Guillory argue that it was in response to this issue that the notion of "aesthetic value" emerged historically. From this point on, "exchange value" explained the exchange of commodities based on labor. In contrast, the concept of "aesthetic value" was used to explain the exchange of art works based on artistic merit. However, as Guillory argues, exchange value remained as the *hegemonic model* for the comparison of works of art against each other; that is, the *most* artistic merit would be measured (and represented) by the highest price. Thus, with the emergence of the market economy, aesthetic judgment was henceforth issued "by *analogy to exchange value*" (317, italics in the original).

For Guillory, this illustrates the historical emergence of the hegemony of the discourse of exchange value over other "value domains" (323). In other words, this "universalization" of exchange value resulted in a kind of totalizing discourse, in reference to which calculative agents enacted transactions. Because diverse commodities are exchanged using money, they are made to be commensurate in a market—thus works of art, religious artifacts, or *any material sign* could be assigned a price and exchanged (323). In this sense, all subcultural value discourses are subordinate to the hegemony of exchange value. The judgment of the "worth" of any material sign is made in reference to its exchange value. Whether judging the merits of a painting, or judging which artifact is more sacred, merit is "represented" by money (see 322–23).

Thus, for Guillory, the "modern *discourse of value*" (323, italics in the original) extends the "measurement" of value to "all acts of judgment" (324). Considering the insights of quantum physics (see Barad 2007), we see that historically in the West the economic "measuring apparatus" shaped the production of social forms in a particular way—such that judgments about merit occurred relative to the constraining "logic" of the exchange value frame. In this way, exchange value became the universal *measure* of the presence of other subcultural values.

For example, inquiring into the origin of the exchange value of diamonds—as did Adam Smith—economists might theorize that a diamond ring commands a higher market price because it is rare in terms of supply and demand, or because it takes a lot of human labor to extract. However, considering Guillory's argument, we might say that it is because a buyer has invested so much in "labor value" in order to earn enough money for the ring that it simultaneously comes to have an increased romantic value to the recipient. When a more expensive ring is given (relative to a worker's wages), the ring itself—while not ceasing to have a certain "exchange value" in the market—also becomes a measure of the level of emotional commitment of the giver toward that relationship.

In the language of citationality, the ring itself simultaneously cites or grafts two value discourses together (i.e., those of exchange value and emotional commitment). This grafting has (interpellative) *identity consequences* for both the giver and recipient. Exchange value has grafted itself onto all other types of value in such a way that subcultural values can hardly be signified without a consideration of the worth of the material signifier in "representing" those values. In this way, exchange value appears to be necessary for the construction of the meaningful "identity" of any other subcultural value domain—as well as the identity of any subcultural actor who cites their material representations.

As W.F. Haug has shown in *Critique of Commodity Aesthetics* (1986), in advanced capitalist culture all types of commodities are sold using advertising techniques which link particular products to an "aesthetic" related to other value domains. Thus, in the contemporary economy we find cars sold with ties to sexuality or jewelry with links to romance. Contemporary subjects come to take it as natural that love be grafted with the exchange value of jewelry. This graft between non-economic valuations—such as love—with exchange value has become so pervasive in contemporary culture that to a certain extent jewelry has changed the performance of "love" itself. For many, the commodity of jewelry *must* be cited if the value of "love" is to be normatively expressed, or properly dramatized. In other words, the performance of subcultural value domains are necessarily *mediated through exchange value* in order to be properly communicated. In this way, subcultural values become marketable. As the Frankfurt School has argued, in late capitalism *all* of culture is potentially subject to commodification (see Jay 1973).

In a performative frame, however, we must switch from the language of the Frankfurt School—which focused on reified *consciousness*—to the language of *practice*. For example, the giving of a diamond ring can be considered as a citational practice, where the materiality of the cultural artifact grafts the contexts of romance and exchange value. The ring, as a citational resource, interpellates particular social identities for both the giver and receiver. In this way, the citational practices of late capitalism interpellate "valued experiences," measurable in exchange value, for subjects involved in even the most intimate of social interactions.

The Exchange Value of Language

Bakhtin and Derrida both retained a tension in their work between the singularity of language in situated context, and the repeatability of language in multiple contexts. It is precisely the repeatable, abstractable "meaning" of language which enables its exchange value to be calculable, as a cultural commodity which can be quoted or cited into new contexts. As we will see in Werner Hamacher's reading of Marx (1967), while the abstracted exchange value transcends the situated material use of the commodity, it is not entirely divorceable from that materiality. In this section, we will consider the exchange value of the language commodity, as a measure of its "worth" when grafted or cited into a new situational context.

In his reading of Derrida's (1994) *Specters of Marx*, Hamacher (1999) notes that what Marx calls "commodity-language" (Marx, cited in Hamacher 1999, 170) is a language of "equivalence"—that is, all commodities can be exchanged for each other. This "exchangeability" means that a standard of exchange-value emerges as a universal measure, abstracted from the unique use-value of each material object. This abstraction, which occurs in the process of the exchange of commodities, means that the object loses its historicality, and instead enters into an abstract relationship with every other commodity—based on this mutual exchangeability (172).

Marx argues that money becomes the "transcendental of commodity-language" (174); in other words, the normative form in which exchange value will be measured. Of course, Marx (1967) argues that what is "really" exchanged is "labor-time," abstracted from the actual historical labor of workers. However, for Marx, this fact—that labor is the source of all value—is *hidden* in the materiality of the object. As Hamacher notes, for Marx, "The object 'cloth' must be the veil over the actual *cloth* which is woven by historical social life" (176, italics in the original). In other words, for Marx the material object readied for exchange hides the *historicality* of the material object produced by workers. The universal "exchangeability"—once abstracted—re-incarnates itself into particular material forms, and in so doing, "efface[s] the singularity of everything it encompasses" (177).

Inasmuch as the commodification process obscures the *historicality* of the material form, its language is that of the "present"—the presence of exchange value (see 177). While this exchange value *appears in the same materiality* as that of everyday language, it denies the historicality of this materiality. In other words, the "exchangeability" of language—as a commodity—abstracts from the materiality of language, even as it inserts itself back into the situated materiality. In so doing, the past and future of the meaningful materiality are denied; the material sign presents itself only as a language claiming the *"presence" of value*. In a Marxist sense, the discourse of the exchange value of language, in its ideological function, seeks to obscure the historical dimension of language, and instead continually re-asserts its "abstract" exchange value.

As Derrida would argue, however—as implied in his criticism of Marx's use/exchange value dichotomy (Derrida 1994; see also Sherlock 1997)—

there can be no strong distinction between "commodified" and "non-commodified" language. For Derrida, the marketability of all language would always already be implicated in its material form. Any socially meaningful utterance is *potentially* "ready" for a market—especially now in the United States where the cultural economy has expanded, and where linguistic commodities can be quickly distributed over the Internet on a wide, and mobile, scale. Using a linguistic suffix favored by Walter Benjamin (Weber 2008), the "-ability" of any strip of language to be served up to a market always already involves the *anticipated valuation*—or abstract marketability—of the money-making potential of that linguistic strip. Perhaps instead of the "commodified" versus "non-commodified" distinction, the notion of a continuum might better characterize how some linguistic forms are more readied or entextualized for the market—while other linguistic forms (such as art) may not be shaped into a marketable format.

In other words, to "commodify" is to abstract, but the abstraction of exchange value is *indicated from materiality*. While any materiality can acquire a market value, the "difference" here concerns the extent to which the material form is readily conducive to a normative abstraction of exchange value, or whether its material form resists that normative interpellation. Normative citational practices involving cultural commodities not only signify particular *subcultural* values, but—using a term from Bakhtin—simultaneously "double-voice" or re-cite *exchange* value. On the other hand, non-normative citational practices—especially those involving less marketable (and more aesthetic) linguistic forms—may resist interpellations of exchange value.

It is the materiality of the cultural form which marks one cultural commodity as having more exchange value than another. In the case of televised auto racing, for example, one race may be *marked* or marketed as more important or valuable than another race. In other words, the citational practices of the subject—in bringing a particular linguistic commodity into the material environment of the home via television—involve not only the interpellation of a self-identity as one who enjoys racing, but also the interpellation of a self enjoying *hierarchically valued* "experiences" (i.e., "watching the Daytona 500" as differentiated from a lesser valued racing experience). In the language of citationality, the market in the cultural economy is a mechanism for the delivery of differentially valued citational resources, and the interpellated subjective experiences and identities normatively associated with them. The commodification of citational practice involves not only the *referential* dimension of language—in delivering a certain experience (i.e., "racing on television") to a subject—but also involves its "value" in *indexing* (see Silverstein 1976), or interpellating, a particular type of social identity (i.e., a "racing fan").

In the case of television, we find a citational technology which presents commodified language prioritized *spatially* to different regional audiences (i.e., sharing geographically patterned citational practices), as well as prioritized *temporally* (i.e., "prime time"). This commodified language is materially positioned in the home of the subject (i.e., the location of the television screen), in a constellation with the other social objects within the home. The commodified words and images on the screen are thus prioritized by the subject within the overall material arrangement of the home environment.

All of the material signs in the home compete for prioritization both spatially and temporally in the citational practices of the subject. The positioning of the constellation of commodities relative to the subject interpellates an experiencing identity, relative to that material form. In the language of the Cartesian assumptions built into contemporary commodity forms, what is marketed is the experience of the temporal and spatial positioning of the subject relative to the "presence" of valued material signs.

Keying the Exchange Value Frame

Just as citational practices can evoke a sense of the political or the religious in everyday interactions, so can they evoke a sense of the economic. We now turn to Erving Goffman's work on the keying of frames. It will be argued in this section that the exchange value frame is keyed through syntactical, material forms. In this way, Goffman's work on frame analysis—as the "organization of experience"—will be extended to a subject's "experience" of the worth of the commodified words and images of others.

In *Frame Analysis: An Essay on the Organization of Experience* (1986), Goffman argues that frames are schemas for interpretation, and a "central element" of culture (27). Events and situations are interpreted within a frame, which allows for the organization of social action into meaningful typologies. In this work, Goffman is particularly interested in the keying of frames, where the normative meaning of activities is "transformed into something patterned on this activity but seen by the participants to be something quite else" (44). Common examples include actors performing on a stage or people "playing" at fighting, where the "reality" of the behavior becomes "something different." In other words, in pretend-fighting, real fighting techniques may be mimicked or cited, yet keying switches the cultural frame from fighting to play (45). For Goffman, all types of "make-believe activities" (such as today's vicarious video game experiences), or types of "dramatic scriptings" (such as today's television shows), are examples of keyed experience (53). Clearly, such keyed experiences, generated by particular citational practices, have become a central aspect of the contemporary cultural economy.

For Goffman, to "key" experience is to transform its interpretation—from "real life" to an alternative frame where reality is "played upon." In a sense, the transformation of language from something merely enabling communication, to a cultural commodity with a market worth, can be seen as a type of "keying" which transforms its interpretive context. In commodification, an everyday human activity—like a dialogue in social interaction—becomes keyed in such a way that a strip (10) of language is considered relative to an economic frame. Language uttered in one context becomes *marketable and valuable for other contexts*. In the contemporary cultural economy, the "experience of meaning" has been normatively keyed as something consumable—and measurable—for Cartesian subjects. In this sense, we might speak of "keying the exchange value frame."

Thus, while actors can give convincing performances in everyday interactions, high-quality performances may be considered to have market value on a television show or website. Both "serious" language use, as well as its keyed parodies, are increasingly marketable as they now travel easily from everyday interactions to the Internet. Today, *any* citational utterance can be assessed as to its marketability.

When the exchange value frame is invoked relative to the subject, *social identity* is keyed in terms of the worth of its accumulated experiences. Exchange value is increasingly becoming the dominant frame for the construction of identity in late capitalism, especially as language is increasingly commodified. When commodified, the materiality of language is shaped in such a way so as to "key" the exchange value frame. Relative to this interpretive context, language becomes a citational resource which is normatively perceived to deliver *worthwhile* experiences to consuming subjects.

Thus, the "difference" between language which is, or is not, "commodified" is that the former has been keyed to the exchange value frame, and thus assessed in terms of its *marketability in another context*. Given the proliferation of distributional technologies in late capitalism, *all* language is subject to such keying and is thus marketable—although it is certainly true that some strips of language have been more heavily prepared or entextualized for marketability than other strips (i.e., "entertainment" versus "academic" commodities). The exchange value frame is re-mobilized whenever marketability is considered.

Syntactical forms which report the speech of others key various frames, through which the relationship between social identity categories is re-enacted and re-interpreted. Those syntactical forms which have become institutionalized in late capitalism are generally those which bring the most profit. Linguistic techniques used in reporting the words of others abide by "framing rules" (see Berger 1986, xvi) which key different *valuing* frames. In the U.S. cultural economy, the normative framing rule has become that virtually any social meaning is eligible for commodification, and available as a citational resource for the construction of social identity.

As Bennett Berger points out, framing rules not only limit the choices of social interactants, but also can perpetuate inequality (xvi). In this sense, the systematic keying of the exchange value frame in institutional utterances can limit the citational resources available for identity construction in everyday life, as well as maintain the unequal relationship between normative identities—as in the case of gender. In other words, framing rules can regulate the way that institutions (and their customers) cite the words of others, in order to maximize the exchange value of the keying practice itself.

The invocation of any frame involves "boundary markers," which give cues as to what frame is to be employed in a situation (Goffman 1986, 251). Goffman shows that these boundary markers include both "temporal and spatial brackets" (252). In the case of the keying of exchange value, such markers would include the scheduling of a television show in "prime-time," or starting it on the hour—ways of indicating the boundaries within which the "presence" of value is marked. Thus, although "reality television" supposedly includes slices of real life, it is the entextualization of that slice—its filming, editing, scheduling as a "show" with a title, and so forth—which key the exchange value frame through the use of bracketing techniques.

Interestingly, Goffman notes that when framing *language*, the "bracketing practices" used involve "the *syntactical organization of sentences*, where sequential placement, punctuation marks, and part of speech determine what one or more words are to be bracketed together and what syntactic role is to be performed by the constituent unit thus formed" (255; italics added). Here we can see that the preparation of language for marketing as a commodity, or for keying into an exchange value frame, involves a particular *syntactical arrangement* of the slice of language—as in the case of a news program which incorporates only short "sound bites" within the newscaster's reporting of an event. The syntactical form becomes important to the marketing of the cultural commodity.

Thus, the keying of the exchange value frame can be readied ahead of an utterance, when the most "market-able" syntactical form is considered by producers. This process precisely involves the selection and preparation of language on the basis of its anticipated market value. In other words, the commodity form of language is *syntactically organized to key the exchange value frame*, in its later recontextualization and re-citation by consumers. Linguistic commodities are materially shaped in such a way so as to be re-cited as a valued experience for subjects. Just as television and computer viewers appear to enjoy the "gazing technology" itself—sometimes regardless of content (see Jhally 1987)—so generations of youth appear to enjoy particular syntactical formations, such as the rapid switching of images which today characterize the organization of action films, video game environments, or other fast-paced television programming. We thus find that the syntactical styles by which language is commodified themselves come to have a market value.

One of the consequences of this situation is that consumers learn to recognize those syntactical arrangements or signifying codes by which exchange value is normatively keyed, such as television conventions for shows and commercials. Of course, as Goffman shows, the recognition of basic techniques allows for the further keying of variations, as when unusual commercials or programs appear which seem to violate the expected conventions. In fact, just as avant garde playwrights or other artists "break frame"—Goffman cites Beckett, Brecht, Godard, the Dadaists, and John Cage as some examples—television producers find markets for the *commodified* performance of "frame-breaking," as Goffman discusses in the case of televised wrestling (416). Even those aesthetic constructions which may initially challenge normative frameworks and identities can eventually acquire a market value as commodified experiences.

The Re-Citation of the Exchange Value Frame

In citational practice, the words of others are grafted into the utterances of the subject, as strips of language received from others are recontextualized into new syntactical arrangements. This grafting of the words of self with the words of others simultaneously graft the differing valuing *contexts* which the words interpellate or imply. Multiple valuing contexts, grafted together from particular syntactical arrangements of meaningful materiality, are prioritized into particular value ratios. Social identity is interpellated from these valuing ratios, as "types of people" are aligned in various proportion with differing subcultural groups. These multiple valuing contexts are organized under the umbrella of the interpellated exchange value context. In other words, the interpretive context of exchange value is continually grafted onto citational practices interpellating family, religion, or subcultural memberships.

Just as Derrida's work has taken up the question of the iterability of words—repeatable across contexts in order to be meaningful, yet singular in context—we can consider the iterability of valuing *contexts* across situations. In this sense we can speak of the iterability of the exchange value context or frame, where the *meaning* of exchange value is both socially recognizable across situations, and yet singular within a situation. Particular words, images, or events are given value or worth as representational instances of the exchange value category, and interpreted in reference to that contextual frame.

In this sense, the meaning of the exchange value *context* or generic category is repeated, as citational usages continually re-invoke the exchange value frame for their interpretation. While these citational practices are always situated, the meanings interpellated from them abstract from the local situation. In other words, the value domain of exchange value *abstracts* from situations, in measuring the worth of differing citational practices and their associated experiences—but is only invoked *within* socially situated citational practices. In this way, Derrida's argument regarding the iterability of meaningful marks applies to interpretive frames and evaluative contexts themselves (see Derrida 1988, 65).

In the case of non-aesthetic configurations, material signs simultaneously signify multiple valuing contexts which are ranked in a hierarchy—one social value over another. Inasmuch as valuing contexts compete with each other for "interpretive dominance," the politics (and ethics) of the entextualization and recontextualization of utterances concern these hierarchical arrangements. For example, politicians or religious leaders are not supposed to issue utterances which appear to put their own economic interests ahead of the interests of those persons they serve; rather, the values of the public good or spirituality are supposed to be the dominant contexts interpellated from their utterances. Given that any citational utterance, in its materiality, is simultaneously positioned relative to all other signs, we can see that citational practice involves a continual re-mixing of the competing value contexts available within the culture. Citational resources, normatively considered as "representing" different value contexts, are thus differentially valued for this function—and more or less marketable as political game pieces in such maneuvering.

The movement of particular words of others, into particular utterances of the subject, necessarily play one valuing context off against another. As discussed earlier, Goffman's concept of "role distance" can be used to consider how any particular citational practice interpellates values which can "stand against" other values. Thus, any particular syntactical grafting of the words of self and others in an utterance can be assessed as to its "embracement of," or "distancing from," the multiple value contexts which are interpellated from the graft. The exchange value frame is interpellated not only as particular representations of values are *embraced*, but also as the subject uses citational resources to *distance* themselves from other valuing contexts. Exchange value is hegemonic in the way that all non-aesthetic citational resources can be given a worth, as they function to both affiliate subjects with particular valuing communities, and to simultaneously distance the subject from others.

Even non-normative citational practices, which seek to interpellate values which *oppose* the hegemony of exchange value, thus find themselves marketable in their role-distancing function. As Dick Hebdige (1996) discusses, "punk rock" citational styles, which seek to distance themselves from normative practices, are all too easily assimilated as a kind of fashion (130). As in the de Certeau examples discussed above, we find that the citational practices of "marginal" social groups are politically contained by being "reported upon." The intended invocation of an alternative value context is lost as oppositional utterances are grafted or appropriated into a normative "reporting" syntax. In this way, the fashion world is able to cite these oppositional styles within its own utterances—a commodified form which mutes the political impact of these "words of the other." Thus, those who seek to politically distance themselves from normative values find that their distancing practices, and preferred citational resources, can always be recontextualized and marketed in unwanted ways. The interpretive context they intend to evoke is not necessarily the predominant context which is interpellated when recontextualized.

Once entextualized into material form, a citational resource is available for anyone to recontextualize; of course, those who control mass distribution (citational) networks are able to more easily influence the continued framing of the entextualization—and thus the value contexts interpellated from the recontextualization. In Inoue's example discussed above, the "voice" of the schoolgirls, when used to sell commodities, interpellated an exchange value context which was beyond the influence of the schoolgirls themselves (see Inoue 2006, 53). As Inoue notes, in the schoolyard the girls could report on their own previous utterances to clarify or alter their meanings; however, as their voices became a commodity, the schoolgirls could not politically compete with the syntactical reframing of their words in the mass media.

An important issue in the contemporary political economy thus concerns this ability to issue "metapragmatic commentaries" (56) on prior speech—that is, to re-frame the entextualized words of others (or self) in various ways in new situations. The speech of oppositional groups loses political force when reframed as a media commodity, given that the groups are no longer able to "provide context." Even as groups politically struggle to control the "valuing contexts" which are interpellated from particular words, the words themselves come to have a market value. Those who struggle to resist the commodification of their words may instead find that their oppositional utterances have a certain marketability.

We can also see the hegemony of the exchange value frame in so-called "reality" television, where even the "direct" reporting of the experiences of others becomes framed as an entertainment commodity for subjects. The words and images of others become mediated, vicarious experiences for consumers. Today, the "experiences of others" are increasingly consumable in everyday life, given the unprecedented transmission capabilities of today's citational technologies. Thus, in Mead's (1969) terms, the human ability to "take the role of the other"—to "experience" the world through the referential positionality of others—has been systematically reframed as the consumable "experience" of another's social positionality. Again, we find that the citational practices of the other are reducible to vicarious, mediated experiences for the pleasure of subjects—and assigned a "worth" as the exchange value frame is keyed.

The grafting of valuable citational resources into new social situations—the re-citing of exchange value—involves the interpellation of a subject as a representative of an imagined *community of consumers*. If all citational resources in the contemporary cultural economy are potentially commodifiable, and translatable into a discourse of economic worth, then all social identities interpellated from these resources involve the "consumption" of valued experience. This interpellated community of consumers shares the normative assumption that experiences are measurable in terms of economic worth, and that the lives of members of such a community can be evaluated as to the worth of their accumulated experiences. Thus, fashionable subjects normatively re-cite those citational forms which signify the presence of value, aligning their identities with a community of "like" consumers. In Baudrillard's (1981) sense of a system of "sign values," the interpellated identities of subjects are differentiated in terms of their social positioning relative to these material signs; that is, important people are taken to have more "valuable experiences."

Brands and Endorsements:

The Mark of the Fashionable Other

The act of consumption can be seen as a kind of citational practice, by which social objects, events, and experiences are purchased and used as symbolic resources to construct social identity and affiliated social values. In a summary of Colin Campbell's work, Jonathan Friedman (1994) points out that for Campbell, the identity of the modern individual is constructed "in the very act of consumption" (21). In the language of citationality, the "consumption" of particular citational resources interpellates particular social identities and social values.

Expanding on the insights of Thorstein Veblen (1953), Pierre Bourdieu (1984) has shown how upper-class members, through consumption, create and maintain status distinctions relative to those lower in the stratification system. For example, Michael Silverstein (2003) shows that wine consumption and "wine talk" at social events is an indexical indication of social status (222). Thus Silverstein speaks of the "indexical value" of "identity-by-visible-consumption," or the value of "the correctly-indexical 'life style'" (227). Here, both the ability to actually *taste* distinctions in wine, as well as *talk* about these distinctions, become citational practices distinguishing class membership. Thus, to be "indexed" as fashionable comes from citing fashionable words, or having fashionable tastes in citational performances.

The fashionable subject thus learns to make fashionable citations, a phenomenon which—as Bourdieu and Veblen have shown—is closely associated with class. As Thorstein Veblen argued, fashionable dress involves both "conspicuous leisure" and "conspicuous consumption"—that is, the *time* to learn about the fashions and the *money* to purchase them (1953, 85). The voicing of "fashion" within the utterances of the subject therefore makes for an excellent status symbol. Of course, fashion is an *intertextual* phenomenon, in that one becomes fashionable oneself by citing fashionable others—designers, celebrities, and so forth. The intertextual citationality of value can also be seen when events are marked as sponsored by other cultural commodities—as when, for example, a television program is "brought to you by" a film company promoting their latest movie. In other words, not only does fashion signify the present (Miller 1987, 126), but the fashionable present is often itself *sponsored*—through a citational reference to the entity responsible for bringing such a valued experience to the consumer.

In the consideration of "brands," as citational markers which indicate the presence of value, it may be worthwhile to revisit Derrida's writings on the signature—normatively taken to indicate the "presence" of the subject. In *Limited Inc* (1988), Derrida argued that within the "metaphysics of presence," the signature is taken to have an authenticity which guarantees the presence of the signatory, and thus the presence of their intentionality. In a similar way, the autograph of the famous person, or the brand name "signature" of a designer on a commodity, seems to guarantee the presence of its value. The "name of the other," whether a brand or a proper name, is affixed to commodities to attest to the authenticity or the quality of the product—much like the marker which announces the value of tourist sites. Brands thus indicate the presence of the "fashionable" other, when re-cited by the subject.

We can find in the entertainment industry all sorts of commodities which seem to derive much of their value from the presence of the brand name or celebrity endorsement. As Haug pointed out in his *Critique of Commodity Aesthetics* (1986), advertising increases the exchange value of goods through an association with a particular "aesthetic," or promise of a particular experience. The citation of the commodity links the identity of the subject with the aesthetic associated with the celebrity or brand—as well as with a particular subculture of users. As Haug argued, this aesthetic value may be nearly detached from the "use value" of the commodity; for example, the fact that a winter hat with a sports team logo may also be a warm hat is almost incidental to its price. The names of celebrities, sports stars, and even social institutions are used to conjure such aesthetic value when they mark or brand a product.

While, in a Marxist sense, commodities "do not bear the signature of their makers" (Jhally 1987, 50), they do bear the signatures of their *endorsers*. From a Marxist perspective, the value is generated from a kind of *counterfeit signature* —that of the endorser, rather than the laborer. Of course, in a Derridean sense, this signature—and its interpellated value—is also "counterfeit" in that it is never fully authentic as the mark of an originary "presence" (Derrida 1988; see also Derrida 1992).

It may also be interesting here, when discussing the inscription of endorsement marks or brand names onto the materiality of commodities, to return to Durkheim's (1965) discussion of marks of the "sacred." In *The Elementary Forms of the Religious Life,* Durkheim argued that as clans engaged in ritual behavior directed toward the totemic representations of group consciousness, they were "worshiping" the group itself—that is, they experienced the "social." In contemporary secular culture, we might say that fashionable cultural commodities have assumed this function—as quasi-sacred materialities taken to represent the "collective consciousness" of a valuing community concerned with the fashionably "present." As subjects engage in normative citational rituals relative to the valued commodity, they reinforce the dominant cultural consciousness of consumerism.

As discussed above, Durkheim points out that in totemic religions, both the "totemic animal" (the animal serving as the totem of the group), and the "totemic representation" (emblems which included paintings, carvings, or tattoos representing the totemic animal), were considered to be sacred (165). In "elementary" religions, objects which bore the painting or carving of the totemic animal *themselves* were regarded as sacred, due "solely to the fact that they bear the totemic emblem" (147). For Durkheim, the totemic "mark" alone confers the quality of sacredness to the material object. Referring to a totem used by the Arunta, he notes that "the churinga are objects of wood and stone like all others; they are distinguished from profane things of the same sort by only one particularity: this is that the totemic mark is drawn or engraved upon them. So it is this mark and this alone which gives them their sacred character" (144). In fact, Durkheim points out that in these clans, "*the images of totemic beings are more sacred than the beings* [animals and plants] *themselves*" (156, italics in the original). These images or inscriptions have the power to transfer the sacred quality onto usually profane objects like wood and stone.

It is hard to miss the affinity of the practices which Durkheim describes with the contemporary function of today's linguistic "markers"—such as brand names or celebrity endorsements. These "emblems" are taken to confer quasi-sacred "value" onto commodities. We can also see an affinity to advertising generally, which serves as a marker of value—as well as foreshadows the experience of that value. As in Durkheim's examples, the presence of the "linguistic" emblem means that value is present; as Durkheim puts it, "It is the emblem that is sacred" (147).

Whether functioning as a brand name or in advertising, language confers a "quasi-sacred" quality to citational resources—in Durkheim's sense that the totemic mark confers religious "value" to objects. Further, language has itself *become* the "sacred" commodity as distributed via mobile devices, computers, and televisions, and as marked by advertising (i.e., other language). In Durkheim's terms, commodified language today both bears the "totemic mark," and is itself the "totem." It was Durkheim's general argument that the ritualized practices of "elementary" forms of religion have persisted into modern cultures; perhaps the commodification of language itself in late capitalism is a good example of this process.

For Durkheim, subjects are socialized or integrated into the "collective consciousness" by learning ritual ways of acting toward material totems. Similarly, individuals today are socialized into the discourse of exchange value as they learn to re-cite that which manifests the "presence" of value—particular quasi-sacred material signs which effectively "represent" other subcultural values. Durkheim showed how the religious community distinguished between the sacred and the profane in their ritual actions directed toward material totems; today, individuals distinguish between commodified citational resources as more or less "valuable." In this sense, it is the materiality of language, as cultural commodity, which is considered to be "quasi-sacred"—and it is through sedimented *citational rituals* that children are now taught to conflate "sacredness" with exchange value. The most fashionable citations are those which most intensely signify the presence of the "quasi-sacred" in the contemporary cultural economy.

In a diverse culture, social groups differ as to what material forms to valorize, and which to subordinate. Just as Derrida (1981) argued that the West has systematically favored the "presence" of speech over writing, we also find that certain forms of *writing* have been normatively favored over others. For example, while graffiti has come to be a citational practice favored among urban street gangs, this "mark of the other" has often been *devalued* as a form of writing within the larger culture. Just as Derrida (1981) shows that writing was feared as a contaminant to the Greek polis by Plato (77), graffiti is a kind of "feared writing," and perceived as threatening to normative community identity in the United States (Sherlock 2000). While we have seen that the signatures of celebrities or athletes may confer exchange value to cultural commodities, we can see that the *exclusion* of the "signature of the other" can also be performative of exchange value—as in the relationship between the real estate market, gated communities, and graffiti. Exchange value can be generated both through the inclusion, as well as the exclusion, of particular "signatures" of the other.

The Value of Role-Distancing Resources

The exchange value of a commodity is normatively perceived as its worth, when grafted into a new context, in delivering an experience to a consumer.

Yet, from the perspective of a theory of citationality, the graft does not represent a new value in its "presence." Rather, in a Saussurean sense, citational practices enact differences in relationships and values. Exchanges which recontextualize material signs thus, in addition to delivering experiences to a consumer, continually re-negotiate relationships between the differential values of self and those of others.

In the case of a teenager's "oppositional" music, for example, it is the precisely the difference between the teen's relationship with the youth subculture, as opposed to the family subculture, which is continuously re-enacted through the music. In other words, when the materiality of the music is brought into a graft or material configuration with the materiality of the home environment, the values of the imagined communities of youth and family subcultures are interpellated *in their difference*. The exchange value of the citational resource involves this re-enacted difference.

For Erving Goffman (1961), "role distance" involves one's distaste for the role one is playing, and for the social identity implied by that role. Moving Goffman's work into a performative framework, we can see that many material signs are valued precisely in that their re-citation distances the interpellated subject from social roles. For example, certain types of clothing may be valued as role-distancing resources to enact a gender parody. The gender parody is a citational practice which—as Butler (1999) points out—potentially dislocates normative gender roles and the values typically interpellated from them. Some citational resources are thus valued for their ability to signify an oppositional difference relative to normative value hierarchies.

Particular citational resources are marketed precisely in such a way as to allow consumers to express such role distance against normative roles and social relationships. In a commentary on Goffman, for example, Charles Lemert gives an example where "a teenage boy wears the shoes of M. Jordan as a way of keying up a sense of social status against the one with which he must live" (Lemert 2003, xxxix). Here we see how "keys" can be mobilized by a particular material form, as a resource for enacting role distance and "playing against the reality presented to us" (xxxix).

In an individualistic society, subjects often dramatize the ways in which their individual valuations differ from those of the larger culture (see Kopytoff 1986). In such performances, social actors may use *deviant* citational resources, as well as engage in citational practices which re-value or re-prioritize *normative* citational resources. For example, teenagers may move material signs of youth culture to prominent places in their lives, re-enacting the difference in value rankings which adults and youth give to the same commodities.

Marketers, in turn, are eager to sell goods which can be used as resources by individuals or subcultures who wish to display their unique styles of valuation—thus playing to the contemporary concern for displaying one's individuality in a increasingly "rationalized" culture (see Weber 1968; Ritzer 2008) homogenized by exchange value. Thus, *individual* citational practices may enact values which take a stand against *institutional* citational practices, even as the resources which enable such practices themselves have an exchange value and contribute to the profits of those same institutions. In this sense, the production of individualized role-distancing resources, which may function to express one's dissatisfaction with the economic structure and the dominant culture, is in fact integral to their reproduction.

The value ratios of individual identities come into play as subjects employ both normative and oppositional resources in their everyday citational practices. For example, some subjects are highly committed to traditional religious or family values in late capitalist culture, while others may simply manage the appearance of such (see Berger and Luckmann 1967, 172–73). We can see that each social identity becomes a unique constellation of adherence to, and distancing from, dominant value categories as interpellated from citational practices. As Bakhtin has pointed out, a person whose "inner speech" is in total conformity with a particular normative value discourse is not really an individual or "self" at all; yet a person who totally distances self from all "outer speech" lives in a private world unintelligible to others (Holquist 2004, 52).

In between these extremes are all types of combinations of, in Goffman's terms, "role embracement" and "role distance" as indicated through citational practice. Relative to dominant social institutions—as Goffman puts it in *Asylums*—the individual can be seen "as a stance-taking entity, a something that takes up a position somewhere between identification with an organization and opposition to it" (Goffman, in Lemert and Branaman 2003, 90). In fact, any utterance simultaneously embraces one value domain, while distancing its implied social identity from another.

For example, as we see in the case of the ritual practices of juvenile gangs, the same citational practices which re-integrate members into the gang are precisely those which simultaneously express a distancing from the normative values of the larger culture. In addition, this oscillation between role-distancing and role-embracing occurs as subjects continually change roles in everyday life when interacting with different audiences, as they recite different identities in those situations. Any citational resource becomes valued for its functionality in both aligning, as well as distancing, a subject from differing value discourses. In contemporary postmodern culture, individual and group identity categories are rapidly shifting, with traditional categories such as gender and race perhaps one day becoming mere historical reference points—against which other identity stylizations take their distance.

The normative "exchange value discourse" is both a value discourse *against* which individuals seek role-distancing experiences, as well as the mechanism *for* the economic valuation of role-distancing resources themselves. The citation of non-normative values in role-distancing behavior thus does not really dislocate the exchange value discourse; rather, in a Derridean sense, role-distancing is necessarily tied to the normative value discourses against which it sets itself apart. Thus, in the economy of alienation, particular commodities come to have an exchange value precisely as "distancing" resources. In short, the resources employed in the citational practices of oppositional politics themselves come to have an exchange value, which ironically results in the reproduction of the political economy.

Commodities associated with particular subcultural values may be desirable to oppositional actors precisely in order to "play against" the system of exchange value. The meaning of such a commodity—as in the case of the rebellious youth's t-shirt or music—oscillates between dominant and supplemental value discourses. Thus, even in the form of a commodity, material signs are able to "double-voice" particular religious, ethnic, or political values. The materiality of the commodity thus marks a site where differing valuing contexts are grafted together and differentiated, in various ratio. This is the site/cite where alternative value discourses are at once subordinated to the dominant discourse of exchange value, yet continue to play against it.

Because, in a Derridean sense, the supplemental or excluded alterity is always already contained within any meaningful identity, we can see that the citation of an oppositional resource is actually a re-citation of that which has *already been abjected* in the normative or dominant identity. For example, if a community excludes graffiti in the initial construction of its identity as a "safe" neighborhood, oppositional groups may precisely use graffiti as a political resource. This practice is thus a re-citation of that which was already abjected in the formation of the community's identity. The re-citation of this "alterity of the other" has value as an oppositional resource, and functions as the basis of the role-distancing experiences of the oppositional subjects.

Thus, in the case of social class, upper-class members who attempt to exclude certain things from their "experiences" find that oppositional groups precisely re-cite those excluded forms as the basis of their resistance. To take another example, the performance of a gender parody appeals to those alternative conceptions of gender which have been abjected in the construction of gender categories in the first place. In this sense, efforts of the powerful to abject the values of the excluded simultaneously create citational resources for those who seek to oppose those dominant values—as well as generate a market value for such oppositional resources.

As in de Certeau's example discussed earlier, powerful groups often seek to manage excluded others by using syntactical forms which "report" on them and for them—thus seeking to eliminate direct expressions of "role distance," and direct challenges to dominant values. In other words, if powerful groups are successful, the oppressed will not be able to effectively re-cite that alterity which is excluded in the construction of the normative identity of the dominant group, and thus become unable to mobilize political opposition. Rather, that which is excluded is strategically, and *syntactically*, maintained and controlled within the citational practices and meaningful material forms produced by the dominant group.

Regarding race, for example, bell hooks (1992b) has shown that white audiences have historically supported a whole industry around the marketing of "blackness" in U.S. culture. Commodities "representing" black culture are distributed in the market and are vicariously experienced by persons who desire a type of "mass-mediated danger" (26). As she notes, "It is within the commercial realm of advertising that the drama of Otherness finds expression. Encounters with Otherness are clearly marked as more exciting, more intense, and more threatening. The lure is the combination of pleasure and danger" (26).

Rather than reciprocal dialogue, or the direct political negotiation of differences, the words of those excluded from the opportunity structure are instead commodified as "vicarious experiences" for consuming subjects. Through strategic syntactical maneuvers, oppositional potentialities are managed in advance, and normative identities and social relationships are maintained—which serves both the political and economic interests of dominant groups. These syntactical maneuvers can, in Goffman's (1961) sense, be considered as a "screen" which allow only limited amounts of social resistance into the political economy, while maintaining its overall structure.

While some critics have charged that mass-mediated entertainment is a form of escapism from the troubles of everyday life, Erving Goffman—in his essay "Fun in Games" (1961)—has instead argued that an important dimension of "fun" is the particular amount of "outside reality" which is allowed into the "game." Many corporate utterances in the entertainment industry are syntactically arranged to make the experience "fun" for consumers. These institutions entextualize their utterances into those syntactical forms which allow *some* alterity in, even while re-differentiating and reproducing dominant social values. In commodity form, the words and images of others are materially shaped in such a way as to maximize their exchange value—as they are marketed as citational resources for consumers. If the words or images "of the other" are to valorize the referential context of the contemporary subject, then their commodified words must re-cite the differences between self and other in an *entertaining* way.

For Goffman, the "transformation rules" (33) of a game determine how much, and in what ways, "outside reality" is made "relevant" to the play of the game. For example, as Goffman notes, gender may be made relevant to a bridge game, or social class made relevant to a party. Goffman argues that just the "right amount" of outside reality must be allowed into the game in order to maximize the fun. In other words, the rules of the game must act as a screen to keep out real world conflicts (33), even while allowing in enough real world tensions to keep the game interesting. For Goffman, the social inequalities of the real world must be "disguised" behind the screening rules of the game (73–79). We might directly apply Goffman's insight to television sitcoms, where real world issues are confronted in an amusing, lighthearted way behind the television "screen." Just as in the politicized syntax of reported speech, games "screen in" some social conflicts, while simultaneously managing the full force of their oppositional potential.

In this sense, the *material form* of the cultural commodity can be seen as a kind of screen. As a syntactical configuration, the real life words and images of others enter into the institutional utterance, yet their contextual relationship to various social issues is disguised. Goffman's argument can be more generally extended to suggest that in the contemporary U.S. economy, culture is widely marketed precisely in order to allow consumers to "play against" the inequalities of the larger social structure (Sherlock 2005)—even as these oppositional resources themselves acquire a market value, and thus ultimately re-cite the exchange value frame. Entire sectors of the cultural economy now produce citational resources through which oppositional stances can be taken toward the political economy—not in order to directly confront real world inequalities, but in order to "experience" them in vicarious fashion. To be marketable, inequality must be transformed into "fun"—or at the very least, into an interesting "information commodity."

While the value of citational resources involving social inequalities *could* be measured in terms of political value (i.e., in provoking social change), it is *normatively* measured in terms of exchange value—as providing marketable "experiences" for consuming audiences. Excluded others are thus "reported on" in the institutional utterances of the entertainment industry, for re-citation by consumers in everyday life. The delivery of vicarious experiences of the "other" has become a multi-million dollar business in the United States, dependent on consumers who want a bit of the experiences of socially excluded others—but not too much. Within a political economy structured to exclude certain others, some of the words and objects signifying alterity are "screened back" into the entertainment experiences of consumers—who purchase these cultural "souvenirs" in order to play within, and play against, that same political economy. The increasing growth of the entertainment industry attests to the amazing ability of the U.S. economy to re-incorporate cultural resistance to its own institutional structure.

THE TEMPORALITY OF EXCHANGE VALUE

The Value of Past Experience:

Historical Rankings and the Value Archive

Journalistic recaps, or retrospective accounts of valued events, are normatively considered as "supplemental" to the presence of the live event itself. These "after-the-fact" news accounts are devalued in the normative value hierarchy as a kind of lesser reproduction of a prior moment, for the benefit of those persons absent from the original citational experience. In a Derridean sense, this kind of after-the-fact "writing" is thus perceived to be a presence of an "absence" (1973; 1988)—a stand-in for the prior, and now absent, experience or event. A hierarchy of value is thus created which extends temporally from the "originary" event forward, as the passing of time devalues retrospective accounts.

In the contemporary U.S. cultural economy, the "originary events," after they have occurred, are themselves ranked and filed in a kind of value archive. Archival technologies (see Derrida 1996) are developed for the housing of cultural commodities, for later recontextualization.This archive serves as a reference for the ranking of all kinds of "greatest moments" in history, which can be re-presented or re-cited as valorized experiences for consuming subjects. The normative subject, constructing a social identity in reference to a particular subculture, is expected to re-cite the institutionalized archives of that subculture in normative citational practices.

For example, we find that news or sports archival footage is retained by television networks to rebroadcast as memorable events from the past. Particular "moments" from certain historical events are valued as delivering decisive experiences to viewers. Archival-based rankings of events, images, and other commodified experiences flourish in the contemporary cultural economy and become commodities in themselves—such as "top-10 lists." Similarly, there are often stories in the media which rank commodified experiences and events in various sectors of the economy, based on the prior experiences of others: top tourist destinations, best-selling books to read, best barbecue spots in the United States, and so forth. The highly regarded experiences of some can thus be re-cited by others—whether in person or as mediated experiences.

In addition, new achievements, as in the case of athletic accomplishments, are continually measured as to where that new achievement would rank against the historical value archive—in the greatest moments of that sport, that city, or even to that television network. Even as these important events first occur, attendees "experience" their *anticipated* "historical value," knowing that they will likely later join the historical archive high in the value hierarchy—as in the case of personally attending an emerging no-hitter in baseball. The later retrospective ranking can thus be anticipated and enter into the event itself; attendees at live events are often aware of what kinds of moments will later be re-cited as newsworthy.

Finally, it may be interesting to here reconsider—along with the issue of value archives and the retrospective assignment of value—the problem of *aesthetic value*, or judgments about the worth of works of art. In discussing the complexity of the issue, Peter Bürger (1990) summarizes the limitations of the perspective that value inheres only in the artwork itself. He argues that to see value only in the work itself is an "ahistorical" approach, which neglects how the discourse of criticism shapes the reception, and thus the future production, of works of art (27). Following this line, the experiential "value" of cultural commodities might be considered less as "present" in events themselves, but rather as emergent with their *retrospective* accounts—which can in turn be anticipated by subjects.

In this sense, the discourse of media criticism, like advertising, is not to be considered as an activity which is merely supplemental to the value of the media commodity itself, but rather as integral to it. The events, and their later critical accounts, become grafted together in the social construction of valued experience. Thus, the *future* accounts of others—such as anticipated critical reviews—enter into the present experiences of event-going subjects. In this way, present citational practices are grafted together with the anticipated retrospective accounting of others. In addition, from a poststructuralist perspective, subjects construct the meaning and value of what they have experienced only after it occurs, in a new social and historical context. Thus, the value rankings of experiences and events are continually open to recontextualization, as social identity is continually reconstituted and recontextualized.

The Live and the Mediated: Value Hierarchies and the Presence of Experience

As discussed above, the ideology of "presence"—associated with speech in the Western philosophical tradition—continues today even in what de Certeau (1988) has called the "scriptural economy." A hierarchy of value emerges which valorizes speech and presence, even as the citational mechanisms which distribute this speech are based on a model of writing—distribution across contexts. While continually shifting and transforming, the cultural economy places "presence" at the top of the value hierarchy, and lesser reproductions of this "live presence" lower in the hierarchy. In this ideological formulation, value is not only perceived as present, but present in a hierarchy.

This value hierarchy involves both temporal and spatial dimensions. Temporally, the live event, where fashionable experience and value have historically been considered to be most fully present, tops the hierarchy. Ticketed events such as fashion shows or sporting events are marked in advance by promoters, or in retrospect by critics, as experiences where value is or was present. To be in the presence of an artist or celebrity at a performance is to experience the greatest value. In other words, to position one's self so as to cite the live event as it happens in "real time" enables the interpellation of a particular type of subject—one who experiences the full presence of value. The fashionable subjects able to afford the hottest ticket in town purchase the "presence of fashionable experience." As Daniel Miller has remarked, "What makes an object fashionable . . . [is its] ability to signify the present" (1987, 126).

Following the live event, a "trickle down" effect occurs relative to the lesser distributional markets. For example, mass reproductions of the "original" event take their places lower in the value hierarchy. Though a recording of a live event is still somewhat of a valuable experience, its exchange value falls below that of actual attendance at the event. A *temporal* chain is thus established regarding the perceived value of the reproduced experience relative to the live event—today involving distributional technologies such as cable television rebroadcasts or DVD recordings. This hierarchy of value—often based on perceived temporal distance from the "origin" of value—continues all the way down to televised accounts of the event on the entertainment news, on talk shows, or in newspaper accounts of the event. These "late" experiences finally become affordable to most consumers, considered as poorer substitutes or supplements for those absent from the original event. As mass-mediated commodities have proliferated, the dichotomy of "live" or "real time" events—versus "after-the-fact" mediated events—has persisted as a basis of differentiating the value of commodified citational resources. In this sense, one's class-based "habitus" (Bourdieu 1984) involves one's temporal positioning relative to the normatively perceived origin of value.

While mass reproduction undermines the "aura" or authenticity of a unique work (Benjamin 1968), the corporations which distribute citational resources attempt to re-establish this aura of presence, even when no uniquely "original" phenomenon exists. In the case of movies, something like an "originary presence" is created via the film's premiere on opening night (in Westwood or Hollywood)—attended by celebrities who bring their aura of presence to the event. In other words, their already-entextualized social identity as a "famous celebrity" is recontextualized at the event. The citational practices of the fans may include attending the event, as well as getting autographs which document the presence of attending celebrities.

Jody Berland (1992) has argued that we also have to understand entertainment and other "cultural technologies" in *spatial* terms (39). Valued experiences today occur in living rooms, sports bars, or via audio players in cars, and thus are spatially differentiated. For example, the purchase of experience at an event involves the claim that a subject was *there*, as evidenced by the ticket stub—an entextualized material sign which can later be cited as a "previously present" experience of the subject.

The spatial location of the material graft—*where* citational practice occurs—is thus an important component of its value. Audiences will normatively value live, public performances more in person rather than as mediated through television and experienced from home. Thus some places are considered more fashionable as citational resources, at certain times, than others. In terms of the "inequality of experience," there is clearly an exclusivity regarding private access to particular citational spaces. An important aspect, then, of the contemporary U.S. cultural economy is *when and where* a subject incorporates the language of others into one's own citational utterances. Alternately, when and where a person—whether a film star or an author—is cited (sighted) is an important component of their celebrity within the cultural economy.

These "citational experiences" not only become the basis of how others attribute status to social actors, but also of how subjects construct and interpret their own social identities. Subjects become the kinds of persons who attend certain kinds of events, or own certain kinds of citational resources. Fashionable persons have access to the experiences and significations which cut closest to the "present" moment of fashion—which enables them to incorporate these experiences into their social identities more quickly. Investors who are able to anticipate these valuations are able to get into the market at a fashionable time, and not show up too late—after the particular phenomenon has become routinized and devalued.

Having argued, however, that "live" events have topped the value hierarchy within the cultural economy, it also appears that mediated forms have become so pervasive that even "live" performances now seem to mimic them (Auslander 1999). Indeed, the very distinction between the historically dominant term of "liveness," and the subordinate term of the "mediatized," may itself be untenable. In his work *Liveness: Performance in a Mediatized Culture* (1999), Philip Auslander notes, for example, that the "live" rock concert—whether seen in person or on television—must now approximate the audio recordings or music videos to which fans have become accustomed (160).

The result, for Auslander, is the devaluation of live performance in contemporary culture. Not only do "live" performances now imitate mediatized performances, but even incorporate mediatization into the live event itself—as when an instant replay screen is used at a sporting event (7). Because of the "devaluation of live presence in mediatized culture" (37), Auslander argues against those theorists who suggest that live performance is an arena outside of the contemporary "economy of repetition," or that live performance offers a privileged site for political resistance to mass reproduction (see Phelan 1996).

However, the cultural belief that live performance provides an "authenticity" which is lacking in mediatized reproductions—which Auslander sees as ideological (42)—still persists within contemporary Western culture. Despite his prediction for the continued devaluation of the live (see 59; 85; 162), he points out that the ideology of the presence of the live has persisted because live events have retained their "symbolic capital" (57); the status derived from one's attendance or presence at the live performance. He notes that "live performances are still worth more symbolic capital within our culture than mediatized performances, even as live performance becomes more and more like mediatized performance" (59). In addition, Auslander argues that live performance still fulfills an important function in "authenticating" the mediatized reproductions—particularly in the case of those rock concerts which mimic the band's music videos (79; 160).

Auslander's central point is that the simple dichotomy between live and mediatized performances is no longer tenable, and that such an ideology is "itself a product of the age of mechanical reproduction" (83). In the Derridean terms of the "logic of the supplement"—and in accord with Auslander's historical account—we might say that the "purity" of the live performance is reasserted when threatened by its mechanized and mediatized supplement—all the while failing to acknowledge its dependency on the supplement. Just as Derrida showed that speech could not be considered as prior to writing, but instead depended upon it (Derrida 1981; 1988; 1997), Auslander argues "in favor of a view that emphasizes the mutual dependence of the live and the mediatized and that challenges the traditional assumption that the live precedes the mediatized" (11).

Thus, considering Auslander's argument, we can see that historically in the U.S. economy the "live" was, and perhaps to some extent still is, highest in the hierarchy of value. In this situation, even while the live in fact depends upon the supplement of the mediatized, and while the "live" and the "mediatized" are in fact mutually interdependent terms (Auslander, 53), the ideology of the presence of value in the live performance persists. Auslander himself wonders whether the "live" will remain the privileged term, suggesting that perhaps a cultural tipping point has recently been reached. Clearly, however, "live" performances still remain an important marketing tool within the industry as "semiotic markers of authenticity" (70), and thus as signifiers of the presence of value.

Thus, even as the contemporary cultural economy is based on the distribution of cultural commodities across contexts—based on the model of writing—the ideology of "live" speech or presence persists. As Auslander recognizes, the "live" performance still retains a certain symbolic capital as a more "authentic" citational experience. This ideology also persists despite that fact that, considering here the work of Richard Schechner (1985) on "restored behavior," live performances are typically the result of careful polishing over several previous "rehearsals" (52)—acts of performative *recitation*.

The distributional network in the U.S. economy has thus developed in such a way so as to structure any citational resource into a hierarchical and rankable structure—whether temporally or spatially. Within such a hierarchical structure, it seems that there will always be a number-one song, a best-selling book, a most-popular television show, or a top-ranked travel destination indicating the "presence" of value. The distributional networks which generate citational resources have become institutionalized to such an extent that cultural commodities are predesigned (or entextualized) to fit these already-sedimented social forms. Jody Berland has noted, citing Kealy, that a three-minute pop song produced in the 1970s had to fit a format designed for car radios (Berland 1992, 39). In other words, the syntactical *forms* in which citational practice occurs in late capitalism have already been thoroughly shaped by market considerations. These linguistic, material forms both limit, and enable, the communicative utterances and the social identities of consumers interacting within such a cultural economy.

Advertising and the Promise of Value

As discussed above, Derrida (1997; 1981) has argued that in Western philosophy, speech has been regarded as an original, authentic mode of communication, while writing has been regarded as a mere "supplement." For Derrida, this "'logic of supplementarity'" relegates the lesser term in a dichotomy to an auxiliary position (Norris 1987, 34). The supplement, like writing, is regarded as inferior, extra, and indeed a threat to the primary term. One term is thus established in a structure of dominance as a "primary presence," through the abjection of the second. Derrida's project of deconstruction was to show, however, that the subordinate, second term in a hierarchy was in fact necessary for the construction and maintenance of the identity of the dominant term all along. The supplement is shown to be crucial in the very constitution of the "original," and not simply an after-the-fact "add-on." Yet Derrida does not invert the hierarchy, but rather shows the mutual interdependence of the differential terms (Gasché 1986, 210).

Advertising, like retrospective accounts of events, is usually considered as supplemental to the more valuable entertainment commodity. For those who cannot afford advertising-free "sights"—for example, by purchasing a premium television channel or a recording technology designed to skip ads—advertising language must be endured as a distraction from the "language-commodity" itself. In the case of the Internet, "popup" ads, like television or radio commercials, are seen to contaminate the purity of the entertainment site/cite. The citational practices involving the experience of linguistic commodities are thus perceived to be devalued by advertising.

In *The Codes of Advertising* (1987), however, Sut Jhally has shown how advertising cannot be regarded as merely supplemental to a commodity's value (see also Haug 1986; Culler 1981). His work shows that in the case of television, advertising and programming cannot be neatly separated, and sometimes the supplemental advertising even *becomes* the commodity or program. This ambiguity between advertising and commodity continues today; for example, some Internet websites are constructed as mostly containing links to other websites. In other words, the website "commodity" itself is comprised of links which function as advertisements for other "cites" by the traveling subject. In fact, most websites, as part of their own content, contain links to other sites/sights—the link functioning to graft the two web contexts together.

While considered only a "supplement," advertising is in fact integral to the meaning and value of the commodity, as well as to the interpellation of the subject who experiences this value—and in some cases, the advertising becomes a commodity itself. In short, the strict distinction between ad and commodity becomes untenable, especially when considering that commodities can also be advertisements for, or signs of, themselves (see Culler 1981, 127; 137; see also MacCannell 1976, 22). It is not altogether clear whether subjects cite the advertising, the commodity, or both in their utterances.

While in the U.S. cultural economy value is said to be present in commodities, the advertising which precedes the cultural commodity also affects its meaning and value. As mentioned earlier, Haug (1986) has argued that advertising itself increases the price of commodities, as aesthetic language is linked to the commodity. Haug shows that contemporary commodities are marketed less in terms of their practical "use value," and more in terms of an aesthetic or mythology created by the music or visual images used in the advertising. A more abstract type of value is promised, though never delivered—for example, that the consumption of the commodity will bring happiness or success.

Haug argues that this aesthetic style of advertising has come to constitute an increasingly greater share of the exchange value of objects in late capitalism; for example, more fashionable, heavily advertised clothing will bring a higher price even if it does not cost more to produce than other brands. He points out that this "aesthetic value" of the commodity becomes almost completely divorced from the technical properties of the object. It is this aesthetic dimension which becomes linked to interpellated social identity. For Haug, then, subjects increasingly "experience" the value of the commodity as mediated through advertising. The language of advertising "infuses value" as it is associated with particular commodities. The commodity comes to signify particular meanings and values, as its advertising creates links between the commodity and particular interpretive contexts. The social identity of the subject which is interpellated from the citation of commodities is also, in this sense, constructed via advertising (see Appadurai 1986b, 56).

Advertising "pre-interpellates" a (Cartesian) subject readied for a particular type of experience. Knowledge of commodities gleaned from advertising markers—like advance knowledge of tourist sites (see Frow 1997, 66–67)—thus shapes the experience of the commodity itself. In this sense, advertising serves as a "marker" for the value of a commodity—in a way similar to those tourist markers which indicate a tourism commodity (see MacCannell 1976, 110; Culler 1981, 132). For example, Jonathan Culler points out that the marker for a Civil War site guarantees the authenticity of that site—as distinguished from any other plot of land. We might say that this marker serves as something of a brand regarding the officially designated site—supposedly guaranteeing or advertising the presence of value in the commodity. We also see that the marker or advertisement is a kind of "entextualized promise": that the commodity-site (cite) will deliver a valuable experience to the subject.

Culler argues that because "authenticity" is marketed in tourism, this authenticity of a site must be "marked" (133). In this sense, we might think of cultural commodities as sites for valued experiences, and advertising as markers for the authenticity of those commodities. Inasmuch as the marker can be purchased, as in the case of a brochure which advertises value elsewhere, what is actually purchased is a *promise* of value. In fact, the markers which guarantee the authenticity of the commodity sometimes become the actual destination of tourists—as when the Civil War marker is visited (139; see also MacCannell (1976, 113-15). Again, we find that both the marker and site—the advertisement and the commodity—together contribute to the "experience" of tourists, and cannot be neatly separated from each other.

As the citational practices of self involve the markers or representations of commodities—such as a movie or sports poster in a teenager's room—the markers themselves can interpellate the experiencing subject. We might even say that a "quote" from another context—like a sports poster with a player's image—simultaneously serves as an *advertisement* for that (value) context, as well as a commodity to be cited in identity-construction. Or, to use a different example, a subject engaged in the citational practice of wearing an Eiffel Tower t-shirt simultaneously *advertises* Parisian tourism (and the t-shirt manufacturer), as well as cites the signifying t-shirt *commodity*. In short, it is not clear at all where advertising ends and commodities begin.

Generalizing from the travel industry, we can see that events in the culture which are *marked* as valuable (or "mark-etable") are experienced and valued as such. Just as a plot of land must be marked as historical, a television "site" must be marketed as a more valuable experience for viewers than sights from everyday life. The excitement generated over events and images which are assumed to be timely, fashionable, and present can, in this sense, be seen as a fetishism of the very experience of mark-etability. Today's cultural commodities can hardly be experienced apart from the advertising which promises the presence of their value. The experience of the marker becomes the experience of the promise of value; that is, the marker *anticipates* value. In fact, many consumers have become as adept as producers and editors at recognizing what will become marketable, even in its nascent stages—whether the talent of emerging young basketball players, or the look of emerging fashion models. In this way, the future of value is folded into the temporality of presence.

The promise of value in advertising helps the subject organize future citational practices around an existing identity or construct an identity to which one aspires. In configuring the materiality of their social environment, consumers choose between what books to buy, which television shows to watch, and which websites to frequent. Advertising assists in the organization of one's purchases, as subjects anticipate the value of particular resources and the construction of a particular identity. The advertising of cultural commodities thus enables subjects to rank and assemble particular role-embracing and role-distancing resources, which will play against each other at the site of a particular identity.

The semiotic dichotomy of "authentic/inauthentic" regarding tourist sites (see Culler 1981) can also be applied to the temporality of the U.S. cultural economy. As mentioned above, the fashionably "present" event is taken to be more authentic than its later reproductions, regarded as lesser supplements. The citational positioning of a subject at a gala event is normatively considered to be a more fashionable experience than watching its later, less authentic rebroadcast on television. This "fashionable time"—closest to authenticity—is assumed to be the temporal point where the *anticipation* generated by advertising crosses over to the *experience* of the presence of value. Those who participate at a temporal or spatial distance must rely on the fidelity of the streaming or reproducing equipment to get as close as possible to the original or authentic live event—a kind of second-hand citational practice.

Just as in the case of travel, the dichotomy of authentic/inauthentic is difficult to maintain in regard to any commodified experiences and events. This also underscores Guillory's (1993) argument regarding the hegemony of exchange value relative to other value discourses. The attempt to find and mark subcultural artifacts of authentic ethnic or religious value—outside of the "taint of mark-etability"—always already becomes trapped in Culler's "dilemma of authenticity" (1981, 137).

Regarding the "promise of value" in advertising, we might here consider Thomas Keenan's (1993) reading of Marx's comments in *Capital* on "'the language of commodities'" (Marx, in Keenan 1993, 176). While Marx insists that commodities in exchange have no "materiality"—as they do in actual use—Marx argues in an example involving coats and linens that "One thing uses the other as the medium of its expression as value" (Keenan 1993, 175). For Keenan, this means that their exchange is "unavoidably a matter of signification" (175), in that one commodity "represents" the exchange value of another. Keenan thus argues that Marx is forced to make a "linguistic turn" (174).

The "materiality" of a coat in *exchange* is thus not in its use in the winter; rather, its materiality in exchange *is that of language*; in Keenan's words, "material in the sense that language is material, not phenomenal or sensible" (177). While others, as in this book, might argue even more forcefully regarding the "materiality" of language, the point in this reading is that one commodity can be considered as the marker or advertisement for another commodity. By extension, every commodity in a differential valuation system *can be taken as an advertisement for every other commodity*—"promising" the delivery of value when that other commodity is cited by an experiencing subject. We can thus see that when language itself becomes a cultural commodity, it simultaneously becomes an advertisement for other language-based commodities.

For example, when a commodity like a popular soft drink is advertised at, or perhaps "sponsors," a professional golf tournament, not only does the golf tournament attest to the value of the beverage, but in turn the golf tournament "gains value" by the mere presence of advertising—in that the tournament would be considered an "important-enough event" that major advertisers would be present. In this sense, the presence of advertising markers, even for a different commodity, are taken to confer value upon that event or experience. Thus, experiences are said to be valuable because of the "presence" of advertising itself. Commodities sponsor or *advertise each other*—each becoming the supplemental marker needed to construct the identity and value of the other.

We have seen that cultural commodities, in their material form, graft contexts in such a way that the referential context of the experiencing subject is perceived to be valorized with the represented context of the other—as in the case of the purchase of an Eiffel tower travel souvenir. When displayed in the home of a U.S. subject following a visit to France, the souvenir plays against the differing materialities of social objects in the home, which are taken to represent other values. In this way, the home context is valorized. The Cartesian subject experiences the graft of materialities, and interpellates a social identity which both combines and re-differentiates the valuing contexts.

However, we can see that the Eiffel tower souvenir statue, in addition to being a *commodity* which functions as a more or less authentic representation of French cultural values, can also function as an advertisement or marker for another cultural commodity—such as a trip to France. In its "commodity function," the souvenir supposedly makes values *present*; however, in its advertising function, it *promises* value elsewhere. Both "functions" operate through the material grafting together of contexts; however, in a Derridean sense, what never quite arrives is the presence of the promised French cultural values.

This process of the "grafting" of contexts in *advertising*, in order to promise value, has been explored by Judith Williamson (2005), Goldman (1992), and Goldman and Papson (1996). For example, in her book *Decoding Advertisements*, Judith Williamson shows that the promised value of advertised perfume is enhanced when a famous movie actress is used in the advertisement. The meaning which the actress's face connotes in the referential system of film is, in the advertisement, brought into the "perfume system." Given that the actress connotes "glamour" in the social world of film (the "referent system"), the perfume *acquires* the connotation of "glamour" within the differential meaning system of perfumes. As the perfume and actress are materially linked in the advertising image, the connotation of "glamour" is transferred from one semiotic system to the other (2005, 25). The perfume's position within its differential system is enhanced through this valorization of its meaning—its "enhanced" promise of value to the consumer. Williamson thus speaks of the "translation" of meaning from one referential system to another, which continually occurs in advertising. As Williamson notes, the value is merely promised in advertising, but is never present. As she puts it "There is no real present in advertising . . . in the actual present you are looking at the ad, anticipating but not enjoying" (154–5; see also Haug 1986).

Robert Goldman also emphasizes that ads recontextualize and graft meanings in order to promise value. In *Reading Ads Socially* (1992), he argues that "Advertisements photographically isolate meaningful moments, remove them from their lived context and place them in the ad framework where their meaning is recontextualized and thus changed" (5). Like Williamson, Goldman argues that this recontextualization of meaning enables the transfer of meaning from one semiotic system to another, in order to increase exchange value (5). Goldman stresses the material configuration of the words and images in advertisements which enable this transfer of meaning; advertisements thus "provide an arena in which to transfer and rearrange meanings" (38). Considering this literature on advertising, we can see that the grafting of contexts occurs not only when a *commodity* is actually purchased and moved into the referential context of the subject, but also in the *advertisements* which promise value. In other words, the "promise of value" is itself constructed through syntactically formed grafts of meaningful materiality.

In a Derridean sense, advertisements which promise the coming presence of value are *performative*—in that the *promise, as speech act, is itself perfor-*

mative. Further, in his reading of Paul de Man, Derrida states that the very "*act* of language is that of a performative promise" (Derrida 1989, 95; italics in the original). As discussed above, a performative speech act purports to produce, rather than simply describe, social realities. In this sense, language purports to produce meaning; that is, language *promises* meaning. Language also promises *value*, inasmuch as—in a Bakhtinian sense—linguistic utterances necessarily enact (meaningful) values.

However, because of the inherent iterability of language, any intended meaning "behind" the issuance of a performative—such as an *intended keeping of a promise*—cannot be stable or secure on its way to eventual fulfillment (see Loxley 2008, 99–100; 109; Derrida 1988; Derrida 1989, 94–95). Meaning, and value, cannot be *delivered* and present-ed; rather, meaning and value—which are continually deferred—can only be performatively *promised*. In the specific example of a "promise," we find a speech act which initiates the expectation of its eventual fulfillment, but this fulfillment cannot be guaranteed in advance—given its projection into an unknown future. The promise that a particular action will be forthcoming, or that advertised value will in fact be delivered, can never actually be fulfilled.

Thus advertising, as a *performative promise of value*, cannot actually guarantee that the commodity will deliver what is promised. As Williamson shows in an example regarding chocolates, advertising goes beyond a representational claim to make a performative one. Using her example, it is not just that the advertised chocolate "represents" happiness, but rather that chocolate can "create happiness" (2005, 36)—in a performative sense. In other words, advertisements performatively *promise* that commodities will performatively *deliver* (value)—a promise whose fulfillment, however, cannot be guaranteed. In fact, as Derrida shows, the promise *cannot* be fulfilled. Subject to the rule of iterability, the meaning or value of the cultural commodity—which has been promised—will never quite be present.

In a Derridean sense, the "performativity of value" is an *aporia of capitalism*. Like meaning itself, "value" is re-citable and repeatable across situations. It enables shared interaction relative to a shared material world, with real social consequences as the economy is re-performed. On the other hand, meaning and value are promised, but never quite present; they are necessarily altered in repeated instantiations. The promised experience of value is never quite present. New commodities are required precisely because former commodities cannot fulfill or deliver what was promised in their advertising (see Haug 1986). Summarizing the work of Laikwan Pang on brand performativity, Constantine Nakassis (2012) also notes that with brands the "ultimate signified"—that is, the brand's promised aesthetic or brand "type" (627)—is "never quite reached," because the anticipation of later iterations or "tokens" (627) of the brand serve to continually re-generate consumer desire, and thereby continually defer satisfaction (634–35).

The contemporary cultural economy in the United States continually re-enacts a *promise of value*. If in addition to the promise of advertising, it is true that every commodity is also an advertisement for itself—as well as for every other commodity—we see that what is circulating in the cultural economy is a promise of value. In a sense, we might say that exchange value "measures" the experiential worth of a performative promise of value, rather than what it is normatively taken to measure—the presence of value. In this sense, the *exchange value* of the cultural commodity—which is the supposed *measure* of the worth of the promised experience *as delivered*—is itself never quite secure.

The commodified promise of any subcultural value is potentially assigned an exchange value in the contemporary cultural economy—which is taken to indicate the experiential worth of that promise. Derrida's notion that language itself enacts a performative promise has become increasingly apparent in today's cultural economy. Language not only promises meaning, but it also promises "value." However, at the same time that the meaningful experience of the commodity's "promise" has become marketable with real economic consequences, it is simultaneously undermined by its own performative structure.

The very nature of commodification, involving the grafting of advertising and commodity, thus involves a promise to valorize the "present." The value of mundane experience is thus seen as intensifiable when "double-voiced" with commodities. However, the valorization of some events and moments, as intense and valuable, necessarily leads to the *de-valorization* of other events and moments. The attempted purchase of that which enhances the everyday "context" simultaneously leads to the devaluation of everyday life as merely mundane. Thus, a kind of vicious cycle seems to fuel the relentless and continual drive in U.S. culture toward the next fashionable experience of "value."

Using Goffman's term, the "action of consumption" (1967, 197) consists in the consumer's belief that the citation of cultural commodities will improve the experiences in their life, and valorize the referential context of the self. Consumers of commodities thus continually seek to re-subordinate or re-abject the mundane experiences of everyday life, in favor of more intense and valuable experiences. Given that the newest, most fashionably present commodities are perceived to be the mechanism by which the subject's experiential situation can be improved, we might say that the contemporary consumer is addicted to the *promise* of valorized experience—which, however, is itself never quite delivered. At the same time, the re-citation of this promise materially re-enacts the very cultural economy which manufactures and distributes such promises.

CONCLUSION

The chapter began by showing that the form of reported speech involves a political stance toward the words of others. Subjects can agree with, or challenge, the words and values of others as they cite them into their own utterances. In addition, as the work of de Certeau and Inoue suggests, the appropriation of the words, images, and objects of the subordinated—into the utterances of the powerful—means that the subordinated lose control over the meanings and the destinations of those forms. An important dimension of politics thus concerns who speaks for whom, and how the words of others are represented in later interactions. Individuals and groups find that they can no longer control the trajectory of their own words and values as the powerful appropriate these words for their own purposes.

Not only do powerful individuals and institutions appropriate the words of others for political gain, but also to generate market value. Inasmuch as language itself has increasingly become a commodity in today's cultural economy, the words, images, and cultural objects of some can be marketed for the economic gain of others. Access to the means of designing and distributing cultural commodities—of institutionally "reporting" speech—is an important factor in the contemporary political economy. Profit is generated as the language which represents the values of one subculture is marketed in a different subcultural context.

A particular type of subjectivity underlies this movement of cultural commodities across contexts in late capitalism—that of a Cartesian subject whose values are considered to pre-exist the commodities which represent them. If subcultural groups value differently, then it seems natural for them to exchange commodities which match those values. This logic of representationalism underlies not only the metaphysical assumptions regarding the "presence" of the Cartesian subject, but also the "presence of value" in capitalism. Within this ideology, consumers are able to re-enact their subcultural values, and display their social identities, via the purchase of commodities. Markets allow the movement of cultural commodities across contexts, to meet the identity construction needs of differing valuing communities. The exchange value of cultural commodities is measured in their ability to fulfill this representational function.

Language, in the broadest sense, becomes a cultural commodity as television shows, films, websites, or text messages are marketed and moved across subcultural contexts. These cultural forms are typically readied by commodity producers in order to generate exchange value, promising to provide an experience of worth to a Cartesian subject. Using Goffman's term, the exchange value frame is "keyed" from the syntactical arrangement of the materiality of cultural commodities, readied by producers precisely for such keying. For Goffman, "frames" organize experience in particular ways. Today, the exchange value frame has become the hegemonic ordering mechanism, inasmuch as meaningful material forms are organized as to their ability to deliver valued experiences. When language becomes a commodity, it is no longer merely assessed relative to its functioning in an everyday communicative context, but rather is assessed according to its marketability.

Just as meaningful "texts" are subject to Derrida's rule of iterability, so are the "contexts" in reference to which these texts are interpreted. The exchange value frame, as the interpretive context for the economic worth of cultural forms, must itself be repeatable across situations—that is, re-citable. This contextual frame of exchange value is re-cited as the commodified words, images, and social objects of others become citational resources for consumers. In this sense, the citational practices of consumers, as they construct identities in everyday life, are performative of exchange value.

For those who *embrace* normative identities and values, brands and celebrity endorsements are seen as a guarantee of the presence of exchange value. Just as Derrida's (1988) work on the signature revealed its entanglement with the metaphysics of presence, we find today that the presence of the celebrity endorsement of a material form increases its exchange value. This contemporary phenomenon bears some resemblance to the rituals studied by Émile Durkheim (1965) in *The Elementary Forms of the Religious Life*. In that book, Durkheim shows that the totemic mark used in rituals conferred sacredness to material forms; today, brand names and celebrity signatures are seen as conveying a "quasi-sacred" quality to citational resources. It is through citational practices that subjects today conflate sacredness with exchange value.

On the other hand, those who use cultural forms to *distance* themselves from normative identities and values find that the citational resources used in resistant practices themselves have an exchange value, and thus their citation re-enacts the exchange value frame. Material forms which interpellate non-normative values and identities simultaneously re-cite the exchange value frame, even as they play against it. Their potentially oppositional force is muted when the materiality representing the oppositional subculture is "reported upon" in marketable forms. In this sense, the commodification of culture involves the proliferation of all kinds of social forms which promise to "play against" the normative social structure, even as they mostly reproduce it. Oppositional resources, including illicit drugs, are commodities sold with a promise of valorized experience for Cartesian-based subjects—that is, sold with the same promise as normative citational resources.

This temporality of presence becomes, in Bakhtin's terms, the dominant "chronotope" in contemporary culture. Past and future are folded into an exchange value frame promising the *presence* of value. We can find this temporality of value, for example, in media stories which recount a valued event. These "after-the-fact" reports are considered as lesser supplements to the event itself. However, the anticipation of such retrospective accounts now enters into the experience of the event itself, as consumers attending events anticipate its later news coverage. In other words, the perceived worth of the event, in the present, is already influenced by the way it is likely to be later re-cited.

The ideology of this temporality of value persists in the continued valorization of the "live" event, even as events themselves have become increasingly mediatized. Philip Auslander (1999) argues that in fact, live events today often mimic their mediated forms, as in the case of a band's live performance reproducing the sounds and images previously recorded on albums or videos. Auslander's work deconstructs the opposition of "live" versus "mediated," as he shows how the very notion of the "live" already depends on the supplemental term of the mediated. Despite his critique, the ideology of the "live" persists in late capitalism.

Regarding future events, advertising is also typically considered as "supplemental" to the actual commodity which follows. If advertising is normatively perceived as *promising* value, commodities are normatively perceived as *delivering* it. However, commodities and their advertising cannot be strictly separated. Sometimes the advertisement itself *becomes* the commodity, as in the example from tourism where travelers visit the "markers" of sites (Culler 1981). In the case of sponsorship, commodities can become advertisements for each other, as when a soft drink is affiliated with a movie or sporting event. In addition, the advertisement *prepares* consumers for the experience of commodities, and thus enters into the "event" of commodity delivery itself. If advertising is performative—in that it helps to bring about the exchange value it purports to merely describe—we might say that the performative "promise of value" found in language-based *advertising* has become an integral part of the measured "presence" of the exchange value of language-based *commodities*.

The chapter thus shows how the citational practices of consumers re-cite the system of exchange value. As consumers re-cite commodified forms—advertised with the promise to valorize experience—they re-generate demand for such forms in the marketplace, which increases their market value. This "performativity of exchange value" not only reproduces the cultural economy itself, but also reproduces the dominant temporality of "presence" operating in the economy. However, while advertising promises the *presence* of exchange value, it can never quite be delivered—given the iterability of the meaning of "value" itself. Thus, what actually is re-cited in the cultural economy is the continual *promise* of exchange value—as syntactically configured in commodity forms.

Chapter Five

The Marketing of Citational Resources

This chapter considers how assumptions from Western metaphysics regarding the "presence of exchange value" not only persist in today's cultural economy, but are also projected into the future. Producers and investors attempt to both anticipate and shape future citational practices, as they research and market new cultural commodities and new citational technologies. Decisions on which cultural commodities to market, and in what way brands will be developed, rely on economic formulas which speculate on the future exchange value of language.

In order to shape the future citational practices of consumers, firms appropriate the subcultural values of consumers into the marketable, material utterances of the institution. As consumers re-cite these citational resources in identity construction practices, the exchange value system is itself re-cited. The co-production of value by consumers and firms thus becomes "co-performative" of the exchange value system. Inasmuch as measures guide this process, the measure itself becomes performative of the cultural economy (see Muniesa 2011; Adkins and Lury 2011; Moor and Lury 2011). Just as Michel Callon (2007) argued that the formulas devised by economists to describe economic functioning have themselves become performative of market conditions, we now find that the accounting and marketing formulas used by firms to calculate the future exchange value of language have also become performative of the cultural economy.

This chapter also considers the empirical research from a number of fields regarding the importance of consumption practices for social identity, and how consumers use commodities and brands to align themselves with subcultural groups. Firms incorporate subcultural values into the design of their brands, and consumers re-cite these brands in the process of identity construction (see Lury 2004; Arvidsson 2006; Nakassis 2012). As this research indicates, brands thus become performative of exchange value. Similarly, recent work in the sociology of tourism literature indicates that tourists themselves participate in the construction of the tourist experience. In this way, the citational practices of tourists also become performative of exchange value.

MARKETS, MEASURES, AND THE PERFORMATIVITY OF EXCHANGE VALUE

Securing the Future: The Metaphysics of Capitalism

To look more closely at the relationship between Western philosophical assumptions regarding "presence," and the workings of a cultural economy based on the "presence of exchange value," we might consider both Heidegger's critique of Cartesian subjectivity, as well as Hegel's notion of universality. In his work, Samuel Weber (1996) analyzes how Heidegger linked Cartesian assumptions regarding subjectivity to modern technology, and how Walter Benjamin linked the universalizing tendencies of Hegelian metaphysics to capitalism (2008). It is worthwhile to consider these critiques, inasmuch as many assumptions from the Western metaphysical tradition have persisted into contemporary U.S. culture, and are re-cited in contemporary economic practices.

As Weber discusses, Martin Heidegger (1977) argued that one consequence of the emergence of Cartesian subjectivity in the West has been the attempt to control nature through technology (79). The Western subject seeks to dominate and control both the natural and social worlds, attempting to achieve Cartesian "self-security" through technology. Weber links television to Cartesian subjectivity, in that it extends the subject's ability to "gaze" at the world (123). In Heideggerian terms, subjects attempt to fix the world as an objectified "picture," which in turn would secure the Cartesian subject. Heidegger argues, however, that because the Cartesian subject can never achieve complete control over the social and natural worlds, the new technologies—which promise to deliver such control—necessarily fail, and thus continually re-generate anxiety (73–74). Ironically, as Weber argues, the modern subject returns again to technology to achieve control and alleviate these anxieties (69–70).

In the contemporary cultural economy, we find an almost addictive, obsessive-like quality in the use patterns of television or computer use. In a Derridean sense, the more that citational technologies—like television or the Internet—are used to try to re-establish the secure "presence" of the subject, the more their citational nature dislocates that identity. Thus, the contemporary subject is caught in a vicious circle, where the repetitive, technology-driven practices which promise to secure one's identity are the very re-citational practices which unsettle it.

We need only look to the Internet to find the types of anxiety which proliferate in a technological environment capable of extending the abilities of humans many times over. There are hackers or viruses threatening to destroy the "archives of value" which technology has built. There are continuing threats to the privacy of users, given contemporary techniques of surveillance. The "secure" boundaries of the family are now threatened as children are exposed to online dangers in new ways. For all of these reasons and more, new security technologies are continually required—to assert control over the online environment, to secure the future, and to protect the online traveler from the dangers posed by the citational technology itself. An important aspect of the contemporary political economy thus concerns the high costs of providing technology-based security, or at least the illusions of such security, to online consumers.

In his reading of Walter Benjamin's texts on capitalism, Weber (2008) also shows the affinities of capitalism with *Hegelian* metaphysics. Hegel's model continually attempts to reincorporate the negation of present levels of human consciousness into a higher-order system; history becomes an unfolding of moments on the journey to the perfection of consciousness. In other words, for Hegel, the "future" is the culmination of a universal system which continually *re-appropriates alterity* (37).

Weber finds a similar logic in capitalism, in that its universalizing tendencies continually reincorporate or re-appropriate opposition into itself. Weber describes this as "a logic and economy of appropriation in which the realization of 'value' remains the dominant goal" (37). In this sense, exchange value becomes the "universal idea" toward which the future is always oriented. In the contemporary U.S. cultural economy, just as in the Hegelian system, the "play" of language is always re-appropriated into this universal idea. Language which resists, or plays *against*, the exchange value system comes to be re-incorporated into its frame. In a commentary on Walter Benjamin's "Capitalism as Religion," Weber notes that in capitalism, the future becomes the (eternal) re-occurrence of the "presence" of value (see 274–75). It is not really a "future," but rather the re-citation of the "present."

We thus find that the Cartesian assumptions of Western metaphysics continue in the contemporary cultural economy. New citational technologies—from television to the latest mobile devices—not only re-cite the exchange value system, but also re-enact the Cartesian subject who "experiences" the value of autonomous objects. However, this same re-citation process, which supports the identities of these subjects and objects across contexts, simultaneously unsettles their identities—in accordance with the rule of iterability. Contemporary citational technologies, involving the commodification and marketing of language itself, continue to be caught up in the Cartesian and exchange value frames.

The Anticipation of Exchange Value

As John Kenneth Galbraith (1978) argued in regard to manufacturing, an important aspect of capitalism is planning for the future behavior of consumers. This remains true, even as the U.S. economy has transitioned toward the marketing of services and cultural commodities. In this effort, producers must anticipate new markets, and, as much as possible, control the future context in which value is constructed. Capitalists thus attempt to shape the exchange value of the future experiences of consumers, and anticipate the marketability of tomorrow's commodities. In other words, producers try to anticipate future citational practices, and predict trends regarding the interpellation of future social identities.

What is needed for investments in the cultural economy is therefore an *anticipation of the marketability of language*; that is, an anticipation of the ways in which language will be syntactically grafted in future citational practices, in order to produce exchange value. This involves not only an anticipation of the value of the content, but also the syntactical form of future entextualizations. Particular syntactical forms, and their distributional networks, are set up for maximum profitability; for example, the nightly news is structured to allow for "sound bites" only. Material configurations for the delivery of citational resources are thus always already taking shape for investors.

Today's investors must consider consumer demand for particular forms of commodified language, which will be used in the citational practices of subjects in everyday life. Producers and investors attempt to control the markets of the future by not only shaping the types of commodities produced, and controlling the distribution forms by which citational resources are delivered, but also by encouraging the construction of certain types of social identities. Corporations conduct market research in order to build "knowledge of the consumer" into the product, attempting to influence future citational practices.

Copyright and trademark laws attempt to secure value through the *authorized* citation of objects, images, and experiences. These laws seek to control the recitation of cultural commodities in the marketplace; in this sense, owners and investors seek to copyright "experiences." In the contemporary cultural economy, owners attempt to protect the dissemination of language—the travels of value and meaning—across contexts. Important legal questions today thus concern the control of the *movement of language*—such as the right to broadcast events, or the right to graft the words and images of celebrities into new contexts. Today, even "virtual properties" are bought and sold in the marketplace, and thus are protected as areas of investment. As new cultural forms emerge, investors busily anticipate the marketability of language in those formats; in other words, how to link the distribution of language to exchange value, and how to generate profit by calculating the future citation of cultural commodities.

Martin Jay, tracing the notion of "experience" in historical commentaries on U.S. culture, suggested that it may be "an exaggeration to claim that America has *always had* a culture fundamentally based on the valorization of experience" (2005, 268; italics added). It *now* seems, however, that the cultural economy is increasingly moving in precisely that direction—as cultural commodities are re-cited in order to intensify the "experience" of the words and images of others. If exchange value will be re-generated through the future experience of citational utterances, then the anticipation of—and the influencing of—those cultural trends will be highly profitable. Investing has become an exercise in the anticipation of the potential exchange value of language in future contexts, and marketing has become an attempt to deliver cultural commodities into those contexts.

The Performativity of the U.S. Economy

In his essay, *What Does It Mean to Say That Economics Is Performative?*, Michel Callon (2007) asks whether the economic formulas developed by economists simply *describe* existing economic conditions, or, in a performative sense, *influence* those conditions—given their actual use in investment decisions. For Callon, material worlds *emerge from* economic formulas; the formulas then come to actually describe this economic "reality" (320). Callon sees the field of economics as a kind of self-fulfilling prophecy, where "As discourse it can change into a system of beliefs that infiltrate agents' minds and colonize them . . . Everyone ends up aligning himself or herself to the model and everyone's expectations are fulfilled by everyone else's behaviors" (323).

In Mead's sense, these formulas become emergent significant symbols, in reference to which social actors align their economic behaviors. After becoming an environment of shared meaning, economic actors are able to anticipate the behaviors of others; or, as Callon puts it, the formulas become a "coordination tool that allows mutual expectations" (322). For Mead, meaning is precisely located in behavioral expectations, which can be anticipated.

Having said this, however, Callon is careful to point out that his formulation of economic performativity is not reducible to a mere self-fulfilling prophecy which involves only beliefs (322). Rather, the interactions conducted on the basis of the shared assumptions provided by the formula have real *material* consequences—which, in Butler's sense, both enable and constrain future interactions. For example, Callon discusses how an economic formula concerning the electricity market, after reaching acceptance within the field, might eventually lead to the installation of electricity meters (331)—as well as increase the profitability of a company which manufactures this material form.

While Callon is especially interested in "economic performativity" as a contribution toward the general perspective of Actor-Network Theory, the concern with "economic" performativity in this book has to do with the way that exchange value is continually regenerated through the re-citation of material forms, in the identity construction process. From this point of view, the cultural economy is "re-performed" as shared consumer demand for normative citational resources results in their continued production. As shared behavioral expectations re-emerge in the culture regarding normative social identities, the demand for particular citational resources is re-generated.

Subcultural "formulas" shape contemporary identity construction processes, and the effective presentation of self. Corporations also enact their strategic formulas in order to produce and market citational resources relative to consumer demand. All of these "formulas"—used by economists, by marketers, and by consumers—are performative of the economy. Just as, in Callon's sense, formulas regarding economic investments have particular material consequences—which both enable, and constrain, the behavior of actors—so do the marketing formulas according to which institutions produce and distribute citational resources, and the *subcultural formulas which guide consumer identity construction.*

In another work, Callon (1998a) has argued that a capitalist economy based on economic contracts favors a particular type of agency—that of "calculative agents" (4). For exchange to occur efficiently, calculative agents must agree on what factors should enter into the economic exchange, and what factors are considered to be irrelevant. In economic theory, Callon notes, the notion of "externality" refers to "out-of-frame" factors which social actors precisely "do not take into account in their calculations when entering into a market transaction" (16). For example, in the case of buying and selling a car, the presumed ownership of a title is clearly within the frame of calculation, whereas individual responsibility for global warming typically falls outside of the contractual frame. Thus, when a social actor decides to list a car for sale, they can usually expect that potential car buyers will discuss the transfer of title, rather than the issue of climate change.

Callon's discussion shows how a cultural economy based on exchange value necessitates an agency based on calculation—consistent with the Cartesian and capitalist subjectivity normative to U.S. culture. This process involves shared calculations, or shared anticipations of how the other will "frame" economic contracts, and what will be perceived as relevant to them. For Callon, this process involves not only, in Mead's terms, the ability to "role-take," but also involves a whole set of meaningful *materialities* in order to "perform" the economy.

In addition, *marketers* "re-perform" the economy as they syntactically frame the materiality of their advertisements and their branded products in particular ways. Callon argues that marketing "has contributed powerfully to the setting up and deployment of the framing devices of calculative agencies" (26). In other words, when potential car buyers are shown an advertisement, the syntactically-configured material form of the advertisement precisely does not encourage concern for global warming. Callon cites the work of Nicholas Thomas, who has argued that an important aspect of the exchange value of commodities is their "alienation" from prior context (19). In this example, it becomes apparent that the successful selling of a car involves "decontextualizing" the car from the "context" of fossil fuel consumption, and recontextualizing the car solely in terms more desirable attributes. The marketing frame defines "relevancy" within that frame.

Earlier, it was discussed how commodities valorize the context into which they are quoted, which simultaneously valorizes the "experience" for the (Cartesian) subject who confronts that material form. As cultural commodities are cited into new contexts, only certain aspects of their material form are taken as relevant to the new context, whereas other aspects are considered to be "external" or irrelevant. The valorization of context involves only the valued features. Marketers are quick to advertise only those aspects of the commodity which they expect will valorize the consumer's experience.

Recalling Goffman's argument in his article "Fun in Games" (1961), we can see that advertisers frame the materiality of their ads in such a way as to exaggerate the anticipated "fun" of their commodities—and exclude undesirable connotations. Normative marketing techniques enact a system of behavioral expectations into which consumers are socialized. As Callon's (1998a) work shows, it is through marketing that certain values of subcultures can be associated with "certain characteristics of products" (26–27). Once this association is promised in advertising, then consumers in everyday life can *meaningfully* re-cite the commodity as "representative" of those subcultural values. In short, as Callon puts it, "marketing tools perform the economy" (27).

Interestingly, Callon cites Goffman's work on frames, and recognizes how an exchange value frame limits social interactions. The interactants must frame a particular interaction as an economic one if it is to be performed properly; as mentioned, they must agree on what is relevant to, and what is external to, the economic contract (1998b, 250). Whereas actors may attempt to create a "closed interactional space" (251), where they can effectively role-take the economic actions of others, Callon notes that unexpected "overflows" beyond the boundaries of the frame often occur because "agents are simultaneously involved in other worlds from which they can never be wholly detached" (253). In other words, economic actors interacting on the basis of exchange value cannot entirely divorce themselves from *other social values* when involved in interactions. While capitalist subjects may attempt to make contracts within a "closed interactional space" which excludes unexpected and threatening surprises, even in the economic "game" some outside reality enters in. Even the most calculative of agents in economic transactions cannot prevent an "overflow" of alternative social values.

Of course, one of the greatest external dangers to calculable economic contracts is unknown future risks. Lee and LiPuma (2002) have argued that new finance instruments, such as the Black-Scholes equations used to price derivatives in options trading, are precisely used in order to control future risk—and even make money from the volatility which risk usually imposes. Lee and LiPuma argue that in the current situation of "post-Fordist finance capital" (203), the use of currency derivatives "can reduce risk by locking in a fixed exchange rate over a specific time period" (206). The action of controlling risk, through the use of derivatives and the purchasing of options, can be seen as a type of citational utterance by investors—which positions the investing subject relative to future market conditions.

This type of investment utterance is based on a certain type of *calculative anticipation*—that of generating capital through a favorable positioning of the subject in regard to the future. As Lee and LiPuma put it, "options allow investors to create profitable positions that rely only on the volatility of the underlying security; for example, by using options strategies such as straddles or strangles, one can make money whether the stock goes up, down, or nowhere in price" (204). As such, it is an attempt to close off the risk of the future. In Callon's sense of economic performativity, we can see that the formulas used to price derivatives can be considered as citational utterances of economists which, when further "cited" by investors, actively shape economic conditions.

If, hypothetically, the underlying security involved in these transactions was to involve a language-based cultural commodity—as is increasingly the case in the post-industrial economy—we can see that exchange value is being anticipated, and re-created, through the taking of an economic position relative to the *future materiality of language*. In such calculations, the future exchange value of language is stabilized, closed, and not subject to overflow. Here, "anticipation" becomes a calculative and strategic part of the process of controlling the future, for the purpose of maximizing profit.

Inasmuch as Callon's work on performativity is correct, competing algorithms not only *predict* the future worth of financial assets, but also performatively *shape* the material environment within which identity construction will occur. Investors and product designers "bet" on particular economic equations, thereby *enabling* a certain type of cultural economy to unfold. When today's trading practices are accelerated by computer programs, "futures" may be quickly decided as algorithms regarding various financial scenarios compete with, and react to, each other—a kind of "futures market" for language.

Investors thus attempt to control the future positioning of material signs, and the shaping of future material environments. Today, technology is used to construct global networks for the dissemination of language into the future, as both entertainment and information commodities. For example, global satellites are able to graft tomorrow's language-commodities into local contexts around the world. Horkheimer and Adorno (1972), in an early analysis of this phenomenon, discussed the importance of the political economy of distribution networks for the commodification of culture, noting, "The gigantic fact that the speech penetrates everywhere replaces its content . . . The symphony becomes a reward for listening to the radio" (159; 161). Today, investments are made into the mechanisms by which language will be marketed and moved into a variety of contexts, as citational resources for the construction of social identities and social relationships worldwide.

Shaping future citational environments, in an economy based on exchange value, also means the marketing of a particular *temporality*—that of "presence." The chronotope of presence severely limits the possibility of a future—in that a future predefined, and marketed as merely a time and place for the recurrence of "presence," is never really a future. In terms of *spatiality*, we see that places themselves are marketed as citational resources for the positioning of fashionable subjects. Thus "New York" or "Paris" become merely branded spaces where certain types of experiences are said to occur, and thus become spaces typified for, and advertised to, global tourists.

Investors thus seek to shape the meaningful material environments of the future—strategically placing images, social objects and the materiality of linguistic commodities in such a way as to maximize the presence of exchange value. The metaphysical assumptions supporting Cartesian subjectivity, favoring "presence," are thereby materially re-enacted. Given that the utterances of today's economic institutions shape the meaningful material environments of the future, we can see that the politics of the future necessarily involves the *material placement or grafting of language into future contexts*. In this type of situation, access to the means of positioning language becomes an important political and economic concern.

Markets and Measures

In his work in economic sociology, Luis Araujo (2007) largely agrees with Michel Callon that in economic exchanges, a "frame" is created which screens out particular real-life concerns. Callon shows that whereas social objects have their own unique biographies as they travel from one situated context to another, "at the moment an entity, product or service is made tradeable," there is "a stabilization of characteristics" (213)—such that the commodity can be priced and exchanged. In other words, many interesting aspects regarding the biographies of things, such as the situational contexts in which they were formerly embedded, come to be screened out of the frame as irrelevant to the economic transaction (213–14). In this sense, the citation of the exchange value of a particular entity involves the mobilization of a frame, which abstracts from the situated nature of everyday life. Inasmuch as *markets* provide this type of framing—which allows exchange to take place despite the many contingencies involved in the real-life biographies of both persons and objects—they can be viewed as contributing to the "performativity" of exchange value.

Araujo wants to mediate between two positions in the economic sociology literature regarding the nature of markets. While Callon, according to Araujo, correctly shows that markets—as structures or social institutions—enable the type of abstraction or "disentanglement" from the contingencies of everyday life as required by economic transactions, he is concerned that Callon's model abandons the "consumption identities" which consumers bring to those exchanges (213–14). Araujo notes that Daniel Miller is critical of Callon on this point, as Miller emphasizes that subjects are precisely motivated to participate in exchange given their lifestyles and "entanglements" in various social contexts (213–14). For Araujo, there is a "paradoxical nature of market exchange" which, on the one hand, "allows it to be framed as an instantaneous act, as Callon . . . argues." On the other hand, market exchange is "a recurrent activity that is deeply entangled in processes of production and consumption, as Miller . . . counterposes" (223).

While this book agrees with Araujo that market exchange simultaneously abstracts from—yet remains entangled with—the lifeworld of social actors, it does so from a slightly different perspective than that developed by Araujo. It is the position of this book that exchange value has become a hegemonic measure of the presence of all other subcultural values, and in this way remains "entangled" with those subcultural values—even while grafting a universalizing exchange value frame onto the material forms taken to represent those subcultural values. As discussed earlier, an important assumption enabling trade in the capitalist marketplace is that individuals and groups come to the market with *pre-existing* subcultural values, which differ from those of others. It is taken as "natural," given the unique Cartesian identities of individuals and groups, that they value differently, and are thus willing to make "unequal" exchanges (in terms of labor time) in the capitalist marketplace.

Social actors are able to make exchanges, despite the differences in their lifeworld entanglements, precisely because exchange value functions as a common measure of the *presence* of all other subcultural values. It is not so much that the market makes these other subcultural values entirely "irrelevant" to the interaction, but rather that exchange value allows their relevance to the particular lifeworlds of interactants to be temporarily suspended during the exchange process itself. These lifeworld concerns can be set aside precisely because of the fact that the economic measure "represents" the presence of *any* other subcultural value. Because of the universality of the measure, the particular subcultural value—whose presence the commodity is taken to "represent"—becomes irrelevant to the framing of the economic transaction. Thus all social actors, regardless of subcultural affiliations, can participate in the same marketplace.

In this sense, it is the *measure* of exchange value which enables economic transactions to occur across individuals and groups with varying subcultural affiliations. However, as discussed above, Callon's work shows that economic formulas designed to *measure* this exchange value do not merely *describe* the pre-existing worth of cultural entities, but also—influencing the decisions of investors—bring that economic value into being. The *measure itself becomes performative* of the exchange value it purports to objectively "report upon." The measure itself, as a material utterance of economists or accountants, has performative effects (see also Barad 2007).

This issue of the performativity of measurement, and the contemporary valuation of financial assets, has been taken up by Fabian Muniesa. Muniesa (2011) suggests that the work of John Dewey on valuation remains important today, in order to move past two dichotomous perceptions regarding the source of the value of entities. Rather than suggesting that value is either an inherent feature of objects, or merely a matter of belief, Dewey asserted that "valuation" should be considered as a social action (24). Muniesa sees this as important in the contemporary valuation of the worth of assets in corporations.

Muniesa suggests that financial valuation has a performative dimension, in that this act itself becomes the basis of further economic decisions (27-28). In corporate finance, estimates must be made about the likelihood of future earnings when investment decisions are considered. In other words, assets of companies are not only evaluated as to their present worth, but are acquired by other companies—or financed by banks—given an anticipation of their future value. In this sense, valuation measures drive investment decisions, and thus become "performative" of the economy which unfolds as a result of those decisions.

In their review of Muniesa's article, Lisa Adkins and Celia Lury (2011) state that Muniesa "not only compels us to think of value as an activity rather than a thing, but also shows how this activity is itself a source of (economic) value" (8). In other words, the process of measuring value is a behavioral practice which itself re-cites the exchange value "frame." As Muniesa puts it, "Valuation is about considering a reality while provoking it. It implies the virtual act of 'obtaining value', as is made clear in the very notion of capitalization" (32). Muniesa goes on to characterize the situation in the U.S. economy, following the financial crisis beginning in the late 2000's, as a "crisis in the representation of value" (33)—as valuation processes are "exposed" as "a form of performance" (33). For example, citing the research of Karen Ho, Muniesa particularly calls attention to the "performative staging of 'shareholder value'" (33) in investment banking decisions.

In their work, Liz Moor and Celia Lury (2011) discuss the contemporary valuation of brands, and how this valuation process enters into the strategic development of the brand—a performative dimension. In addition, relevant to the thesis of this book, they show how dimensions of the lifeworld of consumers are incorporated into the brand, and become monetized as part of its worth (443). In other words, the development and the valuation of the brand involves translating the subcultural values of consumers into financial assets for the corporation. This performativity of brand valuation has become important to global corporations, as the worth of their brands provide an increasing share of their total worth.

Moor and Lury argue that most firms use an "income-based approach" to evaluate brands, which is a measure estimating "likely future earnings that can be attributed to the brand" (442). Discussing the work of Eve Chiapello, Moor and Lury point out that the use of this accounting model "can be understood as an instance of the performativity of economics" (442). The model puts into practice the assumption that "value is forward-looking—value in potentia, one might say—and that, crudely put, a brand's value can only be understood through an estimation of its own potential (in the future) rather than through comparison with other brands (in the present)" (442). As the firm chooses between products to develop under the brand name, various calculations can reveal the most profitable course of action. Citing the work of Salinas and Ambler, Moor and Lury thus point out that the accounting measure, by helping to develop the brand, guides the firm into the future (443).

These corporate calculations regarding future earnings involve the lifestyle preferences of consumers, who "co-participate" in the process of brand development. Firms use market research measures to sort out which aspects of the social worlds of consumers will be incorporated into the brand, and ultimately sold back to them. Moor and Lury note that in the process of measuring brand equity, firms are particularly interested in how "consumer relationships" contribute to market value (450–1). It is thus through their *measure* that subcultural values today enter into the dynamics of brand development. The measure of the value of the brand is not only performative of the brand's future expansion (451), but in turn, we can see that such a measure also becomes indirectly performative relative to social identities—as consumers later re-cite these brands in the process of identity construction.

The Materiality of Institutional Utterances

Judith Butler's formulation of performativity has been criticized as a discursive-based "post-Marxism" which neglects the continuing importance of social class, the exploitation of labor, and the material aspects of social inequality—thus betraying Althusser's emphasis on the "material existence" (Althusser 1971, 166–67) of ideology. For example, Geoff Boucher (2008) has argued that discursive approaches to identity construction and identity politics—including that of Butler, LaClau and Mouffe, and Slavoj Žižek—amount to a new "idealism," unfortunately divorced from political economy. He argues that in the work of Ernesto Laclau, the focus on new social identity movements comes at the expense of class struggle (55). In regard to Butler, Boucher argues that she "neglects the all-important institutional context of the speech act" (157). In contrast, Boucher favors the structuralist Marxism of regulation theory as informed by Althusser, to which he appeals in order to "radicalise postmarxian discourse theories toward a postmodern Marxism" (4).

On the other hand, Boucher does approve of particular insights from what has been termed "poststructuralist Marxism." For example, he finds value in Laclau and Mouffe's work in that it sees "social relations as inherently dialogical"—citing its affinity with the work of the Bakhtin Circle (94). Boucher also argues that while in his view the discourse theory of Laclau and Mouffe is "indifferent to the constraints of social grammar and institutional syntax" (98), he suggests that when more appropriately conceived within regulation theory, their work on linguistic practices can be more closely linked to political economy (236).

In other words, Boucher is interested in how discourse is regulated "syntactically" by what Althusser calls an "ideological apparatus"—that is, a social institution. Boucher also agrees with the theoretical position that "discursive practice implies a limited agent, restricted by the materiality of social relations" (94). In doing so, he emphasizes the importance of the "problem of structuration," or the ways that social institutions, which limit social interactions and identity formations, themselves evolve (15). This position clearly shares some affinity to Butler's notion of "enabling constraint" (1997, 16)—which draws from Spivak (see Butler 1993, 122)—as well as Butler's work on how the persistence of institutions relies on re-citational practices.

These areas in particular—the syntax of institutional utterances, the limits which meaningful materiality places on individual utterances, and a focus on the re-citation or continual re-structuration of the social world—would seem to be areas of overlap between the positions of Butler and Boucher. This book argues that what is needed to bridge their positions is *what Bakhtin's approach provides*; namely, an insistence on the materiality of language and the syntax of utterances. This insight can be extended to include the "utterances" of those social institutions which simultaneously cite, yet syntactically control, the language of individuals. In short, what is needed is a theory of social performativity and citationality which can account for both institutional and individual utterances—while retaining the possibility of recontextualization and material social change.

Within those corporations which produce cultural commodities, employees receive differential wages and salaries based on the perceived worth of their citational practices relative to the profitability of the organization. For example, middle-level managers cite corporate policies and marketing strategies in their bureaucratic utterances; other employees like illustrators, writers, or website designers engage in different citational practices which actually construct the marketable cultural commodities. Employees speak or "cite" in accordance with what is required by their institutional position, as motivated by individual wage and institutional profit considerations.

Media conglomerates also sign or contract with "outside" artists whose music or books will receive mass distribution through the institution. In all, differential amounts are paid to differentially positioned associates of the corporation based on their perceived contributions to the profitability of that economic institution. For their part, the stockholders or private owners of the means of cultural production attempt to gauge the marketability of language, as they try to invest in those corporations whose "institutional utterances" are syntactically arranged in ways which will bring the most profit. Thus, corporations which produce cultural commodities in the contemporary United States economy re-enact social class differences, as they differentially reward the "citational labor" of owners and workers. As will be discussed below, firms have historically been slow to reward the appropriated labor of *consumers* who "co-create" value, expecially in online environments (see Cova and Dalli 2009).

We can see that preparation for employment or investment in such an economic environment involves *learning the exchange value of language*—how to *produce* marketable citational grafts, or how to *invest* efficiently in such an language-based economy. In this sense, workers and owners do not "speak for themselves"; rather, they are socialized to speak in the *voice of exchange value*. As Bourdieu (1984) describes in his notion of a "habitus," the knowledge of *how* to speak in the "voice of exchange value" is differentially distributed across social classes. Thus, both in the construction of fashionable social identity on the "consumption side," as well as in the preparation for occupational positions on the "production side," the meaningful materiality of a class-based habitus "matters." Subjects are socialized to take their position within the exchange value system.

By considering the *materiality of language* in terms of both individual and institutional utterances, this book attempts to ensure that the theory of citationality does not necessarily lead to an idealism which neglects social class. Whether or not theorists like Butler, Laclau and Mouffe, or Žižek are indeed guilty of developing a "discursive-based" approach which downplays the importance of political economy, Boucher's insistence on the continued relevance of class to contemporary identity formation is a point well-taken. Boucher's main argument concerns the continuing relevance of the unequal distribution of economic resources, and of class-based opportunities, for the analysis of contemporary identity formation. This book attempts to retain the importance of these economic factors within the theory of citationality, through an insistence that language-based citational utterances are *material*. In a Derridean sense, it is precisely the "materiality" of words and images which enable them to be recognizable and meaningful across situational contexts.

In his work, Althusser (1971) famously suggested that ideology has a "material existence" (166–67) as grounded in social practices—as opposed to being only a false *consciousness* (see also Boucher 2008, 89). At the same time, Althusser recognized that there are varying types of "materialities" (Althusser 1971, 166). Meaningful materiality takes many differing forms, as Barbara Bolt points out in her discussion of Bruno Latour's notions of "mobility" and "immutability" (Bolt 2004, 24). As indicated earlier, "materiality" can be considered as whatever can be given meaning through its repetition across situational context; in other words, that which has an iterable form which can be divorced from the intentionality of the author. This book, informed by the work of Butler and by the Derridean theory of citationality, has emphasized the materiality of all meaningful utterances—consistent with the work of the Bakhtin Circle.

Increasingly in the contemporary U.S. economy, language *is* the commodity. Language is marketed in material, syntactical formations by institutions—such as a media network producing a television show or a website. Access to the distributional system is unequal, and generally only the utterances of *institutions*—such as a news network—receive mass distribution. In this sense, institutional utterances become a normative, hegemonic constraint on social interaction and identity construction in contemporary U.S. culture. This is because corporations produce the material, citational resources used by individuals in everyday life—thus continually *re-shaping the materiality of the social world* in light of profit considerations.

The theory of performativity developed by Judith Butler, drawing upon Derrida's notion of citationality, benefits by being read with a strong emphasis on the materiality of utterances—an emphasis which the Bakhtin Circle provides. Whether or not Boucher is correct in his claim regarding "post-marxism's tendency to reduce politics and economics to ideological struggles" (16), he has stressed an important point regarding the future direction of poststructuralist theorizing. It is essential, as he claims, to recognize the continuing importance of political economy in shaping "subject-positions"

(58)—as Butler's work on gender also suggests. Citational utterances are always situated in a *particular social position*—and necessarily take an evaluative stance toward class-based material environments.

In Butler's sense, the meaningful materiality of the everyday social environment is an enabling constraint, largely shaped through institutional utterances which re-cite inequalities, which control alterity, and which commodify the words and images of others. Citational resources, produced and distributed by institutions, are used by individual subjects to *respond* to those utterances of institutions—albeit in new syntactical configurations. Individual utterances re-cite institutional utterances to a greater or lesser degree, and thus more or less reproduce normative identities and values. In this way, the citational practices of individuals either increase, or lessen, overall demand for particular cultural commodities, which in turn relates back to the profit of those investors and owners who enable the institutional utterances. The performativity of exchange value thus involves the re-citation of institutional utterances, in the material form of cultural commodities.

This discussion of the materiality of individual and institutional utterances draws attention to the very nature of materiality itself. Slater (2003) has challenged the traditional distinction in social theory between the "physicality" of objects and the supposed "immateriality" of signs (95). Rather, his emphasis is on the "processes of materialisation" by which entities are stabilized, or destabilized (96). Slater argues that materiality is stabilized through social networks, rather than through the properties of goods (101). Appealing to the "semiotic concept of *découpage*" (101; italics in the original), he suggests that "the idea of a stable object—like that of a stable signifier—involves making a cut or incision in the world, cutting out a set of relations and oppositions that are in reality continuous, and could be divided up quite differently" (101).

In fact, Slater sees the social construction of materiality as increasingly important in contemporary economic processes. He argues that advertisers and marketers plan for how an entity will be re-materialized or re-designed in the marketplace (101). Slater argues that firms themselves have begun to recognize the tentative nature of materialization, which enables them to configure entities in new ways in a changing economy (103). In this effort, "a firm attempts to materialise a given product in a given way by intervening in all the social processes through which things come to be given things," which Slater lists as "design, packaging, perceptions, consumer practices, media environments, [and] retail spaces" (107).

Slater points out that the marketing of experiences like events requires "purpose-built, materially bounded spaces" (110), and also requires certain types of materialization in order to be "transactable," such as the printing of tickets (110). Here we might also recall that for Derrida, "meaning"—and by extension, the meaning of "value"—must have a repeatability across situations. This "materiality" across situational contexts can be thought of as that which enables its economic transactability, apart from the intentionality of any particular subject. Thus, exchange value requires a certain amount, and certain kind, of materialization for transactability. A "transactable" materiality must recognizably frame interactions as (measurably) economic ones, and provide the interpretive context against which—in a performative sense—economic transactions will "work."

Slater cites the work of Callon and Gadry to note that the semiotic "cut"—enabling "a particular set of socio-technical effects"—is what renders the event or object "transactable" (110). Of course, it becomes transactable precisely in order to generate exchange value, as measured by various economic formulas and statistics. This suggests an interesting parallel to the work of Karen Barad (2007). As Barad has noted, experiments in quantum physics show that the measuring apparatus performs a particular "cut" in the material world, which results in particular ontological properties of phenomena (127-28). In other words, the measuring apparatus is itself performative of the value it measures—an insight which, as mentioned earlier, is becoming increasingly prevalent when it comes to the valuation of brands.

Barad has suggested that Judith Butler's formulation regarding performative citationality—while groundbreaking—does not go far enough in emphasizing the *materiality* of meaningful forms. In her book *Meeting the Universe Halfway* (2007), Barad argues that what is needed in a theory of performativity is not merely an appreciation of the process of "iterative citationality," but rather that of the "iterative intra-activity" of configurations of matter (208; see also Kirby 2011, 96). Barad's provocative work, drawing on insights from quantum physics, can help situate and expand the argument as developed in this book, especially regarding the status of "materiality" in a theory of the performativity of value.

For example, while Barad's work focuses on what she calls the "entanglements" of meaning and matter (2007, 33), this book focuses on what might be called the "entanglements" of *value and matter*, taking seriously the contention that language—especially as a cultural commodity—has a meaningful materiality that both limits and opens the possibilities for social agency. It should be noted, however, that the argument in the present book—which addresses patterns of human behavior mainly from the perspective of social psychology—admittedly does not directly engage an issue central for Barad and others working on "posthumanist" materialisms—namely, the very reproduction of the human/nonhuman distinction and the question of "nonhuman agency" (see Barad 2007; Kirby 2011; Latour 1993). Having said this, it might be interesting to re-consider how some of Barad's insights might be brought into further dialogue with the argument advanced in this book.

As mentioned, Barad notes that within the quantum physics of Neils Bohr, the particular *measuring apparatus* used in a scientific experiment performs a particular "cut" in materiality during the measurement process, thus creating a "phenomena" (140)—a *material configuration* which includes both the object measured, as well as the measuring apparatus itself. Importantly, Bohr and Barad argue that it is this cut which gives the material world its ontological status (127–28). Barad notes that experiments in quantum physics reveal that a Newtonian/Cartesian world emerges only when a particular measuring apparatus "cuts" the material world in a particular way (97). When materiality is measured differently, a different "reality" emerges. For example, quantum experiments on both light and matter have shown that their "determinate" properties, as wave or particle, depend upon the type of measuring apparatus used (19). Considering the implications of Bohr's work, Barad uses the term "agential separability" to refer to the determinate "entities" which emerge as part of the phenomenon, following the cut of the measuring apparatus—entities whose "ontological presence" is contingent upon the measurement process (174–75).

Expanding on some of the insights from Barad's interpretation of Bohr relative to the problematic of this book, we might say that the "measuring apparatus" in the United States is the system of economic formulas, stock values, retail pricing mechanisms, and so forth used to assess the "worth" of language-based commodities. The "exchange value" of the cultural commodity is what is measured. The exchange value measurement, while in fact *emergent from the measuring process itself*, is normatively interpreted as a "representation" of the extent to which other subcultural values are "present" in the measured material form—such as religiosity or "authentic" ethnic traditions. Social actors in everyday life go on to re-cite the measured exchange value through citational practices involving the commodity—as in the case of status symbols (see Veblen 1953; Bourdieu 1984). Material forms continually re-evoke exchange value, as they are continually re-cited as being able to deliver valued experiences. Measured exchange value is taken to indicate the quality of those "experiences."

Such a "phenomena" was not put into place once and for all at a particular point in Western history; rather, it is continually *re-enacted* through the everyday citational practices of social actors. When "exchange value" is "objectively" measured in the market—through such measures as stock values or retail prices—what is more precisely "measured" is *consumer behavior relative to meaningful materiality*. As consumers "cite" cultural commodities through trips to websites, or watching movies, the exchange value of those language-based commodities increases—as consumer demand shapes market worth. The "agential cut" of the economy enables everyday utterances to re-cite normative values and identities through the use of cultural commodities as citational resources—which also have an exchange value.

Importantly, from the performative point of view as developed by Barad—interpreting Bohr—these values do not exist as ontologically separate, determinate, pre-existing entities, but instead are contingent upon the "cut" performed, and re-performed, by the economic "measuring apparatus." In other words, the very notion that commodities "cross" pre-existing and determinate contexts, and "add value" to new contexts, only emerges from *within* a representationalist perspective. From a performative point of view, valuing "contexts" persist as normative only through the re-enactment of the agential cut of the economic apparatus itself.

Combining insights from both Butler and Barad's versions of performativity, then, we might say that the "exchange value" of linguistic utterances, which re-cite the words of others in particular syntactical formations, is part of the "phenomena" enabled by the capitalist cultural economy. Perhaps a strong emphasis on the *materiality* of linguistic-based commodities helps make Butler's theory of performativity, based on a process of "iterative" citationality, a bit more compatible with Barad's theory of performativity—based on what she calls the "iterative (re)materialization of the relations of production" (Barad 2007, 35).

As Butler has shown, such "cuts" in, or syntactical configurations of, materiality also enact "enabling constraints" regarding social identities such as gender. Turning to social psychology and considering Mead's notion of meaning—that meaning refers to normative patterns of behavior relative to the materiality of symbolic forms (see Joas 1997, 105)—we can see that agential cuts not only enable the interpellation of "values" or "identities" in a conceptual sense, but rather enable or restrict *particular types of behaviors*. In this sense, "value" refers to preferred behavior patterns (Graeber 2001, 49)—"normative" behavior at the group level, as well as anticipatable behaviors at the individual level (Mead 1969).

Agential cuts which differentiate value domains arrange them into a hierarchy, enabling some preferred behaviors while restricting others. In this sense, the economic apparatus *measures normative consumer behavior toward materiality* (i.e., their citational practices), and gives it a mark of exchange value which indicates these patterns. At the same time, the re-citation of this exchange value—as materialized—both restricts and enables future citational practices. In addition, as discussed above, *anticipated* consumer behavior guides actual production, and thus the availability of citational resources. In Richard Schechner's sense of "restored behavior" (1985, 35–36), consumers re-perform actions which focus groups have already rehearsed, which marketers have already advertised, and which accountants have already anticipated.

To think of the economic apparatus as measuring patterns of citational behaviors helps to counter the normative or ideological interpretation of what "exchange value" measures—that is, the "presence" of the value of cultural commodities. In actuality, the value *promised* in advertising is never quite *present* in commodities. Indeed, in a Derridean sense, meaning and value are never quite "present," as they are necessarily altered in repeated re-citations. Inasmuch as exchange value purports to measure the worth of the cultural commodity in delivering a particular experience, the measurement itself is never quite secure. In other words, the normative *meaning of the measurement* is itself never quite present—both in the sense that the pre-existing "value" it supposedly measures is not quite present, as well as in the sense that the re-citation of "exchange value" necessarily alters its meaning across contexts. We might even say that the measurement of "exchange value" does not indicate its *presence* in a meaningful material form, but rather the appeal of that materiality's *promise* of value.

We might thus consider that the cultural economy in the United States can be seen as a kind of "measuring apparatus," which measures and assigns an exchange value to language. The "exchange value" of any particular strip of language reflects patterns of consumer behavior relative to that meaningful materiality—in the sense that the number of viewers of a particular television show, or the number of hits on a website, affects the cost of advertising in that location and thus the "worth" of that cultural commodity. Barad's work helps to emphasize the importance of considering the materiality of language within a theory of performative citationality, as applied to the performativity of exchange value in the U.S. cultural economy.

The Unequal Distribution of Citational Resources

As Judith Butler has shown in her discussion of gender performativity, citational practices are issued from a social positionality which is largely assigned by others. Citational practices are not only limited in this political sense, but also, as we can see from the work of Veblen (1953) and Bourdieu (1984), in an economic sense. Citational resources are unequally distributed—limiting the expensive, fashionable citations of cultural commodities to the wealthier classes.

As Pierre Bourdieu has shown, access to those performative resources which have value in particular "linguistic markets" is restricted (1993, 79). For Bourdieu, upper classes shape and defend "a market for their own linguistic products" (80). This occurs especially through schools, which legitimize upper-class linguistic styles through academic credentials—which can in turn be marketed in the economy. As Bourdieu puts it in an example, "the people who are currently trying to defend their value as possessors of Latin are obliged to defend the existence of the market in Latin, which means, in particular, the reproduction, through the school system, of the consumers of Latin" (81).

In other words, the "values" of privileged subjects are defended in the linguistic market through the regulation of citational practices. Particular citational practices come to have a market value as "indexes" of skilled persons (see Silverstein 1976). A hierarchy of citational practices and valuations becomes institutionalized as a result of this "linguistic domination" (Bourdieu 1993, 82). Bourdieu has shown that in this way, communication styles or citational practices vary by social class, and are integral to the social reproduction of inequality.

Using Bourdieu's term, we can say that the meaningful identity of an upper-class "habitus" is constructed through the abjection of alternative values and identities. Those who learn to speak in the voice of exchange value are precisely not citing less-marketable cultural values. Access to desired social *identities* is secured through class-based temporal and spatial access to citational resources. This access to the means of cultural production (see Guillory 1993) occurs through social positionality relative to institutionalized syntactical practices, which re-generate exchange value as well as upper-class identities.

Butler has argued that re-citational or recontextualization practices have the potential to dislocate normative meanings and identities. On the one hand, it seems that the writings of Pierre Bourdieu and Jean Baudrillard on cultural capital and "sign value," respectively, underestimate this potential by sliding into a near-deterministic position regarding social reproduction (see Butler 1997, 147; Kellner 1991, 21; 28). For Butler, drawing from Derrida, the very fact that the "system" or "structure" must be re-produced or re-cited in order to be maintained opens the possibility for its alteration.

On the other hand, the political difficulty still persists that a *widespread* positioning of non-normative and potentially politically resistant material signs requires access to an institutionalized network of citational resource distribution. As seen from Bourdieu's work, *schools* often reproduce precisely those citational practices which reinforce the class standing of the wealthy; at the same time, the *mass media* distribution of language in the U.S. is almost entirely driven by profit considerations. In other words, the resistant citational practices described by Butler may occur only locally, with little impact on the overall linguistic market—that is, on the political economy of "cultural capitalism." In this sense, despite the possibility of resistance, the probability of economic reproduction continues.

In addition, Bourdieu (1984) argues that communication styles characteristic of a class-based habitus become largely "unconscious" or "automatic" to users, in that they are incorporated into the physical body as behavioral preferences. From this point of view, citational practices come to have market value precisely in that they are used as the basis of identity-construction within class-based subcultures, into which children are routinely socialized. In Bourdieu's sense, the citational resources available and "preferred" within each class—through consumer demand and normative citational practice—come to reproduce the hierarchy of valuations which systematically favor upper-class styles. Citational styles said to be "preferred" in lower-class subcultures have little educational or economic currency; for Bourdieu, this becomes the cultural basis for the social reproduction of inequality. Thus, we find that when working-class youth apply for office jobs they may "cite all the wrong things"—in other words, their cultural capital is limited in ways that fail to meet normative expectations for language use at that institutional site (see MacLeod 1995).

Linguistic Markets and the Appropriation of Subcultural Capital

For Pierre Bourdieu (1991), the French educational system reproduces the official "linguistic market," which is used to value the worth of utterances—as cultural capital (67). Bourdieu's work on France particularly focused on the nexus between education and the state; for Bourdieu, "It is in the process of state formation that the conditions are created for the constitution of a unified linguistic market, dominated by the official language" (45). While Bourdieu recognizes that non-official styles thrive in particular subcultures, he notes that the dominant market ultimately is linked with power. Because of this, during subcultural usage the dominant linguistic market is only "provisionally suspended" (71). When speakers return to more formal markets, their informal styles are "annihilated" (71).

In the contemporary U.S. cultural economy, social actors not only find that their utterances are evaluated in the formal education system, but also are more or less marketable within the mass media. Remembering the work of Daniel Bell (1976) concerning "cultural contradictions" within capitalism, we find that citational styles are valued differentially in the business world, in education, and in the social world of the mass media. In fact, as discussed above relative to the work of Goffman, a linguistic market can thrive where citational resources precisely derive their value as role-distancing resources. Utterances have differential worth in competing linguistic markets, and in a sense, play one market against another. Cultural commodities advertised within the popular media market may serve as resources which distance subjects from their roles in work and schools. Indeed, it is probably because social actors lack citational resources in one linguistic market that they may prefer to participate in another. In turn, those performers who excel at particular oppositional styles, relative to educational or occupational roles, may be financially rewarded when their words and images are appropriated into institutional utterances for the mass media market.

Just as in Bourdieu's France, it is true that in the United States more transgressive citational styles may be of little value in the employment or education "linguistic markets." In the U.S., however, it will be interesting to see in what ways the proliferation of language-based commodities in the mass media affects the linguistic markets of business or education. For example, many firms in the "culture industry" in the U.S. economy precisely market citational resources through the popular media market, drawing from popular culture. These businesses often seek to employ persons already immersed in—that is, who speak in the language of—contemporary subcultural styles. In regards to education, Guillory (1993) has pointed out that some subcultural groups, who have traditionally been excluded from the literary canon, have successfully won representation in the educational curriculum—even while sometimes voicing opposition to normative identities and values.

The increasing commodification of language in the U.S. may thus lead to the merging of historically separate "linguistic markets." In other words, while Bourdieu's work in France focuses on the state/education hegemony over subcultural styles, in the U.S. the cultural commodities distributed through the mass media may have the potential to challenge the more official or literary communications of business or education. However, social change—as a result of the media dissemination of cultural commodities—is often minimal. The economics of "reporting the speech" of the dominated mostly results in the continued commodification of oppositional language. As discussed above, the words and images "of the other" can be syntactically controlled within the utterances of institutions, and robbed of their political impact. Words and images produced by the dominated classes can be appropriated into the syntactical utterances of corporations, and marketed as commodities whose entextualized material form belies their oppositional intent. On the other hand, the appropriation of the words and images of others always has the *potential* to challenge normative identities and values.

We can find some global examples regarding how reporting the speech of others can lead to a reformulation of subcultural values and identities. In his work, Alastair Pennycook (2003) discusses some of the issues involved when English is used in performances by rap and hip-hop artists globally. This appropriation of English occurs as youth, in countries where English is not the native language, challenge normative identities—which Pennycook refers to as the "performative aspect of identity refashioning" (529). Citing Mitchell, Pennycook thus draws attention to how *global* citational resources can be used in practices which challenge *local* identities (525). Building on this literature, Park and Wee (2008) explore "how the language of the Other can be appropriated to serve as a resource for the formation of identities" (242–43). Consistent with the thesis of this book, the work of Park and Wee suggests that the words and images of the other can be recontextualized into a subject's own utterances in identity construction practices.

Drawing on Bourdieu's work, Park and Wee argue that the words and images generated from "autonomous," or localized, linguistic markets may be used as subversive resources to challenge the identities and values representing the more "unified," official linguistic markets of the government and educational institutions (247). However, this resistance seems to have currency only *within* the boundaries of the autonomous market; as Park and Wee put it, "the more autonomous a market, the greater the potential for resignification" (247). They go on to suggest that Butler's work on recontextualization—and the subversive potential of the performative—may best describe *autonomous* markets, while Bourdieu's work recognizes the more limited opportunities for resistance in *unified* markets. As they put it, "Recognizing the existence of multiple markets thus helps to resolve the different understandings of performativity that we find in Bourdieu and Butler" (247). The political question regarding Bourdieu's work on linguistic markets concerns the extent to which the "refashioning" of identity in smaller, subcultural markets can ultimately lead to a dislocation of normative values and identities in other linguistic markets. Regarding the cultural economy in the U.S., we might also consider how developments in the mass media might affect the hegemonic discourse of the more general exchange value system.

David Hesmondhalgh (2006) argues that Bourdieu mainly considers cultural production in terms of small-scale artistic production—a "field" which Bourdieu finds to be largely autonomous from that of political economy (214). Because of this, Hesmondhalgh argues that Bourdieu undertheorizes large-scale and commercial cultural production, and thus is unable to recognize how developments in the mass media might alter the field of political economy. In an analysis of Bourdieu, Judith Butler also inquires as to whether "the field itself might be altered by the *habitus*" (2000,117; italics in the original)—a question which Bourdieu's analysis seems to close off (117–118). For Butler, the field itself may be contested through unauthorized or transgressive re-citations (124–25). Both Butler and Hesmondhalgh are thus concerned that Bourdieu's formulation of the unified field of political economy makes it immune to alteration—for example, by interactions in other linguistic markets (see Butler 2000, 117–18). As this book has suggested, citational resources acquire exchange value not within an individual frame or field, but as they play against or valorize a differentiated field into which they are cited.

Butler goes on to point out that for Bourdieu the linguistic "market" (field) is taken as a "preexisting context," in which subjects are differentially "positioned" (119). For Butler, re-citational practices might alter the field or linguistic market itself, and thus "the way in which social positions are themselves constructed through a more tacit operation of performativity" (122). Whereas for Austin and Bourdieu, performatives "work" inasmuch as they are issued by authorized speakers in authorized situations, Butler argues that oppositional utterances may in fact lead to changes in the nature of authority itself. Butler thus asks "whether the improper use of the performative can succeed in producing the effect of authority where there is no recourse to a prior authorization; indeed, whether the misappropriation or expropriation of the performative might not be the very occasion for the exposure of prevailing forms of authority and the exclusions by which they proceed?" (123–24).

Utterances may be more or less oppositional, given the material configurations of the various linguistic markets into which they are inserted. It may be true, as Park and Wee suggest, that the extent to which unauthorized speakers can resist normative identities and values depends on the autonomy of the market, and becomes more difficult in unified markets (2008, 247). Indeed, Bourdieu has forcefully shown how unified markets can perpetuate inequality through the differential ranking of linguistic utterances. On the other hand, as Butler suggests, re-citational practices may lead to changes in authorizing institutions and "fields" themselves (Butler 2000, 124)—perhaps even in unified markets. In this sense, citational practices with currency in autonomous, subcultural markets may also have currency as role-distancing resources in more unified markets—and effectively challenge the hegemony of the "universal" exchange value frame. Perhaps one linguistic market may be successfully played off against another. Even today's commodities—as institutional utterances materially designed to generate exchange value—may enter into unknown, material configurations in the future with unexpected political effect.

THE CO-PERFORMATIVITY OF VALUE

Consumption and the Co-Creation of Exchange Value

In the introduction to her study of consumer culture, Celia Lury (1996) cites sociological work, including that of Lunt and Livingstone, as well as that of Anthony Giddens, which indicates the importance of consumer culture to individual identity formation. In addition, several empirical research studies in fields such as marketing, consumer research, sociology of the economy, and anthropology have also shown the importance of consumption in social identity construction. In this section, we will see how marketers try to turn the performativity of *subcultural values* into the performativity of *exchange value*. As consumers seek to incorporate particular meanings and values into their lives, through the citation of those cultural commodities taken to represent such meanings and values, marketers hurry to bring such citational resources to market.

Grant McCracken (1986), citing work by Marshall Sahlins, as well as by Douglas and Isherwood, notes that consumer goods are valued by consumers not only for their technical properties and instrumental use value, but also for their symbolic dimensions (71). In particular, McCracken notes that the differing materialities of commodities lead to differing attributions of identity categories (73). Citing Austin's work, as well as that of Stanley Tambiah,

McCracken sees consumer objects as "performative" of the cultural meanings that they signify (73).

In his survey of the empirical research on the relationship between material possessions and identity, Russell Belk (1988) concluded that "Evidence supporting the general premise that possessions contribute to sense of self is found in a broad array of investigations" (160). For Belk, one of the reasons possessions are valued by self is that they align one's identity with subcultures of family and friends. He notes that because we belong to several subcultural groups which we value to varying degree, the perceived value of the consumer objects we purchase also varies. For Belk, "the individual has a hierarchical arrangement of levels of self, because we exist not only as individuals, but also as collectivities. We often define family, group, subculture, nation, and human selves through various consumption objects" (152). Using Belk's term, commodities "extend" the self into meaningful materialities, as they align individual identity with subcultural group identity.

Marsha Richins (1994) has found a relationship between the meaning of a possession and its value (505), which is linked to the process of identity construction. Citing work by Rochberg-Halton and Mihaly Csikszentmihalyi, Richins discusses the importance of "repeated interaction" (i.e., re-citations) with the possession by subjects as a source of "private meaning" and value (506). Richins is particularly interested in the gap between the market worth of the object as commodity, and the personal attribution of value given by individuals after purchase. As she notes, for some people "economic value is not the most important form of value" (505), as in the case of possessions bearing sentimental memories. This finding by Richins could be interpreted as showing that while exchange value has not yet become completely hegomonic over other types of value, it does continually draw upon the memories and emotions of subcultural lifeworlds for its sustenance. The finding could also indicate the continuing importance of role distancing practices in a culture dominated by exchange value.

The research also underscores Derrida's point that while "exchange value" has to be abstractable and stable across situations in order to remain meaningful, it also is altered and negotiated within individual contexts. Richins suggests that it may be precisely because of identification with intermediary subcultures that individual, private attributions of value and meaning come to differ significantly with their "public" meanings. She notes that "For individuals with strong reference group identification, acquisition and use behaviors and the private meanings of goods may be influenced more by the shared meanings of reference group members than by the meanings held by society at large" (518).

These individual and subcultural meanings—and values—are increasingly being incorporated by businesses into the design and advertising of commodities. Citing their earlier work, Prahalad and Ramaswamy (2004) have introduced the term "co-creation of value" into the marketing literature, to indicate the contemporary trend whereby "The meaning of value and the process of value creation are rapidly shifting from a product- and firm-centric view to personalized consumer experiences . . . active consumers are increasingly co-creating value with the firm" (5). Whereas in the past, value creation was considered the sole purview of the producer, today's consumers have "their own views of how value should be created for them" (6). Prahalad and Ramaswamy thus suggest that marketers should become more sensitive to the subcultural values of social actors, in order to co-create products in tune with consumer life experiences.

Using the example of video games, Prahalad and Ramaswamy show that the co-creation of value involves the production of environments in which consumer experiences will occur (10). While the firm provides the "space" in which the experiences will unfold, the end-user actively creates the "experiences" (11). Thus, as Prahalad and Ramaswamy indicate, today firms consult with consumers in the design of "value co-creation space" (11). Considering this research by Prahalad and Ramaswamy on the co-creation of value, we might say that the appropriation of subcultural meanings and values by marketers results in the performativity of exchange value.

So far, we have seen that empirical research indicates the importance of consumption to the construction of identity. It also shows that individual identity is aligned with that of the group, via valued materialities. Marketers have increasingly recognized how their products become integrated into consumer lifestyles, and have begun to involve consumers in the production and design of goods and services. However, in his work, Douglas Holt (1997) has questioned some of the assumptions and limitations of these trends in both business and in marketing research. In particular, he attempts to make a "poststructuralist turn" in marketing research, and critiques some of the representationalist assumptions of prior research in the field.

When it comes to consumer "lifestyle," Holt wants to adopt an approach which neither assumes that "lifestyles are behavioral expressions of personality traits," nor that "lifestyles are structured by quantititative differences in universal values across groups" (327). In addition, he argues that meaning is neither an inherent or essential feature of objects (328), nor equally accessible in the same way to all members of a particular social group (328; 333). Holt's approach is to focus on the ways in which consumers differ in how they incorporate commodities into their own lifestyles. For this reason, Holt suggests that even if consumers purchase the same good, they may not do so for the same reasons, nor give the object the same meaning.

Marketing research will therefore be misleading, Holt argues, if it assumes that consumption patterns reveal pre-existing sets of values or meanings in objects, or that an object has a singular meaning which represents the values of a collectivity (326). Rather, consistent with the approach of this book, Holt suggests that "Since consumption objects are polysemic, they are more aptly considered resources that facilitate and constrain consumers' meaning construction rather than fully realized meanings that consumers acquire" (344). Holt argues that a poststructuralist approach—which he applies in his study to interview analysis—overcomes this flaw, and argues instead for the grounding of meaning in consumer practices. Recognizing that individuals belong to several groups simultaneously, he concludes that consumption practices must also be hybrid and "conflicted" (341).

In certain ways, Holt's poststructuralist argument aligns with the approach of this book, and its focus on citational practice. For example, in his study he notes that for some working-class informants, employment at the local university was a source of pride (337). In other words, their everyday citational practices involving the university became important in the construction of their social identity, aligning them with a subcultural group perceived to be prestigious. Holt's research leads him to conclude that it is through "consumption practices" that identity differences, or "symbolic boundaries," between groups are maintained (343). In the language of citationality, the citation of cultural commodities leads to the re-interpellation of subcultural group identities, in reference to which individual identity is aligned. Some subcultural affiliations are embraced, while subjects distance themselves from others. Holt, then, locates consumer values not in pre-existing "lifestyle" groupings, but rather in imagined group affiliations which are re-cited through consumption practices.

Holt points out that consumer practices can "transform" collectivities (344), an argument which is consistent with Butler's notion of how citational practices can dislocate normative identities. He also notes the instability of the meaning of "cultural objects," which he attributes to their simultaneous membership in more than one "semiotic system"—resulting in a multiplicity of semiotic associations for any particular social form (329). Again translating Holt into the language of citationality, this suggests that the meaning and value of any social object depends on its positioning within the unique assembly of citational resources which shape the overall material environments of consumers—as one interpellated value context is played off against others. As Holt puts it, the "meanings of a particular cultural object for a particular individual in a particular context are produced typically through negotiation between or syncretic combination of available discourses" (329). While Holt does not follow these poststructuralist moves with an extended Derridean critique of the presence of value (see 328; n2)—nor use the word "performative"—his work is helpful as a description of the functioning of current economy, as well as an effective critique of representationalism in the marketing literature.

We have thus seen in this section that one central thesis of this book—that consumers cite cultural commodities in order to construct their social identities—seems supported by empirical evidence across several literatures. Researchers have taken up the notion of performativity, and many marketing researchers are shifting away from the representationalist model which has historically prevailed in that field. Even though some of the empirical research today still uses the language of representationalism, while some adopts the language of performativity, we can generally conclude that there is much evidence for a central thesis of this book—that social actors use commodities in the construction of their social identities, as well as to align individual identity with that of social groups.

As might be expected, given that much of the literature presented in this section has been drawn from business and marketing, rather than critical social theory, it does not generally develop a critique of the model of the "presence of value"—even if it does increasingly adopt the language of performativity theory. Given this limitation, the literature implicitly re-cites some of the same assumptions shared by social actors in the cultural economy regarding the "presence of value"—and in this way itself re-cites the system of exchange value. Having said this, the marketing and business literature is helpful in providing a description, if not a critique, of the way in which the performativity of exchange value occurs in the contemporary U.S. economy. Translating these studies into the language of citationality, it can be argued that both subcultural values, and exchange value, are re-performed through the citing of the words, images, and objects "of the other." In the next section, we will continue looking at the empirical literature related to the performativity of exchange value, through the specific mediation of brands.

Brands and the Performativity of Value

In the formation of their social identities through the citation of cultural commodities, social actors do not so much cite particular commodities, as cite the social meanings indicated by those commodities. Brands have become important carriers of cultural meanings, and are carefully managed by firms across the entire range of their products. This section presents a literature review of some selected empirical and theoretical literature in consumer research, marketing, anthropology, and sociology regarding brands to provide interdisciplinary research in support of a central thesis of this book—that the performativity of exchange value in the contemporary U.S. cultural economy occurs as social actors re-cite cultural commodities. Branded commodities are cited in the identity construction process, as subjects align their individual identities with those of subcultures and their affiliated values. As the research indicates, brands have become central to the continual re-production of the cultural economy.

In her consumer research, Susan Fournier has studied how consumers develop "relationships" with particular brands (1998, 368). Fournier's research indicates that consumers not only develop relationships with products for their technical use-values (351), but also for their lifestyle or symbolic features; as she puts it, "the meanings they add into their lives" (361). Fournier argues that within the field of marketing there has been an increasing recognition of the "relationships" that consumers develop toward particular brands (343–44). For Fournier, this relationship is not merely between the consumer and an inanimate, branded product, but rather between the consumer and the entire network of people involved in marketing the good. Social actors in this production network make decisions and engage in actions "enacted on behalf of the brand" (345). Fournier sees the relationship between this network of actors and the consumer as important for consumer identity.

Fournier's research shows that brands indicate "cultural categories" (367), and are used by consumers to align their individual identities with subcultural identities and values. Other studies have suggested the same. Citing the work of Holt, as well as that of Elliott and Wattanasuwan, Borgerson's (2005) review of the consumer research literature indicates that field's concern with how brands are used as resources in identity construction (439). Another thread in the field of consumer research, focusing on what has been called a "brand community," suggests that social identity is accomplished through active participation with others in the consumption of a particular brand.

For Muniz, Jr. and O'Guinn (2001), the nature of "community" has changed, especially with the proliferation of the mass media in Western cultures. Instead of being formed in shared geographical space, they argue—citing Anderson and others—that today community has become more of an "imagined community" (413; 419; 426). This includes what they call "brand communities." Muniz, Jr. and O'Guinn point out that brand communities differ from what others—noting Schouten and McAlexander's research on Harley-Davidson riders—have called a "subculture of consumption." Muniz, Jr. and O'Guinn suggest that brand communities differ in that they are not marginalized socially, are always defined relative to a commercialized product, and typically embrace the ideology of commercialization (414–5).

Muniz, Jr. and O'Guinn see the development of brand communities in a positive way, in that they enable consumers to remain "connected to other consumers through the benefit of community" (427). They suggest that marketers attempt to develop brand communities as part of "relationship marketing," and point out that the formation of such communities increases the economic value of the brand (427). In this research, we again find that consumers "cite" brands as they construct identities relative to subcultural groups—even if the boundaries and identities of subcultural groupings are shifting in postmodern culture.

Schau and Muniz, Jr. (2002) extend the concept of brand communities to the Internet, and particularly focus on the ways that brand communities are incorporated into self-presentation strategies in cyberspace. They find that individuals differ in the extent to which they immerse themselves in various brand communities online. Consumers use the brand differently in various self-presentation strategies, leading to variations in how individual online identity aligns with that of the larger brand community.

Celia Lury (2004) has shown the increasing importance of brands in the contemporary economies of the United Kingdom and the United States. Her work demonstrates that just as the production and design of *individual products* increasingly incorporate consumer information and input, so does the development of *brands*. Lury notes that the brand becomes an "interface" (7), which allows for the "exchange of information between 'producers' and 'consumers'" (74).

Citing the work of Callon and Cochoy, Lury finds marketing to be a "performative discipline" (17), in that it actively shapes markets through the appropriation of subcultural values and practices into brand design (18). Marketers work to anticipate the future practices of consumers, and incorporate these projections into the development of the brand (39). In this way, marketers appropriate emerging subcultural trends into the brand. In turn, brands shape future economic transactions as they are marketed back to consumers—a process which Lury refers to as the "performativity of the interface of the brand" (51).

Like Lury, Adam Arvidsson (2006) argues that brands generate value for firms through the appropriation of subcultural values, including—citing Hebdige—the resistant "styles" of oppositional groups (68–69). As he notes, "Brands . . . rely on the productivity of consumers not only for the realization, but for the actual co-production of the values that they promise" (35). Consumer behavior within social groups is both anticipated, and shaped, in ways that will generate value for the firm. He notes that brand managers are in the business of "controlling, pre-structuring and monitoring what people do with brands, so that what these practices do adds to its value" (82).

Arvidsson cites the consumer research literature which indicates the importance of brands for contemporary identity construction (5). Consistent with a central thesis of this book, he argues that "brands are primarily to be understood as resources for the construction of a self and its social moorings" (82). For Arvidsson, one of the ways in which this is accomplished today is that brands provide an environment within which consumers co-create value, as they co-create social identities within branded contexts. Arvidsson notes that in contemporary Western cultures, traditional subcultural boundaries may be changing, and that brands now provide a reference for individual identity formation. As he puts it, "Like older forms of community, sustained by tradition, class or local culture, brands provide a context . . . that enables a person to become a subject" (83; see also 132; 76). Brands thus become performative of economic value, as they function to align individual identity with a branded "identity context." Citing Lury, and Lury and Shields, he argues that brands become a "context for life" (13), or a "predetermined frame of action" (8).

The work of Arvidsson and others suggest that branded "commodities" today are best thought of as environments or spaces within which consumers generate value, rather than as individualized citational resources. As Arvidsson puts it, "Content thus becomes environmental, rather than representational" (96). In other words, while firms do still generate cultural commodities which are cited by consumers, they also increasing design the branded spaces within which citationality occurs—especially on the Internet (96). Also, as mentioned, Arvidsson suggests that these spaces become a kind of identity context themselves, replacing subcultures as the reference against which individual identity is aligned.

For Cova and Dalli (2009), the "co-creation" of value on the Internet, to date, has not been an equal partnership, in that consumers have rarely been compensated for their participation in the process (316; 335n2). In addition, citing the work of Franke and Piller, Cova and Dalli point out that "the more consumers are involved in co-production and design, the more they are willing to pay for the products" (327). Citing their earlier research, Cova and Dalli thus speak of the "'double exploitation of working consumers'" (as cited in Cova and Dalli 2009, 327). They are thus opposed to those versions of "co-creation" theory which portray "an idyllic marketscape with consumers and producers living in harmony" (334), and instead focus on how consumer subcultural practices—increasingly online—become translated into market value for companies.

Extending this argument more specifically to brands, Hugh Willmott (2010) provides examples which suggest that the largely unpaid contributions of consumers toward the development of global brands have become "an increasingly significant source of privately appropriated wealth" (522). Willmott notes that in "internet-based businesses" in the contemporary economy, organizations especially rely on "feedback on goods and sellers that contributes to the appeal, and thus to the brand equity, of those companies" (525). In those cases where consumers upload words and images to websites, they contribute to the value of those sites—but are often not financially rewarded by firms for their labor (518).

For Willmott, consumer contributions build "brand equity," which firms then "monetize" (519) into "brand value" (527). Willmott points out that the "intangible" assets of firms, like brands, "now far outstrip traditional accounting assets as a percentage of market value" (529). While such firms are certainly instrumental in developing the spaces or environments within which the consumer contributes, they heavily rely on the contributions of end users to develop those spaces in innovative ways. As Willmott notes, both "brand communities," and "brand managers," are together involved in building brand equity, which is then monetized by the firm and returned to shareholders (521). For Willmott, it is the process of "brandization" which enables the appropriated labor of consumers to be "converted into privately appropriated wealth" (534). Again we find, in the language of citationality, that today's firms not only provide the citational resources which consumers use in identity construction, but also provide the branded spaces within which that citationality occurs.

In an interesting development regarding digital gaming, Herman, Coombe, and Kaye (2006) discuss how one company allowed players in an online multi-player game to acquire intellectual property rights for their co-creation activities in the game (184–85). They suggest that this allowance by the company, regarding the "*performativity* of intellectual property" (186; italics in the original) was meant to generate "goodwill" toward the brand. The company hoped that this goodwill would translate into "customer loyalty," and thus continued use of the branded environment by players (186). In other words, the goodwill generated by such a strategy "enables corporations to claim as economic value consumers' affective relation to the corporation" (186)—a kind of performativity of exchange value via an emotional affiliation with the brand. Thus, while the producer of the digital product no longer appropriated consumer labor directly, they hoped for the "performativity of exchange value" more indirectly—through the mediation of "goodwill." In doing so, firms clearly hope to avoid negative perceptions from participants who "consider their activities within the virtual space of the game as creative work, not simply leisurely play" (188).

In the anthropology literature, Constantine V. Nakassis (2012) also explores the relationships between consumers and brands, incorporating the language of citationality into his approach. Nakassis recognizes the importance of the brand for the performativity of market value, and the ways in which this process is tied to identity construction. He notes that since the 1960s, businesses have recognized that the "value" of the commodity is increasingly located in the brand, rather than in the labor involved in its production (629). Citing the work of Robert Foster, of Adam Arvidsson, and of Terry Hanby, Nakassis points out that consumers develop relationships with brands, and use brands in the construction of the self.

Nakassis develops the concept of "brand citationality" (627), where to cite a *particular* branded commodity, or "brand token," is to evoke the *general* aesthetic or meaning which marketing practices have associated with the brand—its "brand type" (628). For Nakassis, it is this re-citational practice which "is central to the brand's coherence and intelligibility, and to its ability to generate surplus meaning and value" (629). Consistent with the argument in this book, Nakassis points out that the brand's performativity relies on its citation by consumers. As he notes, "The brand is citational, and this makes it able to be performative" (625). Nakassis's contribution thus reveals how the citation of brands by consumers is performative of markets, and thus of market value.

Discussing the work of Michel Callon, and Celia Lury, on "market performativity," he agrees that today's firms interact with consumers to co-create value, and suggests that the brand has become integral to this communication process. Nakassis cites Lury's research on the brand as an "interface" between consumer and firm, noting that for Lury the "brand is performative in the sense that it structures consumer-producer relationships and thus the market through its 'interface'" (634). Referring to these "feedback loops" between consumers and firms, as mediated through brands, Nakassis speaks of the "citational performativity" of brands (634). The meanings entextualized into brands, themselves drawn from the lifeworlds of consumers, are reincorporated back into the lives of consumers and given new meanings and values (629). As consumers thus recontextualize the meaning and value of the brands in new ways, firms try to research and reincorporate these emergent developments into the brand itself.

Considering the research and theory described in this section, we can clearly see the reciprocal relationship between individual utterances, and institutional utterances, as they relate to brands. Firms "re-cite" the subcultural values of consumers, and consumers "re-cite" the brands which are taken to represent those values—in an ongoing dialogue within a linguistic market. The purchase of branded citational resources by consumers, used in the process of identity construction within particular *localized* linguistic markets, re-cites the larger cultural economy based on the *universal* measure of the exchange value of language.

The Performativity of Value in Contemporary Tourism

Several contemporary theorists in the sociology of tourism—some working in the United Kingdom and others in the United States—have together developed a critique of the notion that tourists are simply the passive receivers of an inauthentic culture marketed by the tourist industry—as delivered within highly regulated and self-enclosed spaces. This literature instead emphasizes that tourists are active participants in the phenomenon of tourism, and help shape the sites and spaces in which tourism occurs. If indeed the paradigm of tourism bears some affinity to everyday life in late capitalism, as discussed above, the implications of such notions regarding the "performativity of value" in tourism are worth considering.

We have seen that in the contemporary literature on marketing there is an increased recognition that consumers are co-creators of value. Similarly, tourism researchers are starting to move away from the notion that tourists "gaze" (see Urry 1990) at pre-packaged sites, toward the idea that tourists participate in the co-production of the value of their tourist experience. For example, David Crouch (2002) has argued, citing Selwyn, that the discipline needs to move beyond a paradigm which has historically "prioritised vision as detached," thus "over-emphasising the object of the gaze and the decentralised observer" (207). Similarly, in their edited collection, Simon Coleman and Mike Crang (2002) found that contributions went "beyond the visual to performance" (11). In research regarding family photography at tourist sites, Jonas Larsen (2005) notes that "Tourist places are produced places, and tourists are coproducers of such places" (422).

Larsen's research in northern Europe, which presumably holds for the United States as well, reveals that not only is contemporary tourism itself performed, but also individual and group *identity* is performed at tourism sites. Larsen's article *Performativity of Tourist Photography* argues that family photos taken at the ruins of a medieval castle are quite carefully staged to idealize family relations in the photograph (2005, 424; 430). Individual identities are thus aligned with the "happy" family, as represented by the photo. As Larsen notes, "Places are not only or even primarily visited for their immanent attributes but are also, and more centrally, woven into the webs of stories and narratives people produce when they sustain and construct their social identities" (425–26). Larsen points out that for some, the tourist site can become "a backdrop for family staging" (429).

We thus increasingly see the language of performativity being incorporated into the tourism literature, to describe the active practices through which tourism itself is constructed—as well as the social identities of tourists. Part of the reaction against the passive "gaze" of visitors toward a site has been to instead emphasize that performativity is an *embodied* experience, involving more than just visuality (Coleman and Crang 2002, 10). For example, in developing their concept of "performative authenticity," Britta Timm Knudsen and Anne Marit Waade (2010) discuss how "the gaze, the place and the imagined audience play an important role, but the concept of performativity covers more than visual signs, gaze and imaginations. Performativity also includes a tactile body, movements, actions and emotions" (12).

As an embodied experience, Knudsen and Waade go on to suggest that "authenticity" is performative; that is, it is neither a condition of a cultural object, nor of the gazing subject (10–11), but rather "something which people can *do* and a feeling which is *experienced*" (1; italics in the original). They use the term "performative authenticity" to refer to the ways that tourists, in the "new affective economy" of Sweden (5), are "re-investing in authenticity as a way of intensifying experience, while the local tourist managers and authorities are re-investing in authenticity to brand their city or region" (5). For Knudsen and Waade, authenticity in tourism now involves the intensification of bodily experience, as "a feeling you can experience in relation to place" (5).

This version of "performative authenticity," as an embodied and emotional tourist experience, might be effectively contrasted with another discourse regarding authenticity in the sociology of tourism—the loss of cultural authenticity in staged tourist venues. This discourse was historically influenced by Dean MacCannell's (1976) classic book *The Tourist* (Coleman and Crang 2002, 4; see also Chaney 2002). In that book, MacCannell characterized the modern tourist as searching for an authentic alternative to the "staged authenticity" (MacCannell, quoted in Urry 1990, 9) of the experiences marketed by the tourism industry (Urry 1990, 9–10; Larsen 2005, 419).

In his work, Crang (2006) takes a different approach regarding the relationship between tourism and the authenticity of tourist experience. He points out that the debate surrounding this issue actually rests on an often-unquestioned assumption; namely, that place itself is stationary, stable, and thus representative of the local cultures to a greater or lesser extent (48–49; see also Coleman and Crang 2002, 4–5). Quoting Celia Lury, Crang links this issue regarding the authenticity of place to "a presumption of not only a unity of place and culture, but also of the immobility of both in relation to a fixed cartographically coordinated space" (Lury, quoted in Crang 2006, 54). From this point of view, tourists are seen as disrupting the "authenticity" of the local space and culture (Crang 2006, 54–55).

In contrast, Coleman and Crang (2002) advocate for "a sense of performativity of place rather than just performance in place" (10), noting that places are "fluid and created through performance" (1). In this sense, the "performativity of place" refers to the idea that the spaces of tourism should not be thought of as stable and self-enclosed sites whose tourist value pre-exists visitors, but rather as spaces brought into being with behavioral practices. In a similar way, David Crouch (2002) has noted that tourist space should not be considered as "inert," but rather a result of an "embodied practice" (208) on the part of the tourist.

Coleman and Crang (2002) also note that the traditional tourism model—that of tourists traveling from one autonomous, local space to another—itself is dependent on "a buried notion of self-presence" (10). This comment by Coleman and Crang raises an important issue regarding the recent body of work on the "performativity" of tourism, as well as on the performativity of authenticity and place. On the one hand, this recent literature rightly shows the limits of past theories and research regarding the "visual gaze" of tourists, and regarding tourist spaces as self-enclosed and fixed spaces. As we see, some in the field have been moving toward the notion of an embodied performativity, through which tourists actively construct tourist spaces, and actively bring about their own physiological experiences. On the other hand, an oft-unquestioned assumption—regarding the "presence of value" in the tourism experience—is reproduced in the literature, which thereby re-cites the ideology at the heart of the contemporary cultural economy. This issue can also be framed as the difference between two differing notions of performativity, as discussed earlier.

One notion of performativity in tourism studies assumes that the "co-creation" of tourist experience, by the embodied performer, actually involves the *presence* of valued experiences. This notion of performativity follows Austin's sense of the performative utterance—which actually brings about a social reality rather than simply describing one. In this version of performativity, tourist sites—including virtual ones—actually *deliver* valued experiences as visitors co-create valued spaces.

The second notion of performativity, which draws upon the citational aspects of performativity as developed by Derrida and Butler, would argue instead that the meaning and value of tourist experiences are never quite present. Inasmuch as researchers in this field adopt the first version of "embodied performativity"—that the tourist actively participates in *making value present*—they are subject to this Derridean critique. From the point of view of a performativity theory which draws upon Butler or Derrida, the active engagement of tourists re-enacts the *promise* of value, as opposed to the co-creation of an experience whose value becomes "present."

Regarding the issue of embodied "experience," it may be worthwhile to recall Howard Becker's work (1963) regarding the interpretation of the physiological changes induced in the body during a drug experience. Becker, from a symbolic interactionist perspective, showed that purportedly "individual" physiological sensations were actually subject to social—and thus shared—interpretations. In a similar way, tourism-related interpretations of intensified bodily experiences—if they are to be anticipated or communicated socially—must be repeatable. As marketable and meaningful experiences, those tourist events which are designed to engage the body and induce physiological changes must also be *measurably* valuable. In this sense, the valorization of "embodied" or "authentic" experience, as a tourist phenomenon occurring in meaningful material environments, must be socially organized—into shared cultural categories through which individual physiological experiences are interpreted. However, as Derrida has shown, the meaning and value of such experiences are not "present" across iterations—given the singularity of each re-enactment.

In his version of the performativity of tourist spaces, Tim Edensor (2000; 2001)—like Judith Butler—emphasizes that tourist performances are re-enactments of prior performances. As reiterations which necessarily differ across situational contexts, a possibility is opened for resistance on the part of tourists to the normative identities and normative values associated with the typical tourism experience. On the one hand, Edensor argues, it is true that the tourist industry materially organizes the space in an attempt to regulate, and standardize, each performance given by visitors (2000, 326; see also 2001, 71). Citing the work of Judith Adler, Edensor notes how each tourist is guided in advance to repeat normative performances, through the use of "programmes, brochures, accounts and guidebooks" (2001, 71). On the other hand, despite the efforts of the tourist industry, each performance necessarily differs as a situated and singular act; as Edensor puts it, "performance is an interactive and contingent process" (72). Because of this, there is the potential for a tourist performance to disrupt the regulatory expectations of the tourist managers (75–77).

Because the production of tourism necessarily relies on the repeated behaviors of active participants, there is always a possibility for disruptive practice. Like that of Butler, Edensor's version of performativity theory suggests that the very nature of tourism—the repetition of visits to particular "sites/cites"—involves potentially disruptive elements. Regarding the repetition of normative tourist spaces and experiences, Edensor notes that "this (re)production is never assured, for despite the prevalence of codes and norms, tourist conventions can be destabilized by rebellious performances" (60). In fact, Edensor challenges a binary logic which would characterize iterations are either normative or disruptive (78), noting instead that the variety of performances available to tourists can be "ambivalent and contradictory" (78).

Edensor points out that it is often the case that the prescriptions of the tourism industry are followed "unreflexively" (62). When challenged, however, not only are normative tourist practices and experiences potentially disrupted, but so are the social identities normatively associated with tourism. As Edensor recognizes, "tourist performance maps out individual and group identities" (71). Given that these identity categories are in fact re-cited through tourist practices, there is the possibility that resistant or subversive practices can dislocate them.

Edensor thus argues that despite the best efforts of the tourist industry, with several powerful media technologies at their disposal, there is always the "potential for innovative performance" (79). Edensor (2000) has also shown that performances given at a tourist site can vary on a number of differing factors, including the nature of the tourist space, the amount of regulation imposed by the management of the tourist site, and the varying abilities of tourists to give normative or unexpected performances (325-27). Given this variation in "performative processes," he argues that the "symbolic values of sites" are always in the process of being "ceaselessly reconstitute[d]" (326). These insights regarding tourism have a general affinity with a thesis of this book—that re-citational, performative practices on the part of consumers have the potential to dislocate normative values and identities.

In addition to Edensor, other theorists have emphasized the potential of tourist practices to disrupt the normative meanings and identities within the industry. Cohen and Cohen (2012), for example, in their review of recent tourism research, reach a similar conclusion regarding the potential of the performative to dislocate norms and values. As they put it, citing the work of Obrador, Pons, and Carter, "performatives do not only (re)produce social entities, they can also critically counter hegemonically imposed public sites or attractions, especially through acts of resistance" (2184). Citing Minca's research, Claudio Minca and Tim Oakes (2006) also note that "while the performativity of tourist 'places' seeks to make them unreflexive stages where subject-object binaries are maintained and where particular experiences are regularized and commodified, that performativity always renders this process of order and control incomplete and vulnerable to disruption" (11). By extension—and relevant to the thesis of this book—such resistant practices found in the tourist industry can also disrupt the market or exchange value of the tourist "experience."

In addition, Edensor suggests that much of what we are discussing in the specific example of tourism—namely, the power of the performative to disrupt normative identities and values—also applies more generally to *everyday life* in post-industrial cultures like the United States or United Kingdom. Edensor points out that for John Urry, "we are tourists much of the time whether we like it or not" (61), as contemporary culture "obscures the distinction between tourism and the everyday" (61). If, as Edensor argues, performative practice is potentially disruptive of the regulatory norms of tourism, *and* everyday life is becoming less distinguishable from tourism, then we re-arrive—through Edensor's work—at Judith Butler's point regarding how re-citation practices in *everyday life* can disrupt normative identities and values. Precisely because, as Edensor puts it, "the everyday is . . . the realm of repetition" (61), the re-citation of cultural commodities and commodified experiences always involves the potential for resistant and disruptive performances.

In considering how the concept of performativity has been, and can be, taken up within the sociology of tourism, we have seen that one discourse regarding the performative practices of tourists suggests that tourists themselves co-produce the "presence of value" at tourist sites. This discourse seems to align with that typically found in the contemporary marketing literature, which suggests that consumers co-produce the "value" of goods and experiences in the contemporary post-industrial economy. On the other hand, an alternative version of performativity theory as applied to tourism—drawing upon the theory of citationality from Derrida and Butler—suggests that the normative meanings and values typically claimed by the tourist industry are never quite present. This argument—that the performativity of tourist places and identities may dislocate the *presence* of value in tourism—is especially interesting to consider relative to Eve Meltzer's (2002) work on how tourist space and location is performed relative to *absent* places.

In the article *Performing Place: A Hyperbolic Drugstore in Wall, South Dakota*, Meltzer describes the advertising efforts of a drugstore in South

Dakota which—going back to 1931—has involved placing "hundreds of thousands" of roadsigns in nearby states, as well as in several other countries (162). Meltzer takes an interest in how the value of this tourist phenomenon—as a cultural experience—has been constructed. Meltzer suggests that the fame of the drugstore as a cultural phenomenon has been achieved not so much through the delivery of goods or experiences in a particular spatial and temporal location, but is "present" only inasmuch as it is semiotically constructed relative to other places. In other words, the drugstore's "being there" (165) is not solely about being fixed in time and space, but its "location" is better thought of as a performance which dramatizes its position relative to somewhere else (166). Meltzer, citing the work of Christian Metz and Jacques Lacan, notes that all signification involves the "presence of an absent referent" (166). In this example, the drugstore becomes "present" as a worldwide phenomenon inasmuch as it is advertised from "unlikely locations such as Pakistan . . . , Korea, Saudi Arabia, and Germany, among others" (162).

Relevant to this book, we can see that the "exchange value" of the drugstore "brand" has been constructed by being situated relative to other places—its experiential value has been *promised* by advertising from other locations. In Derridean terms, its value is not quite present, but rather is continually deferred—that is, its value as a brand is continually promised but not actually delivered. Meltzer points out that if tourists are not to be disappointed upon actually arriving in the geographical location, they must instead find value from participating in the "hyperbolic" experience of advertising itself—the semiotic, rather than cartographical, "space." Meltzer clearly shows that its value has been constructed from its outside—from another, differentiated "context" such as Pakistan or Germany. The tourist experience is thus derived relative to the context of the other, with which it is grafted in the materiality of the advertisement—in other words, the *alterity from which it is advertised*. Meltzer thus shows that the value of the cultural experience is actually never really present in a particular cartographical location.

In the same sense, cultural commodities do not derive their value from what they *deliver* when purchased and experienced by consumers in a particular spatial-temporal location; rather, consumers participate in the semiotic space opened in the distance between the commodity and its advertisement. It is the advertising, located in a different context, which promises that the commodity will valorize the referential context of self upon "arrival." We again, in Meltzer's work, see a critique of "place" as a self-enclosed site for the delivery of valued experience. As Coleman and Crang put it in a commentary on this article, "Place is, as it were, disseminated through these signs" (2002, 15).

In his work, Crang (2006) attempts to deconstruct the notion of "presence" in tourism studies—both the presence of the tourist, and that of the site (63). He notes that "the tourist seeks to travel to be present at a place, but as we examine those places we find they are shot through by absences where distant others, removed in space and time, haunt the sites" (49). If neither the tourist nor the visited site can be considered as entirely present, and are indeed constituted through a relationship with absence, then—by extension—the *value* of the tourist experience is never quite *delivered.* Hypothetically, then, if Wall Street traders were to assess the value of the drugstore's brand, for the purpose of assessing the market value of the company—we can see that the value being measured is not quite "present." While the measurement purports to measure the *presence* of value in the market, this effort actually involves trying to quantify the *allure of a promise*—the semiotic *claims to value* which tourists chase from sign to sign.

CONCLUSION

Investors and managers attempt to extend the temporality of the "presence" of exchange value toward the future citational practices of consumers. In order to maximize the exchange value of language in the future, they attempt to anticipate, and to shape, how identity *will be* constructed. This process involves not only *anticipating* the marketability of language—as a citational resource—but also performatively *bringing about* particular citational practices. Callon (2007) has argued that economic investors are guided in this effort by formulas developed by economists. He suggests that the work of economists—by influencing investments and product development decisions—become performative of the economy itself. Future projections regarding anticipated value, as measured through the application of economic formulas, can drive product and brand design, as well as marketing and investment decisions. In this sense, the economic *measure* becomes performative of the economy itself.

As firms attempt to invest in the marketability of language in the future, and bring about exchange value through the design of particular citational resources, consumer input is solicited. Several studies have shown that marketers increasingly appropriate from the subcultural lifeworlds of consumers in the design of their products and brands. Consumers thus "co-create" value with firms (Prahalad and Ramaswamy 2004), and assist in producing the citational resources which will be used in identity construction practices. As consumer lifeworlds expand on and alter traditional identity categories—in today's postmodern culture—firms incorporate and accelerate these changes with cutting-edge citational resources. In addition, corporations and consumers not only co-create individual citational resources, but also co-create value using branded *environments* within which consumer citational practices can unfold—as in the case of the Internet gaming industry.

Social identity and affiliated values are not only interpellated from the material forms of individual utterances, but from *constellations* of meaningful materialities. In the advertising and business literature, the term "consumption constellation" has emerged to refer to a group of products which are typically associated with a particular social identity (Englis and Solomon 1996, 185; see also Englis and Solomon 1995). A "cluster" (Englis and Solomon 1996, 185) of products together allow individuals to align their identities with those of particular subcultures.

For Englis and Solomon, marketers and managers should understand the ways in which products are perceived to be "complementary" (185) with each other, and, as a grouping, be affiliated with various "types" of people and social roles. Their recommendation (187–89) is that firms might, for example, design advertisements, sponsor events, solicit celebrity endorsements, find product placements, or engage in collaborative marketing efforts in order to achieve a consistency of desired "symbolic associations" (189) with particular products. The concept of "consumption constellations" is thus useful in *describing* the ideological processes involved in the contemporary U.S. economy, particularly as it affects consumer identity construction processes.

In chapter six, however, the alternative notion of "aesthetic constellations" of materiality will be used to develop the critique of the contemporary cultural economy—as opposed to its mere description. The term "constellation" has been used in the critical theory of Theodor Adorno and Walter Benjamin, who attempted to show how both art, and art criticism, could dislocate normative meanings. In the next chapter, their argument is extended from the aesthetic dislocation of *meaning*, to the potential dislocation of *value*—as it is brought into a framework of performative citationality. This version of performativity theory differs from that emerging within marketing and business, in that the emphasis on citationality opens a space for the critique of the "presence" of exchange value. In other words, while "consumption constellations" may generally re-cite the normative frame of exchange value, the recontextualization of cultural commodities into "aesthetic constellations" may have the potential to disrupt it.

In chapter six, then, it will be argued that in the case of aesthetically configured material forms, the interpellation of both valuing contexts and social identities becomes ambiguous. When value contexts are disrupted, subjects cannot be clearly aligned with any imagined valuing community. In the experience of "aesthetic negativity" (Menke 1998, xi), no interpretive context can be interpellated which clarifies the value of either the citational resource, or the identity and values of the subject. While it is true that such aesthetic re-configurations cannot be controlled in advance by subjects, it is also true that certain citational resources are more or less conducive toward "breaking" the normative valuing frames which are interpellated from them.

Such aesthetically configured citational resources thus make the interpellation of the exchange value frame problematic.

III

Toward a Poststructuralist Critique of the Commodification of Language in the U.S. Cultural Economy

Chapter Six

The Promise of Value

This chapter argues that in addition to a political advocacy regarding equal access to—and adequate rewards for—the "co-creation" of exchange value by social actors, there is also a need for a critique of the exchange value frame itself. It is through that economic frame that language is increasingly commodified, as the words and images of social actors are shaped into marketable material forms. This chapter turns to the aesthetic theories of Theodor Adorno and Walter Benjamin, and integrates them into the theory of performative citationality. Relying on Christoph Menke's reading, Adorno's thesis in *Aesthetic Theory*—regarding the dislocation of normative *meanings* through the work of art—is extended to the potential dislocation of normative *values*.

It is also argued in this chapter that in addition to the potential for the utterances of *artists* to generate "aesthetic negativity" (Menke 1998, xi), *everyday social actors* might issue utterances—as well as participate in interactive dialogues—which have the potential to dislocate normative values and identities. This argument is tied to Butler's work on how recontextualization processes open a space for the dislocation of normative identities. The work of Erving Goffman on "frame-breaking" is also discussed in this regard. Finally, the work of Benjamin on the aesthetic potential of modern media technologies is also considered—especially given the "citational" aspect of photography.

BREAKING FRAME:

UNSETTLING EXCHANGE VALUE

Aesthetics, Politics, and the Critique of the Hegemony of Exchange Value

In his discussion of the controversies regarding the inclusion of various subcultural groups in the educational canon, John Guillory (1993) distinguishes between "cultural representation," "political representation," "aesthetics," and "aesthetic value." These distinctions will be useful to us in speaking of cultural values, political values, and *that which potentially dislocates value discourse itself*—"aesthetics." Guillory's main point in his book is that cultural representation, as regards the inclusion of a particular minority group in the educational canon, should not be confused with political representation, which concerns the access of group members to the means of cultural production (13; 18).

Guillory argues that the question of "aesthetic judgment"—evaluating the quality of works regardless of subcultural origin—is obscured in the curriculum debate by a contemporary relativism advocating for the mere inclusion of the works of various subcultures into the literary canon. For Guillory, this kind of advocacy for cultural representation addresses neither the question of access to the means of cultural production, nor appreciates the autonomy of "aesthetics" from other contemporary value discourses.

While Guillory's critical interest is much the same as Bourdieu's—to critique the inequality of access to "cultural capital" (an issue in the value domain of politics)—his analysis is also applicable to the main concern in this chapter; namely, the possibility of an "aesthetic" disruption of valuing discourses themselves, and of the exchange value system which measures their worth. Of particular relevance is Guillory's argument that the canon debate regarding educational curriculum in the United States has reduced art to merely cultural capital, and thereby launched an attack on "aesthetics" itself. In consequence, such a move limits the operation of aesthetics in resisting the exchange value frame—and instead assimilates aesthetics into the current hegemonic discourse of exchange value by way of "aesthetic value."

As Guillory argues, cultural representation is not the same as political representation. For example, de Certeau (1988) has shown that certain syntactical forms are used by dominant groups to "report" on the speech of subordinate groups. This results in *cultural* inclusion or "representation," while simultaneously denying the *political* agency of subordinate groups. For Guillory, the voice of the excluded other may "return" through inclusion in the educational canon, but still be excluded from full economic and political participation in the larger society. The political question, as Guillory sees it, concerns who has control over the "social conditions governing access to literacy" (16). In the language of citationality, this involves control over normative citational practices, and over the production and distribution of citational resources. In other words, following Guillory, "exclusion" cannot simply be defined as "exclusion from representation" (18) *within* normative citational practices, but rather in terms of access *to* the normative distributional network of these citational resources.

This question of greater equality within the political economy, as advocated by Guillory, is indeed urgent. However, this strategy—of greater "access to the *means of cultural production*" (18; italics in the original)—must be combined with a *critique* of those same cultural practices, inasmuch as they are implicated in the continuing re-citation of the consumer economy itself. In other words, contemporary critical theory must graft together the political question regarding "access to value," with the question of the performative re-citation of exchange value itself.

As Derrida argued in *Specters of Marx* (1994), this latter endeavor involves the dislocation of any anticipated, desired, or even identifiable political values of the future—because any critique of "value" demands an unknown future in which its repetition and re-citation necessarily occurs. Despite the uneasy relationship between critical theory and poststructuralism to date, a graft of these projects may not be altogether incompatible; indeed, the *material forms* which perpetuate unequal access to value within capitalism are the very same material forms which re-cite the ideology of the "presence of value" itself. Commodified material forms tend to close off alternative futures as they re-cite the temporality of exchange value—which not only generates class inequality, but interpellates the very identity of class-based "consumers."

For Guillory, then, the simple insertion of a particular author into the literary canon—who supposedly "represents" the collective identity, values, and experiences of a subcultural group—cannot be taken as an adequate political strategy to improve group access to the economic and political means of cultural production (10). Extending Guillory's argument, such *political* access to the means of identity production must be combined with access to particular *aesthetic* citational resources; that is, resources which have the potential to dislocate the interpellation of class-based Cartesian subjects. As discussed above, this type of Cartesian individualism has historically supported the development of capitalism itself, and is necessary for the contemporary re-citation of exchange value. Recognizing this (poststructuralist) point does not lessen the importance of the political question regarding access to cultural capital—the specific concern of Guillory, Bourdieu, and of critical theorists generally.

This question of dislocating normative citational practice, in *addition* to an advocacy for full political participation within the existing hegemonic structure of value, is especially urgent today given the contemporary reduction of politics to the mere marketability of one's "political" words—as we see with the proliferation of politically oriented talk radio, Internet sites, or cable television stations. Clearly, the mere inclusion of the voice of a subordinated group within institutionalized, syntactical forms—designed to generate exchange value—perpetuate the current political economy more than challenge it. Increasingly, it seems that in this age of media politics the question of political legitimation becomes simply one of citational hierarchy—which political authority is cited where. Thus, we find that political decision-making is too often moved not by the force of the better argument, but rather by those words and images which have a better market value—that is, those words and images can be valorized as better experiences for those who consume cultural commodities marked as political.

While Guillory and Bourdieu have implicated the educational institution in the unequal distribution of cultural capital, we can also recognize the school's critical location as a potential site for the dislocation of normative citational forms. Schools are one of the last non-commercial alternatives to the mass media for the distribution and positioning of language in society (see Guillory 1993, 8)—especially as family life is increasingly plugged into commercial media, and contemporary social interaction has become saturated with a mobile and commercialized Internet. In this sense, the canon debate over the exposure of students to aesthetics, as an alternative to the more marketable material forms of the consumer economy, becomes an important site of contestation regarding the commodification of language generally—and thus over the construction of social identity itself.

Because cultural commodities shape the materiality of the future social environment, and thereby shape the citational resources through which future identities will be interpellated, certain political questions become crucial—such as the ownership of media networks for the distribution of language, the control of and commercialization of the Internet, and the commercialization and rationalization of educational curriculum. However, as Butler (1993) has shown in her discussion of the work of Slavoj Žižek, because of the iterability of political language itself, the effectiveness of particular challenges to hegemonic economic formations cannot be guaranteed in advance—in alignment with known political positions. Rather, those who would change contemporary articulations of values and identities must seek to open unknown future contexts which may provide, rather than foreclose, opportunities for alternative identity and value formation. If "present" politics concerns the negotiation of already-known values and identities, then *aesthetics*—in disrupting the existing "identity of value" itself—opens the space for a (tentative) new politics, and a (contingent) new articulation of identities and values. As Derrida (1994) has shown, the *anticipation of such an unknown future* is not the same thing as the *calculative anticipation* of political or economic strategies.

The next sections of this book address the question of "breaking" the hegemonic exchange value frame, in order to instead provide an opening for an unknowable future. If meaningful cultural forms have increasingly become commodities in the closed system of exchange value, it is precisely in the "play" of language, meaning, and value—given their iterability across contexts—where the possibility of opening the future lies. The critique developed by the Frankfurt School regarding the culture of late capitalism—as dominated by exchange value—is thus moved into a discussion of performativity and citationality.

Aesthetics and Breaking Frame

As suggested earlier, Erving Goffman's (1986) work in *Frame Analysis* might be used to consider exchange value discourse as a "frame," within which social reality is organized in a particular way. In that work, Goffman was not only concerned with the construction of the frames by which experience was organized, but also was concerned with the "vulnerabilities" of frames (10). The work of Goffman on "breaking frame" might be considered when discussing the possibility of an aesthetic configuration through which an utterance might unsettle normative value discourses—particularly the dislocation of the hegemonic frame of exchange value.

For Goffman, when an individual "breaks frame," they have a "negative" or non-normative experience (379). Goffman discusses how the anxiety experienced by some when normative frames are broken might become pleasurable experiences for others—as when a practical joke is played. Interestingly, Goffman cites as examples of "breaking frame" both cultural *commodities*, such as televised wrestling, as well as the work of avant-garde *artists* (see 401–08). For Goffman, both art and commodities have the potential to disrupt normative frames and experiences.

Goffman points out that the dislocations of normative value frames are usually only temporary. In addition, frame-breaking techniques can themselves become routinized. Yet, as Goffman points out, routinized and *repeated* violations of the boundaries of frame, as normalized violations, might over time result in a *change in the boundaries of the frame itself* (420). Using Butler's (1999) example, we can imagine that initial performances of a gender parody—which might produce a temporary "negative experience" for audiences—also could become a more regular occurrence in television shows—as a gendered cultural commodity. Applying Goffman's insight, we can see that while any particular citation has less "aesthetic negativity" (see Menke 1998, xi) following its routinization, the *cumulative effect* of such commodification might be an alteration in the frame itself. We can see here the affinity between Judith Butler's argument regarding the political potentialities of recontextualization, and Goffman's notion of frame-breaking (Sherlock 2011).

In other words, as gender parodies become routine, the category of gender itself might itself be altered. Thus, as a political strategy, Goffman's "micro" approach to interactional "frame-breaking" becomes interesting as a way of "disorganizing the world" (Goffman 1986, 493). Routinized frame-breaking, he notes, will result in "a generative effect, systematically transforming all instances of the class, and, incidentally, systematically undermining the prior meaning of the acts" (493). In this sense, perhaps even the commodification or routinization of certain "aesthetic" citational practices may undermine the value frame or identity category itself. To use Derrida's (1981) notion of the *pharmakon*, the commodity may be both "poison" and "cure" relative to the exchange value frame.

As Butler has shown, gender categories not only limit subjectivity, but *enable* a particular subjectivity at the same time. The dislocation of identity categories by "enabled" subjects must therefore occur *within* situated action, through repetitions which re-cite the categories "with a difference." In Goffman's sense, while any citational configurations which temporarily dislocate gender or value categories might easily be re-commodified, the cumulative effect of such recontextualizations might be an alteration of the sedimented meaning of the value category itself. Thus, the dislocation of identity categories involves the effort to alter those very frames which simultaneously enable one's own agency; Butler has noted the "uneasy sense of standing under a sign to which one does and does not belong" (1993, 219).

It must be remembered that, as Butler shows, citational practices are not just a matter of choice. As in the case of gender, social sanctions enforce normative citational practices. Yet, as Derrida and Butler have shown, even enforced repetition necessarily involves alteration, and thus also involves the potential for the dislocation of sedimented meanings. Although normative utterances interpellate normative interpretive contexts, the grafting of utterances into unknown future contexts always opens the possibility for alterations of frame. For Butler, this possibility "is precisely the *political promise of the performative*, one that positions the performative at the center of a politics of hegemony, one that offers an *unanticipated* political future for deconstructive thinking" (1997, 161; italics added).

Thus, like Derrida, Butler locates the hope for alternative citational practices in an open and unknown future, as opposed to an alignment with known political values. At the same time however, as Butler points out, no political subject has agency outside of contemporary regulatory (value) discourses; rather, contemporary subjects are always already constituted *by* such discourses, and configure their utterances within the existing constellation of normative discourses (1993, 15).

In developing her argument, Butler appeals to Žižek's work on the performativity of political signifiers. According to Butler, Žižek argues that political signifiers should not be taken as "representative" of pre-existing political constituencies, but rather that these communities are themselves interpellated from such signifiers (191). Like Anderson (1991) or Guillory (1993), Žižek argues that such "imagined communities" lack the value consensus which is typically attributed to them—the signifier can never guarantee the adequate representation of a "pure" valuing community (Butler 1993, 191). Integrating this insight with Derrida's work on citationality, Butler argues that "It is this open-ended and performative function of the signifier that seems to me to be crucial to a radical democratic notion of futurity" (191).

Any regulating "unity"—including group norms—as interpellated from political signifiers must be continually re-cited to maintain its regulatory effect; however, this re-citation also opens it to alteration (193). Butler follows Žižek in arguing that the recognizable political values supposedly shared by a community are, in fact, subject to the "contingency" of signification (193). In this sense, the re-citation of normative subcultural values are always subject to the possibilities of "breaking frame."

Just as Žižek and Butler have suggested that *political* signifiers can be considered as performative, we can also consider those *economic* signifiers—which continually re-cite exchange value—to be performative. The re-citation of exchange value interpellates the subject to be a member of an imagined subculture which in fact lacks the "valuing unity" attributed to it—as does the abjected collectivity required for the identity of the "valuing" group. For example, the maintenance of the "fashionable" subculture, as a social location where value is presumed to be present, requires the continual abjection of those who reciprocally emerge as the unfashionable. The inherent instability of *both* identities require their continued re-citation; for Butler, this requirement simultaneously opens the possibility of their dislocation and alteration. While objecting to certain Lacanian aspects of Žižek's political theory, Butler embraces Žižek's argument that this possibility can be called the "democratic promise" of the political signifier (195). We can also here see its applicability to the *economic* signifier which re-sites the presence of exchange value.

Along with the contributions of both Goffman and Butler on "frame-breaking," Henry Louis Gates's (1988) work in *The Signifying Monkey* also shows how re-citation can dislocate normative value categories. Gates shows how aesthetic citational configurations, such as the "Monkey tales" told over generations in particular African-American communities, can disrupt normative signifying practices. For Gates, this community tradition has long made use of the repetition and variation of particular themes in new contexts—a *repetition with alteration* (see xxii–xxiii; 50–51). The *way* stories are repeated—that is, the citational style by which traditional themes are voiced—becomes more important than the content of the story. Gates notes, in discussing the work of Roger D. Abrahams, that what is important in these tales is that "one does not signify something; rather, one signifies in *some way*" (54, italics in the original). These aesthetic styles thus "play with" the syntactical forms of citational practice itself.

For Gates, the emphasis in the telling of the tales is less on the referential meaning, and more on the "play of language"—an emphasis on the material, syntactical *form*. Like Butler, Gates argues that resistance to dominant meanings occurs not from their "outside," but from *within* normative citational practices and their associated identities. In fact, Gates argues that the very usage of the alternate term "'Signifyin(g),'" within the black community, has the rhetorical function of challenging "the nature of (white) meaning itself"—that is, of normative "signification" (46–47). In other words, an aesthetic modification in linguistic form is used to disrupt normative value contexts, as it dislocates normative referential meanings.

For Gates, a particular "rhetorical strategy" (47)—that is, a particular citational style or syntactical arrangement—is meant to unsettle the *values* of the dominant group; here, the normative system of racial categorization. Importantly, as Gates points out in reference to the Monkey poems, it is the *materiality* of the signifier which is involved in this play of language. This materiality signifies differently than normatively assumed.

Gates cites Bakhtin's notion of the "double-voiced word," which for Bakhtin involves "inserting a new semantic orientation into a word which already has—and retains—its own orientation" (Bakhtin, in Gates 1988, 50). Thus, the normative meaning of a word is repeated "with a signal difference" (Gates 1988, 51)—a difference which grafts a usually excluded context onto the normative referential context. Thus, while the normative context and usual meaning exists, the usually excluded context is simultaneously cited—distancing itself from and playing against the normative meaning. Both meanings are kept in tension in the "play" of language. Gates recognizes this dimension of language in literary (aesthetic) tropes, and describes their predominance in African-American language use (52).

Thus, Gates shows that aesthetic citational configurations can dislocate dominant value discourses, as the play of language dislocates the interpellation of normative referential contexts. In this sense, we can see how such play of aesthetic language might resist the automatic signification of exchange value. Words with exchange value as a cultural commodity, such as a literary tale, may signify differently as they are re-cited in an aesthetic way which resists their normative commodification. Aspects of materiality which are normatively taken to signify the "presence of value" can be made problematic through aesthetically configured citational forms. Despite the hegemony of exchange value—that all language can signify a market "worth"—aesthetic citational configurations have the potential to unsettle this interpellated context through the generation of "aesthetic negativity" (see Menke 1998, xi). Language itself has a certain "play" such that its connotations cannot be controlled in advance; it cannot be made entirely subservient to the demands of commodity circulation.

Recalling our discussion above regarding reported speech, it is interesting to note that in the traditional Monkey poems, it is precisely reported speech which usually starts the "trouble"—employing a technique of "indirection" (Gates 1988, 77). Typically, in these tales the monkey reports on what the elephant previously said about the lion, which leads to a conflict between those two. The "play" is between strips of language (supposedly) spoken in different contexts—the "absent" conversation is re-cited in the present conversation. Gates notes that such "indirection" is also how tropes function: an absent or excluded meaning comes to problematize the automatic understanding of "present" meaning (80).

Thus while "reported speech" can be used to *marginalize* groups, as in the de Certeau or Inoue examples discussed earlier, we can also see how particular syntactical forms (like aesthetically configured reported speech) can *disrupt* normative referential contexts—both in a subject/author's utterances when narrating a story, as well as in the character's utterances speaking within the story. As another example, Gates discusses how Zora Neale Hurston, in her novel *Their Eyes Were Watching God*, uses a "double-voiced narrative mode," mixing syntactical forms of "reported speech" to create a particular aesthetic effect (xxv–xxvi).

In this sense, aesthetics can be considered as a kind of "playing with context," disrupting normative referential links between the material sign and its typically interpellated context. What is at stake in the "playing," however, are not just the social relationships and values involving a *single* context; rather, the materiality which disrupts normative signification processes involves the negotiation of multiple contexts—and their implied social relationships. Aesthetics involves "playing" with several contexts simultaneously—both dominant and subordinated contexts.

For Bakhtin, the modern novel is precisely an aesthetic form which grafts or plays with several contexts simultaneously; in the novel a "heteroglossia" of voices might disrupt the "monologic" voice of any modern political ideology (Allen 2006, 30). The aesthetic form of the novel showcases the intertextuality of language, as in the case of Dostoevsky's novels (Allen 2006, 25). "Intertextuality," as Julia Kristeva has argued, necessarily disrupts the identity or values of any individual subject (Allen 2006, 44–45). For example, according to Graham Allen, Gates argues that in the Hurston novel white and black speech patterns were blended into a "hybrid voice beyond any notion of singular or stable identity" (171). This revealed the "tradition of the

African-American people's struggle to find identity between imposed and self-designed linguistic forms" (172).

Considering the intertextuality of language in everyday life, it can be argued that beyond the literary text, *everyday* utterances might be "poetically" configured so as to disrupt exchange value contexts. Utterances issued in everyday life, like those formulated in novels, can be more or less aesthetically configured to "break" anticipated interactional frames—even though, unlike dialogue written into novels, their outcomes cannot be controlled in advance by the intentionality of the "artist."

While literary artists may be able to control the responses of other characters to their protagonist *within* the novel, they have no control over the responses of others in real life *to* their novel; the latter situation parallels that of the subject issuing utterances in everyday life. The aesthetic negativity of the novel, as a work of art, is only achieved to the extent that the novel disrupts normative meanings and values in its "external" reception in unknown future situations. The responses of others to aesthetically configured utterances—whether to the entextualizations of subjects issued in everyday life, or to novels presented for public reception—are beyond the "present" intentionalities of the artists.

AESTHETIC NEGATIVITY AND CITATIONALITY

Re-Siting Adorno: Aesthetic Negativity and Citationality

Judith Butler has argued that resistance to the identity category of gender must occur from within that normative category, since the same categories which restrict citational practices simultaneously enable them. Similarly, if normative *value* categories, such as the hegemonic exchange value discourse, are to be resisted, then literary or everyday utterances—which can themselves be given an exchange value—must be configured in such a way as to simultaneously resist that exchange value framing. In Goffman's sense, in order to "break frame," the exchange value context must be systematically altered, even as it repeated. Although the focus of the Frankfurt School was on the reification of consciousness, their work on the commodification of culture and the possibility of such an "immanent critique" (see Buck-Morss 1979) can be "re-sited" into a poststructuralist perspective. In this section, Theodor Adorno's aesthetic theory, as interpreted by Christoph Menke, will be reconsidered within the theory of performative citationality.

In *The Sovereignty of Art: Aesthetic Negativity in Adorno and Derrida*, Christoph Menke draws upon the work of Adorno to argue that art is both "autonomous" and "sovereign" (1998, x-xi). The autonomy of art means that it is distinct from other spheres which are "not art." The sovereignty of art, in Menke's words, positions the aesthetic as a "subversion of the rationality of all discourses"—what Menke refers to as "aesthetic negativity" (1998, xi). Menke wants to develop the critical potential of art, as the basis of criticizing other non-aesthetic discourses, by appealing to the concept of aesthetic negativity—which he finds in the work of both Theodor Adorno and Jacques Derrida. Although ultimately Menke's position is closer to that of Adorno than Derrida, he also disagrees with that reading of Adorno which conflates art and social critique—in Menke's view, violating the autonomy of art (7-8). For our purposes in this book, Menke's emphasis on the sovereignty and autonomy of the aesthetic will be specifically considered relative to those other *valuing* discourses over which exchange value has become hegemonic—such as political, religious, or other subcultural values.

It is important at the outset to emphasize that the aesthetic theories of Adorno (1997) and Menke are not being introduced here as part of an argument that the aesthetic realm is somehow transcendental to that of value or meaning. Rather, it will be argued that the "aesthetic" has to do with a particular syntactical arrangement of *material* forms, where the situated singularity of particular aesthetic configurations play against the normatively-signified meanings of the materiality involved. If, in Derrida's sense, "meaning" and "value" are identifiable as they are interpellated from the repetition of recognizable materialities, an *aesthetic* configuration of such materiality plays against those referential meanings and values. As Gates argued, the aesthetics of "Signifyin(g)" has to do with the *way* citational practices can dislocate normative referential meanings—and here, normative value discourses.

In short, the "aesthetic" effect emerges *through* material forms as they are repeated—with a difference (see Gates, xxii-xxiii; 50-51). Aesthetic effect does not belong to a transcendental realm apart from meaningful materiality. Menke argues, in his reading of Adorno, that *aesthetically configured material forms* can be contrasted with the *materiality of cultural commodities*, in the way that aesthetic forms tend to resist normative meanings. This argument will be extended from Adorno and Menke's concern with the aesthetic dislocation of normative meaning, to the possible dislocation of normative *values*.

Citing Horkheimer and Adorno's *Dialectic of Enlightenment*, Menke argues that for Adorno, the "commodified pleasures" derived from culture industry products differ from the pleasure derived from aesthetic experiences. In the case of commodities, Adorno argued that pleasure simply becomes amusement, as "aroused by the 'automatic' recognition of something already known" (Menke 1998, 11). As opposed to this kind of pleasure, as when an audience easily anticipates the progression of a popular song, Adorno contrasts the pleasure or enjoyment derived from aesthetic experience—which he characterizes as "non-conceptual" (12). In other words, for Adorno, aesthetic experience disrupts understanding, or in a Derridean sense, the "presence" of normative meaning (12). This aesthetic experience is based on the *failure* of a subject's "automatic understanding" of a material form. Menke argues that this is Adorno's understanding of "aesthetic negativity."

As Menke discusses, Adorno sees aesthetic experience as involving an active role of the subject. In confronting the art object, the subject initially seeks an understanding of the object in non-aesthetic terms, attempting to derive its normative meaning. However, the *materiality* of the aesthetically-formed object blocks such "automatic" understanding. For Adorno, Menke argues, aesthetic experience is thus an experience of the *failure* of the material form to signify in an automatic or normative way.

In the language of poststructuralism, the "experience" of aesthetic negativity occurs when normative values or identities cannot be readily interpellated from the material form. The material form itself does not automatically summon normative interpretive contexts, to be applied to its interpretation. Importantly for Adorno, that which *subverts* normative understanding (and value) is *within* the material form. It is the materiality of the art object itself—the "utterance" of the artist—which resists or subverts the attempts of the subject to understand its meaning.

It is important to note that this subversive quality, for Adorno, relates to the material form of the work of art as sign, which is materially entextualized in such a way as to block or resist normative significations. This is in contrast to the way that *commodities* signify—where a material form readily and easily signifies recognizable identities and values. Menke shows that for Adorno, the automatic understandings achieved in all *non-aesthetic* discourses—which, for our purposes, includes all *value* discourses—are based in the identification of signifier with signified (36). In other words, it is only the materiality of *art* which has the potential to disrupt the signification of normative values and identities. To put it differently, what is called "art" is that type of material configuration which plays against normative interpellations in particular ways.

In everyday life, it is only certain *aspects* of material forms which signify normative meanings. Menke emphasizes the importance here of not confusing the *entire* materiality of the object with those particular aspects or elements of it which signify; in other words, the signifying elements are a subset of the comprehensive materiality of the object. Beyond those particular signifying characteristics of any material form is what Adorno finds to be a "superabundance" (113) of "excess" materiality—to which he appeals in his aesthetic theory. In non-aesthetic and non-problematic understanding, subjects quickly focus only on particular aspects of material forms, which they have been taught are relevant to the signification of normative identities and values. In other words, there are taken-for-granted links between certain aspects of the material form—as signifiers—and particular signifieds.

Whereas it is true that understanding in non-aesthetic processes is occasionally disrupted, Adorno argues that this confusion usually occurs only temporarily, and is resolvable—eventually resulting in the re-establishment of some normative understanding or meaning (59). In these non-aesthetic processes, as Menke discusses, this resolution of occasional ambiguity typically occurs with the *restoration of social context*—the selection of an alternative, culturally-available interpretive context. In other words, if one interpretive context cannot be evoked in order to interpret a particular aspect of the material form, another interpretive context is quickly evoked instead. If this misunderstanding is not eventually resolvable through the restoration of some normative, interpretive context, the non-aesthetic object does not signify—it lapses into a "mere thing" lacking social meaning.

By contrast, Adorno and Menke argue, in *aesthetic* experience there can be no such easy appeal to alternative interpretive contexts to restore meaning, since the disruption of normative signification lies *within* the materiality of the art object itself. In other words, precisely because the material form of the aesthetic object is non-normative, it cannot invoke *any* of the typical interpretive contexts—such as any normative value domain. The material form of art continually resists the socially meaningful restoration of *any* interpretive (valuing) context (60). This is because for Adorno, as Menke shows, the materiality of the aesthetic object has been entextualized into a "*self-subverting* signifier formation" (59, italics in the original). In poststructuralist terms, the syntactical configuration of the material form resists the ready interpellation of any normative context.

If the subject, attempting understanding, cannot appeal to any culturally-available interpretive context in the search for meaning, Adorno argues that they can only *return to the aesthetic object* for a closer examination of its materiality—of precisely those "superabundant" or "unselected" aspects of the materiality usually ignored (or abjected) in normative signification processes (67; 69). Thus for Adorno, the aesthetic experience involves a dislocation of understanding and meaning (58)—that is, the loss of a normative context which guides interpretation. Because the total materiality of the object always exceeds those particular aspects which signify, the disruption of normative meaning keeps the audience of the work searching, in vain, for normative signification in the *rest* of previously "unselected materiality" (67) However, no definitive meaning emerges from aesthetic objects. Extending this argument to the signification of exchange value, we might say that the aesthetically configured form cannot be identified or experienced as a materiality of *known value*—that is, as a "measured" representation of known subcultural values.

Whereas even non-aesthetic signs are ambiguous in the sense that elements of their materiality may signify differently in different contexts (i.e., multiple *understandings* may be taken from any cultural "text"), it is only in aesthetic experience that these normative associations between material aspect and signified understandings are *themselves disrupted* (68). It is not just that one understanding or valuation is favored over another; rather, it is that *understanding or valuation is itself disrupted*. For Adorno, the aesthetic object thus attains a status somewhere between a mere thing, and a signifier with automatically-linked meanings. The superabundance of the materiality stands against, or takes a position in resistance to, normative interpretive contexts.

Applying these insights to the problematic of this book, we can see that while the work of art clearly is a social product and not a mere thing, no normative meanings are readily available for its interpretation; instead, in the experience of art *all normative (and meaningful) valuing contexts are disrupted*. In poststructuralist terms, the work of art is an utterance which resists the interpellation of any known value discourse. While in normative signification processes identifiable cultural values are cited, in the case of an aesthetically configured citational resource, subjects are unsure of its "value"—and thus become *unsure of their own interpellated identity relative to that materiality*. The Cartesian subject becomes unsure of what subcultural values the materiality represents, or of its exchange value as an "experience" of those values.

As Menke points out, for Adorno "interpretive speech," as aesthetic *criticism*, is the attempt in words to describe or assess this experience of aesthetic negativity (110). While this attempt can never wholly succeed, Adorno argues that the best aesthetic criticism approximates, in its own material form, the experience of aesthetic negativity. In other words, the critical essay must *itself*—within the conceptual, discursive form of language—employ self-subverting tactics which resist automatic or normative understanding. This is why Adorno paid so much attention to the material form of his own writings, trying to create a "discontinuity" of meaning—in order to approximate aesthetic experience as much as possible (110; Nicholsen 1999, 110). The interpretive speech of criticism *performs* its own inadequacy as an "expression" or "representation" of aesthetic experience (Menke 1998, 111). The materiality of "aesthetically configured" language—in both aesthetic works as well as in aesthetic criticism—is thereby configured in such a way as to resist the interpellative grafting of normative values and identities.

Adorno was drawn to Walter Benjamin's notion of a "constellation," applying it to the configurative arrangement of interpretive statements in his essays, in such a way as to potentially resist automatic understanding (see 110). Thus, while aesthetic experience itself is nonconceptual, the critic might configure an essay about the aesthetic object in such a way as to enable "aesthetic experience to lodge itself *within* interpretive speech" (111, italics in the original). Menke points to two ways to achieve this "configurative discontinuity" in the interpretive speech of critics (112). We will here extend

Menke's work to consider these two ways more generally—as applicable to *any* instance of reported speech—given that an art critic is "reporting on" the utterance of the artist.

The first strategy of dislocating normative meaning concerns Derrida's deconstructive methodology, whereby—according to Menke—the critic is able to reveal an "*undecidability* of interpretations" (112; italics in the original) of a material form. Menke argues that this method reveals that any particular interpretation of an aesthetic object is incompatible with another possible interpretation (112). Derrida's work shows that no *particular* conceptual discourse or interpretive frame can adequately cover the aesthetic object. The ambiguity generated from the *tension between multiple interpretations* thus disrupts any particular, identifiable meaning of the material form.

The second type of critically-formulated speech creates discontinuity in another way, favored by Adorno and Menke. As Menke notes, this type of "configurative discontinuity" involves "the superabundance of the aesthetic object itself" (113). Rather than showing the relativity of competing interpretive contexts (i.e., differential value domains), the *materiality* of the aesthetically configured critical essay itself resists *any* interpellated context by which normative understanding can be achieved. Citing Paul de Man, Menke notes that this method attempts—in the material configuration of the critical essay—to re-perform the subversive "strategies" entextualized into the aesthetic object—rather than, as for Derrida, supporting diverse readings by different audiences (112-13).

While it would not be correct to differentiate "art" vs. "commodity" as pure categories with differing properties, it would be true for Adorno that the "stringency" of works of art is greater than that of most commodified forms—that is, their self-subverting material forms have a greater potential to evoke an "experience of aesthetic negativity." Unlike art, many commodified forms are entextualized in such a way as to readily and clearly evoke particular value contexts—especially that of exchange value. Thus for Adorno, as Menke notes, social objects like art or commodities can be critically evaluated as to the "degree of stringency" experienced from their material forms (131). The "experience" of the exchange value of commodified language can thus be contrasted with the "experience" of aesthetic negativity, as generated by aesthetically configured language (see 131)—whether in the art object itself, or in aesthetic criticism.

Menke argues that Adorno describes the material configuration of an aesthetic work as a kind of "'thing of a second order'" (146; Adorno 1997, 99)—which is not the material status of a mere thing, but is also not the materiality of a sign with an automatically-understood meaning (Menke 1998, 146). According to Menke, citing Derrida (147), it is here that Adorno locates the "beauty" of aesthetic works. In blocking or subverting normative signification, this "thing of a second order" is itself showcased or performed. In his reading of Heidegger, Adorno argues that in the experience of aesthetic negativity, it is the *materiality* of the "thing of a second order" which comes forth (146)—as opposed to a signification of its referential meaning (or, by extension, its *value*). This materiality is described by Adorno as the "aesthetic image" (149), which exists *between* the non-meaningful materiality of a mere thing, and the "surpassing of the thinglike in the *presence* of a meaning" (155; italics added). In a Derridean sense, we might say that the "value" of the aesthetic image—as an identifiable domain with a "presence" of meaning—is dislocated or deferred. In other words, in the experience of aesthetic negativity, a subversion of the normative *temporality*—of the "presence" of value—occurs.

Thus for Adorno, the "stringent" resistance of the aesthetic object to normative, automatic significations results in a "transfiguration" of its materiality (156). In poststructuralist terms, this resistance—and resultant transfiguration—makes the normative interpellation of evaluative contexts problematic. While the identity or value of the *non-aesthetic* object is secured through the interpellation of normative interpretive contexts, in aesthetic negativity *all* evaluative contexts are disrupted—in Menke's terms, the aesthetically-transfigured materiality "distances us from the contexts in which we have always stood in our non-aesthetic, understanding-based use of representations" (229; see also 156). Aesthetic negativity thus loosens the one-to-one correspondence between the materiality of the object, and the normatively signified value context—as well as dislocating the social identity typically interpellated with that value. Unlike commodities, aesthetic objects no longer "represent" valuing subcultures. The material form of aesthetically configured language or objects—both art works and "self-subversive" art criticism—has instead been entextualized in such a way as to potentially dislocate normative significations of identity and value.

Menke argues that Derrida attempted to extend the moment of "aesthetic negativity"—the disruption of normative understanding (and by extension, value)—to *all* texts, including the non-aesthetic (162-63). Menke calls this a "non-aesthetic sense of negativity" (167). The issue at stake, regarding the problematic of this book, is whether only an *aesthetic* transfiguration "motivated" by the stringent form of the object itself, or also a Derridean deconstruction brought to the reading of the social object, can result in the dislocation and subversion of the normative signification of exchange value.

It is Menke's position, which will be followed here, that Derrida is ultimately unsuccessful in this attempt to generalize the experience of aesthetic negativity to non-aesthetic textuality. Menke argues instead, following Adorno, that the moment of aesthetic negativity—with the potential to disrupt meaning (and value)—*must remain within the autonomous sphere of art*. The reason Menke favors the approach of Adorno over Derrida on this point—

regarding the applicability of aesthetic negativity to non-aesthetic discourses—has to do with claims regarding the "presence" of meaning in Western metaphysics.

For Derrida, the establishment of meaning in Western metaphysics and culture involves an "absolute" claim involving the recognizable "self-identity" of the mark (195). As discussed earlier, Derrida's critique of metaphysics reveals the ultimate failure of this claim. For Derrida, the replication of any identity across contexts, as well as its internal reliance upon an abjected and differential supplement, dislocates the claimed "presence" of this identity (195). For Derrida, the experience of this failure to secure identity—as a negative experience—applies to both aesthetic objects as well as to non-aesthetic "texts." *Any* "positive" identity or meaning necessarily excludes alternative identities and meanings, and is therefore never quite "present."

Menke, however, argues that in the case of non-aesthetic texts, meaning (and value) tend toward normative understandings—even competing interpretations of a text can be resolved through negotiation in everyday life. Following Adorno, Menke argues that the assertion of strong metaphysical claims to "identity" and "truth" only arise as a *result* of a prior disruption of these normative significations and "automatic" understandings—in an experience of "crisis" which occurs only when the subject confronts *aesthetic* forms (216-17; 227). It is this initial disruption of signification through an encounter with *aesthetic* forms which leads to the subsequent assertion, and ultimate failure, of metaphysical claims—as an (ideological) attempt to ground the meaningful identity of signs in intentional subjectivity. By contrast, in interaction involving non-aesthetic forms, "automatic" or normative assumptions proceed in an unquestioning way—without the need for absolute claims regarding the "presence" of meaning and the autonomous self-identity of signs (195).

Menke shows that both Adorno and Derrida agree that the aesthetics of negativity are grounded in the failure of metaphysical claims to "presence" and "self-identity." Both would agree that the failure of these metaphysical claims reveals (what Adorno would call) their "unintentional truth" (see Buck-Morss 1979, 77)—that their identity is neither "present" nor secured (Menke 1998, 205; 216-17). However, in his reading of *Negative Dialectics*, Menke argues that only Adorno is able to show why the metaphysical claims must be *raised in the first place*—following the *aesthetic* disruption of normative signification processes, which in turn initiates the assertion of metaphysical claims regarding the presence of meaning (217; 239; 241-42). Menke thus concludes that Derrida is unable to ground the necessity of the metaphysical impulse—or the ultimate experience of its failure—in *non-aesthetic* discourse (241).

For Adorno, when the appeal to "reason" (in understanding) undergoes a crisis, as when the subject encounters (or cites) the aesthetic object, the recourse is to raise "infinite" claims in order to ground itself—the "metaphysical impulse" (217). Interestingly, Menke terms this metaphysical impulse for universal grounding, citing Adorno, the "'*desire for presence*'" (220, italics added). The difference here is that Derrida argues that there is, in *all* discourse, a *structural* alterity undermining the metaphysical "presence," which deconstruction techniques can reveal. Adorno is arguing that *socially produced* forms of materiality—such as commodities or aesthetic forms—have been entextualized with lesser or greater degrees of self-subverting strategies within their material, syntactical forms. Materialities must repeat "with a difference," if their meanings and values are not to be re-cited as "present."

We here re-arrive at the same divergence from Derrida as that of Judith Butler: in favor of a *social* rather than a *structural* iterability (Butler 1997, 152). For Adorno, the material form which dislocates the "presence" of value is *socially produced*, as in the case of aesthetically configured utterances. In a Bakhtinian sense, the entextualized form of the aesthetically configured utterance takes a particular shape and stance relative to normative social meanings and values. Having said this, it is also true that critical readings of non-aesthetic texts can themselves *become* aesthetic utterances in particular material configurations—in Adorno's sense that aesthetic criticism can itself approach the kind of aesthetic negativity experienced in art.

Derrida is correct in emphasizing that the "aesthetic reception," or political consequences of art's later recontextualization, can never be controlled in advance—either by the audience or by the artist. Similarly, commodities may in fact end up in future syntactical arrangements with aesthetic effect. Thus, a rigid distinction between aesthetic and non-aesthetic texts (like cultural commodities), cannot be fixed once and for all. However, the more general point is that any contemporary syntactical arrangement is more or less conducive to the aesthetic disruption of normative meanings, values, and identities—even recognizing that this effect is not guaranteed in future re-articulations. It is not that value is "present" in non-aesthetic forms, while "dislocated" in aesthetic forms; rather, in non-aesthetic forms the "presence of value" is re-assumed and re-cited in a relatively unproblematic manner.

Thus for Menke, art must be considered as both autonomous and sovereign. It must remain *autonomous,* rather than extended to a general textuality, because the false claims of the metaphysics of presence—which Adorno's negative dialectics and Derrida's deconstructive methodology rightly expose—are claims grounded in a "crisis of reason" (216-17) provoked only by *aesthetic* forms. This crisis which initiates aesthetic negativity cannot be *first* provoked in non-aesthetic discourses, because the normality of less-stringent, non-aesthetic material form tends to provoke normative significations (i.e., meaning, value, and understanding).

It is precisely because aesthetic experiences do not work according to the logic of these less-stringent discourses (like commodities) that it has potentially destabilizing consequences for normative meanings and values—thus the *sovereignty* of aesthetic subversion. This *politically* subversive result is what Menke calls the "'postaesthetic'" consequence of aesthetic experience (179; 225). Thus, Menke argues that although aesthetic experience is autonomous from non-aesthetic (value) discourses, such as politics, it is *not without consequences for them*—it is just that this aesthetic experience is "logically prior" to these consequences (225).

Applying this argument to the problematic at hand, we can see that the disruption of the "presence of value" must occur as a *result* of the experience of the failure of metaphysical claims regarding the presence of value—which can only originate from their prior assertion and ultimate inadequacy. The material form which first "motivates" metaphysical claims to value, and thus ultimately initiates the experience of the failure of such claims, is *aesthetic* form—that *materiality* which disrupts normative significations and interpretive (value) contexts. Thus, following Adorno and Menke, the "last refuge" for the critical disruption of exchange value discourse must be aesthetic form.

It is in this sense that it might be suggested that Western metaphysics functions as a defense against the *threat* of aesthetics, inasmuch as art threatens normative reason, Cartesian-based understanding, and—for the purposes of this book—normative *value*. In the contemporary cultural economy, metaphysical claims specifically function to defend against aesthetic disruptions regarding the "presence of exchange value." Cultural commodities are said to both represent subcultural values, and themselves "have" an exchange value—as inherent features present in their material forms. In contrast, aesthetic objects are of ambiguous value—both as a commodifiable object, and as a representation of subcultural values. The metaphysical assertion of the "presence" of exchange value—the *process of commodification*—responds to the aesthetic constellation of materiality by attempting to reframe its ambiguity into known and recognizable domains of value.

While Menke does not follow Derrida in generalizing the processes of aesthetic negativity to *non-aesthetic* discourse, he does follow both Adorno and Derrida in arguing that aesthetic negativity has "destabilizing consequences for non-aesthetic discourses" (173). Having undergone an aesthetic transfiguration, Adorno argues, aesthetic materialities become "things of a second order"—as estranged from normative contexts (229). Extending this argument to the question of value, we can see that the materiality of a "thing of a second order," as a *citational resource*, potentially disrupts the interpellation of *value* discourses—including that of exchange value. In addition, this book argues that the syntactical configuration of citational resources is not limited to the utterances of an artist, an art critic, nor even the utterances of a solitary subject—but can be extended to the material configuration of *interactive dialogue*. Entextualized strips of language taken from the ongoing flow of social life can be more or less "stringently" configured, as they are "reported" in new social situations.

Interestingly, in a critique of Kierkegaard, Menke characterizes the destabilization of meaning, generated by the experience of aesthetic negativity, as a "devaluation" of meaning (230-31). In this sense, the *exchange value* of the material signifier, as it "represents" normative meanings and values, is *devalued* in aesthetic configurations. Thus, both subcultural valuing discourses—as well as their exchange value—are "devalued," as the material configurations from which they are interpellated become "things of a second order." We can see here a direct application of Adorno and Menke's aesthetic theories to the potential dislocation of normative value discourses—including the exchange value discourse.

As Menke points out, aesthetic transfiguration does not refute the "validity" of non-aesthetic (value) discourses on their own terms, nor assert an alternative validity (231). In other words, "aesthetic negativity" does not enter into a political arena regarding the appropriate prioritization of social values, nor an economic arena as a kind of "aesthetic value" (see Guillory 1993). The aesthetic disruption of value is not an appeal to *irrational* social action. Rather, what is disrupted is the "presence" of the automatic understanding, or normative signification, assumed by value discourse (232). In other words, aesthetically configured utterances open a space which unsettles the automatic re-citation of normatively-interpellated grafts of identity and values. This experience of aesthetic negativity *precedes* any tentative re-articulation of social identities or social values, in potentially new configurations or proportions; that is, it precedes any new "hegemonies" or new "universal values" such as democracy or social justice (see Laclau and Mouffe 1994; Butler, Laclau, and Žižek 2000).

For Adorno, as Menke describes, when automatic understandings are frustrated, and normative meanings and values are disrupted, repeated attempts are often made at understanding what the aesthetic object (or utterance) might mean. For Adorno, these become only *tentative*, speculative assertions (Menke 1998, 59-60). In other words, meaning is drawn into question and becomes *estranged* (59), rather than *rejected* (i.e., the object does not revert to "mere thing"). As Menke notes, eventually some social meaning will often be re-affixed to even the most ambiguous works of art (59).

As automatic contextual assumptions are disrupted following the experience of aesthetic negativity, new assumptions and interpretive contexts are tentatively—rather than automatically—applied to the aesthetic object, in a continuing search for its meaning and value. Interestingly, Adorno argues that these new tentative re-applications of interpretive context, which might tentatively ground the now-unsettled meaning of the work, are "quoted"(60).

In Menke's words, "This reference to the *context by quotation* rather than by application creates distance: contextual assumptions that guarantee understanding become ambiguous when they are quoted" (60, italics added). In other words, it is "quotation," or re-citational practice, which retains an element of "tentativeness" in the re-generation of meaning following aesthetic negativity—as opposed to a reified, automatic re-application of a pre-existent meaning. In this sense, the process of citationality is not only involved in the *disruption* of meaning and values—as in the case of aesthetics—but also is crucial for their (always-tentative) *restoration.*

In this formulation, the re-articulation of meanings and values, following the disruption of hegemonic forms, are tentative or provisional, rather than naturalizing and reified. The tentative "quoting"—by which meaning and values are re-cited following aesthetic negativity—leads neither to nihilism, nor to the re-installation of a reified universal discourse following a dialectical negation, but rather reveals the contingency and tentativeness of all (universal) claims to identity and value (see Laclau and Mouffe 1994).

Thus, the *disruption* of any particular value discourse—such as exchange value—cannot be achieved through a mere appreciation of the diversity of valuing domains, or the (political) citation of alternative value contexts; rather, it can only be achieved through the *aesthetic* dislocation of "value" itself. This type of "immanent critique" opens the space for a *tentative* restoration of "values," and perhaps opens, appealing to the language of Laclau and Mouffe (1994), a space for an ongoing critique of the universalizing, hegemonic claims of any particular value discourse—including that of exchange value.

This discussion of aesthetic negativity not only has implications regarding the value or meaning of a (more-or-less) stringent material form, but also for the social *identity* of the subject who incorporates that form into their citational utterances. When a subject cites an aesthetic object, their interpellated identity is destabilized or made tentative, inasmuch as the meaning and value of the citational resource is itself tentative. We see here how the citation of an aesthetic object may unsettle the (Cartesian) identity of subjects, in a way that the citation of less-stringent resource (i.e., commodities) does not. Following the experience of aesthetic negativity, the process of "quotation as tentative understanding" does not automatically re-establish *secure* Cartesian identities and values; rather, the material form of the "self-subverting" aesthetic object continues to frustrate any perfect fit of these tentative identity contexts (see Menke 1998, 61). The identity and exchange value of the Cartesian object, and the interpellated identity and values of the Cartesian subject, are de-stabilized by aesthetically configured material forms.

In this section we have extended Menke's reading of Adorno's aesthetic theory to argue that the experience of aesthetic negativity not only disrupts normative *meanings*, but also normative *values*—including the hegemonic exchange value discourse. Of course, Adorno himself saw the realm of aesthetics as perhaps the last refuge for critical thinking in late capitalism—where culture had become commodified and a discourse of exchange value prevailed (Rose 1978, 48; Jay 1973). This insight can be moved from a perspective emphasizing the reification of consciousness into a framework based on Derrida and Butler's notions of performative citationality. Following up on Adorno's insistence that it is the *materiality* of the aesthetic form which generates such a disruption of meaning, and thereby value, we can see that citational utterances—whether issued by artists, everyday subjects, or social institutions—may be more or less configured in aesthetic ways to initiate such disruption.

While no strict dichotomy can be maintained between commodities and aesthetic objects as citational resources, it is clear from Adorno's work that aesthetically configured utterances have greater potential to unsettle normative value discourses, as well as the identities interpellated from the utterances. Recognizing this, we can re-site Adorno's aesthetic theory into a theory of performativity which emphasizes re-citational practices. As Butler argued, re-citational practices have the potential to re-install, or to resist, normative values and identities. This occurs not through a process involving the implementation of a pre-existing political intentionality, but rather through the aesthetic reconfiguration of normative material forms—including linguistic utterances.

As Menke argues, the disruption of contextual frames depends on an aesthetic negativity which cannot be generated from non-aesthetic textual configurations—such as that of politics. As Adorno suggests, it is the stringent qualities of the material configuration itself which resists "automatic" abstractions—such as the universalizing measure of exchange value. This is why political (non-aesthetic) opposition itself cannot generate the aesthetic negativity necessary to unsettle the re-citation of the exchange value context. The strategy of a contemporary critical theory must therefore include not only *political* opposition to inequality—and, in Guillory's sense, an advocacy for full inclusion within the system of cultural production—but also the *aesthetic* disruption of the automatic interpellation of the exchange value frame itself. Using Laclau and Mouffe's terms, the articulation of a new, more democratic "universal" must *follow* the aesthetic disruption of the current, reified, hegemonic formulation—that of exchange value. In short, aesthetics is not a "new politics," but rather precedes it as the dislocation of the "old politics." In this sense, it is the *materiality of aesthetic form* which continually reveals, and re-performs, the tentative nature of any particular system's claim to universal truth or universal "values."

Aesthetic and Commodified Citational Forms

As discussed earlier, Guillory (1993)—drawing on the work of Howard Caygill (1989)—argues that "aesthetic value" emerged historically as a category with the development of the market economy, and with the accompanying hegemony of exchange value. The work of art was considered as a sphere separate from that of the commodity (317). However, as Guillory points out, this strict separation can be maintained neither in theory nor in practice—even Marx reintroduced aesthetics in his theory to explain consumption as "the object's capacity to produce a need in the consumer that did not exist before" (321).

Perhaps, following Adorno and Butler, it is better to distinguish between meaningful social objects—such as "commodities" and "works of art"—to the extent that they re-cite sedimented meanings and automatic understandings, or whether they incorporate self-subverting strategies which allow for a greater possibility of the experience of aesthetic negativity in future constellations and contexts. Given that, in a Derridean sense, any identity always already incorporates alterity and thus cannot be a pure category, we might—using a term from Bakhtin—speak of the ratios in which citational forms like art or commodities embrace or distance themselves from normative understandings and values, in given constellations with other citational forms. For example, several gender parodies might differ in the extent to which they disrupt normative gender categories, or are marketable as commodified experiences (see Butler 1999, 176-77). The extent to which any particular performance is a commodity or work of art becomes a matter of ratio or proportion, relative to normative understandings and values.

Utterances—whether as everyday words, text messages, photographs, songs or video clips—are more or less marketable. Some are marketed against the wishes of the subject who uttered the word or was captured in the photograph; other utterances have been entextualized by subjects precisely for mass media distribution. Some utterances are artistically designed to prevent ready incorporation into current distributional forms, while others are formulated precisely to fit such forms. While the distributional technology is often ideologically considered to be a neutral transmitter of value and experience, in fact the materiality of the distributional form always already "takes a stand" relative to normative meanings and values. This raises the question of whether aesthetic negativity can be achieved within those distributional forms and networks precisely designed to deliver commodified language.

As Gillian Rose (1978) has pointed out, at times Adorno seemed to suggest that the culture in late capitalism had become "'completely reified'" (48). Adorno argued that not only did the reification of consciousness obscure the inequalities of the capitalist system, but also obscured any possible alternatives to existing conditions. The ability to critically analyze the political-economic system was severely limited by mass culture; Adorno thus turned to aesthetics as the refuge of critical consciousness in such a reified culture (Jay 1973). Inasmuch as contemporary citational technologies "re-cite" exchange value, then the writings of the Frankfurt School on the critical potential of the aesthetic remain relevant. With contemporary citational technologies, any utterance can quickly achieve national media distribution into virtually any referential context, and language itself is thus increasingly commodifiable.

Peter Uwe Hohendahl (1995) argues that Adorno's work on the "culture industry," and his accompanying pessimism toward the future, was historically situated relative to "Fordist capitalism" (128). The focus of production in that 1940s economy, according to Hohendahl, was on pre-packaged, pre-planned culture (130)—against which Adorno strongly reacted. However, Hohendahl points out that Adorno, especially in his essay "Culture Industry Reconsidered," shifted the focus of his analysis as the economy itself shifted. Citing Miriam Hansen, Hohendahl points out that in that essay, Adorno is more sympathetic to the struggles of modern filmmakers or musicians (131).

In that later essay, we find Adorno giving less of a sweeping indictment of mass culture, and instead offering a closer analysis of the materiality of the particular artwork in question, and the extent of its stringency (135). Hohendahl argues that the work of the later Adorno explores the progressive potential of modern art—especially film (131). It is this later work which is most compatible with the notion that aesthetically configured citational resources may be disruptive of normative values and identities, especially when combined with the Derridean insight that the re-citation of normative identities and meanings necessarily involve their alteration. Having said this, however, Adorno also recognized that modern art could never be "pure," and was necessarily tied to the commodity form (172).

This later work of Adorno becomes relevant to the analysis of contemporary citational resources, and the extent to which they self-subvert their own commodified form. Despite a more sympathetic treatment of modern art in his later work, however, Adorno never abandoned his concern with commodification. Instead, he argued that the modern artist must work to undercut normative expectations through the formulation of the materiality of the work—using techniques which "in-cite" critical reflection on the part of the audience (135).

In Derridean terms, the aesthetic form occupies the space between the normative and unquestioned repeatability of the meaning and value of its material elements, and an unintelligible singularity with no recognizable meaning or value across situational contexts. This syntactically-configured tension involves the repeatability of meaning and value "with a difference." In Goffman's (1961) sense, the materiality of the aesthetic form has to screen out a certain amount of "difference," in order to remain at least minimally intelligible—as opposed to a mere thing. On the other hand, the aesthetically configured screen must allow in some difference in order to challenge normative valuing contexts. Aesthetic tension, playing against normative identities and values, becomes commodifiable when the material screen receives an exchange value within the cultural economy. However, as opposed to easily-commodifiable forms, the aesthetically configured material form resists the "automatic" measure of its exchange value, and its unquestioned assimilation back into the exchange value frame. Rather, its stringent qualities disrupt the reified nature of the exchange value frame itself.

Cultural Commodities as Pharmakon

In his critique of Plato's *Phaedrus*, Derrida (1981) shows how Plato's text—which attempts to exclude writing from the Greek polis—in fact is forced to admit to the dependency of speech on writing. For Plato, speech becomes a "'good' kind of writing that is inscribed in the soul" (Norris 1987, 35). Derrida's analysis focuses on Plato's use of the Greek word "pharmakon" to describe writing. In Plato's text, the word "pharmakon" at various times is used to mean either "poison" or "cure" (Derrida 1981, 97; 99). Derrida's critique shows that writing will not remain in a subordinate position in Plato's text; rather, Plato at times is forced to concede the necessity of writing for communication. For Plato, as Christopher Norris notes in his work on Derrida, "Writing is both poison *and* cure, on the one hand a threat to the living presence of authentic (spoken) language, on the other an indispensable means for anyone who wants to record, transmit, or somehow commemorate that presence" (1987, 37-38, italics in the original).

The writings of both Theodor Adorno and Walter Benjamin seem to oscillate between considering the commodity as a source of reification, and alternately, as a potential site of redemption. In this sense, we might say that the commodity could also be described as a "pharmakon"—both a potential poison as well as potential cure. More so than Adorno, Benjamin explored the possibilities for the "redemption" of commodities and political change. For Benjamin, commodities of the past could perpetuate the ideology of capitalism, yet also had the power to "explode" into the present in images which would challenge that ideology.

Benjamin argued that modernity threatened the memory of cultural traditions and values (Wolin 1994, 217). However, Benjamin argued that when faced with the possible loss of this cultural memory, the current generation may yet redeem the sufferings of past generations. Benjamin was attracted to the poet Baudelaire's use of "correspondences," through which an almost-forgotten past could be returned to the attention of the current generation, and potentially be redeemed (235). In other words, Benjamin longed for a method by which the sufferings and experiences of the past could be brought forth from their past contexts, and grafted or cited into contemporary contexts in critical ways. Thus, while Benjamin agreed with Adorno's assessment of the reification process in late capitalism, he held out hope for the redemption of commodities—and at times moved Adorno's thought in this direction as well.

In her analysis of Benjamin's *Passagen-Werk*, Buck-Morss (1983) finds the central argument of Benjamin to be that "the recently out-of-date objects of mass culture possessed political, indeed, revolutionary power for his generation" (211). For Benjamin, the "dream-images" (214) of previous generations become embodied in commodities as a kind of collective unconscious, which the present generation reifies as natural (217). While this process could result in the perpetuation of ideology across generations and even contribute to fascism (238), there also was the potential that such commodities could be "read" by future generations within a more critical constellation.

Once the exchange value of commodities had receded, their historical "truth" could potentially burst into the present—in such a way as to make apparent that the promises of the commodity were illusory (214-15). For Benjamin, the promise of an alternate society lay not in the desires of consumers for the current fashions, but in recovering the memories of the past from ruin (222, n24). New technologies, especially film, had the potential to re-cite the *promise* of unfulfilled desires. In the language of performative citationality, while commodities re-cited exchange value, they also re-cited the unfulfilled desires of past generations for those alternative values abjected within the commodity form.

Benjamin thus argued that the new technologies of mass culture could contribute to either destruction or redemption. On the one hand, capitalism had the ability to absorb the desires and hopes of people into all types of technology-based commodities. On the other hand, the utopian hopes of the past, brought into the present and grafted into new contexts via these new technology-based commodities, could awaken or "shock" the current generation into political action.

Both Adorno and Benjamin shared the view that a critical reading of any "commodity-text" must develop its critique even while employing the language of commodification; that is, critique is bound together with that which it confronts. This type of "immanent critique" tries to discover possibilities for alternative futures, as well as discover traces of unfulfilled pasts, from within the commodity form itself—and transform the commodity through the very process of critique (Buck-Morss 1979, 154-55). For Benjamin, in Howard Caygill's words, the point of criticism was to "keep open as many futures as possible for the works criticised" (1998, 79). In other words, Benjamin argued that critical theory disrupts the temporality of the commodity's "presence," by opening the future and redeeming the past.

Caygill points out that Benjamin's "speculative" criticism meant that criticism addressed not only what was "present" in the commodity-text as constructed by capitalists, but also considered how the text-at-hand was only one historical possibility. Speculative criticism would reveal traces, within the commodity-text, of abjected possibilities and unfulfilled wishes; in addition, it would reveal potentialities for its future development (35). In this sense, for Benjamin the "commodification" of an object, event, or of language limited or fixed its interpretive possibilities (see 131). The commodification process limited the interpellated context to only that of exchange value, and thereby restricted possible futures.

Benjamin's method of criticism, whether of a work of art or of a commodity, thus looked both to the past and to the future (92). Given that the configuration of now-outdated commodities may have foreclosed the futures of past generations, a critical reading of the traces of their unfulfilled wishes and desires may lead to their redemption in new contexts. In this sense, a reading of the commodity-text involves not only what values are claimed to be "present," but also what values have been abjected in the text. The commodity becomes a historical record or archive of what has *not* happened historically; what Adorno refers to as its "unintentional truth" (see Buck-Morss 1979).

Of course, some texts would be more receptive than others to these types of transformative, critical readings—those aesthetically configured texts with high degrees of stringency would especially encourage such a re-citation. However, *any* meaningful material form could potentially be "translated," or transformed, via that kind of recontextualizing critique which revealed that the commodified configuration of the text was only one possible syntactical construction. When recontextualized in unknown future grafts, the commodity could have an alternative "afterlife," which retrieved "those of its possibilities which had neither been realised in the work itself nor in previous critiques" (Caygill 1998, 47). Caygill concludes that for Benjamin, "Critique disturbs the identity of the work by opening it to future possibilities" (46). In other words, the recontextualization or re-citation of the commodity may later retrieve those alternative values abjected in its once-present "identity"—based only on its market value.

Setting aside for a moment some of the important differences between Adorno, Benjamin and Derrida, we can also see some clear affinities here between critical theory and Derrida's "poststructuralism." As Max Pensky has noted, both Adorno and Derrida developed methodologies of textual criticism which "dedicate themselves to the gleaning of unintentional moments of interruption, resistance, deferral, or negation that are cryptically encoded within the material that dominant totalizing discourses marginalize or repress. In this sense both Adorno and postructuralism still understand philosophy as containing the promise, however fragile, of preserving the possibility of thinking differently or thinking difference" (1997, 6). Like Benjamin, Adorno looked to outdated commodities, no longer perceived as valuable, for this abjected other (6).

Commodities whose exchange value had faded and were no longer given a "present" value—could potentially return as oppositional citational resources. Both Adorno and Derrida, according to Pensky, are thus thinkers of "alterity" (6), and, like Benjamin, attempt to indicate a future beyond those processes of commodification and rationalization which characterize contemporary Western cultures. For an alternative to the metaphysics of presence, they all looked to the materiality of citational resources—including commodities.

If Benjamin and Adorno saw the commodity as both poison and cure, using the language of the "reification of consciousness" (see Buck-Morss 1979; Jay 1973; Rose 1978), we might apply the same insight using the language of performative citationality. The citation of cultural commodities may re-interpellate unequal social relations, or may potentially disrupt them in new situational contexts. The commodification of language is the basis of re-producing exchange value in the current cultural economy, yet language-commodities are also re-cited in new syntactical configurations—such that their meaning cannot be precisely fixed once and for all.

Contemporary media technologies are instrumental in shaping the distributional networks for cultural commodities. Strips of social life have become easily entextualizable and marketable, as images or words are delivered as experiences for consumption. In Heidegger's (1977) sense, this commodity-form has become so pervasive that contemporary subjects now perceive the world as a "picture." Similarly, Norman Denzin (1995) has noted the cinematic quality of everyday life; the movie-going experience has resulted in the normative practice of citing strips of reality as if taken from a movie. Music heard in a car may thus be experienced as a "soundtrack" to everyday life, as if one is driving in a scene from a film. In short, the technological processes shaping the ways in which cultural commodities are delivered, and cited by the subject, have also shaped the meanings of everyday life as marketable strips of "experience."

Photographs taken in everyday life might therefore be instantly recognized as having a marketability—especially if they capture a moment which a national magazine, newspaper, or website might profitably distribute. Similarly, one's own backyard might be perceived through the lens of a national home or garden magazine. In this sense, photography can be considered as part of the societal apparatus which measures or documents the "presence" of exchange value (see Barad 2007). Advancements in digital photography amount to refinements in the measuring apparatus which enables the re-citation of exchange value—as technological advancements in the performativity of exchange value. Photography participates in the performativity of exchange value in that every marketable image taken re-cites that interpretive frame.

Walter Benjamin's work on photography in particular, and technology more generally, might be helpful in understanding these processes. For Benjamin, photography can be considered *as a form of citational practice* (Cadava 1997, xvii). In addition, as Cadava notes, Benjamin views history as something which is also cited or quoted (xvii). What the citing of history and photographable images share, as does citationality generally, is the "interruption" of context—as when a quote is lifted out of a text to be inserted elsewhere.

According to Benjamin, the thinking of history, or memory generally, involves the interruption of the "flow" of past events—as a particular event is "cited" into the present (xviii). Photography, like thought or memory itself, fixes or freezes a moment; in Cadava's words, "photography names a process that, seizing and tearing an image from its context, works to immobilize the flow of history" (xx). History thus becomes an "image," entextualized for reciting in another context. As discussed above, the materiality of "texts" are formed through the interruption of the flow of socio-historical "discourse" (Silverstein and Urban 1996). In Benjamin's words, "interruption is one of the fundamental procedures constitutive of form" (Benjamin, quoted in Weber 2008, 99)—as in the case of photographs "taken" from the discourse of ongoing social life.

As Cadava notes, citing Benjamin and Junger, noteworthy "events" are constructed in modernity through their "technological reproducibility" (1997, xxiii), given that they can be repeatedly reinserted into multiple temporal and spatial contexts. Thus, images from the past can continually return as an "eternal *present* made possible by the technical media" (xxvii; my emphasis). As Kracauer noted, this reproducibility has in turn affected the modern subject's very *perception* of everyday life; in Cadava's words, "the world's 'photographability' has become the condition under which it is constituted and perceived" (xxviii). In a consumer economy, the marketability of cultural commodities involves such a recognition or anticipation of their potential exchange value, when recontextualized or re-cited in other contexts.

Benjamin was acutely aware of the destructive possibilities of such a technical re-presentation of the past; not only for the perpetuation of economic inequality, but also for political propaganda as in fascism (xxiv). Especially in an age of technical reproducibility, the question continually arises as to whether citational forms like art or commodities can open a space for an alternative future, or simply be recontextualized into the articulations of dominant political and economic groups. On the one hand, Benjamin understood the dangers of modern technology, especially in the context of fascism.

Citational technologies like photography have indeed been used, in both politics and in the marketplace, to shut down a potentially redemptive dialogue with the past, and to restrict possible futures (see Caygill 1998, 95). On the other hand, as Caygill notes, Benjamin felt that the new art forms of photography and film had the potential to "create unprecedented experiences of space and time, which will bring with them the dissolution of previously valid experiences of identity" (107).

We thus find in Benjamin's work a kind of "aporia" or "pharmakon" of photography—the potential of this citational technology for destruction, yet also for redemption. As Cadava notes, for Benjamin it was precisely photography's link to death which also enabled new identities. As with writing for Derrida, for Benjamin the photographic image "allows us to speak of our death *before* our death. The image already announces our absence . . . It announces the death of the photographed" (Cadava 1997, 8; italics in the original). This possibility, using Derrida's term, is inscribed into "iterability" of the image—in that it outlives the initial context of the photographed (10). As with Derrida, the meaning of any material form requires that it function in the absence, or death, of any particular sender or receiver; in this sense, absence or death *constitutes* the photograph.

For Benjamin, the photograph thus announces death, yet also outlives that which dies; as Cadava puts it, "the photograph, like the souvenir, is the corpse of an experience" (128). If experience—and the value of experience—is said to be "present," its iterability in fact requires the "death" of that "presence" in order for its meaning to persist across contexts. It is in this sense that photography may be considered a "pharmakon," enabling a history where "something lives in its death" (128). For Benjamin, this is also the "citational temporality" of history itself. Whenever a strip of language is entextualized in order to travel across contexts, the death of the authentic, original "context" occurs.

Thus, for Benjamin, it is *citationality itself*—and in particular modern, technological forms of "aesthetic citationality" such as film and photography—which has the potential to open alternatives to "present" political and economic structures. Benjamin's own form of writing attempted to develop a visual "constellation," where various images of the past could be brought into a critical configuration with the present—as we see in the unfinished *Arcades Project* (see Cadava 1997, xxi). Such a constellation of images, where past and present are grafted together, might "in-cite" critical awareness through new syntactical configurations. Benjamin's own aesthetic construction of texts attempted to replicate the "radical temporality of the photographic structure" (61), where the "past and the present moment flash into a constellation" (Benjamin, in Cadava 1997, 61). Here in Benjamin we can clearly see one way in which critical theory might be moved into a poststructuralist theory of citationality—via aesthetic theory.

Thus we can see not only the influence of Benjamin's work on Adorno's aesthetic theory, but also the implications for the problematic at hand. For Benjamin, an aesthetic configuration of words and images can potentially dislocate the claimed "presence" of the exchange value of commodified language. Benjamin refers to the "occasion" of the grafting together of images from different times and places as the "now," as distinct from the temporal "present" (Weber 2008, 51). For Benjamin, as Samuel Weber notes, the "event" of the now enables "a past that opens—imparts itself—to the future" (51).

Weber argues that what is important for Benjamin is the *configuration* of words or images—their *syntactical* relation to each other rather than their semantic or referential meaning (75-77). Similarly, in a discussion of Benjamin's notion of the "'historical image,'" Weber points out that the temporality of the constellation forming such an image does not derive from its "representing" or "belonging" to a particular time period, but rather from the "event" in which various contexts become "synchronic" (230). Citing Sterne's strategies in *Tristram Shandy*, Weber notes that such syntactical positioning of language, as in an aesthetic configuration, can alter the normative value of the elements (76).

In other words, while the Bakhtin Circle argued that the syntactical formation of the words of self and others in utterances necessarily *enacted and negotiated* values, here the argument is that an aesthetic constellation of meaningful elements—as they play against each other—may be potentially *disruptive* of "value" itself. We can see that for Benjamin, the material, syntactical arrangement of words or images in an aesthetic configuration can disrupt normative values—as well as potentially disrupt the temporality of "presence." Reified and automatic meanings usually taken for granted can be dislocated through the syntactical arrangement of material signs.

These insights also apply to the potential dislocation of social identity, as interpellated from material signs. An ambiguous materiality also renders ambiguous the social identity interpellated from that citational resource. Even commodities have the potential to contribute to aesthetic experience when grafted into particular syntactical configurations, and re-cited by subjects. In this sense, the type of "anticipation" found in a closed system of exchange value—that is, predicting the calculative behaviors of economically-motivated actors with known and stable identities—may also be interrupted.

We have seen that whenever the words of the other are cited, or a photograph of the other is taken, a strip of meaningful materiality is decontextualized from the flow of everyday life, to be grafted into a new context. The new context always differs from the former context, in that certain aspects of the former context are left out whenever the utterance of the other is entextualized and recontextualized. Even in a verbatim quote of the other's speech, certain words of the other are selected while others are omitted, as the situated context in which the words were first uttered is lost. In this sense, the words of others are "translated" into new utterances, necessarily involving an alteration of the meaning of those words.

As Cadava notes, Walter Benjamin has argued in his work on translation that a good translator should not simply "render a foreign language into one we may call our own, but rather . . . preserve the foreignness of this language" (1997, 17). In the sense that the words of the other are necessarily "foreign" to the referential perspective of self, we might generalize this insight to inquire as to the ethical responsibility of self toward the words of the other—in other words, to what extent are the words of the other simply consumed as experiences for the (Cartesian) subject, or respected and preserved in their alterity? As de Certeau has shown, the *way* that the words of the other are incorporated into the subject's reporting practices is a political matter—the new syntactical form re-presents the intent and interests of the other to a greater or lesser extent.

To cite the words of the other necessarily involves a change of context of those words. As in photography, Benjamin argues that "translation demands the death of the original" (18). In this sense, any citation of the words of the other—not just the translation of a text from one language to another—means the "death" of the original context, and the survival of the words in translation in the new context. Benjamin refers to this as the "afterlife" of the work (Weber 2008, 66). As Samuel Weber points out, for Benjamin the *significance* of the original words or work has to do with this afterlife—the way that the words of the other are *grafted* into new contexts—rather than the "semantic" significations of those individual words or works (62). Or, as Weber puts it, "To signify is to be transformed" (63). In other words, the meaning of any word or work is continually deferred, and changing, as those words and social objects are translated into new citational grafts.

Clearly the "words of the other" can be transformed or cited in various ways in the utterances of subjects. These syntactical forms can be more or less marketable within a hierarchical system of valuation, just as various translations of "foreign" texts can be considered to be of differing quality. Thus when cultural commodities, involving the words and images of others, are produced with an eye toward maximum marketability, they are precisely "translated" into those syntactical forms which make them easily re-citable by subjects as valuable experiences—that is, shaped into normatively recognizable "forms of value." We can see that the ethics of translation involve *how* the words of the other are cited—not only by producers who market them, but by everyday subjects who incorporate those words of others into their own citational practices.

The syntactical arrangements which translate these words and images into new contexts can be considered as more or less "critical" relative to particular political values, and more or less "aesthetic" relative to value discourses in general. As discussed above, aesthetic configurations have the potential to unsettle all discourses of value. Thus, regardless of the *actual* citation or translation of any particular work, we can speak of the potential "marketability" or potentially aesthetic "translate-ability" of any linguistic form into future, unknown contexts (see Weber 59).

Regarding the potential for cultural commodities to disrupt the hegemonic frame of exchange value, we might end this section with a consideration of the work of Constantine Nakassis (2012) on brand performativity. In a discussion of how the "performative citationality" of Derrida and Butler might be effectively revised given some semiotic considerations, Nakassis argues that there are "structural instabilities" within the semiotic configuration, or "citational structure," of brands (635). While brand managers are often able to recover when brands signify in unexpected ways, Nakassis notes that "not all excesses are necessarily recoupable" (635). For Nakassis, there is always the possibility that the materiality of the branded commodity may signify differently than anticipated by a company, noting the "excesses of materiality, intelligibility, and ontology that haunt the brand" (635).

This argument has an interesting parallel to the earlier discussion of Adorno, especially regarding how the materiality of the work of art may generate "aesthetic negativity"—that is, disrupting normative interpretive contexts in reference to which the work might be given meaning (Menke 1998, xi). That insight from Adorno was extended in this chapter to suggest that art works might disrupt normative *values*—in addition to normative meanings—and also that *commodities* could potentially disrupt normative values and identities in particular aesthetic constellations. Applying these insights, we might be consider here—relative to the work of Nakassis—how the *materiality of the brand* has the potential to signify differently when entering into particular social environments or syntactical configurations. The exchange value frame—as the normative interpretive context for the branded commodity—may be dislocated when the materiality of the brand begins to signify in unexpected ways. In short, the recontextualization of any material form—whether art, branded good, or language-based commodity—always imparts the *chance* that the material form will signify something other than exchange value.

The Aesthetics of Interactional Framing

As Briggs and Bauman argue, citing Bakhtin and Julia Kristeva, a "genre"—such as a literary structure or aesthetic form—is intertextual (1992, 146). Considering the work of Adorno and Menke, we can recognize that the stringent qualities of aesthetic forms involve intertextual *relationships*—to other signs and ultimately to other people. As discussed earlier, for the Bakhtin Circle any utterance posits a relationship between self and other—including an "aesthetically configured" utterance. Thus, the disruption of normative value discourse, in the experience of aesthetic negativity, also disrupts normative relationships between self and other—and opens a space for alternative relationships. If the "automatic understanding" within contemporary U.S. culture is that subjects normatively *consume* the words and images of the other as a valuable experience for the subject, then the aesthetic disruption of such an assumption necessarily involves a re-negotiation of social relationships between self and other.

In everyday life, the frame or context for social interaction is *mutually sustained* by co-participants, as when both parties understand that they are "playing a game." The construction of any interactive dialogue, and its interpretive frame, occurs through both inclusions and exclusions. Appealing to Goffman's work on games, Adam Kendon (1997) has shown how these mutually-constructed frames are *achieved* in interaction, as social actors treat some meanings as relevant and some as irrelevant—as we have seen in the work of Callon on economic contracts (1998a; 1998b). Frames are *changed* as participants give cues to each other within the interaction, indicating a readiness for "frame alteration" (Kendon 1997, 331). In other words, contexts are not pre-existing entities within which subjects assume fixed positions—as Butler points out in her critique of Bourdieu's notions of "field" and "market" (2000, 119)—but are themselves sustained through normative re-citation, and are thus vulnerable to alteration.

These insights regarding the emergent nature of interactive context have broader implications for the dislocation of value frames. The stringent materiality of works of art—as utterances issued by artists in an ongoing social dialogue—can be considered as "interactional cues" for the transformation of cultural frames. As strategic moves in social dialogue which can indicate a "readiness" for frame shift, "words of art" can configure with the words of others is such a way as to potentially dislocate normative value and identity interpellations. Any utterance in everyday interaction can signal a shift away from normative interpretive frames, and introduce a stringent quality into the mutually-constructed and mutually-sustained frames of everyday life.

As the Bakhtin Circle showed, the utterances issued by a subject are always already "dialogical," incorporating the words of the other into syntactical arrangements with the words of the self. Like the "utterances" of artists, they cannot be considered as "individual" or autonomous, but are always already social and intertextual. In addition, conversational exchanges between interactants can be entextualized as "strips of interactive dialogue," and decontextualized from the flow of everyday life. Like the syntactical form of a work of art, the material forms of the *social dialogues* between self and other can be considered as more or less stringent in their potential to dislocate normative meaning and interpellated value frames. As Michael

Holquist reminds us, Bakhtin considered the negotiation of values between self and other, through syntactical utterances issued in interactive dialogue, to be a "problem in *aesthetics*" (2004, 29; italics in the original). Everyday utterances and strips of interactive dialogue not only *negotiate* social values between interactants, as Bakhtin shows, but—when configured in aesthetic ways—may *disrupt* normative values as they are grafted into unknown future situations.

In normative dialogue in everyday life, typified value frames are continually invoked and assumed, and normative social identities are shaped in reference to those valuing contexts. However, when utterances begin to alter or dislocate frame—introducing the potential for aesthetic negativity into interactive dialogue—normative social *relationships* are no longer automatically assumed or re-cited. Rather, in Adorno's sense, after normative (value) contexts are disrupted by aesthetic negativity, they can only be *tentatively* quoted in the attempt to re-establish meaning and interpretive context. In this sense, the meaning of interactive dialogue is made tentative following the stringent characteristics introduced by the (performing) social actors. As John Lucy (1993) has stated, "verbal *art* is a form of creative metalinguistic play with the power to affect social reality" (21; italics added).

In this sense, we can speak of the "aesthetic negativity" induced by performance, as in the case of performance art, or even regarding the more or less aesthetic citational performances of everyday life. Commenting on "verbal art," Lucy has noted that "Alternation of direct and indirect speech can be used to create both practical and aesthetic effects" (18-19). In a Bakhtinian sense, the way that the words of others are *reported upon* in everyday life, or double-voiced in one's own interactive utterances, can have *aesthetic* significance—and thus can be considered as a critical move in social interaction. Such moves produce more or less stringent qualities within the interactional sequence itself—as potentially disruptive of normative meanings, values, and identities. Although the flow of everyday dialogue is ongoing, the particular strips of language selected from this discourse will, in Adorno's sense, come to have more or less "subversive" qualities.

Thus a "performance artist"—whether or not officially recognized as such—may make a move in social interaction, potentially introducing a disruptive element into social dialogue. This performance—as a re-citable resource—may enter into a number of future constellations, as grafted into the utterances of unknown future others. Each newly-entextualized graft will in turn have more or less stringent characteristics as it is re-cited—that is, it will either "automatically" re-instate, or potentially dislocate, normative value domains and identity categories.

For example, as Judith Butler (1999) argues, gender parodies in performance art may re-cite gender in such a way as to disrupt the normative understanding of gender—such that the gendered body can no longer support "automatic" understandings. In parody, the entextualized performance has a material form which resists the automatic application of gendered significations, to a greater or lesser extent. Instead, the meaning of the performance, and the meaning of the performing body as "aesthetic object," involves the tentative quotation or citation of alternative interpretive contexts, following the initial disruption of their meanings. In addition, the "meaning" of gendered *identity*, as an iterable and recognizable social category involving particular social values and social relationships, is itself made ambiguous. The same applies to any mutually sustained, interactive performances in everyday life—which are entextualize-able from the ongoing flow of interaction, and thus available for recontextualization in future situations.

In this way, Adorno's argument concerning "aesthetic negativity" applies not only to traditional works of art or performance art, but to *any* interactive strip or dialogical sequence taken from everyday interactions—as more or less "stringent" in various future recontextualizations. In fact, the traditional art work itself is never a self-enclosed utterance of an autonomous artist, but is itself always a *response* to—in dialogue with—the pre-existing words and images of others. All utterances are, in this sense, more or less "aesthetic" citational grafts of the words of self and other.

The task of the "critical" performer—whether the author of written essays, or a street artist—is to entextualize or form their utterances in such a way as to potentially disrupt the automatic application of the exchange value frame. Of course, the performer cannot control future recontextualizations, nor control the potential re-assimilation of the utterance back into normative value frames. As Menke has argued, even the most ambiguous of aesthetic material forms will eventually be assigned some meaning or "value." On the other hand, utterances do vary in the extent to which they embrace or resist easy assimilation into normative frames. While many commodities are entextualized into a material form which "automatically" signifies exchange value, particular entextualizations of a given performance may not be so readily marketable. The materiality of the performed utterance, or strip of interactive dialogue, may have stringent qualities which resist attempts at re-incorporation into normative value frames. In order to incorporate this new materiality, existing frames may themselves have to be altered.

Aesthetic Forms and the Interpellation of Social Identity

Aesthetic negativity has the potential to disrupt or dislocate any cultural value discourse, including that of exchange value. While any linguistic utterance made in today's technological environment can be quickly commodified and given an exchange value, it is also possible that any utterance of a subject can enter into an aesthetic constellation with the words of others in subsequent recontextualizations so as to subvert normative, sedimented meanings. Such aesthetically configured citational practices, precisely because of their ambiguity of meaning, have the potential to resist automatic re-citations of value, and disrupt the interpellations of normative "experiences"—as associated with recognizable social identities.

As discussed earlier, material signs graft at least two contexts; in the case of reported speech, the referential context of self is grafted with the "context of alterity." When the normative subject cites cultural commodities, the words of others signify exchange value, and become a rankable, consumable experience for the interpellated (Cartesian) subject. In other words, the materiality grafting the referential context of self with the context of exchange value involves a commodity; the exchange value of this commodity is measured in terms of the value of the experience it can deliver. In the case of the *aesthetically configured* object or utterance, however, the normative grafting process is disrupted. The stringent material form does not automatically signify "exchange value," as do most commodities; thus, the social identity of the "present subject having valuable experiences" cannot be automatically interpellated through its citation.

Returning to Butler's example of gender, a male audience member attending a performance involving gender parody may find that the normative experience—in which the female body is displayed for his viewing pleasure (see Mulvey 1989)—is disrupted. In other words, those citational practices entextualized as the "performance" disrupt the normative citational practices of the male audience member, who finds himself now positioned relative to a non-normative citational resource. The material form of the performance no longer serves as a stable and unquestioned resource to be re-cited by the securely-gendered subject, in the "experience" of his masculinity (see Dworkin 1989; MacKinnon 1987). Rather, the normative grafting of the value context of gender, with the identity context of the experiencing subject, is disrupted.

We can see that in this case the meaning and "worth" of the aesthetic performance, the identities of both the performer and audience member, and the value categories themselves are all *made tentative*. While material forms which objectify women are normatively assigned an exchange value, the aesthetically configured performance makes the automatic citation of exchange value problematic—as well as the normative identity of the "gazing" consumer. The *aesthetic* construction of citational forms—always already a grafting of the referential contexts of self and others—potentially dislocates normative value discourses. In doing so, such utterances open a space for alternative *relations* between self and other—as mediated through social identity categories.

In a discussion of the work of William F. Hanks, Silverstein and Urban (1996) have noted that each new citation of a social category or "genre"—for example, "gender" or "value"—remains in a kind of tension with the normative or sedimented meanings of that category; that is, with prior citations of it (8). Not only are particular value domains or social identities subject to this tension (between repeatable category and situated instance), but so are the normative *relationships* between the value and identity categories—which are (re-) interpellated from the citational instance.

Using Goffman's language regarding role distance, we might say that each new situated re-citational practice plays against those *generic* meanings, re-producing or resisting the normative, sedimented meanings to a greater or lesser extent. For example, the performative citational practice which parodies gender is a material form which exists in tension with other entextualized citations of gender, and "takes a stand" relative to normative relationships between gendered social identities. Of course, often part of the strategy of performance art is precisely to position the performance—as an entextualized strip of behavior in a particular setting—in tension with normative meanings (see Carlson 1996). We might thus speak of singular, situated, "citational constellations" involving the words of self and the words of others, which conform to or resist the sedimented meanings of past citational practices.

However, this process involving aesthetic negativity is not a total *rejection* of normative identity categories; rather, the restoration of meaning to aesthetic configurations, following disruption, results in the *estrangement* of identity. As Menke's discussion of Adorno revealed, aesthetic negativity involves a continued attempt by the subject to re-establish (previously-subverted) meaning with a tentative "quoting"—here, of *possible* identity contexts. Thus, even as identities are dislocated and made ambiguous (for all interactive participants) through the construction of aesthetic interactional configurations, new and tentative interpellations are attempted (or quoted) within the social psychological situation. In addition, utterances often embrace or distance themselves from several identity categories at the same time. The aesthetic configuration of a gender parody, for example, may not only estrange the normative understanding of gender categories, but perhaps those of age or social class as well. Following the experience of aesthetic negativity, the tentative reconstruction of social identity begins.

In thinking about social identity, relative to "aesthetically-formed materiality," we must also distinguish between the instance of the subject "experiencing" an aesthetically-constructed utterance made by others, and the instance of the subject issuing an utterance which has the potential to be aesthetically experienced by others. In other words, we must distinguish between the self as audience of aesthetically configured utterances, from the self as performer of potentially aesthetic utterances.

In the *first case* of the self confronting an aesthetically configured entextualization issued by others, the subject finds the automatic or normative signification of value to be disrupted—as when an audience member encounters a gender parody. Here, the usual interpellation of an experiencing, valuing Cartesian subjectivity is disrupted given the aesthetic configuration; that is, the material configuration does not interpellate a normative subject. Instead of the subject using the cultural form to interpellate exchange value (i.e., the worth of the experience), attention is drawn to the *materiality* of the citational configuration (in Adorno's sense). The *form* of the citational resource—here, the materiality of performed language—is itself drawn into question.

Thus, the subject must respond to a situation where their (Cartesian) identity is not secured by the object—in Mead's (1969) sense, the "I" of self cannot respond to a securely-interpellated "me." The audience member attending a gender parody is thus positioned relative to an ambiguous materiality, which not only disrupts the "presence" of the normatively-valued "experience" (i.e., of the objectification of women), but also the presence of the interpellated Cartesian subject who so experiences. The ambiguous material form thus disrupts the normative *temporality*, and normative *exchange value*, of Cartesian, capitalist experience—as "present."

In confronting the aesthetically configured materiality, the interpellated identity of the audience member is no longer that of one who experiences events of a recognizable and normative "worth." Rather, the social identity ("me") interpellated from such an aesthetic configuration—to which the "I" must respond—becomes ambiguous, and estranged from its usual referential context. The self's response to such a situation becomes problematic given their positioning within it; a male audience member who grows uncomfortable at a gender parody may begin to worry about the attributions of others as to "what kind of person" with "what kind of values" would attend such a performance. The ambiguity of a calculable worth of the experience may draw into question the investment of time "spent" at the performance. Positioned as an unstable subject by the performance itself, the subject may begin to reconsider not only the meaning of gendered identity, but also the social relationships in which the female identity category of "gender" is normatively experienced as subordinate by males. The citational resources which the subject is citing (i.e., is positioned relative to—have become unstable, as well as the social identities normatively interpellated from them).

On the other hand, even if a performed utterance is *potentially* "aesthetic," it is never necessarily so. Each singular subject, located within a unique social addressivity, brings multiple social identities into each situation—and necessarily enters into a different "constellation" with the potentially aesthetic utterance. Thus the "aesthetic configuration" does not necessarily invoke the experience of aesthetic negativity for every subject in any particular situation. Because subjects are simultaneously positioned differently relative to multiple citational forms, the identities and values of subjects are "differentially disrupted." In Goffman's sense, subjects are distanced from, or embrace, multiple citational resources simultaneously. Thus each socially-positioned subject necessarily assumes a unique social stance; the experience of aesthetic negativity becomes a question of ratio relative to multiple identity and value categories.

In addition, particular audience members may lack the semiotic codes typically brought to the interpretation of aesthetic objects (and their stringent qualities). Traditionally, works of art are prepared, or entextualized, with particular audience codes in mind—codes which, as Bourdieu and Guillory argue in the case of social class, are unevenly distributed. Thus, a configuration which some audience members interpret as subversive, in reference to other known material signs, may lapse into unintelligibility as "mere things" for other audience members. While the experience of aesthetic negativity does indeed depend on the self-subversive characteristics of the material object, the future "interpretive situations" into which the object will be grafted cannot be known in advance. No one can entirely anticipate the future travels of entextualized cultural forms, their likelihood of generating aesthetic negativity in future situations, or their political implications.

However, this does not mean that aesthetic negativity remains altogether a private, subjective experience. Those who share (Cartesian) identity categories—despite their simultaneous membership in other, differentiated groups—may share an "experience" of disruption. This sense of disruption of Cartesian identity, like any meaning, can be communicated across contexts. While there are certainly limits as to the communicability of subjective experience—including the experience of aesthetic negativity—it is also true that the utterances of self may be more or less successful in this communicative attempt.

We have now arrived at the *second case* to be considered—that of the subject issuing utterances which are potentially aesthetic to others. Adorno argued that one of the functions of aesthetic criticism was precisely the attempt to put into understandable language the experience of aesthetic negativity—the ironic attempt at "communicating the disruption" of normative understanding. Following the reception of an aesthetic utterance, a subject may attempt to communicate their experience of aesthetic negativity to a wider audience—as in the case of telling others about a work of art or a gender parody. This type of interpretive speech or aesthetic criticism is difficult, because it seeks to shape the experience of aesthetic negativity into understandable, iterable forms; that is, meaningfully communicating the disruption of meaning. As discussed, for Adorno this endeavor means using conceptual language in such a fashion as to self-subvert its own "understandable" form, thus mimicking the self-subversive strategies of the aesthetic object it seeks to re-enact (Buck-Morss 1979, 98; Nicholsen 1999, 3).

As Sherry Weber Nicholsen notes, Adorno's form of writing was itself "constellational" or "configurative," seeking to create such a discontinuity of understanding—employing techniques such as the lack of paragraphing or lack of linear argumentation (1999, 96). In such a constellation, concepts were "set in relation to one another" (107), often cross-referencing each other (10). For Nicholsen, Adorno's sentences in *Aesthetic Theory* formed a "*constellation composed of contexts*" (174; italics added), in such a way that connections between sentences could be drawn by readers (175).

Bakhtin has shown us that the syntactical form of the utterance—its "aesthetic" construction (Holquist 2004, 29)—negotiates values between self and other. This argument has been extended, via Menke's reading of Adorno's aesthetic theory, to argue that interactive dialogue—as a more or less "stringent" configuration of the words of self and other—can generate the experience of "aesthetic negativity." Now we see that, for Adorno, aesthetic configurations not only play words, sentences, or *texts* against each other, but also play interpellated *contexts* against each other. In other words, Adorno's work used the materiality of language to graft together contexts in such a way as to disrupt the usual semantic meaning of the words and sentences—using a particular citational or syntactical configuration. While the grafting of the *commodified* words of others may indeed valorize the referential context of self—re-enacting the system of exchange value—Adorno shows that a "constellation of contexts" may also have *aesthetic* effect.

Adorno wanted to simultaneously embrace the importance of non-aesthetic social criticism—which appealed to a "nondiscursive rationality" in the critical analysis of society—as well as to embrace the realm of aesthetics, which disrupted normative understanding and opened a space to possible alternative social relations (Nicholsen 1999, 3). In this sense, his essays themselves oscillated between the *enactment* of particular political values, as well as the *disruption* of "value" itself. On the one hand Adorno, in "The Essay as Form," argued that a critical essay itself was not "art," in that criticism relied on concepts while art undermined normative understanding (Nicholsen 1999, 106). On the other hand, Adorno's essays—as opposed to more "rationalized" modes of expression—were configured in such a way as to dislocate such meaning and thus potentially approach aesthetic status themselves (106-107). Both aesthetic performance, as well as the "reporting" on such a performance, are re-citational practices with the potential to disrupt normative value and identity categories.

The subject as potential artist or performer has no control over the future contexts into which their "stringently-configured" utterances will be received. Each utterance in face-to-face dialogue, as an entextualized grafting of the words of self and others, may later be experienced by others and responded to in unpredictable ways. The "understandings" which the aesthetically configured utterance potentially disrupts in future recontextualizations depends upon the understandings which others already hold. Thus, any potentially aesthetic utterance *takes a chance* in its attempt to disrupt normative meanings, with no controllable interpretive outcome, and no guarantee of delivering "aesthetic negativity" to audiences. The utterance may be misunderstood, or may be subsumed into existing value discourses despite its attempt to subvert them. The only defense against such assimilation is to build into the materiality of utterances those self-subversive qualities which might disrupt their easy assimilation into known value and identity genres.

Similarly, the subject might intend an utterance to be a "rational," conceptual critical commentary on the works of others, but it may instead, in some unknown future configuration, itself initiate an aesthetic experience. For example, Derrida's commentary on Shakespeare, or Adorno's essays, may themselves come to be considered as aesthetic objects. In this sense, Shakespeare's plays are citational forms which are always open to recontextualization—as are the utterances of Adorno, or Adorno's critics. Subjects can only make utterances—citing the words and works of others—in entextualizations which are more or less stringent relative to normative values and identities.

We have seen that syntactically-arranged citational forms can themselves be seen as "aesthetic objects"—not only in the case of the literary work, but also in the case of interactive dialogues between self and others. Just as Menke, Adorno, and Derrida argued that the experience of works of art can dislocate normative understandings, it has been argued in this chapter that "aesthetically-constructed" citational forms, issued by subjects in everyday interactions, can disrupt normative value discourses within the culture—particularly the hegemonic exchange value discourse.

Such a disruption also makes ambiguous the social identities normatively affiliated with those values, as well as the social relationships between persons categorized into those identities. The aesthetic negativity derived from such aesthetically configured citational forms may initiate a critique of normative value discourses, as well as open the possibility of differing social relationships—considering that utterances always already re-cite social relationships. In addition, such citational practices in everyday life may unsettle relationships with co-present others. Aesthetically-configured utterances which disrupt sedimented gender relations, or other cultural value domains, thus have consequences for interpersonal relationships—as in the case of two people who disagree over the "value" of a gender parody.

Such a dislocation of normative understanding has implications for the assembly of self—as constructed through language. While the normative subject in late capitalism cites the commodified words of others as a valuable experience, the subject experiencing aesthetic negativity becomes dislocated or estranged. Rather than experiencing the "presence of value," the subject is re-positioned relative to an ambiguous materiality. The interpretive context against which the experiencing subject is normatively defined becomes problematic. This disrupts the *temporality* of the normative subject (as one who continuously experiences "presence"). Thus, a materiality which disrupts the presence of *value* also disrupts the temporality of the Cartesian *subject*. Rather than the "self" as automatically understood and unthinkingly re-cited, the self-construction process is "made tentative." Experiences of unknown value thus unsettle the archive (of valued experiences) by which the contemporary subject is defined. Opening such a space for critical reflection is especially important today, given the ever-increasing proliferation of cultural commodities used in the construction of normative social identities.

THE FUTURITY OF VALUE

Mead, Derrida, and the Critique of Presence

Just as Bakhtin argued that the differential perspectives of the self and other are required for self-constitution and human perception (see Holquist 2004, 20-21), George Herbert Mead also argued that role-taking involves the referential context of others. Influenced by Einstein's relativity theory in a way similar to Bakhtin, Mead argued that role-taking involves the simultaneous consideration of two differing perspectives, those of self and other (Joas 1997, 158; 173).

Mead appears at times to define a significant symbol precisely in terms of an "identical" meaning shared within a community of users. From that point of view, it is because we share meaning with others that we can predict or anticipate the reactions of others—in other words, significant symbols make role-taking possible. Inasmuch as Mead's theory interprets "significant symbols" to have an identifiable meaning across contexts, it becomes subject to a Derridean critique—that is, of wrongly assuming that some kind of stable meaning is "present" across contexts (Sherlock 2007).

Importantly, however, Hans Joas argues that Mead, in his theory of role-taking, moves in a more "pragmatic" direction than many theorists, focusing on the "reciprocal anticipation of behavioural expectations" (153)—a reading more consistent with Butler's notion of a "sedimented" citational practice. In other words, the anticipation of the citational practices of others concerns the expected *behavior* of others toward self, rather than a focus on a shared *conceptual* consensus as to the meaning of significant symbols. For Mead, it is not a matter of a pre-existing "group consciousness" enabling multiple applications of intended, normative meanings across situational contexts; rather, meaning is located in social interaction in (what we might call) reciprocal "citational expectations."

According to Joas, in one essay Mead precisely defines meaning "not with reference to the actual reaction of the other, nor to the mere awareness of one's own attitude of response, but rather as the consciousness of the relation between one's own actions and the responses of the other to them, which one can anticipate" (105). Here for Mead, "meaning" is subtly shifted toward an awareness of the normative practices (relative to materiality) which typically govern social interaction, as based on a social history of objectively-accomplished utterances and actions—as well as in our assessment of the *probability* that they will be repeated in future situations. This "awareness" of social meaning is emergent *from* reciprocal behavioral practices, rather than—to use Durkheim's term—a shared "collective consciousness" pre-existing practices.

However, while this shift may spare Mead from Derridean criticism regarding a shared, "present" meaning located in a group consciousness and abstractable from social action, Mead's position still seems to imply an equivalence between the attitudes of self and the attitudes of the other toward objects and situations—albeit rooted in behavioral expectations. For example, in *Mind, Self and Society*, Mead argues that "What language seems to carry is a set of symbols answering to certain content which is *measurably identical in the experience of the different individuals*. If there is to be communication as such the symbol has to mean the same thing to all individuals involved" (Mead 1969, 54, italics added).

We have seen that while Derrida (1988) has also noted the necessity of the repeatability and recognizability of linguistic signs across situations for communication to occur, he also insists that each repetition necessarily differs in each occurrence—an "aporia" of singularity and repetition. For Mead, we can anticipate the responses of others because we can "arouse" in ourselves the same response, and this enables us to adjust our future actions accordingly (1969, 73-74). This language seems to move Mead in the direction of positing a shared, "present" meaning to utterances and citational practices among members of society, "whereby individuals can indicate to one another what their responses to objects will be, and hence what the meanings of objects are" (122, n29).

However, returning to Bakhtin, a *stable* "other" in time and space *must* be assumed for anticipation and meaning construction to occur in the first place. Like Bakhtin's assumed "addressee" in the utterances of self, the perspective of Mead's "other" in the role-taking process *has to be* repeatable, recognizable, and stable in time and space. In other words, the "moment" of abstracted meaning, as *shared behavioral expectation*, must abstract a *stable* perspective (i.e., that of the other) from which to view the meaning of one's own anticipated utterances (and the consequent identity interpellations). For Mead, the "me" phase of the self, as a normatively-typified social identity, occurs precisely through the eyes of this *stable* other.

When the anticipated responses of others toward one's own citational practices "arouse" in the self the same responses, the subject is seeing one's own "meaningfully" identifiable utterances from the perspective of a stable, socially recognizable "viewing position." It is precisely against this "synchronic" moment—of a shared behavioral expectation toward meaningful materiality—that Mead contrasts the dynamism of the "I" phase of the self. Like Bakhtin and Derrida, Mead thus retains a tension between singularity and repetition—recognizing that the existential actions of the *self* are not limited to those normatively attributed to a particular *social identity*. In other words, the "I" phase of one's "self" can respond to (and against) the normative "meaning" of the anticipated social identity—an identity interpellated from normative behavioral practice (the "me").

Any "trouble" between Mead and Derrida on this point concerns the definition and location of "meaning" relative to these processes. Derrida's insistence that meaning is never quite "present" does seem incompatible with the way that meaning is defined at times in *Mind, Self and Society*. As discussed, in those accumulated lecture notes Mead tended to suggest that meaning is located precisely in the "identical" responses of self and other to social objects and social situations. The trouble arises in that we are using the same word, "meaning," to describe two distinct "moments" or processes. On the one hand, the term can be used, as Mead and Bakhtin do, to refer to the repeatable, shared aspect of language which enables the *responses* of others—toward "identifiable" signs—to be *anticipated*. On the other hand, the term can be used more generally to refer to an assumption in Western metaphysics that meaning is "present" in the shared consciousness of subjects—a sense of "meaning" to which Derrida objects, and is precisely *not* the emphasis which Mead wants to give to the term.

For example, in Mead's *Philosophy of the Present* (1959), we can immediately see that his notion of the "present" is not the "metaphysical present" which Derrida challenges. Commenting on that book, Joas notes the importance of the "event" in Mead's theory of the temporality of self. He states that for Mead, "Without the interruption of the passage of time by the event, no experience of time would be possible" (1997, 176). As Joas points out, Mead defines time *differentially* in terms of the event, in that each event "in its relation to other events gives structure to time" (Mead 1959, 21). For Mead, the event necessarily involves a change in the material environment. In this process, he argues, past and future enter into the "present" (33).

For Mead, every new event becomes the occasion for the reinterpretation of the past. However, it is also true that the material changes in the environment, as a result of events, to some extent condition the future. All social action, which necessarily occurs in the "present," objectively changes the material environment in such a way that both *enables, yet limits,* future behavioral possibilities. Here we see an affinity with Butler's notion of meaningful materiality as an "enabling constraint."

In Mead's view, this change in material conditions is necessary for the emergence of time, because the event creates two different "referential systems" (Joas 1997, 182). The event, as a change in material conditions, involves a "passing"—from the "old" to the "new" referential system (i.e., before and after the material change). It is important to stress that the "time of the event," for Mead, is in the *passing* between the systems—the "simultaneity of . . . membership" (183) in both the old and new referential systems, or the *simultaneous signification of each*. In the language of citationality, this passing would be the temporality of the graft—the simultaneous bringing together, and differentiation, of referential contexts through the materiality of the citational "event." A temporality which "splits" the present, as described by Mead, does not coincide with the way that the Western philosophical system characterizes the "presence" of meaning.

For Mead, as Joas puts it, "The simultaneity of this membership, or participation, in two systems is thus a defining characteristic of presents" (Joas 1997, 183). Here, the "present" is not that experienced by an autonomous, Cartesian subject; rather, the present is split by the "simultaneity of membership" *in multiple referential contexts*. In the language of citationality, we can say that every citational grafting of the words of self and others, in a new syntactical (material) arrangement, splits the "present" by uniting and differentiating referential contexts.

As mentioned above, we see here the influence of Einstein's theory of relativity on Mead. Mead, like Bakhtin, applies this framework of relativity to human interaction (Holquist 2004, 20-21; Joas 1997, 173). For Mead, social interaction takes place in a present, interpretable by two observers, each of whom "embodies a different time-perspective" (Joas 1997, 190). Because the self is able to "role-take," or simultaneously adopt the referential system of the other in addition to their own, two differential perspectives emerge within the self. Each new event brings an occasion for the self to imaginatively occupy the "passing"—a process through which the self is able to consider the meaning of one's actions, as well as re-consider the meaning of their social identity, from multiple referential perspectives. According to Joas, by emphasizing the situated and simultaneous referential viewpoints of at least two social actors, Mead "*is laying the corner-stone of an intersubjectivist theory of the consciousness of time*" (188, italics in the original). Mead's theory of temporality is clearly not that of the Cartesian subject, but has to do with an intersubjective grafting of contexts which unsettles the "present."

Although Mead shares with Cooley (1964) the position that the other is important in the emergence of the self concept, he objects to the "mirror" image of the "looking-glass self" in that it distorts the *temporality of the self*. For Mead, as Joas puts it, "In self-reflection the actor does not turn back upon himself in a frozen present—as in a mirror—but reflects upon the future possibilities in the present conditions, which issue from the past" (Joas 1997, 192). For Mead, the process of seeing any "me" (before or after considered action), through the eyes of others, indeed requires a synchronic, "frozen" moment. However, this synchronic moment is itself embedded in a complex temporality involving past and future, and thus is not quite "present."

The "moment" of self-reflection, in the planning of future behavior, necessarily involves knowledge of sedimented citational practices which interpellate normative social identities. Agency within social constraints thus necessarily involves *past* social identities, *anticipated* future behaviors, as well as an "anticipation of a retrospective" social glance (by self and others) at behaviors now considered, but not yet completed. In addition, the "frozen" moments of anticipating, or retroactively interpreting, social identity is necessarily *disrupted by actual, situated behavior*—the actual utterances of the "I" which, for Mead, cannot be reflected upon as they occur. Thus (pre-utterance) anticipated social identity never quite aligns with (post-utterance) interpellated identity, precisely because meaning is never quite "present" in dynamic social action—only in the "synchronic" abstraction of its meaning.

Citational practices are not just *re-enacted* behavior, but are also *anticipated and adjusted* before enacted, based upon the anticipated reactions of others. Just as utterances are re-cited from previous enactments, in Butler's sense of performativity, so are utterances re-enactments of imaginative rehearsals. As Mead has shown, human behavior is radically future-oriented, toward *action*. Like those theorists who emphasize that the process of citationality disrupts the "presence" of intentional subjects, Mead's theory similarly dislocates the "presence" of sovereign subjectivity by focusing on the *temporality* of the self—a self not merely present, but one projecting potential actions into the future.

Mead, like Bakhtin and Butler, recognized that the responses of others limited the agency of the self. For Mead, this profoundly affects the process of anticipating one's own utterances. Even though intentionality cannot govern future contexts, the self is able to *anticipate* whether one's particular citational practices—and the resultant interpellated social identity—will likely be interpreted by others as normative or deviant, and thus can adjust considered utterances accordingly. Meadian theory can re-contribute this dimension of *anticipation* to a contemporary theory of self, although the nature of "agency"—from a poststructuralist point of view—cannot be allowed to lapse back into a theory of Cartesian intentionality. Social identity can never be interpellated from actual utterances in quite the same way as anticipated by self—thus one's "identity" cannot be controlled or assured across temporal or spatial contexts. It is clear, however, that performative citationality can be rehearsed (see Schechner 1985, 35-36).

Having said this, Mead's notion of agency, particularly the nature of the "I" and the "me," seems in need of revision along contemporary poststructuralist lines. The "I" phase of the "self" must be interpreted as an ongoing response to those social identities which are interpellated from *re-citational* practices. Although the materiality of the social world is shaped by institutional utterances, which profoundly restrict the re-citational practices and social identities of individuals, at the same time the agency of subjects is *re-enabled.* The re-citation of institutionally-produced citational resources, when syntactically reconfigured by subjects, necessarily alters the identities and values implied by those materialities—to a greater or lesser extent.

In addition, Mead's concept of "anticipation" needs to be reconsidered in terms of a theory of citationality. In particular, the anticipation of the "known," normative behavior of others must be contrasted with a more Derridean *anticipation of the unknown*—as in the unknown consequences of the future re-citations of meaningful material forms. This is an especially important point given that investors in the contemporary cultural economy attempt to establish a closed system involving the presence of value—as they attempt to "anticipate" both future costs and future profits.

Investors attempt to fold the temporality of the future into the restrictive limits of the "present" economic system. As "events" themselves increasingly become commodities in a post-industrial economy, such investments involve an anticipation of the *worth of future experiences* for consumers. As language has increasingly become a commodity to be delivered via new citational technologies, the positioning of subjects—relative to the future materiality of commodified language—has become increasingly important for investment purposes. If the notion of "anticipation" is to be retrieved in performativity theory, it becomes crucial that it *not* merely refer to the calculative anticipation of the marketability of language—as an investment in an already-closed system of economic exchange.

The Aporia of Anticipation

Entextualized utterances of the self will enter into unknown constellations with the utterances of others in future situations. Like the two dice "thrown" in Derrida's (2007) essay "My Chances, *Mes chances*: A Rendezvous with Some Epicurean Stereophonies," the implications of any grafting of the words of self and other will be retrospectively determined in this future. In that essay, Derrida states: "I will throw out *two questions*. These questions having been cast, imagine that, in one blow, it is a single throw of two dice . . . After the fact, after the blow . . . , once they have fallen, we will try to see (if indeed something still remains to be seen), what sum they form between them: in other words, what their constellation signifies" (347-48).

Let us for a moment consider every singular die as a strip of language—each an entexualization which grafts the words of self and other, and which necessarily interpellates unique value ratios or identities which the die is taken to "represent." One singular "double-voiced die" is cast *today*, and is more or less "aesthetically configured" in its syntactical form, thus more or less socially recognizable in terms of its value. A second double-voiced die perhaps will be added to it, thrown in some *future* situation, by some unknown other in some future game—who for some (now unknown) reason takes the represented "value" of the first-thrown die as somehow relevant to that future game.

Then these two dice—like Derrida's two questions—having both been thrown (or entextualized), are *themselves* available for further recontextualization and re-citation for a new game to be determined in some future situation, where perhaps a third die either adds to the two, or replaces one of them, to form a new constellation and a newly-combined "value." We can see that such activity can continue again and again, with the combined "value of the dice" in any game always being open to further re-contextualization. The value of the dice is thus always deferrable, and always subject to chance.

Like the "value" of the dice, the question of the exchange value of language concerns the nature of these *future* games. As Goffman pointed out in his work on games, the *rules of the game* determine what is or is not to be considered as relevant within that game. In a linguistic sense, these rules are part of a collectively-negotiated context or frame (Kendon 1997), shaping which citational resources will count as relevant within the future interaction. In this sense, the normative regulations of a culture attempt to "precontextualize" the future—influencing the selection, the meaning, and the future value of "thrown" or entextualized strips of language. While investors indeed try to shape the rules of future games, no one can guarantee these rules—which will ultimately determine the relevance and value of previous entextualizations.

Given this uncertainty regarding the nature of future grafts into which they may later enter, entextualizations—like thrown dice—introduce an element of chance into the values of the future. For Derrida, chance is essential for any "event," or any "experience" to occur; both terms imply the occurrence of something *unforeseen* or *unanticipated*. As he notes, "If one anticipates what is coming . . . there is no pure event" (Derrida 2007, 349). Because identity demands repetition across situations, the possibility of *chance*—of singularity and difference within the re-citation process—suggests the potential disruption of identity. Possible alternative relationships between social identities always remain "in play" for future recontextualizations.

In other words, relationships to others can never be finally fixed, and one's "experiences" involving the words of others (and their values) must always remain open to the future and to chance (Derrida, 2007; see also Direk 2000). Indeed, Derrida (1978) finds Hegel's "restricted economy" of meaning to be compatible with the "presence" of exchange value, involving "a knowledge of meaning that always already has been anticipated" (271). That is a universalizing economy where "The *circularity* of absolute knowledge could dominate, could comprehend only this circulation, only the *circuit of reproductive consumption*" (271; italics in the original). Derrida notes that "Hegel has bet against play, against chance" (260). For Derrida, the values and identity of the other—to which the self must remain open—cannot therefore be already known.

Derrida thus introduces a kind of *aporia of anticipation*, where two necessary but differing—even contradictory—aspects of "anticipation" remain in tension. While the future, the "event," and "experience" cannot be anticipated as already known if to occur at all, they must in fact *re-occur* in order to be socially recognizable and meaningful. It is here where Adorno's aesthetic theory is particularly useful; normative identities and meanings are disrupted through aesthetic configurations, yet meaningful social categories are *tentatively* re-applied or "quoted" following the experience of aesthetic negativity. Aesthetic configurations create a space where signifying materiality exists between the automatic signification of normative meaning, and a meaningless lapse into a mere thing. Such a space holds in tension the aporia of meaning as both repeatable (and anticipatable), yet singular as a situated "event." Social meanings can be anticipated, but not absolutely foreseen. Aesthetic configurations *dramatize* this aporia, and thus ensure that the *anticipation of value remains tentative*.

We have seen the importance of anticipation in Mead's theory of social action. In the process of role-taking, the self is able to anticipate the social reactions of others to their own considered behavior. Inasmuch as the self anticipates normative responses, and mentally makes adjustments to considered utterances, orderly interaction becomes possible—but not guaranteed. Because others may not respond in anticipated ways, social interaction involves a continual readjustment to the actual responses of others—an ongoing oscillation between anticipated and actual responses. Derrida does not reject this dimension of human interaction, but indeed emphasizes that one's anticipation can never be completely fulfilled. Anticipated meaning or value never comes to be "present"; the re-citation process always introduces an element of the *unforeseen*.

Chance, for Derrida, always dislocates anticipation as a knowing "in advance" (Derrida 2007, 348). In short, Mead's framework needs to be expanded to recognize this side of iterability—that not only are meanings repeatable and therefore anticipatable, but also that anticipation itself requires a *continual* deferral of all meanings (including the meaning of "value"). Derrida uses the concept of anticipation in this sense of a "waiting for the unknown," and an openness toward it—rather than the anticipation of an already-known identity or value. Thus, chance not only "undoes our *anticipation*" (348, italics in the original), but also enables a kind of eagerness for an unknown future. Like Mead, Derrida emphasizes the future-oriented nature of citational practices; but for Derrida, the anticipation of the future also radically undermines the presence of stable meaning or value.

The Promise of Value

As discussed above, investors in the market attempt to anticipate the value of future citational resources. Of course, their interest is not to dislocate the exchange value frame but rather to profit from it—capitalizing on a kind of "profitability of anticipation." In this sense, the commodification of culture involves the commodification of "anticipation" itself. We also see advertisers involved in the process of marketing the "anticipation of value," when trying to promise the future delivery of exciting events to consumers. Marketing involves the commodification of a promise of value, as advertisers attempt to draw the attention of the consumer or investor to the coming commodity. Contemporary consumers have been socialized into an eagerness for those commodified citational resources which supposedly will delivered the promised value. As both Goffman (1967) and Haug (1986) note, there is an excitement to the shopping experience itself, as consumers gamble on the anticipated value of their purchases.

As discussed earlier, Jonathan Culler (1981)—citing Roland Barthes—has noted that in tourism everything becomes a "sign of itself" (127). Extending this argument to the notion that commodities in general become "advertisements" for their own value (see MacCannell 1976, 22), we can see the "aporia" of the commodity's promise—the commodity as a "pharmakon." On the one hand, the commodity re-cites the ideology of exchange value—that advertised value can be delivered and experienced as *present*. On the other hand, the commodity also re-cites a promise to consumers—of the experience of its value in the *future*.

Value is thus both cited as present, as well as promised in the future. On the one hand, the commodity seems to foreclose the future in a perpetual "presence" through the re-citation of the exchange value frame. On the other hand, it re-cites the anticipation of value in the future—necessarily an unknowable "futurity of value." Capitalism simultaneously involves both types of anticipation—as an investment in a value which will become present, as well as the continual promise of future value.

Exchange value is normatively "re-anticipated," and "re-interpellated," as an ongoing context for the interpretation of material signs in the U.S. cultural economy. Normatively interpreted through the ideology of presence, this exchange value frame is assumed to pre-exist the value of any individual commodity—rather than seen as a frame which is re-constructed through re-citational practices. The value of cultural commodities is taken as pre-existing and natural, as commodities—in Adorno's sense—"automatically" signify their worth.

In semiotic terms, this is a pretense or an ideology that the "signified" has already guaranteed the meaning of its signifier; in other words, that the signified outcome was in fact an already-anticipated identification, and therefore *without chance*. This ideology of presence assumes that what *came to be* signified as value was *already there* in the signifier. In this sense, "value" pretends, retrospectively, to have a natural link with that which socially comes to represent it. This move enacting the "presence of exchange value" in the economy parallels the ideology of presence in Western metaphysics generally.

In contrast, aesthetic negativity problematizes this automatic identification of signifier with signified by precisely disrupting the *context* within which the sign is interpreted—the normative identification between material signifier and signified value. The stringent quality of aesthetically configured utterances makes the interpellation of "already-known" contexts more difficult and less automatic. As Adorno argued, subjects, following an experience of aesthetic negativity, *tentatively* cite alternative interpretative contexts or value domains in an attempt to restore disrupted meaning. This "space of tentativity" can be seen as a kind of *waiting* for meaning or for value. The *tentative* status of the work, following the experience of aesthetic negativity, is one where its meaningful identity has not yet been established—yet the material form has not lapsed into a mere thing. We see, in a Derridean sense, that the aesthetic form has opened a space for the *anticipation* of a meaning or value which is perhaps forthcoming, but not guaranteed.

As discussed above, this space of ambiguity, which involves the tentative re-application of interpretive contexts, forces a re-examination of those "superabundant" aspects of the materiality normatively abjected in its entextualization. This superabundance could mean its *other material features*—that is, art might draw attention to certain material aspects of the work which are usually marginalized as irrelevant. Or, the consideration of superabundance might involve an abjected materiality which has been excluded, and is apparently absent from its current entextualized material form. In addition, "superabundance" can also refer to the way that the same material features are able to signify differently, as in the case of tropes—where differing meanings are held in tension "within" the same materiality. In automatic understanding, the materiality of language is presented and interpreted only in line with normative significations; following aesthetic negativity, other tentative meanings of the superabundant material sign are brought into play.

In encounters with art, as contexts are tentatively quoted rather than automatically applied, the contingency in signification is revealed. Art thus opens the *chance* that signifiers can signify something other than exchange value—something of unknown value in an unforeseen future. Because art demands that attention be given to the superabundant aspects of citational resources, a space opens for a *promise* of difference—that is, of a *different signification*.

This openness to alternate, non-normative signification is simultaneously an openness to *unknown* significations—in future situations into which the work may be grafted. Aesthetics thus problematizes the re-citation of value, through the *injection of chance into the material configuration of citational forms*. This element of chance involves a *waiting* for meaning and value, and a *promise* of difference from the automatic repetition and re-citation of normative value contexts. In this sense, art takes a chance on the future. In his work, Derrida notes the privileged position that art "retains for us, in our experience, as the place of chance and luck. The work provokes us to think the event" (2007, 360).

Although citational resources cannot be neatly separated as "commodity" and "art," they do vary in their ratio of marketability-to-stringency—that is, they are more or less conducive to the experience of aesthetic negativity, relative to contemporary value frames. In this sense, to use the favored Benjaminian suffix (see Weber 2008), while any cultural form can in fact be marketed, some are less market-*able* than others. The stringency of the more aesthetically configured utterances indicates their "willingness" to be altered in translation, and not exactly repeated as identifiable and of calculable value (see 47-48). In this way, citational resources vary regarding their differing *stances toward temporality*. Aesthetic configurations open a space for an unknown future, while more marketable forms are syntactically formed to signify the presence of already-known values.

In an economy increasingly based on the marketability of language, it is interesting to recall Derrida and Benjamin's writings on the "play" or "promise" of language. As Samuel Weber notes, both Derrida and Benjamin were drawn to those words and grammatical forms of language which introduced an element of chance or play, thus disrupting the "present" moment in favor of a more enigmatic temporality (2008, 126; 66). In formulations such as Benjamin's use of the present participle, we see that the syntactical arrangement of language—in its material form—can resist easy incorporation into a metaphysics of presence, where the future is already pre-determined as a continuation of normative meanings and values (66). Rather, these particular linguistic forms are more receptive to a *future*—as their citation introduces an indeterminacy into normative temporal interpellations. In this sense, particular syntactical arrangements might generate indeterminacy as to the "presence of value" in cultural commodities—as opposed to those forms of reported speech entextualized to merely reproduce exchange value.

This disruption of the temporality of the present, via the play of language, involves not only an openness to the future, but also the transformation of the past. When one text is cited into another, as Derrida argues, it is not merely "quoted." Rather, "the two texts are transformed, deform each other, contaminate each other's content, tend at times to reject each other, or pass elliptically one into the other and become regenerated in the repetition" (1981,

355). In addition, the cited text not only maintains its ties to its previous context, but, as Derrida argues, transforms that as well. As he puts it, "Each grafted text continues to radiate back toward the site of its removal, transforming that, too, as it affects the new territory" (355). Thus, when cultural forms from the past are cited, their meanings and values are altered—as well as the exchange value of the utterances into which they are grafted.

There is, for Derrida, a redemptive or messianic dimension to language—even the language of commodities. This messianic dimension of the commodity, its "promise," has to do with the alterity through which the identity of the commodity was originally constituted. For Derrida, anything "present" already contains the "spectral" within, as its other. Derrida appeals to this "constitutive alterity" as the promise of a future, and an alternative to the commodity as presently constituted (see Hamacher 1999, 170). While the language of exchange value attempts to close off both past and future in its claim to present value, the critique Derrida develops attempts to open both of these temporal dimensions (see 177).

However, as Derrida shows in his analysis of the "structure of the promise," there is no *guarantee* of an alternate future. A promise, as Hamacher states, "must play itself out in a mode of saying which corresponds to nothing given, nothing present, nothing extant and therefore can in no way be placed under the logic of representation, imitation or mimesis" (189). Or, as Caputo notes, for Derrida a "promise" is "the very structure of openness to the future, a word given in advance, to the other, to the future, to what is coming" (Caputo 1997, 30).

If, as Derrida and de Man have argued, the very "*act* of language is that of a performative promise" (Derrida 1989, 95; italics in the original), then the *commodification* of language enacts a performative promise of its *exchange value*. As discussed earlier, the promise of the presence of *any* subcultural value is subject to commodification, and the assignment of an exchange value to it. At the same time, however, Derrida speaks of the aporia, or unresolvable tension, between the performative act of promising, and the "truth" of what is promised (1989, 133-37). Whereas the commodity's "promise" is marketed with real economic consequences, its "value" is continually undermined by its own performative structure.

Thus, a different future can be promised, but not necessarily delivered as intended. While "present" structures are necessarily altered through recontextualization and re-citation, it is not necessarily for the better. Derrida thus refers to *possibilities,* which cannot be known or anticipated in advance. What Derrida terms the "messianic without messianism" (1994, 65) is not a known religion, but rather a *future possibility*—an event or a "structure of experience" to come (Derrida 1994, 168). It is not associated with any present political party or religious community (or *any* identifiable value domain). Instead, this possibility is radically oriented toward a future which cannot be politically, economically, or technologically designed in advance (see also Hamacher 1999, 205).

Derrida's deconstructive strategy attempts a recovery of those elements which have been abjected in the texts of Western philosophy, as well as in Western culture. As Hamacher discusses, Derrida's work in *Specters of Marx* is also a re-orientation toward alterity in an unknown future (199). To "become a commodity" is to become an object or experience of *known* exchange value, which a calculating subject can anticipate. This contrasts with a Derridean notion of futurity, where political or economic values cannot be known in advance (203). As Hamacher notes, Derrida sees language as a future-oriented *promise* (199)—or having a "prospective structure" (189). This view of language takes a stand against the contemporary trend toward the increased commodification of language.

In this sense, what is at stake in the "commodification of language" is thus the temporality of language itself. Because of its inherent "futurity," language can never be entirely controlled, or closed off in its entextualization as a cultural commodity; rather, it is a "medium" through which future possibilities are opened (193). Language always "has a play," outside of any structure which attempts to frame its meaning within fixed boundaries. In short, language can never be totally commodified or reified.

Living in an age bombarded with new citational technologies for the delivery of cultural commodities, we must return to the questions raised by Adorno, Benjamin, and others concerning the political and aesthetic "promise" of these modern technologies. Martin Heidegger argued that in Western cultures, the role of the object is to fix and determine the subject (Weber 1996). As Samuel Weber shows, Heidegger links his critique of Western subjectivity with his critique of technology, which takes "all alterity as raw material to be given form and set into place" (50). Those who are able to effectively objectify the words of others into their utterances—using modern citational technologies—are also able to maintain their privileged social identities, and privileged institutional positioning. Heidegger argues that it is fear which drives modern technology, in that subjects attempt to increasingly "secure" a future. While this is one possible outcome of technology, Walter Benjamin argues that the arts which employ the new technologies, such as film, *may* open alternative futures (Caygill 1998, 78). For Benjamin, "Technology can be used to resist the change in experience, to monumentalise the present by closing it off to any other future than the repetition of the present, or it can be used to promote the transformation of experience itself" (95).

Both Derrida and Benjamin found redemptive possibilities within technology itself. However, while Benjamin (1968) ends his "Work of Art" essay with a Marxist hope for political redemption over fascism, Derrida insists that the future situation must be kept open-ended, unknowable, and not reducible to a known political system—we can find Derrida objecting to this kind of "structured" Marxism in *Specters of Marx* (1994). Having said this, and despite Benjamin's concluding remarks in the "Work of Art" essay, Benjamin's view regarding the possible technological transformation of experience often comes very close to Derrida's views regarding the "messianic" and the "promise." As Cadava argues in his reading of Benjamin's work on photography, the photograph is a *promise* "that everything may be kept for history, but the everything that is kept is the everything that is always already in the process of disappearing, that does not belong to sight. What is kept is only the promise, the event of the promise" (1997, 65-66).

Today we see technologies such as computers develop as an archive of value, where entextualized images and words can be saved, stored, and "re-experienced" in ways never before possible. Television networks keep digital libraries where the "valuable" historical images of sports, television, and film are at their disposal for rebroadcast. For Derrida, there is an important connection between such archival technologies and experience, and between the archive and the future. He notes that "what is no longer archived in the same way is no longer lived in the same way. Archivable meaning is also and in advance codetermined by the structure that archives" (Derrida 1996, 18).

In this sense, new archival technologies influence how syntactical forms will be entextualized, saved, and experienced by subjects in the future. The words and images saved on today's computers, or available through the Internet, will be left for future generations who will engage this archive in new situations—they will "experience" our archives of value. Inasmuch as the commodity form limits what our language says to our children, and given that the traces of our "collective experience" have often been reduced to what has sold well in our marketplace, future possibilities have been reduced. On the other hand, "present" cultural entextualizations, and the alterity abjected in their construction, is necessarily open to unexpected re-valuation in the future. Thus for Derrida, the "question of the archive" is "a question of the future, the question of the future itself, the question of a response, of a promise and of a responsibility for tomorrow" (36). The question of the future concerns in what way our archived language—whether produced for today's marketplace, or as aesthetically configured—will be grafted into future situations.

The Cartesian self is normatively considered to be an archive of valued experiences accumulated over a lifetime, and is thus interpreted through an exchange value frame. As such, normative social identity—as currently configured—is relatively closed to the future. Yet, because we think about our self in a language, the play and promise of language always remains at work—even as today the self is continually re-positioned relative to commodified citational resources. If language can never be completely commodified, neither can the "self." The words of others might come to the contemporary subject with a normative worth as a valued experience, but as these words are re-grafted into new situations, the play of language prevents a complete closure of their meaning and value. If re-citations are necessary to re-enact their exchange value, then these very recontextualizations open the possibility for "breaking frame." Neither the self, nor one's values, are ever quite present; the meaning of one's values relative to those of others, tentatively re-enacted through utterances, are always open to reinterpretation.

Values and valuing domains are necessary and inevitable in social life—as Menke noted, even the "aesthetic" disruption of normative value categories usually results in some kind of restoration of meaning and value. Laclau and Mouffe (1994) have shown that a theory of performativity need not lead to political nihilism, because new and contingent hegemonic articulations can construct new "universal" values—such as what they term "*radical and plural democracy*" (167; italics in the original). The re-interpellation of valuation frames *can* be made less "automatic," and the contingency of any particular claim to universality can be made more transparent (see Butler, LaClau, and Žižek 2000, 86).

As Butler points out, subjects are both enabled, and limited, through normative identity and valuing categories; such categories themselves are both repeated and altered through recontextualization. Like Derrida's deconstructive technique, the "breaking of frame" involves not just a reversal of the present hierarchy of valuations, but a displacement of the hierarchical system itself. In other words, in frame-breaking, the ratio of differential social values relative to each other is not simply "re-mixed" following political opposition to normative framing hierarchies—resulting in a mere reshuffling of identifiable political values. Rather, in frame-breaking, the very identity or identification of known value categories is aesthetically contested and thus opened to alternative formulations—in a *future*. If subjects are typically re-positioned relative to normatively-valued signs, then *aesthetically configured* material grafts—of unknown value—force a reconsideration of normative social identities and values. While subjects may always already be socially positioned within dominant values which are *likely* to be re-cited, this re-citation process always re-introduces the possibility or *chance* of difference.

If "value" has a structural iterability, it is "structural" in the sense that its identity is continually *re-structured* in situated citational practice. Subordinate groups and their associated values are thus continually *re-subordinated* through ongoing, normative citational practices. The utterances of both individual subjects and social institutions continually altercast the social identities of others. As Julia Kristeva has pointed out, subordinate groups are constructed through—as Hebdige puts it—their "*positioning in language*" (Hebdige 1996, 120, italics in the original). In this sense, one's responsibility toward others is a responsibility for one's own words—that is, for the *interpellative consequences* of one's own citational practices. Normative social relationships can either be re-cited or resisted to varying degree. "Agency" thus involves the responsibility for one's utterances, which necessarily take a stand relative to the words and values of others.

According to Culler (1982), Derrida "does not dispense with the category of intention" (216); at the same time, however, he asserts that intentionality cannot control or dictate meaning. In his analysis of Austin, Derrida discusses the notion of an "intention-effect" (216), where the author attempts to guide an argument in a particular way, only to have language exceed or displace this meaning (216-18). Similarly, even though a person cannot be entirely responsible for how others may recontextualize or re-cite their utterances in the future, we might speak of a "responsibility-effect." Social actors are responsible for the material forms of their utterances.

As discussed above, the utterances of subjects may be more or less stringently constructed; in other words, more or less ready to automatically signify normative values. In the language of the Bakhtin Circle, utterances are more or less ready to be assimilated into dominant, "monological" social discourses such as the exchange value frame. For Bakhtin and his associates, a "dialogized" work of art, such as the novel, "incorporates a variety of viewpoints that may be artfully played off one another" (Hanks 1989, 114). In a discussion of parody, Butler similarly refers to "an openness to resignification and recontextualization" (1999, 176). In this sense, social actors have a responsibility for entextualizing and double-voicing their utterances in such a way that resists the automatic re-citation of those meanings which perpetuate inequality.

In this effort, actors must anticipate those known strategies by which power typically re-incorporates resistance. As Butler points out, "Parody by itself is not subversive" (176). Rather, social actors must "understand what makes certain kinds of parodic repetitions effectively disruptive, truly troubling, and which repetitions become domesticated and recirculated as instruments of cultural hegemony" (176-77). In other words, responsibility involves a *knowing anticipation* of how power works, in order to open the future as an *anticipation of the unknown.*

Social actors are thus responsible for the material form of their utterances, as well as the social positioning of this materiality. In the global political economy, some social actors are positioned with greater access to wider audiences than others, and actors differ in their ability to speak for themselves (see Spivak 1988; Inoue 2006). Those social institutions and groups with greater access to the mechanisms of language distribution, through which to position their words, thus carry a special responsibility for the re-citation and re-production of material forms. We can here see the importance, as did Jürgen Habermas (1984; 1987), of a non-commercialized "public sphere," where alternative citational resources have a place to *take form.* Having said this, it is also true that there is no predicting how any utterance will be recontextualized in the future, and therefore no predicting its political consequences. As Derrida has shown, language tends not to "stay put," but rather disseminates into situations which cannot be controlled in advance.

Derrida has identified a certain "aporia of responsibility," in that being responsible toward particular, singular others might mean being irresponsible toward "other others" (Derrida 1995)—including "generalized" others. In addition, we can identify a tension between political values based on *reason*, as in the Habermasian formulation of critical theory, and the more *aesthetic* formulations of Adorno, Benjamin, or Derrida. To dislocate known or seemingly rational political values through aesthetic configurations might indeed have disastrous political consequences for unknown others in future situations. There is a "radical" sense of responsibility in play here, where the dislocation of all value domains means that one takes on *responsibility for unknown consequences*; indeed, in a Derridean sense, it is not really "responsibility" if one can already anticipate the outcome. This type of "responsibility without insurance" is to be distinguished from mere recklessness or irresponsibility; that is, of putting others in known or likely danger. Rather, it involves taking a careful chance regarding the future; as Culler summarizes Derrida's strategy in *Dissemination*, "Derrida is not playing with words, he is betting with words, employing them strategically with an eye on larger stakes" (Culler 1982, 146).

To be human is to struggle with this "aporia of responsibility"—that "responsible" political choices, relative to the known words (and values) of particular others may be "irresponsible" relative to other others, including unknown past or future others. Aesthetics moves the agency of subjects away from an anticipation of highly probable consequences, toward an anticipation of unknown consequences—in other words, away from known and identifiable social relationships between self and others. This "promise" of difference assumes material forms—as the entextualized forms of one generation become the citational resources of future generations. In this sense, to entextualize a promise of difference means to allow for the futurity of language, and thus the futurity of value—with unknown political consequences.

This aporia of responsibility, like any aporia, cannot be resolved. Social actors must take responsibility for normative (i.e., probable) political outcomes, as well as "bet" on unknown outcomes. Thus, there is also an unavoidable *aporia of art and reason* at play here. Both "rational" decision-making which anticipates probable political outcomes, as well as an "aesthetic" anticipation of the unknown, are necessary to *responsible* social action. While advocacy for a rational, just society necessarily speaks within the known discourses of value, aesthetic negativity dislocates these known discourses and thus opens a space for the values of unknown others.

Responsibility thus involves a stance toward temporality—a dislocation of the hegemony of "presence" in favor of an openness toward the future. In

Specters of Marx (1994), Derrida means to show that the "present" is haunted by specters—both the ghosts from the past who seek justice, as well as the ghosts of those to come. Derrida "cites" the specters in his critique of presence—a strategy which can also be applied to the contemporary dislocation of those values and practices which re-produce inequality.

Words given to us from the past—and words issued by us to the future—must not be reduced to mere commodified resources for any "present" consumer. Both the past and the future haunt the presence of exchange value. Using Benjamin's favored suffix (see Weber 2008), we might say that there is a "value-ability" to the words of others, which differs radically from the market-ability, or exchange value, of language. In this sense, following Derrida, we might speak of a "messianic structure of value." The "value-ability" of the words of others, as the continuing importance of every voice into the future, takes the material form of a *promise*—the promise of a "value" never quite "present."

CONCLUSION

This chapter began by suggesting that what is needed in developing a contemporary critical theory, informed by recent developments in poststructuralism, is not only an approach which advocates for equal access to the production and distribution of cultural commodities *within* the contemporary exchange value system, but also for the dislocation of the hegemonic frame *of* exchange value itself. If, as argued in chapters four and five, product and brand designers—as well as investors—attempt to anticipate and shape the future commodification of language in accordance with calculative economic planning, then the opening up of the future to "unknown" values becomes an important critical move. The work of the Frankfurt School on aesthetic theory, as well as that of Erving Goffman on frame-breaking, is particularly helpful in this regard—when moved into a theory of performative citationality.

For Goffman, frames can be disrupted through the employment of particular frame-breaking techniques, which generates a non-normative experience. Goffman gives examples of how works of art, as well as particular commodities, can exploit the vulnerabilities of frames. He notes that while the disruption of frames is often only temporary, repeated violations can alter the frame itself. Applied to value frames, we can see how oppositional or subversive re-citations can dislocate normative subcultural values, or exchange value. For example, the work of Gates (1988) on "Signifyin(g)" within African-American communities shows that aesthetic configurations can challenge the norms and identities of hegemonic racial discourses. In other words, aesthetic configurations of the materiality of language can disrupt normative value interpellations.

Theodor Adorno's aesthetic theory, as interpreted by Christoph Menke (1998), shows how the materiality of aesthetic forms can disrupt normative meanings. This book extends this thesis to the aesthetic disruption of the "meaning of value"—and thus argues that aesthetically configured material forms have the potential to disrupt the interpretive context, or frame, of exchange value. Because the realm of aesthetics, for Adorno and Menke, can disrupt any normative meaning, it does not fall under the hegemonic control of the exchange value frame. Rather, as an "autonomous" and "sovereign" realm (Menke 1998, x-xi), the aesthetic arrangement of material forms can potentially disrupt the interpellation of any subcultural value frame—as well as the exchange value frame.

Adorno's theory shows how aesthetic material forms can generate an experience of "aesthetic negativity" (xi), which confounds attempts to commodify the forms as having a known and measurable value. When constellations of material forms—including the materiality of language—cannot generate interpellations of known value, they simultaneously challenge the interpellation of normative identity categories for subjects positioned relative to those forms. In this situation, the "experiences" of Cartesian subjects are no longer measurable in terms of exchange value, and the alignment of individual identity with normative subcultural values becomes problematic.

Even commodities can enter into material constellations with aesthetic effect, just as today's works of art can become commodities in future situations. Benjamin argued that the outdated commodities of capitalism, whose time of fashion had come and gone, had a potentially critical effect if brought into particular constellations with contemporary material forms. Such "quoting" from the past could potentially redeem the commodities, which represented the unfulfilled desires of past generations. Benjamin saw photography as a citational technology which could quote moments of the past into the present; in this sense, it was a potentially progressive technological development. On the other hand, modern technologies like photography or film could extend the hegemonic reach of capitalism into the lifeworlds of its subjects.

Works of art can be considered as "utterances" of the artist—syntactical forms combining the words and images of others with those of self in particular ways. Such utterances can generate aesthetic negativity when inserted into particular, situated, material constellations. These syntactical forms can generate this effect whether or not the "artist" who issued them is officially recognized as such; performance artists need not be officially recognized by institutions for their utterances to have aesthetic effect. Similarly, everyday interactions can produce strips of dialogue which have aesthetic effect when recontextualized into particular situations. In Bakhtinian terms, syntactical forms which incorporate the words and images of others—even in the dialogues of everyday life—have the potential for dislocating normative value frames and normative identities. As Butler (2000) recognized in a critique of Bourdieu, normative values and identities can be dislocated precisely because unauthorized speakers bring forth re-citations in non-normative ways.

If the aesthetic utterances of artists have the potential to dislocate normative identities and values within particular material configurations, then the questions of agency and intent return to the fore. Mead's work is valuable in this regard, as it addresses these issues without slipping back into a Cartesian version of subjectivity. Mead's pragmatic orientation toward behavioral practices allows performativity theory to better emphasize that citational practices can be anticipated and rehearsed, before their actualization. In fact, considering Schechner's notion of "restored behavior" (1985), it is clear that rehearsals—including inner conversations with self—comprise part of the chain of re-citations by which meaning and value are stabilized. In addition, Mead's approach allows for the distinction between the "I" of action and the "me" of social identity. The notion of role-taking—which involves taking the perspective of the other—also undermines any notion of a "self-present" subject.

One consequence of "returning" Mead to poststructuralist theory is that such a move reveals an aporia regarding the notion of "anticipation." This aporia becomes particularly acute in the contemporary economy, given the increased commodification of language. On the one hand, investors and brand developers must calculate—or anticipate—the marketability of language in the future in order to maximize profits. On the other hand, as Derrida and Butler have shown, it is precisely the process of re-citationality which undermines the stability of anticipated meaning and value. At stake in the commodification of culture is thus the temporality of language—whether the words and images of others will be appropriated and marketed as delivering the "presence" of exchange value, or whether the more aesthetic play of language will dislocate that metaphysical frame, and "anticipate" a future with unknown values.

Hans Joas, in his book *The Genesis of Values* (2000), argues that "values arise in experiences of self-formation and self-transcendence"(1). Especially drawing on the "pragmatist ethics" (169) of John Dewey and George Herbert Mead, Joas argues that it is through encounters with others—specifically, through the process of role-taking—that individual perspectives move toward "universalizing" principles of shared morals (169–71; see also 155–23). However, we have seen in this book that the increasing commodification of language affects the role-taking process itself, and thus the nature of the "universal" potential of encounters with others. When the materiality of the language of the other is shaped according to profit considerations, its recitation does not encourage the emergence of a shared, universal morality;

rather, role-taking becomes measured assessment as to the "worth" of the words and images of others for the experiences and utterences of self. On the other hand, the citationality required to re-enact the exchange value frame opens a space for a dislocation of its hegemonic presence, and the potential formulation of a (tentative) new hegemony (see also Laclau and Mouffee 1994; Butler, Laclau, and Žižek 2000).

Samuel Weber has noted that in the work of Walter Benjamin on epic theater, "To cite a text means to interrupt its context" (Benjamin, quoted in Weber 2008, 99). Weber argues that for Benjamin, the quality of "citability"—a defining characteristic of the art form of epic theater—contrasts with a calculative orientation toward the future (105). If, as Weber suggests, the nature of "citability" implies a future open to unknown or possible re-citations (105), then citability precisely works against the closed, contextual framing of calculative agency. Just as in Butler and Derrida's version of "performative citationality"—where the iterability, or citability, of material forms potentially "breaks" the normative framing of meanings and identities—we find in Benjamin the aesthetic possibility of breaking the calculative frame of exchange value. Citational practices—particularly those involving aesthetic forms—can potentially contribute to the dislocation of that contemporary economic frame within which language is increasingly commodified.

Works Cited

Adkins, Lisa and Celia Lury. 2011. Introduction: Special Measures. *The Sociological Review* Issue Supplement s2: 24–38. doi: 10.1111/j.1467–954X.2012.02051.x.

Adorno, Theodor W. 1997. *Aesthetic Theory*, trans. and ed. by Robert Hullot-Kentor. Minneapolis: University of Minnesota Press. (Orig. pub. 1970.)

Alexander, Jeffrey C., Bernhard Giesen, and Jason L. Mast. 2006. *Social Performance: Symbolic Action, Cultural Pragmatics, and Ritual*. Cambridge: Cambridge University Press.

Allen, Graham. 2006. *Intertextuality*. London: Routledge. (Orig. pub. 2000.)

Althusser, Louis. 1971. "Ideology and Ideological State Apparatuses." In *Lenin and Philosophy*, tr. Ben Brewster, 170–86. NY and London: Monthly Review Press.

Amariglio, Jack and Antonio Callari. 1993. "Marxian Value Theory and the Problem of the Subject: The Role of Commodity Fetishism", In *Fetishism as Cultural Discourse*, eds. Emily Apter & William Pietz, 186–216. Ithaca: Cornell University Press.

Anderson, Benedict. 1991. *Imagined Communities: Reflections on the Origin and Spread of Nationalism*. London: Verso. (Orig. pub. 1983.)

Appadurai, Arjun, ed. 1986a. *The Social Life of Things*. Cambridge: Cambridge University Press.

———. 1986b. "Introduction: Commodities and the Politics of Value". In *The Social Life of Things*, ed. Arjun Appadurai, 1986a, 3–63. Cambridge: Cambridge University Press.

Araujo, Luis. 2007. Markets, Market-Making and Marketing. *Marketing Theory* 7(3): 211–226. doi: 10.1177/1470593107080342.

Arvidsson, Adam. 2006. *Brands: Meaning and Value in Media Culture*. London: Routledge.

Auslander, Philip. 1999. *Liveness: Performance in a Mediatized Culture*. London: Routledge.

Austin, J.L.. 1975. *How to Do Things With Words*, 2nd edition, Ed. by J.O. Urmson and Marina Sbisa. Cambridge: Harvard University Press. (Orig. pub. 1962.)

Bakhtin, Mikhail. 1984. *Problems of Dostoevsky's Poetics*. Ed. and trans. by Caryl Emerson. Minneapolis: University of Minnesota Press. (Orig. pub. 1929.)

———. 1986. *Speech Genres and Other Late Essays*. Ed. by C. Emerson and M. Holquist, trans. by V.W. McGee. Austin: Texas University Press. (Orig. pub. 1979.)

Barad, Karen. 2007. *Meeting the Universe Halfway. Quantum Physics and the Entanglement of Matter and Meaning*. Durham: Duke University Press.

Baudrillard, Jean. 1981. *For a Critique of the Political Economy of the Sign*. St. Louis: Telos Press. (Orig. pub. 1972.)

Bauman, Richard. 1996. "Transformations of the Word in the Production of Mexican Festival Drama". In *Natural Histories of Discourse*, eds. Michael Silverstein and Greg Urban, 301–327. Chicago: The University of Chicago Press.

Bauman, Richard and Charles L. Briggs. 1990. Poetics and Performance as Critical Perspectives on Language and Social Life. *Annual Review of Anthropology* 19: 59–88. doi: 10.1146/annurev.an.19.100190.000423.
Becker, Howard S. 1963. *Outsiders*. New York: The Free Press.
Belk, Russell W. 1988. Possessions and the Extended Self. *Journal of Consumer Research* 15(2): 139–168. *Communication & Mass Media Complete*, EBSCO*host* (accessed March 25, 2013).
Bell, Daniel. 1976. *The Cultural Contradictions of Capitalism*. New York: Basic Books.
Bell, Vikki. 1999. Performativity and Belonging: An Introduction. In *Performativity and Belonging*, ed. Vikki Bell, 1–10. London: Sage Publications.
Benjamin, Walter. 1968. The Work of Art in the Age of Mechanical Reproduction. In *Illuminations*, ed. Hannah Arendt, trans. Harry Zohn, 217–251. New York: Schocken.
Berger, Bennett. 1986. Foreword, In *Frame Analysis*, by Erving Goffman, xi–xviii. Boston: Northeastern University Press. (Orig. pub. 1974.)
Berger, John. 1980. *Ways of Seeing*. London: British Broadcasting Corporation. (Orig. pub. 1972.)
Berger, Peter and Thomas Luckmann. 1967. *The Social Construction of Reality: A Treatise in the Sociology of Knowledge*. New York: Anchor Books. (Orig. pub. 1966.)
Berland, Jody. 1992. Angels Dancing: Cultural Technologies and the Production of Space. In *Cultural Studies*, eds. Grossberg et al. London: Routledge.
Blumer, Herbert. 1969. *Symbolic Interactionism: Perspective and Method*. Englewood Cliffs: Prentice Hall.
Bolt, Barbara. 2004. *Art Beyond Representation: The Performative Power of the Image*. London: I.B. Tauris.
Bolz, Norbert and Willem van Reijen. 1996. *Walter Benjamin*. New Jersey: Humanities Press. (Orig. pub. 1991.)
Borgerson, Janet. 2005. Materiality, Agency, and the Constitution of Consuming Subjects: Insights for Consumer Research. In *NA - Advances in Consumer Research* 32, eds. Geeta Menon and Akshay R. Rao, Duluth, MN: Association for Consumer Research, 439–43.
Boucher, Geoff. 2008. *The Charmed Circle of Ideology: A Critique of Laclau and Mouffe, Butler and Žižek*. Melbourne: re.press.
Bourdieu, Pierre. 1984. *Distinction: A Social Critique of the Judgement of Taste*. Cambridge: Harvard University Press. (Orig. pub. 1979.)
———. 1991. *Language and Symbolic Power*. Ed. by John B. Thompson. Trans. by Gino Raymond and Matthew Adamson. Cambridge: Harvard University Press.
———. 1993. *Sociology in Question*. Trans. Richard Nice. London: Sage. (Orig. pub. 1984.)
Briggs, Charles L. and Richard Bauman. 1992. Genre, Intertextuality, and Social Power. *Journal of Linguistic Anthropology* 2(2): 131–172. doi: 10.1525/jlin.1992.2.2.131.
Buck-Morss, Susan. 1979. *The Origin of Negative Dialectics: Theodor W. Adorno, Walter Benjamin, and the Frankfurt Institute*. New York: The Free Press. (Orig. pub. 1977.)
———. 1983. Benjamin's Passagen-Werk: Redeeming Mass Culture for the Revolution. *New German Critique* 29: 211–240.
Bürger, Peter. 1990. The Problem of Aesthetic Value. Trans. Shaun Whiteside. In *Literary Theory Today*, eds. Peter Collier and Helga Geyer-Ryan, 23–34. Ithaca: Cornell University Press.
Butler, Judith. 1993. *Bodies That Matter*. New York: Routledge.
———. 1997. *Excitable Speech: A Politics of the Performative*. New York: Routledge.
———. 1999. *Gender Trouble*. New York: Routledge. (Orig. pub. 1990.)
———. 2000. Performativity's Social Magic. In *Bourdieu: A Critical Reader*, ed. Richard Shusterman, 113–128. Oxford: Blackwell Publishers Ltd. (Orig. pub. 1999.)
Butler, Judith, Ernesto Laclau and Slavoj Žižek. 2000. *Contingency, Hegemony, Universality: Contemporary Dialogues on the Left*. London: Verso.
Cadava, Eduardo. 1997. *Words of Light: Theses on the Photography of History*. Princeton: Princeton University Press.

Callon, Michel. 1998a. Introduction: The Embeddedness of Economic Markets in Economics. In *The Laws of the Markets*, ed. Michel Callon, 1–57. Oxford: Blackwell Publishers/The Sociological Review.

———. 1998b. An Essay on Framing and Overflowing: Economic Externalities Revisited by Sociology. In *The Laws of the Markets*, ed. Michel Callon, 244–269. Oxford: Blackwell Publishers/The Sociological Review.

———. 2007. What Does It Mean to Say That Economics Is Performative? In *Do Economists Make Markets? On the Performativity of Economics*, ed. DonaldMacKenzie, Fabian Muniesa, and Lucia Siu, 311–357. Princeton: Princeton University Press.

Caputo, John. 1997. *The Prayers and Tears of Jacques Derrida*. Bloomington: Indiana University Press.

Carlson, Marvin. 1996. *Performance: A Critical Introduction*. London: Routledge.

Caygill, Howard. 1989. *Art of Judgement*. London: Basil Blackwell.

———. 1998. *Walter Benjamin: The Colour of Experience*. London: Routledge. (Orig. pub. 1997.)

Certeau, Michel de. 1988. *The Practice of Everyday Life*. Trans. Steven Rendall. Berkeley: University of California Press. (Orig. pub. 1984.)

Chaney, David. 2002. The Power of Metaphors in Tourism Theory. In *Tourism: Between Place and Performance*, eds. Simon Coleman and Mike Crang, 193–206. New York: Berghahn Books.

Clark, Katerina and Michael Holquist. 1984. *Mikhail Bakhtin*. Cambridge: Belknap Press.

Cohen, Erik and Scott A. Cohen. 2012. Current Sociological Theories and Issues in Tourism. *Annals of Tourism Research* 39(4): 2177–2202. http://dx.doi.org/10.1016/j.annals.2012.07.009.

Coleman, Simon and Mike Crang. 2002. Grounded Tourists, Travelling Theory. In *Tourism: Between Place and Performance*, eds. Simon Coleman and Mike Crang, 1–20. New York: Berghahn Books.

Collins, James. 1996. Socialization to Text: Structure and Contradiction in Schooled Literacy. In *Natural Histories of Discourse*, eds. Michael Silverstein and Greg Urban, 203–228. Chicago: The University of Chicago Press.

Cooley, Charles H. 1964. *Human Nature and the Social Order*. New York: Schocken Books. (Orig. pub. 1902.)

Cova, Bernard and Daniele Dalli. 2009. Working Consumers: The Next Step in Marketing Theory? *Marketing Theory* 9(3): 315–319. doi: 10.1177/1470593109338144.

Crang, Mike. 2006. Circulation and Emplacement: The Hollowed-out Performance of Tourism. In *Travels in Paradox: Remapping Tourism*, ed. Claudio Minca and Tim Oakes, 47–64. Lanham: Rowman & Littlefield.

Crawford, Sue E.S. and Elinor Ostrom. 1995. A Grammar of Institutions. In *American Political Science Review* 89(3): 582–600. http://dx.doi.org/10.2307/2082975.

Crouch, David. 2002. Surrounded by Place: Embodied Encounters. In *Tourism: Between Place and Performance*, eds. Simon Coleman and Mike Crang, 207–218. New York: Berghahn Books.

Culler, Jonathan. 1981. Semiotics of Tourism. *American Journal of Semiotics* 1 (No. 1–2): 127–140.

———. 1982. *On Deconstruction*. Ithaca: Cornell University Press.

Denzin, Norman. 1995. *The Cinematic Society: The Voyeur's Gaze*. London: Sage.

Derrida, Jacques. 1973. *Speech and Phenomena*. Trans. David B. Allison. Evanston: Northwestern University Press. (Orig. pub. 1967.)

———. 1978. *Writing and Difference*. Chicago: The University of Chicago Press. (Orig. pub. 1967.)

———. 1981. *Dissemination*. Trans. Barbara Johnson. London: Athlone Press. (Orig. pub. 1972.)

———. 1988. *Limited Inc*. Evanston: Northwest University Press.

———. 1989. *Memoires for Paul de Man*, Revised Edition. New York. Columbia University Press. (Orig. pub. 1986.)

———. 1992. *Given Time: I. Counterfeit Money*. Trans. Peggy Kamuf. Chicago: The University of Chicago Press. (Orig. pub. 1991.)

———. 1994. *Specters of Marx*. New York: Routledge. (Orig. pub. 1993.)

———. 1995. *The Gift of Death*. Chicago: The University of Chicago Press. (Orig. pub. 1993.)

———. 1996. *Archive Fever*. Trans. Eric Prenowitz. Chicago: The University of Chicago Press. (Orig. pub. 1995.)

———. 1997. *Of Grammatology*. Trans. Gayatri Chakravorty Spivak. Baltimore: The Johns Hopkins University Press. (Orig. pub. 1967.)

———. 2007. *Psyche: Inventions of the Other, Volume 1*. Eds. Peggy Kamuf and Elizabeth Rottenberg. Stanford: Stanford University Press. (Orig. pub. 1987.)

Direk, Zeynek. 2000. On the Sources and the Structure of Derrida's Radical Notion of Experience. *Tympanum: A Journal of Comparative Literary Studies* 4, http://www.usc.edu/dept/comp-lit/tympanum/4/direk.html.

Duranti, Alessandro and Charles Goodwin. 1997. *Rethinking Context: Language as an Interactive Phenomenon*. Cambridge: Cambridge University Press. (Orig. pub. 1992.)

Durkheim, Émile. 1965. *The Elementary Forms of the Religious Life*. Trans. Joseph W. Swain. New York: Free Press. (Orig. pub. 1912.)

———. *Rules of Sociological Method*. New York: The Free Press. (orig. pub. 1895).

Dworkin, Andrea. 1989. *Pornography: Men Possessing Women*. New York: E.P. Dutton. (Orig. pub. 1979.)

Edensor, Tim. 2000. Staging Tourism: Tourists as Performers. *Annals of Tourism Research* 27(2): 322–344. http://dx.doi.org/10.1016/S0160-7383(99)00082-1.

———. 2001. Performing Tourism, Staging Tourism. *Tourist Studies* 1(1): 59–81. doi: 10.1177/146879760100100104.

Emerson, Robert M. and Sheldon L. Messinger. 1977. The Micro-Politics of Trouble. In *Inner Lives and Social Worlds: Readings in Social Psychology*, ed. James A. Holstein and Jaber F. Gubrium, 2003, 524–535. New York: Oxford University Press.

Englis, Basil G. and Michael Solomon. 1995. To Be *and* Not To Be: Lifestyle Imagery, Reference Groups, and *The Clustering of America*. *Journal of Advertising* 24(1): 13–28. doi: 10.1080/00913367.1995.10673465.

Englis, Basil G. and Michael Solomon. 1996. *Journal of Business Research* 37(3): 183–191. doi: http://dx.doi.org/10.1016/S0148-2963(96)00068-9.

Featherstone, Mike. 1991. *Consumer Culture and Postmodernism*. London: Sage.

Ferrell, Jeff. 1999. Cultural Criminology. *Annual Review of Sociology* 25: 395–418. doi: 10.1146/annurev.soc.25.1.395.

Ferrell, Jeff and Clinton R. Sanders. 1995. Culture, Crime, and Criminology. In *Cultural Criminology*, eds. Jeff Ferrell and Clinton Sanders, 3–21. Boston: Northeastern University Press.

Foster, Hal. 1993. The Art of Fetishism: Notes on Dutch Still Life. In *Fetishism as Cultural Discourse*, eds. Emily Apter and William Pietz, 251–265. Ithaca: Cornell University Press.

Foucault, Michel. 1965. *Madness & Civilization: A History of Insanity in the Age of Reason*. New York: Vintage. (Orig. pub. 1961.)

———. 1994. *The Birth of the Clinic: An Archaeology of Medical Perception*. Trans. A. M. Sheridan Smith. New York: Vintage. (Orig. pub. 1963.)

———. 1995. *Discipline and Punish: The Birth of the Prison*, trans. by A. Sheridan. New York: Vintage. (Orig. pub. 1975.)

Fournier, Susan. 1998. Consumers and Their Brands: Developing Relationship Theory in Consumer Research. *Journal of Consumer Research* 24(4): 343–373. *Communication & Mass Media Complete*, EBSCO*host* (accessed March 11, 2013).

Friedman, Jonathan. 1994. Introduction. In *Consumption and Identity*, ed. Jonathan Friedman. Chur, Switzerland: Harwood.

Frow, John. 1997. *Time and Commodity Culture*. Oxford: Clarendon Press.

Galbraith, John Kenneth. 1978. *The New Industrial State*. New York: Mentor. (Orig. pub. 1967.)

Gardiner, Michael. 1992. *The Dialogics of Critique: M.M. Bakhtin and the Theory of Ideology*. London: Routledge.

Gasché, Rodolphe. 1986. *The Tain of the Mirror: Derrida and the Philosophy of Reflection.* Cambridge: Harvard University Press.
Gates, Jr., Henry Louis. 1988. *The Signifying Monkey: A Theory of Afro-American Literary Criticism*. New York: Oxford University Press.
Gergen, Kenneth J. 1991. *The Saturated Self: Dilemmas of Identity in Contemporary Life*. New York: BasicBooks.
Giddens, Anthony. 1984. *The Constitution of Society: Outline of the Theory of Structuration.* Berkeley: University of California Press.
Goffman, Erving. 1959. *The Presentation of Self in Everyday Life*. Garden City: Doubleday & Company.
———. 1961. *Encounters: Two Studies in the Sociology of Interaction.* Indianapolis: The Bobbs-Merrill Company, Inc.
———. 1967. *Interaction Ritual: Essays on Face-to-Face Behavior*. Garden City: Doubleday & Company.
———. 1986. *Frame Analysis: An Essay on the Organization of Experience*. Boston: Northeastern University Press. (Orig. pub. 1974.)
Goldman, Robert. 1992. *Reading Ads Socially*. London: Routledge.
Goldman, Robert and Stephen Papson. 1996. *Sign Wars: The Cluttered Landscape of Advertising*. New York: The Guilford Press.
Graeber, David. 2001. *Toward an Anthropology of Value.* New York: Palgrave.
Guillory, John. 1993. *Cultural Capital: The Problem of Literary Canon Formation.* Chicago: The University of Chicago Press.
Gumperz, John J. 1997. Contextualization and Understanding. In *Rethinking Context: Language as an Interactive Phenomenon*, ed. Alessandro Duranti and Charles Goodwin, 229–252. Cambridge: Cambridge University Press. (Orig. pub. 1992.)
Habermas, Jürgen. 1984. *The Theory of Communicative Action, Vol. 1: Reason and the Rationalization of Society*. Trans. Thomas McCarthy. Boston: Beacon. (Orig. pub. 1981.)
———. 1987. *The Theory of Communicative Action, Vol. 2: Lifeworld and System: A Critique of Functionalist Reason*. Trans. Thomas McCarthy. Boston: Beacon. (Orig. pub. 1981.)
Hamacher, Werner. 1999. Lingua Amissa: The Messianism of Commodity-Language and Derrida's "Specters of Marx". In *Ghostly Demarcations: A Symposium on Jacques Derrida's Specters of Marx*, ed. Michael Sprinker, pp. 168–212.
Hanks, William F. 1989. Text and Textuality. *Annual Review of Anthropology* 18: 95–127. doi: 10.1146/annrev.an.18.100189.000523.
Haug, Wolfgang F. 1986. *Critique of Commodity Aesthetics: Appearance, Sexuality and Advertising in Capitalist Society*. Trans. Robert Bock. Minneapolis: University of Minnesota Press. (Orig. pub. 1971.)
Hebdige, Dick. 1996. *Subculture: The Meaning of Style.* London: Routledge. (Orig. pub. 1979.)
Heidegger, Martin. 1977. *The Question Concerning Technology and Other Essays.* Trans. William Lovitt. New York: Harper Colophon Books. (Orig. pub. 1954.)
Herman, Andres, Rosemary J. Coombe and Lewis Kaye. 2006. Goodwill and the Performativity of Intellectual Property in Online Digital Gaming. *Cultural Studies* 20(2–3): 184–210. doi: 10.1080/09502380500495684.
Hesmondhalgh, David. 2006. Bourdieu, the Media and Cultural Production. *Media, Culture & Society* 28(2): 211–231. doi: 10.1177/0163443706061682.
Hewitt, John P. and David Shulman. 2011. *Self and Society*, 11th edition. Boston: Allyn & Bacon. (Orig. pub. 1976.)
Hochschild, Arlie Russell. 2003. Emotion Work. In *Inner Lives and Social Worlds: Readings in Social Psychology*, eds. James A. Holstein and Jaber F. Gubrium, 204–226. New York: Oxford University Press. (Orig. pub. 1983)
Hohendahl, Peter Uwe. 1995. *Prismatic Thought: Theodor W. Adorno*. Lincoln: University of Nebraska Press.
Hollywood, Amy. 2002. Performativity, Citationality, Ritualization. *History of Religions* 42(2): 93–115. http://www.jstor.org/stable/3176407.
Holquist, Michael. 2004. *Dialogism: Bakhtin and his World*, 2nd edition. London: Routledge. (Orig. pub. 1990.)

Holt, Douglas B. 1997. Poststructuralist Lifestyle Analysis: Conceptualizing the Social Patterning of Consumption in Postmodernity. *Journal of Consumer Research* 23(4): 326–350. http://www.jstor.org/stable/2489569.

hooks, bell. 1992a. Representing Whiteness in the Black Imagination. In *Cultural Studies*, eds. Grossberg et al. London: Routledge.

———. 1992b. *Black Looks: Race and Representation*. Boston: South End.

Horkheimer, Max and Theodor W. Adorno. 1972. *Dialectic of Enlightenment*. Trans. John Cumming. New York: Herder & Herder. (Orig. pub. 1947.)

Inoue, Miyako. 2006. *Vicarious Language: Gender and Linguistic Modernity in Japan*. Berkeley: University of California Press.

Jameson, Frederic. 2001. *Postmodernism, or, The Cultural Logic of Late Capitalism*. Durham: Duke University Press. (Orig. pub. 1990.)

Jay, Martin. 1973. *The Dialectical Imagination: A History of the Frankfurt School and the Institute of Social Research, 1923–1950*. Boston: Little, Brown and Company.

———. 2005. *Songs of Experience: Modern American and European Variations on a Universal Theme*. Berkeley: University of California Press.

Jhally, Sut. 1987. *The Codes of Advertising: Fetishism and the Political Economy of Meaning in the Consumer Society*. New York: St. Martin's Press.

Joas, Hans. 1997. *G.H. Mead: A Contemporary Re-examination of His Thought*. Cambridge: The MIT Press. (Orig. pub. 1980.)

———. 2000. *The Genesis of Values*. Trans. Gregory Moore. Chicago: The University of Chicago Press.

Joseph, Miranda. 2002. *Against the Romance of Community*. Minneapolis: University of Minnesota Press.

Keenan, Thomas. 1993. The Point is to (Ex)Change It: Reading *Capital*, Rhetorically. In *Fetishism as Cultural Discourse*, ed. Emily Apter & William Pietz, 152–185. Ithaca: Cornell University Press.

Kellner, Douglas. 1991. *Jean Baudrillard: From Marxism to Postmodernism and Beyond*. Stanford: Stanford University Press. (Orig. pub. 1989.)

Kendon, Adam. 1997. The Negotiation of Context in Face-to-Face Interaction, In *Rethinking Context: Language as an Interactive Phenomenon*, eds. Allesandro Duranti and Charles Goodwin, 323–334. Cambridge: Cambridge University Press. (Orig. pub. 1992.)

Kirby, Vicki. 2006. *Judith Butler: Live Theory*. London: Continuum.

———. 2011. *Quantum Anthropologies: Life at Large*. Durham: Duke University Press.

Knudsen, Britta Timm and Anne Marit Waade. 2010. Performative Authenticity in Tourism and Spatial Experience: Rethinking the Relations Between Travel, Place and Emotion. In *Re-Investing Authenticity: Tourism, Place and Emotions*, eds. Britta Timm Knudsen and Anne Marit Waade, 1–21. Bristol: Channel View Publications.

Kopytoff, Igor. 1986. The Cultural Biography of Things: Commoditization as Process. In *The Social Life of Things*, ed. Arjun Appadurai, 1986a, 64–91. Cambridge: Cambridge University Press.

Laclau, Ernesto. 1977. *Politics and Ideology in Marxist Theory: Capitalism-Fascism-Populism*. London: Verso.

Laclau, Ernesto and Chantal Mouffe. 1994. *Hegemony & Socialist Strategy: Towards a Radical Democratic Politics*. London: Verso. (Orig. pub. 1985.)

Larsen, Jonas. 2005. Performativity of Tourist Photography. *Space and Culture* 8(4): 416–434. doi: 10.1177/1206331205279354.

Latour, Bruno 1993. *We Have Never Been Modern*. Cambridge: Harvard University Press. (Orig. pub. 1991.)

Lee, Benjamin. 1989. The Semiotic Origins of the Mind-Body Dualism. In *Semiotics, Self, and Society*, eds. Benjamin Lee and Greg Urban, 193–227. Berlin: Mouton de Gruyter.

———. 1993. Metalanguages and Subjectivities. In *Reflexive Language: Reported Speech and Metapragmatics*, ed. John A. Lucy, 365–391. Cambridge: Cambridge University Press.

Lee, Benjamin and Edward LiPuma. 2002. Cultures of Circulation: The Imaginations of Modernity. *Public Culture* 14(1): 191–213. doi: 10.1215/08992363-14-1-191.

Lee, Benjamin and Greg Urban. 1989. *Semiotics, Self, and Society*. Berlin: Mouton de Gruyter.

Lemert, Charles. 2003. Goffman. In *The Goffman Reader*, ed. Charles Lemert and Ann Branaman, ix–xliii. Oxford: Blackwell. (Orig. pub. 1997.)

Lemert, Charles and Ann Branaman, eds. 2003. *The Goffman Reader*. Malden: Blackwell Publishing. (Orig. pub. 1997.)

Lloyd, Moya. 2007. *Judith Butler: From Norms to Politics*. Cambridge: Polity Press.

Loxley, James. 2008. *Performativity*. London: Routledge. (Orig. pub. 2007.)

Lucy, John A. 1993. Reflexive Language and the Human Disciplines. In *Reflexive Language: Reported Speech and Metapragmatics*, ed. John A. Lucy, 9–32. Cambridge: Cambridge University Press.

Lury, Celia. 1996. *Consumer Culture*. New Brunswick: Rutgers University Press.

———. 2004. *Brands: The Logos of the Global Economy*. Abingdon: Routledge.

MacCannell, Dean. 1976. *The Tourist: A New Theory of the Leisure Class*. London: MacMillan Press.

MacCannell, Juliet Flower. 1985. The Temporality of Textuality: Bakhtin and Derrida. *MLN* 100 (No. 5): 968–988. http://www.jstor.org/stable/2905440.

MacLeod, Jay. 1995. *Ain't No Makin' It: Aspirations and Attainment in a Low-Income Neighborhood*. Boulder: Westview Press. (Orig. pub. 1987.)

MacKinnon, Catharine A. 1987. *Feminism Unmodified: Discourses on Life and Law*. Cambridge: Harvard University Press.

Madison, D. Soyini and Judith Hamera. 2006. Performance Studies at the Intersections. In *The Sage Handbook of Performance Studies*, eds. D. Soyini Madison and Judith Hamera, xi–xxv. Thousand Oaks: Sage Publications.

Marx, Karl. 1967. *Capital, Volume 1*. New York: International Publishers. (Orig. pub. 1867.)

McCracken, Grant. 1986. Culture and Consumption: A Theoretical Account of the Structure and Movement of the Cultural Meaning of Consumer Goods. *Journal of Consumer Research* 13(1): 71–84. *Communication & Mass Media Complete*, EBSCO*host* (accessed March 11, 2013).

Mead, George Herbert. 1959. *Philosophy of the Present*. LaSalle: The Open Court Publishing Co.. (Orig. pub. 1932.)

———. 1969. *Mind, Self, & Society*. Ed. Charles W. Morris. Chicago: The University of Chicago Press. (Orig. pub. 1934.)

Mehan, Hugh. 1996. The Construction of an LD Student: A Case Study in the Politics of Representation. In *Natural Histories of Discourse*, eds. Michael Silverstein and Greg Urban, 253–276. Chicago: The University of Chicago Press.

Meltzer, Eve. 2002. Performing Place: A Hyperbolic Drugstore in Wall, South Dakota. In *Tourism: Between Place and Performance*, eds. Simon Coleman and Mike Crang, 160–175. New York: Berghahn Books.

Menke, Christoph. 1998. *The Sovereignty of Art: Aesthetic Negativity in Adorno and Derrida*. Cambridge: The MIT Press. (Orig. pub. 1988.)

Mertz, Elizabeth. 1996. Recontextualization as Socialization: Text and Pragmatics in the Law School Classroom. In *Natural Histories of Discourse*, eds. Michael Silverstein and Greg Urban, 229–249. Chicago: The University of Chicago Press.

Miller, Daniel. 1987. *Material Culture and Mass Consumption*. Oxford: Basil Blackwell.

Mills, C.Wright. 2003. Situated Actions and Vocabularies of Motive. In *Inner Lives and SocialWorlds: Readings in Social Psychology*, eds. James A. Holstein and Jaber F. Gubrium, 248–254. New York: Oxford University Press (Orig. pub. 1940.)

Minca, Claudio and Tim Oakes. 2006. Introduction: Traveling Paradoxes. In *Travels in Paradox: Remapping Tourism*, ed. Claudio Minca and Tim Oakes, 1–22. Lanham: Rowman & Littlefield.

Moor, Liz and Celia Lury. 2011. Making and Measuring Value. *Journal of Cultural Economy* 4:4, 439–454, doi: 10.1080/17530350.2011.609708.

Mulvey, Laura. 1989. *Visual and Other Pleasures*. Bloomington: Indiana University Press. (Orig. pub. 1975.)

Muniesa, Fabian. 2011. A Flank Movement in the Understanding of Valuation. *The Sociological Review* 59 Issue Supplement s2: 24–38. doi: 10.1111/j.1467-954X.2012.02056.x.

Muniz, Albert M., Jr. and Thomas C. O'Guinn. 2001. Brand Community. *Journal of Consumer Research* 27(4): 412-432. *Communication & Mass Media Complete*, EBSCO*host*.

Nakassis, Constantine V. 2012. Brand, Citationality, Performativity. *American Anthropologist* 114(4): 624–638. doi: 10.1111/j.1548-1433.2012.01511.x.

Nicholsen, Shierry Weber. 1999. *Exact Imagination, Late Work: On Adorno's Aesthetics*. Cambridge: MIT Press. (Orig. pub. 1997.)

Norris, Christopher. 1984. *Deconstruction: Theory and Practice*. London: Methuen. (Orig. pub. 1982.)

———. 1987. *Derrida*. Cambridge: Harvard University Press.

Ochs, Elinor. 1997. Indexing Gender. In *Rethinking Context: Language as an Interactive Phenomenon*, eds. Alessandro Durant and Charles Goodwin, 336–358. Cambridge: Cambridge University Press. (Orig. pub. 1992.)

Park, Sung-Yul and Lionel Wee. 2008. Appropriating the Language of the Other: Performativity in Autonomous and Unified Markets. *Language & Communication* 28(3): 242–257. http://dx.doi.org/10.1016/j.langcom.2008.01.010.

Pennycook, Alastair. 2003. Global Englishes, Rip Slyme, and Performativity. *Journal of Sociolinguistics* 7(4): 513–533. doi: 10.1111/j.1467-9841.2003.00240.x.

Pensky, Max, ed. 1997 Editor's Introduction. In *The Actuality of Adorno*, ed. Max Pensky, 1–21. New York: SUNY Press.

Phelan, Peggy. 1996. *Unmarked: The Politics of Performance*. London: Routledge. (Orig. pub. 1993.)

Pietz, Willliam. 1985. The Problem of the Fetish, I. *Res* 9 (Spring): 5–17.

———. 1993. Fetishism and Materialism: The Limits of Theory in Marx. In *Fetishism as Cultural Discourse*, Emily Apter and William Pietz, eds., 119–151. Ithaca: Cornell University Press.

Plissart, Marie-Francoise & Jacques Derrida. 1989. Right of Inspection. *Art & Text* 32 (Autumn): 20–97.

Poster, Mark. 2001. *What's the Matter with the Internet?* Minneapolis: University of Minnesota Press.

Prahalad, C.K. and Venkat Ramaswamy. 2004. Co-Creation Experiences: The Next Practice in Value Creation. *Journal of Interactive Marketing* 18(3): 5–14. doi: 10.1002/dir.20015.

Preucel Robert. 2006. *Archaelogical Semiotics*. Malden: Blackwell Publishing.

Richins, Marsha. 1994. Valuing Things: The Public and Private Meanings of Possessions. *Journal of Consumer Research* 21(3):504–521. *Communication & Mass Media Complete*, EBSCO*host*.

Ritzer, George. 2008. *The McDonaldization of Society*, 5th Edition. Los Angeles: Pine Forge Press. (Orig. pub. 1993.)

Rochberg-Halton, Eugene. 1986. *Meaning and Modernity: Social Theory in the Pragmatic Attitude*. Chicago: The University of Chicago Press.

Rojek, Chris and John Urry. 1997. Transformations of Travel and Theory. In *Touring Cultures: Transformations of Travel and Theory*, ed. Chris Rojek and John Urry, 1–19. London: Routledge.

Rose, Gillian. 1978. *The Melancholy Science*. New York: Columbia.

Saussure, Ferdinand de. 1974. *Course in General Linguistics*. Trans. Wade Baskin. London: Fontana. (Orig. pub. 1916.)

Schau, Hope Jensen and Albert M. Muniz, Jr. 2002. Brand Communities and Personal Identities: Negotiations in Cyberspace. In *NA – Advances in Consumer Research* 29, eds. Susan M. Broniarczyk and Kent Nakamoto: Association for Consumer Research, 344–349.

Schechner, Richard. 1985. *Between Theater & Anthropology*. Philadelphia: University of Pennsylvania Press.

Sherlock, Steve. 1997. The Future of Commodity Fetishism. *Sociological Focus* 30 (1): 61–78.

———. 1998. Souvenirs: A Sociological Analysis. Paper presented at the annual meeting of the Michigan Academy of Science, Arts, and Letters.

———. 1999. Where Do You Want to Go Today: Computers and the Tourist Gaze. Paper presented at the annual meeting of the American Sociological Association.

———. 2000. Structure & Anti-Structure: Poststructuralist Themes in the Sociology of Deviance. Paper presented at the annual meeting of the Michigan Academy of Science, Arts, and Letters.

———. 2004. Valuation and Self-Identity. Paper presented at the annual meeting of the American Sociological Association.

———. 2005. Fun in Late Capitalism: Erving Goffman and the U.S. Cultural Economy. Paper presented at the annual meeting of the Michigan Academy of Science, Arts, and Letters.

———. 2007. Mead and Derrida: Symbolic Interactionism in Poststructuralist Context. Paper presented at the annual meeting of the Michigan Academy of Science, Arts, and Letters.

———. 2011. Performance and Performativity: Erving Goffman and Poststructuralism. Paper presented at the annual meeting of the American Sociological Association.

———. 2013. Role Distance and Juvenile Delinquency. Paper presented at the annual meeting of the American Sociological Association.

Silverstein, Michael. 1976. Shifters, Linguistic Categories, and Cultural Description. In *Meaning in Anthropology*, eds. Keith H. Basso and Henry A. Selby, 11–55. Albuquerque: University of New Mexico Press.

———. 2003. Indexical Order and the Dialectics of Sociolinguistic Life. *Language & Communication* 23(3–4): 193–229. http://www.journals.elsevier.com/language-and-communication/

Silverstein, Michael and Greg Urban. 1996. The Natural History of Discourse. In *Natural Histories of Discourse*, eds. Michael Silverstein and Greg Urban, 1–17. Chicago: The University of Chicago Press.

Simmel, Georg. 1955. *Conflict and the Web of Group-Affiliations*. New York: The Free Press. (Orig. pub. 1908.)

Slater, Don. 2003. Markets, Materiality and the "New Economy." In *Market Relations and the Competitive Process*, eds. J.S. Metcalfe and Alan Warde, 95–113. Manchester: Manchester University Press. (accessed as Saginaw Valley State University e-book, June 7, 2013).

Spivak, Gayatri Chakravorty. 1988. Can the Subaltern Speak? In *Marxism and the Interpretation of Culture*, eds. Cary Nelson and Lawrence Grossberg, 271–313. Urbana: University of Illinois Press.

Strauss, Terry. 1989. The Self in Northern Cheyenne Language and Culture. In *Semiotics, Self, and* Society, eds. Benjamin Lee and Greg Urban 53–68. Berlin: Mouton de Gruyter.

Taussig, Michael. 1993. *Mimesis and Alterity: A Particular History of the Senses*. New York: Routledge.

Thompson, John. 1995. *The Media & Modernity: A Social Theory of the Media*. Stanford: Stanford University Press.

Torgovnick, Marianna. 1990. *Gone Primitive*. Chicago: University of Chicago Press.

Turner, Jonathan, Leonard Beeghley, and Charles H. Powers. 2007. *The Emergence of Sociological Theory, 6th edition*. Belmont: Wadsworth. (Orig. pub. 1981.)

Urry, John. 1990. *The Tourist Gaze: Leisure and Travel in Contemporary Societies*. London: Sage.

Veblen, Thorstein. 1953. *The Theory of the Leisure Class*. New York: Mentor. (Orig. pub. 1899.)

Vološinov V.N. 1976. *Freudianism: A Marxist Critique*. Trans. I.R. Titunik and Neal H. Bruss. New York: Academic Press. (Orig. pub. 1927.)

———. 1986. *Marxism and the Philosophy of Language*. Trans. Ladislav Matejka and I.R. Titunik. Cambridge: Harvard University Press. (Orig. pub. 1929.)

Weber, Max. 1968. *Economy and Society*. Totowa: Bedminster. (Orig. pub. 1922.)

Weber, Samuel. 1973. The Sideshow, or: Remarks on a Canny Moment. *MLN* 88 (4–6): 1102–1133.

———. 1991. *Return to Freud: Jacques Lacan's Dislocation of Psychoanalysis*. Cambridge: Cambridge University Press.

———. 1996. *Mass Mediauras: Form, Technics, Media*. Ed. Alan Cholodenko. Stanford: Stanford University Press.

———. 2008. *Benjamin's -abilities*. Cambridge: Harvard University Press.

Williams, Rosalind H. 1991. The Dream World of Mass Consumption. In *Rethinking Popular Culture*, eds. Chandra Mukergi and Michael Schudson, 198–235. Berkeley: U-C Press. (Orig. pub. 1982.)

Williamson, Judith. 2005. *Decoding Advertisements: Ideology and Meaning in Advertising*. London: Marion Boyars. (Orig. pub. 1978.)

Willmott, Hugh. 2010. Creating "Value" Beyond the Point of Production: Branding, Financialization and Market Capitalization. *Organization* 17(5): 517–542. doi: 10.1177/1350508410374194.

Wolfreys, Julian. 2004. *Critical Keywords in Literary and Cultural Theory*. Basingstoke: Palgrave MacMillan.

Wolin, Richard. 1994. *Walter Benjamin: An Aesthetic of Redemption*. Berkeley: University of California Press.

Wortham, Stanton and Michael Locher. 1999. Embedded Metapragmatics and Lying Politicians. *Language & Communication* 19(2): 109–125. http://dx.doi.org/10.1016/S0271-5309(98)00021-4.

Index

About the Author

Steve Sherlock is a professor of Sociology at Saginaw Valley State University in Michigan. He received his Ph.D. in Sociology from the University of Notre Dame in 1986. He has taught at SVSU for over twenty five years, and currently offers courses in Sociological Theories, Social Psychology, and Juvenile Delinquency.

CPSIA information can be obtained at www.ICGtesting.com
Printed in the USA
BVOW07*1618131213

338971BV00001B/1/P

9 780739 168615